Sacred Men

GLOBAL AND INSURGENT LEGALITIES

*A series edited by
Eve Darian-Smith
and Jonathan
Goldberg-Hiller*

Sacred Men

LAW, TORTURE, AND RETRIBUTION IN GUAM

Keith L. Camacho

DUKE UNIVERSITY PRESS

Durham and London   2019

© 2019 Duke University Press
All rights reserved

Cover designed by Courtney Leigh Baker
Text designed by Amy Ruth Buchanan
Typeset in Quadraat by Westchester Publishing Services

Library of Congress Cataloging-in-Publication Data
Names: Camacho, Keith L., author.
Title: Sacred men : law, torture, and retribution in Guam /
Keith L. Camacho.
Description: Durham : Duke University Press, 2019. | Series:
Global and insurgent legalities. | Includes bibliographical
references and index. |
Identifiers: LCCN 2019010886 (print)
LCCN 2019016764 (ebook)
ISBN 9781478005667 (ebook)
ISBN 9781478005032 (hardcover : alk. paper)
ISBN 9781478006343 (pbk. : alk. paper)
Subjects: LCSH: War crime trials—Guam—History—20th century. |
World War, 1939–1945—Atrocities—Guam. | Guam—History—Japanese
occupation, 1941–1944.
Classification: LCC KZ1186.G85 (ebook) | LCC KZ1186.G85 C363 2019
(print) | DDC 341.6/90268—dc23
LC record available at https://lccn.loc.gov/2019010886

Cover art: Japanese prisoners being searched at a POW camp on Guam.
Courtesy of U.S. National Archives, College Park, Maryland.

This book is freely available in an open access edition thanks to TOME
(Toward an Open Monograph Ecosystem)—a collaboration of the
Association of American Universities, the Association of University
Presses, and the Association of Research Libraries—and the generous
support of Arcadia, a charitable fund of Lisbet Rausing and Peter Baldwin,
and the UCLA Library. Learn more at the TOME website, available at:
openmonographs.org.

Contents

ACKNOWLEDGMENTS vii

INTRODUCTION 1

PART I   The State of Exception

1. War Bodies 29

2. War Crimes 60

PART II   The Bird and the Lizard

3. Native Assailants 89

4. Native Murderers 116

PART III   The Military Colony

5. Japanese Traitors 149

6. Japanese Militarists 181

CONCLUSION 215

NOTES 225
BIBLIOGRAPHY 269
INDEX 283

Acknowledgments

Many folks supported the making of this book. First and foremost, I want to thank the following individuals for sharing their insights about Chamorro culture and history. Un dangkulu na si yu'os ma'åse to Julian Aguon, Anna Marie Arceo, Ma'ina Arceo, Raymond Arceo, Jay Aromin, Eulalia Arriola, Jil Benavente, Jesi Bennett, Miget Bevacqua, Ifit Borja, Mario Borja, Kisha Borja-Quichocho, Leevin Camacho, Victor Camacho, Keith Castro, Rick Castro, Francine Clement, Michael Clement, Hope Cristobal, Jose Cruz, Micki Davis, Tina DeLisle, Vicente Diaz, Emma Dueñas, Manny Dueñas, Martha Dueñas, Frankie Eliptico, Anita Borja Enriquez, Dave Gardner, Robert Gurion, Mary Hattori, Jessica Jordan, Cinta Kaipat, Gus Kaipat, Tiffany Lascado, Jillette Leon Guerrero, Victoria Leon Guerrero, Tricia Lizama, Fran Lujan, Victor Lujan, Kelly Marsh, Art Medina, Suzanne Medina, Bryan Mendiola, Laurel Monnig, Shannon Murphy, Tiara Na'puti, Lisa Natividad, Rita Nauta, Lou Nededog, Lino Olopai, Andrew Quenga, Heidi Quenga, Joey Quenga, Joe Quinata, Carmen Quintinalla, Zita Pangelinan, Nathalie Pereda, Michael Perez, Malia Ramirez, Raymond Ramirez, Elizabeth Rechebei, Scott Russell, Jaye Sablan, Sharleen Santos-Bamba, Adolf Sgambelluri, Austin Shelton, Gil Shinohara, Jessica Solis, Marie Storie, Tanya Taimanglo, Linda Taitano, Christine Tenorio, Honora Tenorio, Therese Terlaje, Dominica Tolentino, Anthony Tornito, Robert Underwood, Faye Untalan, James Viernes, and Paz Younis.

Elsewhere, I want to acknowledge the staff of the Hoover Institution Library and Archives at Stanford University, the Richard F. Taitano Micronesian Area Research Center at the University of Guam, the U.S. National Archives and Records Administration, and the War Crimes Studies Center at the University of California, Berkeley. In particular, I thank David Cohen, of the War Crimes Studies Center, for identifying relevant archival materials. Alfred Flores, Lawrence Lan, Raymond Ramirez, Angela Robinson, and

Christen Sasaki likewise provided much-appreciated research assistance. In terms of travel funding, the American Council of Learned Societies, the MacMillan Brown Centre for Pacific Studies at the University of Canterbury, and the UCLA Asian American Studies Center generously supported my trips to these collections. In this regard, Cindy Mueller, Karen Nero, David Yoo, and Mari Yoshihara deserve recognition. From 2009 to 2017, I received several opportunities to draft and circulate earlier versions of my book at various institutions. At the University of California, Riverside, for instance, I want to thank Tammy Ho, Jodi Kim, Mariam Lam, Vorris Nunley, Robert Perez, Michelle Raheja, Dylan Rodriguez, Setsu Shigematsu, and Traise Yamamoto for allowing me to discuss my preliminary thoughts about indigeneity, sexuality, and violence in 2009 and 2011. At the American Indian Studies Program at the University of Illinois, Urbana-Champaign, Jodi Byrd, Brenda Farnell, Matt Gilbert, Leann Howe, Fred Hoxie, John Low, John McKinn, Bob Parker, Debbie Reese, Robert Warrior, and Louellyn White welcomed me to their community in 2009. I thank them for pushing my understanding of incarceration and militarization and for broadening my view of indigenous worlds in the Americas and globally. Jose Capino, Jane Desmond, Virginia Dominguez, Augusto Espiritu, Anna Gonzalez, Jerry Gonzalez, Janet Keller, Martin Manalansan IV, Lisa Nakamura, Naomi Paik, Junaid Rana, and Elizabeth Tsukahara also made me feel at home at UIUC. I remain grateful to them as well.

My book has also greatly benefited from the feedback provided by scholars of Japan and Asia more generally. At the David Chu Program in Asia-Pacific Studies at the University of Toronto, I thank Tak Fujitani, Janet Poole, Shiho Satsuka, and Lisa Yoneyama for inviting me to workshop a paper on treason and war crimes. I especially acknowledge Tak and Lisa for creating spaces from which we can decolonize knowledge about Asia and Oceania. In fact, Lisa served as one of the two readers for Duke University Press. Even though she has a demanding schedule, she agreed to review my book and help me refine its theoretical premise. I cannot thank her enough for her generosity and expertise. Of course, all errors are mine. I also want to thank Akira Nishimura and Yujin Yaguchi for allowing me to share my work on empire and war at the University of Tokyo. Greg Dvorak of Waseda University, Shun Ishihara of Meiji Gakuin University, and Miyumi Tanji of Australian National University (ANU) have likewise been supportive colleagues. At the International Institute for Okinawan Studies at the University of the Ryukyus, Yoko Fujita, Ayano Ginoza, and Ikue Kina sponsored a trip for Teresia Teaiwa and me in 2016. While we had productive conversations about soldiering and war in Fiji, Guam, and Okinawa, I still feel saddened by the passing of Teresia a year later. She was an astute thinker and beloved friend who fostered understanding and solidarity among numerous indigenous communities in Oceania, no less the Fijians, I-Kiribati, Māori, Sāmoans, and West Papuans of Aotearoa.

Pacific Islands studies also lost Tracey Banivanua Mar and Paul Lyons, in 2017 and 2018, respectively. Tracey, a historian of indigenous resistance and settler violence in Australia and Oceania, once invited me to give a talk on war crimes at La Trobe University in 2015. Along with Samia Khatun and Nadia Rhook, she convened a fabulous group of folks to explore the "counternetworks" of empires. I sincerely thank Tracey for widening such networks to include Kalissa Alexeyeff, Tony Ballantyne, Tony Birch, Penny Edmonds, Alan Lester, Alice Te Punga Somerville, and many others. Also sorely missed is Paul Lyons, a literary scholar of militarism and tourism at the University of Hawai'i at Mānoa (UHM). He very much inspired my thinking on these subjects, as well as greatly advanced Pacific literary criticism. Don Nakanishi, professor and former Director of the UCLA Asian American Studies Center, also helped to establish the field of Pacific Islander studies in California. Although he passed away in 2016, he created an intellectual community that continues to benefit Pacific Islander faculty and students. For these reasons, Paul Lyons, Tracey Banivanua Mar, Don Nakanishi, and Teresia Teaiwa will be remembered for their many contributions. May they rest in peace and power.

I also want to thank Margaret Jolly, Nicholas Mortimer, and Katerina Teaiwa for hosting me at ANU in 2013. It was a privilege to workshop draft chapters with their colleagues in Asian and Pacific studies. As such, I humbly thank Chris Ballard, Carolyn Brewer, George Carter, Paul D'Arcy, Sinclair Dinnen, Ken George, Nicole George, Nicholas Halter, Brij Lal, Latu Latai, Lotu Latai, Salmah Eva-Lina Lawrence, Katherine Lepani, Vicki Luker, Siobahn McDonnell, Areti Metuamate, Rebecca Monson, Rachel Morgain, Kirin Narayan, Roannie Ng Shiu, Zag Puas, Paul Sharrad, Vince Sivas, Keiko Tamura, Serge Tcherkezoff, and Matt Tomlinson.

At UHM, my colleagues in Chamorro studies, Hawaiian studies, Oceanic ethnic studies, and Pacific Islands studies have also welcomed my discussions on militarism and war. For their generosity, I thank Hokulani Aikau, Brian Alofaituli, Ibrahim Aoude, Leilani Basham, Lola Bautista, David Chappell, Brian Chung, Kim Compoc, Joy Enomoto, Akiemi Glenn, Vernadette Gonzalez, Noelani Goodyear-Ka'ōpua, Monisha Das Gupta, David Hanlon, Betty Ickes, Tara Kabutaulaka, Noel Kent, Scott Kroeker, Kenneth

Gofigan Kuper, Rod Labrador, Monica LaBriola, Joyce Mariano, Alexander Mawyer, Brandy McDougall, Davianna McGregor, Jon Okamura, Jon Osorio, Gary Pak, Craig Santos Perez, John Rosa, Noenoe Silva, Fata Simanu-Klutz, Ty Tengan, Julie Walsh, Terence Wesley-Smith, Geoffrey White, and Erin Wright. In California, I likewise received feedback from Iosefa Aina and Kēhaulani Vaughn of Pomona College; Piya Chatterjee and Jih-Fei Cheng of Scripps College; Yến Lê Espiritu, Frank Ross, and Joseph Ruanto-Ramirez of the University of California, San Diego; Chris Finley and John Carlos Rowe of the University of Southern California; Evelyn Ho and Evelyn Rodriguez of the University of San Francisco; Anita Jain and Jocelyn Pacleb of California State Polytechnic University, Pomona; and JoAnna Poblete of the Claremont Graduate University.

During the researching of this book, many folks also helped me to think deeply about colonialism and law. I thank Maile Arvin, Eiichiro Azuma, Crystal Baik, Holly Barker, Myla Carpio, Iokepa Casumbal-Salazar, David Chang, Connie Chen, Cathy Choy, Kealani Cook, Iyko Day, Rudy Guevarra, Kara Hisatake, Christine Hong, Stacy Kamehiro, Lon Kurashige, Karen Leong, Simeon Man, Fermina Murray, Stephen Murray, Gary Okihiro, Vika Palaita, Rebecca Rosser, Kiri Sailiata, Dean Saranillio, Paul Spickard, Theresa Suarez, Tony Tiongson, Wesley Ueunten, Duncan Williams, and Judy Wu. As I prepared my manuscript for review in 2016, I asked several people to read one or more chapters. For their kind efforts, I thank Victor Bascara, Elizabeth DeLoughrey, David Hernández, Lauren Hirshberg, Miriam Kahn, Uri McMillan, Natsu Taylor Saito, Amy Sueyoshi, and Victor Viesca. At the invitation of Albert Refiti, I circulated two chapters to Vā Moana/Pacific Spaces of the Auckland University of Technology in 2017. I thank Albert, Rafik Patel, and I'u Tuagalu for honing my treatment of Giorgio Agamben's *homo sacer* in colonial and postcolonial contexts. I also thank Alys Moody of Macquarie University and Damon Salesa and Lisa Uperesa of the University of Auckland for allowing me to talk about native gossip and testimony with their colleagues and students.

At Duke University Press, senior editor Courtney Berger supported this book at every stage of the review process. She also selected two excellent external readers. Of these evaluators, only Lisa Yoneyama disclosed her identity. Heeding everybody's criticisms, I then revised my manuscript at the United States Studies Centre at the University of Sydney in 2017. While there, Susan Beal, Shelly Cheng, Sarah Graham, Simon Jackman, Beau Magloire, Luke Mansillo, Jared Mondschein, Aaron Nyerges, Brendon O'Connor, Janine Pinto, Shaun Ratcliff, Jessica Regan, Drew Sheldrick, Rodney Taveira,

Lucas Thompson, and Amelia Trial granted me the resources, time, and space to complete my study. Their support proved invaluable, as did my conversations with Robert Aldrich, Warwick Anderson, Julio Capó Jr., Rebecca Conway, Emelda Davis, Miranda Johnson, Jude Philp, Matt Poll, Ben Silverstein, Vanessa Smith, and Adrian Vickers. I thank Nico Tripcevich for creating the maps. I also thank Suzanne Medina, Austin Shelton, and Gil Shinohara for providing me with several photos for the book, an effort that I greatly appreciate. Assistant editor Sandra Korn of Duke University Press prepared the manuscript for production. Both Courtney and Sandra have been wonderful. My gratitude extends, as well, to Jon Goldberg-Hiller and Eve Darian-Smith for including my book in their new Duke series, Global and Insurgent Legalities.

At UCLA, I thank my colleagues for their counsel, friendship, and humor. They include Randy Akee, Jade Alburo, Victor Bascara, Charlene Villaseñor Black, Maylei Blackwell, Andrew Bottom, Lucy Burns, Michelle Carriger, Michelle Caswell, Janet Chen, Genevieve Carpio, Jessica Cattelino, Mitch Chang, King-Kok Cheung, Jennifer Chun, Sharon Claros, Melany de la Cruz-Viesca, Eliot Delgado, Elizabeth DeLoughrey, Michelle Erai, Kristine Espinoza, Cindy Fan, Kelly Fong, Wendy Fujinami, Jonathan Furner, Gilbert Gee, Anne Gilliland, Mishuana Goeman, Laura Gómez, Pamela Grieman, Akhil Gupta, Sarah Haley, Chris Hanscom, Cheryl Harris, Kelly Lytle Hernandez, Alfred Herrera, Lane Hirabayashi, Alice Ho, Grace Hong, Darnell Hunt, Marjorie Kagawa-Singer, Jerry Kang, Mary Kao, Kris Kaupalolo, David Kim, TK Le, Marjorie Lee, Rachel Lee, Betty Leung, Jinqi Ling, Seiji Lippit, Christine Littleton, Steve Loza, Purnima Mankekar, Beth Marchant, Valerie Matsumoto, Natalie Matsuoka, Kyle Mays, Sean Metzger, LT Rease Miles, Robert Nakamura, Tam Nguyen, Thu-hương Nguyễn-võ, Idriss Njike, Safiya Noble, Paul Ong, Arnold Pan, Kyeyoung Park, Thomas Phillip, Ninez Ponce, Nora Pulskamp, Janelle Rahyns, Barbra Ramos, Gaspar Rivera-Salgado, Michael Rodriguez, Ananya Roy, Markeith Royster, Jessica Schwartz, Suzzane Seplow, Eboni Shaw, Shu-mei Shih, Irene Soriano, Shannon Speed, Renee Tajima-Peña, Lois Takahashi, Sarah Tanase, Wendy Teeter, Robert Teranishi, Meg Thornton, Tritia Toyota, Pat Turner, Karen Umemoto, Melissa Veluz-Abraham, Lori Vogelgesang, May Wang, Eric Wells, Lily Welty, Ben Woo, David Yoo, and Min Zhou. I likewise thank the brilliant students who enrolled in my seminars when I began to make sense of military tribunals. They include Laura Beebe, Ellen-Rae Cachola, Asiroh Cham, Alfred Flores, Lisa Ho, Clara Iwasaki, Angela Robinson, Natasha Saelua, Christen Sasaki, Marie Sato, Pua Warren, and Wendy Yamashita. A special thanks, as well, goes out to the Pacific Islands Students Association, Samahang Pilipino, and other student educators, organizers, and volunteers of the UCLA Community Programs Office.

I also thank my ʻaiga and *familia* in Aotearoa, California, Guam, Hawaiʻi, Saipan, and Sāmoa. I especially extend a heartfelt thank-you to my parents, Barbara and Juan Camacho, and to my mother-in-law, Alice Anesi. Of course, my partner, Juliann, deserves my deepest appreciation. Finally, I reserve my last comment for the descendants of the military tribunals. That is, may we invoke the love and joy of our proverbs. May we become the animals of peace.

Introduction

> Biopower's supreme ambition is to produce, in a human body, the absolute separation of the living being and the speaking being, *zoē* and *bios*, the inhuman and the human—survival.
> —Giorgio Agamben, *Remnants of Auschwitz: The Witness and the Archive*

> An numa' piniti ha taotao
> Nangga ma na' pinitimu
> Maseha apmamam na tiempo
> Un apasi sa' dibimu
> —Chamorro proverb

> When you hurt somebody
> Expect to be in pain
> For even if it takes time
> You'll pay for the pain you caused

On January 21, 1942, Luis C. Crisostomo reported to the Japanese police headquarters in Saipan, one of several islands in the Marianas governed by the Nanyō-chō, or the Japanese South Seas Government. The U.S. territory of Guam, the southernmost island in this archipelago, had already fallen to the Japanese military a month earlier. Like the other Chamorro men who received the order, Crisostomo did not fully comprehend the nature of the request; the sudden directive only indicated an urgent transfer to Guam. Otherwise, he was told to arrive at one o'clock in the afternoon. The Japanese police then informed Crisostomo, a twenty-one-year-old man, of his new role as an interpreter for the Japanese administration in Guam. With no choice in this matter, he relented to the police. As his wife, Marikita Palacios Crisostomo, explained, the police "forced" him to heed these orders. "They just took him."[1]

The next day, Luis C. Crisostomo boarded the vessel *Nantaku Maru* for Guam. Approximately twenty-three men joined him, all of whom were tasked to serve as interpreters. Immediately dislocated from their families in Saipan, they were instructed to perform multiple translation duties for the Japanese administrative, agricultural, educational, medical, military, and police units. They all served one goal: to colonize and change Guamanian attitudes "from the American influence and to obey the rules, orders and regulations of the Japanese, and also to see that they place themselves like Japanese."[2] On January 23, 1942, only two days after their summons, the group landed in the port village of Sumay, a Japanese naval base that once housed the U.S. Marine Corps barracks. They also joined ten Saipanese male interpreters who had previously invaded Guam on December 8, 1941, a few hours before the Japanese military bombed and assaulted the island. With his newfound identity as an interpreter, Crisostomo registered at the Minseibu, the Japanese civil administration, located in the capital of Hågatña. At first, he merely worked as an interpreter. He then briefly returned to Saipan in May 1942 to seek the blessings of the Palacios family and to marry their daughter Marikita Palacios. Afterward, the couple left for Guam and moved to the village of Hågat. Once there, Crisostomo assumed the dual responsibilities of an interpreter and a police officer.

With the arrival of the supplementary force of Chamorros in January 1942, the Japanese conscription of native interpreters and police officers was well under way. By 1944, the Japanese had forcibly recruited seventy-five men and three women as interpreters from the islands of Rota and Saipan. The transformation of Luis C. Crisostomo from the son of farmers into a proper man of Japanese authority and law had likewise begun. Like the other Rotanese and Saipanese interpreters, he adapted to his new roles as an interpreter and police officer in ways that revealed his gendered, material, and political investments in colonial modernity and nationhood.[3] Through investigative methods and torture tactics fashioned by the Japanese military and police, Crisostomo specifically attempted to subjugate the Chamorros of Guam to the Japanese empire, thereby making Guamanians into the likeness of obedient and lawful Japanese subjects. His efforts ceased, however, when the U.S. military reinvaded the island in the summer of 1944. A few months later on January 1, 1945, the U.S. military police located Crisostomo and placed him in a stockade. Suspected of committing "war crimes" against U.S. nationals, he remained in the internment camp until a military tribunal subpoenaed him for trial on June 4, 1945. Until then, he labored, as a prisoner, for the U.S. military. As his wife, Marikita, elaborated, "My husband told me that while he was in prison they were taken out on work details and Guamanians would come up to them and say, 'You are monkeys now. You beat the Chamorros, and now you are monkeys.' Some would say, 'Come here so I can kill you.'"[4]

Now depicted as an animal, Luis C. Crisostomo faced a judge and jury of white military officers, who found him guilty of assaulting thirteen individuals and killing two men in Guam. On June 22, 1945, two-thirds of the military commission voted to execute him by hanging by the neck, a legal process that stripped his ties to Japan, recognized him as an "American," punished him as a "war criminal," and expunged him from the nation as a nonsacrifice. In this manner, he was a sacred man of the war, that is, *homo sacer* to his native community and to the emerging American political order. As Giorgio Agamben argues, homo sacer is a life "that may be killed but not sacrificed."[5] "What defines the status of *homo sacer* is therefore not the originary ambivalence of the sacredness that is assumed to belong to him, but rather both the particular character of the double exclusion into which he is taken and the violence to which he finds himself exposed."[6] This double exclusion (also called inclusive exclusion) allows a sovereign entity to kill with impunity, a violent force over an extrajuridical sphere and a violent inclusion and exclusion of certain beings and actions from the sphere of the law.[7]

As similarly illustrated by the Chamorro proverb, at the beginning of this introduction, abandonment, pain, and suffering result from the failure to maintain native life in the Mariana Islands. In this respect, one's cultural and political obligation to another is read as an expected and mutually beneficial relation; to disregard this custom—what Chamorros describe as *inafa'maolek*, or "to make good"—subjects one, as both self and clan, to shame, violence, and even death. Luis C. Crisostomo clearly knew of these obligations, as did the Guamanians who fell under his disciplinary purview. As the saying goes, "Un apasi sa' dibimu," or "You'll pay for the pain you caused." When placed in the context of what Agamben also calls the "state of exception," here understood as the extrajuridical space between American and Japanese claims to Guam and the wider Mariana Islands, one's relation to a community hinges on the violence of sovereignty, made lawful, between the living being and the speaking being, zoē and bios, the inhuman and the human. One can thus be remade in the image of a community, as in a "monkey," just as much as one can be remade in the image of a nation, as in a "war criminal." Taken together, they constitute homo sacer, the sacred man that dwells outside (zoē) and inside (bios) the rule of law.

In *Sacred Men: Law, Torture, and Retribution in Guam*, I examine the figure of homo sacer in the U.S. Navy's War Crimes Tribunals Program from 1944 to 1949. My argument is twofold. First, I demonstrate that the navy's tribunal prosecuted Japan's nationals and its native subjects in an effort to impose the U.S. rule of law in Guam and other formerly Japanese-occupied

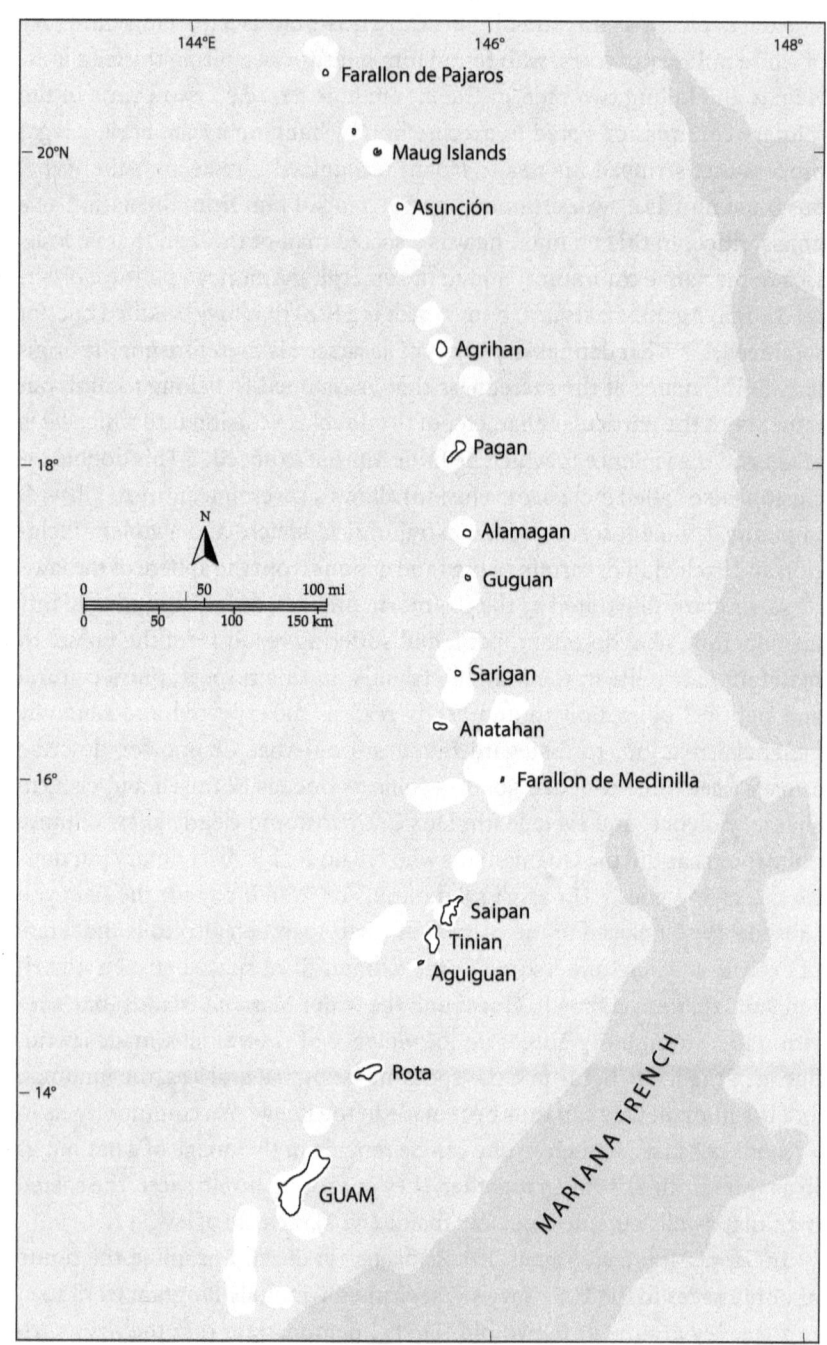

Map I.1. Guam and the Northern Mariana Islands

islands.⁸ Following Agamben, I take the site of the military commission as a threshold from which the matter of sovereignty became highly contested during World War II and its immediate aftermath in the 1940s. More was at stake than the military's classification and separation of the living being, zoē, from the speaking being, bios, among the accused Chamorro and Japanese war criminals. Additionally, indigenous Chamorro memories of being tortured by the Japanese police in Guam had, in fact, functioned as vital testimonies for the navy's court—testimonies that reified the distinctions between loyal wards, on the one hand, and war criminals, on the other. By treating native testimonies as bios, a form of political life that resonates with what I call the ko'ko-hilitai relation, I then arrive at the second part of my argument. Herein I foreground a native proverb about reciprocity and retribution in an effort to highlight the epistemological basis in Chamorro testimonies about harm and injury.

In Chamorro society, numerous proverbs about life and death abound. They illustrate the strength and vitality of cooperation, love, and reciprocity. While they often take the form of short messages, the proverbs also invoke larger and older stories about Chamorro banter, humor, jealously, loss, survival, and violence. Collectively, they impart lessons about how to respect and revere every living thing, including the land and the sea. Whether the proverbs discuss the origin of the coconut tree, the significance of sharing a meal with strangers, or the danger of making too much noise in the jungle, they all seek to foster harmonious relations among the living and the dead. Unlike the U.S. rule of law and its separation of the living being and the speaking being, Chamorros frequently make no distinction between such things. Animals, plants, humans, and spirits share the same space in Guam, a point that the Chamorros of World War II had culturally expressed by way of the bird (ko'ko) and the lizard (hilitai) proverb. But contrary to the plethora of proverbs that encourage reciprocal relationships, the proverb of the ko'ko and the hilitai can also be understood for its lessons about retribution, violence, and death. In this book, I show how this important proverb can shed insight on the political utility and consequence of gossip and rumors—that is to say, testimonies—in a military court of law. My merging of Chamorro and European philosophies of violence is thus intentional. In this respect, the Chamorro proverb of the ko'ko and the hilitai and Giorgio Agamben's theories of biopower can help us unpack the force and meaning of the U.S. Navy's War Crimes Tribunals Program. By employing this methodology, we can better analyze the origins of the U.S. empire in Guam,

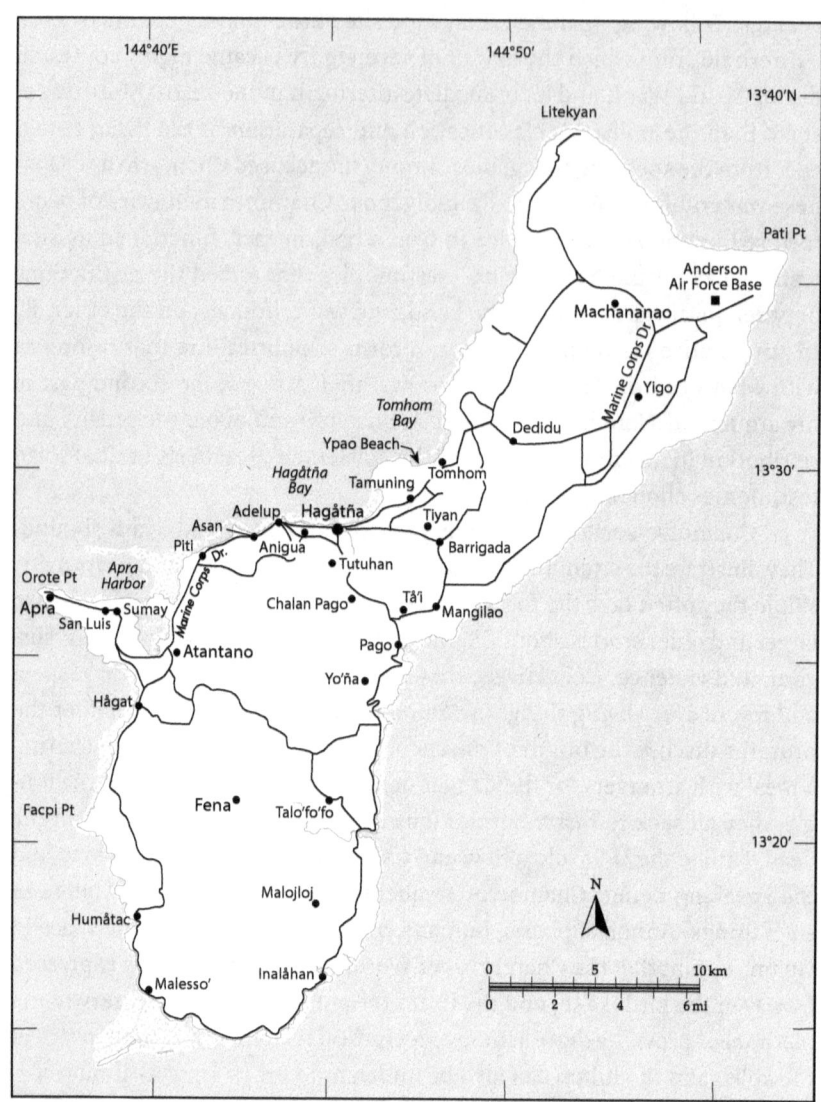

Map I.2. Guam

Rota, and the Marianas and offer new approaches for the study of biopower more generally.

On Agamben and Empires

In this book, I expand upon Agamben's discussions about the state of exception, homo sacer, and the paradigm of the camp. On the state of exception, he writes that it is "neither external nor internal to the juridical order, and the problem of defining it concerns precisely a threshold, or a zone of indifference, where inside and outside do not exclude each other but rather blur with each other."[9] As Agamben explains, the "state of exception is not a dictatorship (whether constitutional or unconstitutional, commissarial or sovereign) but a space devoid of law, a zone of anomie in which all legal determinations—and above all the very distinction between public and private—are deactivated."[10] He makes it very clear, as well, that many countries invoke various states of exception, as in their declarations of civil wars, cultural festivals, or martial laws. Agamben also stresses that the "state of exception tends increasingly to appear as the dominant paradigm of government in contemporary politics."[11] As he argues, "This transformation of a provisional and exceptional measure into a technique of government threatens to radically alter—in fact, has already palpably altered—the structure and meaning of the traditional distinction between constitutional forms. Indeed, from this perspective, the state of exception appears as a threshold of indeterminacy between democracy and absolutism."[12] For Agamben, the mysterious figure subjected to the state of exception, homo sacer or sacred man, is that who therefore may be killed and yet not sacrificed. He clarifies the origins of homo sacer as such: "An obscure figure of archaic Roman law, in which human life is included in the juridical order [ordinamento] solely in the form of its exclusion (that is, of its capacity to be killed), has thus offered the key by which not only the sacred texts of sovereignty but also the very codes of political power will unveil their mysteries."[13] Homo sacer is bare life, the nonspeaking being. As Agamben explains, the "fundamental categorical pair of Western politics is not that of friend/enemy but that of bare life/political existence, zoē/bios, exclusion/inclusion."[14]

As the legal scholar Tom Frost elaborates, bios, or political life, "is not defined imminently by itself, but is defined through its being held in relation to 'natural life,' what it is not, mere existence, zoē, which exists as a universal transcendent referent."[15] Defined in a negative functional relation, political life is held in relation to what it is not, natural life, a negative relationality that, for Agamben, underpins modern political existence.[16] This ban—what Agamben theorizes as the meaning of x being produced by its relation to a non-x—suggests that bios can only gain meaning from what it is not. As Frost details, zoē is thereby not "completely subsumed and transformed into bios, but instead continues to exist. This zoē remains in the political order, existing as politicized zoē, or bare life." Importantly, "The implications of this are that individuals will be de-subjectified, become expendable and be killed with impunity in any political order, because creating leads to the biopolitical creation of human detritus."[17] For these reasons, the biopower of modern democracies—whether by way of colonialism, homophobia, incarceration, militarism, or racism—produces more bare lives as much as it reproduces the economic, political, and social conditions that make homo sacer in the first place.[18]

In Agamben's texts, homo sacer manifests as four creatures: "zoē or biological life, *bios* or political life, bare life (sometimes rendered as sacred life or naked life, from the original Italian term '*nuda vita*') and a new 'form-of-life,' occasionally rendered as 'happy life.'"[19] In this book, I mainly focus on the first three variations of homo sacer as my study does not address Agamben's "happy life" dilemma as to how to make no separation between zoē and bios in the law. Nor do I seek to resolve the means by which sovereignty and right no longer have a hold over life.[20] Instead, I explore the aporia that led to the making of the U.S. Navy's War Crimes Tribunals Program and its declaration of "democracy" in militarist terms. Such an approach lends itself to related studies about why and how indigenous peoples have, as the legal scholar Paul Havemann asserts, become the "paradigm non-people, non-citizens, *homines sacri*."[21] At worst, they "have been excluded and condemned to placelessness in 'zones of exception' such as reserves, mission schools or camps and other forms of segregation under the regime of the sovereign's draconian 'protection.'"[22] Before the law, indigenous people and their claims to "authenticity," however construed, are also suspect; they are "not a representative of objective cultural difference, but rather a membrane of cultural difference," as the anthropologist Elizabeth A. Povinelli once put it.[23] Whether they are Aboriginal Australians struggling to attain native title, American Indians seeking to revise treaties, or Kanaka Maoli articulating a new nation, their efforts for recognition are usually perceived by states as "past tense presences."[24] But by addressing the struggles waged by colonized peoples in Japan and the United States, we can "make visible an active subjectivity that can operate as an alternative to the abandoned and hopeless figure of the Muselmann, that most extreme embodiment of the form of (de)subjectivation defined by Agamben as *homo sacer*."[25] As the political theorists Simone Bignall and Marcelo Svirsky explain, a "renewed attention to Agamben's core concepts such as 'the camp' and '*homo sacer*,' considered in terms of the colonial context and with respect to the rich histories of colonial rebellion and resistance, can enable a more nuanced understanding of the forms of agency available to individuals and peoples that have been rendered *homo sacer* by a politics of 'inclusive exclusion.'"[26] In this respect, I foreground in this book the American, Chamorro, Chamorro-Japanese, and Japanese attorneys, carpenters, farmers, investigators, nurses, prostitutes, and soldiers who engaged the animal life and political life of the American and Japanese empires. We can then examine why and how Luis C. Crisostomo became a police officer under Japan and a war criminal under the United States, as well as analyze the ways in which Japanese civilians and soldiers alike experienced related colonial conditions.

On the Military Colony of Guam

On the material and spatial politics of Auschwitz, a Nazi extermination camp, Giorgio Agamben states that it constitutes "the very paradigm of political space at which politics becomes biopolitical and *homo sacer* is virtually confused with the citizen." He explains, "The correct question to pose concerning the horrors committed in the camps is, therefore, not the hypocritical one of how crimes of such atrocity could be committed against human beings." As he asserts, "It would be more honest and, above all, more useful to investigate carefully the juridical procedures and deployments of power by which human beings could be so completely deprived of their rights and prerogatives that no act committed against them could appear any longer as a crime."[27] With Guam as the main site of this study, I find this island as similarly invoking the juridical procedures of the camp insofar as the Chamorros, Chamorro-Japanese, and Japanese retained no (or partial) political rights. This is not to conflate the violence of the Nazi genocide of Jews with the violence of American and Japanese punishment and possession. By situating Guam as a military colony, I instead focus on its biopolitics of exception and exclusion.[28]

In an act of war with Spain in 1898, for example, the American military invaded Guam, as it did Cuba and the Philippines. The U.S. Navy usurped Spanish rule over the Marianas as well, severing the political ties between Guam and the Northern Mariana Islands. The latter came under German rule from 1898 to 1914, followed by Japanese naval and administrative governance until 1944. The U.S. Navy in Guam appointed naval governors to rule the island like a ship with the indigenous Chamorros as its wards. From 1898 to 1941, the Chamorros, as U.S. nationals, also possessed no rights as per the protections of the U.S. Constitution.[29] As with other territories like American Sāmoa and Puerto Rico, the U.S. plenary doctrine, coupled with the dictates of military rule, determined, by force, which populations received partial or total protections offered by the state.[30] Chamorros, Japanese nationals, and other nonwhite communities that resided on the island garnered none whatsoever under the navy. As the legal scholar Natsu Taylor Saito argues, the Supreme Court has used the doctrine since the nineteenth century to grant Congress and the U.S. government "plenary—full or complete and therefore unchallengeable—power with respect to national security and, by extension, over immigration matters on the theory that regulation of the borders is a power inherent in sovereignty."[31]

With the navy as the governing body of laws, and with the legal support of the plenary doctrine, Guam consequently received an "uneven application of the Constitution."[32] Addressing the historical impact of the Constitution in the colonies, the critic Amy Kaplan states that "there were no consistent guarantees of due process or the right to criminal and civil juries or full protection under the Fourteenth Amendment; in other words, there were no clear rights to be protected against unfair procedures."[33] Given the island's role as a coaling station for naval ships, the American government focused on Guam as a port, with little regard for the civil rights of the Chamorros. The appointed naval governor therefore "exercised complete executive, legislative, and judicial power."[34] In the navy's view, law enforcement never posed a problem because the Chamorros were an "inherently law-abiding and peaceful people."[35]

While the navy's public position on Chamorro relations with colonial law presents an image of interracial harmony, the everyday realities of naval governance, segregation, and militarism were far from peaceful. As the anthropologist Laura Thompson observed, "Social intercourse between the [naval] officers' families and natives was frowned upon and the system of etiquette was designed to 'keep the natives in their place.' Segregated schools were introduced whereby native children of both classes attend schools for natives while the children of the naval colony went to white schools."[36] In many respects, the navy created, administered, and enforced a plethora of laws to discipline Chamorro bodies into subservient, non-rights-bearing subjects of the state.[37] The navy also charged Chamorros for a variety of "crimes," such as assault, battery, burglary, prowling, and sex.[38] With the assistance of Marine Corps personnel and native patrol officers, the navy policed many Chamorro cultural, religious, and social practices, from whistling in the streets to adopting children into their extended clan networks.[39] Trial by jury was also not introduced because, in the navy's estimation, "it was not desired by the inhabitants nor considered suitable." More precisely, the navy refused to introduce trial by jury because of the fear that Chamorro "jurymen would be governed by familial influences rather than by the law and evidence," a position that would change in the course of the tribunal's development.[40] Furthermore, the navy made no concerted effort to criminalize the relatively small community of Japanese nationals in Guam. Prior to the formation of the tribunal in 1944, American naval punishment mainly entailed the cleaning of streets, the drying of copra, the gardening of vegetables, the making of roof tiles, the paying of fines, the raising of pigs, or the sewing of clothes. All profit went to the naval government.[41] Very seldom did crimes like assault and murder appear in its court records.[42] The navy only severely punished individuals suspected of having Hansen's disease, or leprosy, by exiling them to the Philippines.[43]

In Guam, the rule of law under the American naval government subsequently functioned in militarist, racist, and totalitarian terms. It is a colony, then and now. Reflecting on the colony in modern European philosophy and practice, the political theorist Achille Mbembe explains that "the colony represents the site where sovereignty consists fundamentally in the exercise of a power outside of the law (*ab legibus solutus*) and where 'peace' is more likely to take on the face of a 'war without end.'"[44] Elaborating further, he argues that "colonies are zones in which war and disorder, internal and external figures of the political, stand side by side or alternate with each other. As such, colonies are the location par excellence where the controls and guarantees of judicial order can be suspended—the zone where the violence of the state of exception is deemed to operate in the service of 'civilization.'"[45] Understood in these terms, Guam represents a zone where the *normalized* state of exception serves the "civilized" Americans and enables regimes of militarized violence and white supremacist statecraft to converge as legitimate law.

The Nanyō-chō in the adjacent islands of Rota, Tinian, and Saipan differed no less in this respect. For both Japan and the United States, the rule of law aimed to "establish a semblance of order and administrative control rather than to build an elaborate system of justice."[46] As I have argued elsewhere, each empire attempted to indoctrinate Chamorros and others in

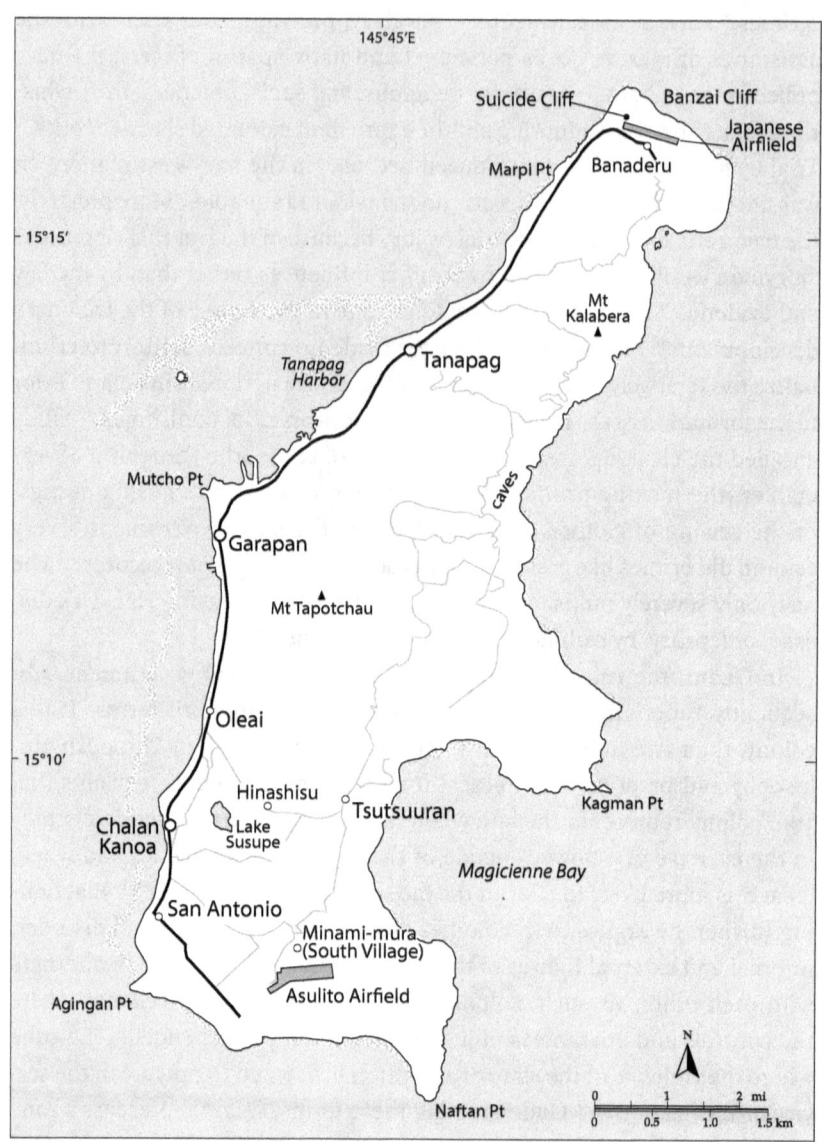

Map I.3. Saipan

an effort to cultivate their loyalties.[47] A loyal population implied an orderly citizenry and noncitizenry. While the archipelago remained divided along this fault line of governance, each colonial power understood the value of law and its threat of violence in subduing the native population. In Saipan, for example, Chamorros equated education and law with discipline and punishment, a point shared by Edward T. De La Cruz. Known as Toshiwo Tamaoki under the Nanyō-chō, he recalled, "At school we sometimes were made to stand in the sun as punishment."[48]

With more than ninety thousand people in Saipan by 1941, most of whom labored for the island's sugar industry, only two police officers were on duty at any one time (figure I.1).[49] As with other Japanese colonies in Korea, Okinawa, and Taiwan, governors-general suspended the rule of law or tailored it to the specific requirements of colonized peoples.[50] Following this seemingly exceptional practice, Japanese government officials and their corresponding police units punished people for almost any act deemed illegal. In Saipan, this carceral apparatus began in 1915 with the Japanese naval police force, followed by the making of the colonial police in 1922. In each case, the Japanese police recruited Chamorros over the Refaluwasch in the Northern Mariana Islands.[51] Believing that Chamorros were more "civilized" than other natives because of their long history with the Spanish Empire, Japanese police officials "tended to favor the Chamorros of the Marianas as the most advanced and adaptable of the Micronesian peoples."[52] Yet the Chamorros remained in subordinated positions to the Japanese in the police.[53] The Japanese police also enlisted young and impressionable Chamorro men because, in doing so, the Japanese government simultaneously sought to erode the authority of native elders and leaders.

In their preparation for invading American-occupied Guam, the Japanese police utilized the labor of native men as "weapons," a tactic frequently employed by colonial powers during World War II.[54] Although it is unclear how many Chamorro police officers from Rota and Saipan became interpreters, the seventy-five males and three females tasked to be interpreters already understood the power of the police. Faced with a partial English-speaking native population, as not everybody spoke English in Guam, the Japanese enlisted these native interpreters to mediate the "signs, intentions, and meanings from one language to another."[55] The first wave of these interpreters comprised ten Chamorro men in their early twenties, all of whom participated in the civic, patriotic, and sport activities of the Seinendan, or Young Men's Association in Saipan.[56] Their recruitment began with the delivery of a four-by-five-inch note to their homes on November 27, 1941.

I.1. Japanese police station in Minami-mura (South Village) in Saipan, ca. 1937.

Addressed to each man, the paper read, "Saipan Govt. Office, Head of Dept., Police Affairs, Nishi Gunzō."[57] On the same day, the young men reported to police director Nishi Gunzō to confirm their affiliation with the Seinendan. Gunzō then ordered them to meet at his house a few days later, on December 5, at five o'clock in the afternoon; he then instructed them to "correct" the trace of an unidentified island on a piece of paper.[58] In the Japanese colonial imagination, the island may have been a map of Guam, and the exercise may have been a way to gauge the men's understanding of its topography. Whether that was the case or not, none of the men succeeded in ascertaining the purpose of this activity.

With no further explanation as to the meaning of these events, Nishi Gunzō ordered the ten Chamorro men to convene at the Naval Guard Unit at Tanapag Harbor on December 6 at five o'clock in the afternoon. As the interpreter and police officer Jose P. Villagomez recalled, the "Chief of Police told us that we could not refuse what was asked by the officials."[59] They were simply told "to help the Emperor and Japan."[60] Specifically, the Japanese navy advised the Saipanese interpreters to warn the people of Guam of an impending military invasion and to encourage them to seek refuge in the mountains. The young men also had to cut any American communication lines and identify any American military fortifications in the shoreline areas of Guam. With no extra clothing or food, they then boarded the Japanese landing craft, *Daihatsu Ranchi*, for Rota around two o'clock in the morning. They landed briefly in Rota to eat and rest, after which they were separated into two groups of five. On the morning of December 8, 1941, Martin Borja, Antonio Camacho, Jose Cabrera, Juan Manibusan, and Francisco Sablan landed off the coast of Inalåhan in southern Guam. Jose Cabrera, Jose Guerrero, Segundo Sablan, Celeste Torres, and Jose Villagomez then arrived in Litekyan in the northern part of the island.

The former group hid in the jungle from both the Americans and the invading Japanese military. However, the other five interpreters encountered American naval personnel who, suspecting them of being "infiltrators," imprisoned them in the Hågatña jail along with the previously interned Japanese residents.[61] Two days later, on December 10, the American naval government surrendered to the Japanese military and released its prisoners. On the other hand, the group in Inalåhan met, by chance, Father Jesus Baza Dueñas, a prominent Chamorro community leader, on December 13. The priest escorted them to his home and prepared a meal for them. In the afternoon, Father Dueñas then drove the interpreters to the nearby village of Yoña, where a Japanese army encampment had been recently erected. Upon their arrival, a Japanese soldier and a Saipanese interpreter exchanged the following conversation:

> *Where are you from?*
> We are Saipan Chamorros.
> *Where are you going?*
> We came here before the war started.
> *By whose order?*
> The Naval Guard Unit.
> *Why?*
> As interpreters.[62]

As these comments reveal, the Japanese military had seized Guam from the American empire. After all, the unknown Japanese soldier spoke as if he governed the island. His ignorance about Saipanese interpreters demonstrated the lack of political agency accorded to Chamorros.

Antonio Camacho, the interpreter involved in this dialogue, remarked, "We came here before the war started." His casual reference not only denoted his involvement in the Japanese invasion of the island but also suggested that "we," Chamorros as political life, always resided in the Marianas long before the invading Americans and Japanese. Without a doubt, this linguistic and political metastructure of translation exacerbated relations among "Americanized" and "Japanized" Chamorros in Guam, a matter that would resurface repeatedly in the war crimes trials examined in this book. In every translation, the interpreters for the American and Japanese empires addressed what the historian Vicente L. Rafael describes as the "irreconcilable demands between a faithful and free rendition of the original, but also between the tendency to reproduce as much as to resist the dominant conventions of meaning and signification."[63] To put it another way, every speaker of the tribunal faced the predicament of asserting, merging, or disavowing one or more linguistic worlds in an effort to render partial meanings about law, torture, and retribution. In these ways, numerous Chamorros faced enormous difficulty in making intelligible their concepts about life and death in a legal and political space dominated by English- and Japanese-speaking military officials who had, for the most part, no regard for them.

On Torture, Testimony, and the Ko'ko-Hilitai Relation

What did the Rotanese and Saipanese interpreters and police officers say and do that warranted their inclusive exclusion in the navy's commission? How did their Japanese military and police counterparts, many of whom saw Guam as their property, become implicated in this assertion of the American political order? In this book, I take torture and confession as the forms of punishment that hardened and ruptured colonial, native, and settler political and social relations across the board. As the legal scholar Paul W. Kahn explains, "The object of torture was confession, which had the dual purpose of providing information and acknowledging sin—whether against God or the sovereign."[64] In Kahn's view, "Confession was a necessary aspect of the ritual of punishment. It was literally the last act of the dying man. This was not because of lingering uncertainty over guilt—whether he actually committed the crime—but because the sovereign's power over life required the moment of acknowledgment."[65] "Without acknowledgment," he emphasizes, "the sovereign might exercise violence but not power."[66]

In Japanese-occupied Guam, torture commenced with a report submitted to one of the many police stations scattered across the island's villages. The memo often detailed an assaulted person, an insulted official, a stolen chicken, or a suspected spy, among other accusations. Around one or two investigations occurred each day. The interrogations also took place in facilities that previously served the American naval government, such as the medical office in Hågat and the records repository in Hågatña. In every case, the interpreters and police officers arrested the alleged criminal, usually a man, and recorded his name, date of birth, place of residence, and marital status. While a person was being investigated, other police officers would depart for the scene of the alleged crime, interview people, assess the site for clues, and cross-check information. The torturing of individuals happened before, during, and after any interrogation session. With no recourse to a trial, the interpreters and police officers often beat, slapped, and whipped the suspected person, as well as exposed him to the sun without food or water for long periods of time. Quite often, the Chamorro and Japanese interrogators used the *chilin guaka*, a bullwhip, as a favored weapon. The Guamanian farmer Joaquin A. Limtiaco, a survivor of numerous torture sessions, described the chilin guaka as "a tendon 3/4" in diameter and about 3½ feet long, tied to a wooden handle about 12 inches in length."[67] During his and other confessions, the accused criminals usually acknowledged their guilt for committing whatever accusation they faced. In doing so, they identified other relatives, neighbors, and rivals as accomplices. As a result, torture emanated outward from the body of the victim to the bodies of his clan, village, and island; its power seemed totalizing.[68]

With respect to the tribunal, what mattered was the way Guamanians understood gossip as testimonies, a form of political life, bios, that very much informed the court's dehumanization of every war criminal. Unlike federal courts that do not admit rumors as evidence, the navy's military commission adhered to its procedures regarding its use of gossip as testimony.[69] Given that the tribunal featured Guamanian and Chamorro-Japanese notions of the past in this regard, I understand gossip, hearsay, and rumor to mean a "form of interaction that in most societies variously provokes scorn, derision, and contempt, but also enormous interest."[70] Discussing the contradictory nature of gossip, for example, the anthropologist Niko Besnier asserts that it "embodies the complexities of social life. . . . Through gossip, people make sense of what surrounds them, interpreting events, people, and the dynamics of history."[71] As testimony, gossip provided Guamanians, especially those involved in the military and police apparatuses of the U.S. Navy, with a political voice. Although the tribunal never viewed gossip as a knowledge system that shaped American precedents, I intend to demonstrate otherwise.

Turning to the Chamorro proverb that opened this introduction, I show how the proverb of the ko'ko (bird) and the hilitai (lizard) informed Guamanian testimonies about what constituted proper and improper native behaviors and attitudes during the war. From this relation, we can then understand how the Chamorro custom of inafa'maolek functioned under extreme duress. As the Chamorro historian Christine Taitano DeLisle explains, inafa'maolek often operates as a system of reciprocity alongside other values like "*respetu* (respect), *gai mamåhlao* (literally, 'to have shame' but loosely 'to save face'), *mangingi*, the sniffing of an elder's hand to take in his or her essence and wisdom as a sign of *respetu*, and *chenchule*, a gift or form of compensation."[72] The Chamorro scholars Tiara R. Na'puti and Michael Lujan Bevacqua similarly explain that inafa'maolek functions "on the assumption that mutual respect must prevail over individualism."[73] They suggest that inafa'maolek compels Chamorros to maintain "positive relationships" among a group.[74] At the same time, this custom informs how they express jealousy, hate, and vengeance. As the Chamorro educator Faye Untalan elaborates, "People try to shape how you think, how you live, how you behave. And it has to meet their norms or their values. If it does not, then the retribution comes in."[75] As such, she stresses that gossip can be "very mean-spirited," even urging some people to chastise and reject others. In this respect, we can ask, what happened to the knowledge system of inafa'maolek when the tribunal utilized gossip to condemn or vindicate war criminals under Japan's empire? And how did Guamanian and Chamorro-Japanese forms of racism and retribution function as political life in rendering the Japanese, Rotanese, and Saipanese as the zoē and bios of "war criminality"?

As one version of the proverb indicates, the "*hilitai* (monitor lizards) were black and could sing beautifully. The *hilitai* was so proud of its voice that it showed off by singing to all the other animals."[76] Yet a few of the animals like the *totot* (Marianas rose-crowned fruit dove) said, "You may have a better voice than me, but my colors are prettier than yours!"[77] Jealous, the hilitai sought the assistance of a friend, the ko'ko (Guam rail), to paint yellow dots on its skin. The ko'ko agreed to help on the condition that the hilitai beautify the bird with white stripes as well. And so the ko'ko kept its promise, but the hilitai only partially painted the bird, in a hurry to show other animals its yellow and black patterns. Angry and offended, the ko'ko caught up to the hilitai and immediately pecked its beak and tongue. Today, the white stripes on the ko'ko appear incomplete, whereas the hilitai, with its forked tongue, no longer arrogantly sings (figures I.2 and I.3). As the educator Lawrence J. Cunningham explains, "The importance of this story is not in the explanations for the characteristics of these animals. The real message is the core Chamorro value. *People who do not meet their obligations will be punished.*"[78] The actions and attitudes of the hilitai, a cunning figure

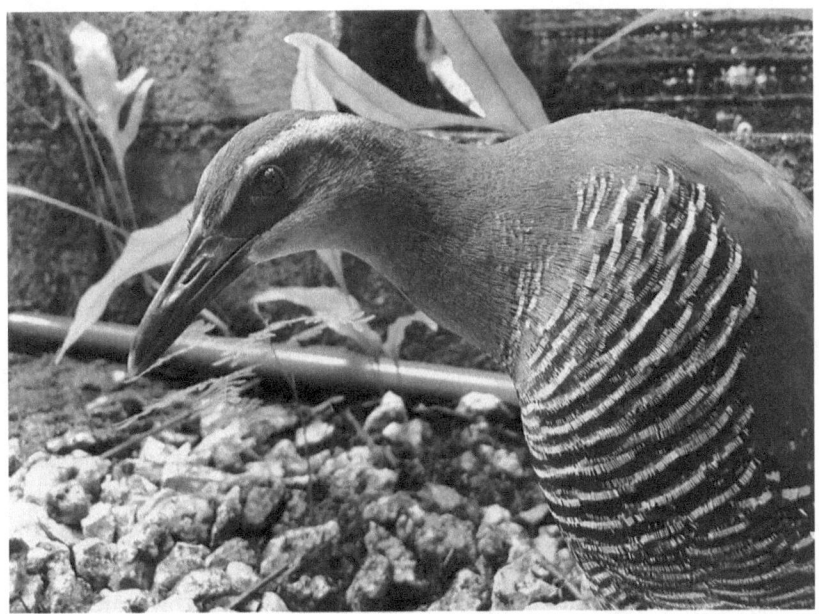

I.2. The ko'ko. Photograph by Anthony Tornito, Department of Agriculture, Guam.

I.3. The hilitai. Photograph by Dave Gardner, Pacific Consultants Group, Guam.

in native thought, portend extreme danger and risk for anybody who does not directly disclose his or her intentions to a group. In this manner, its "forked tongue" can represent the direct and implied texts of the speaking being and the living being. Without the negative relation that the hilitai represents, moreover, the native custom of inafa'maolek would lack influence and relevance in the maintaining of relations.

Other proverbs about the hilitai demonstrate its significance in Chamorro culture and history. As one saying goes, "Yanggen inaca hao ni ayuyu ti hun sinet'ta hasta que palapak i hilo," or "When you are bitten by a coconut crab he will not let you go until the thunder roars." Here, the proverb indicates the strength of the *ayuyu*'s claws, but it also signals the length of time a rumor, good or bad, may adhere to a person. Alternatively, as the Chamorro genealogist Malia Ramirez observes, the proverb warns that one should not get into a violent situation from which one cannot get out.[79] After all, the ayuyu is one of the few animals that can tear apart a coconut's exterior, puncture its hard shell, and consume its fleshy white meat. When placed in the context of the hilitai as a deviant subject, however, the lizard's intelligence outwits the power of the coconut crab. As another proverb reveals, the hilitai "is said to be fond of eating the tail-purse of the ayuyu . . . that it willingly offers its tail to the crab for bait, and while the crab chews on the lizard's tail the lizard twists about and chews at the crab's vitals."[80]

By turning to the proverb of the ko'ko and the hilitai, I demonstrate that Guamanian gossip invoked the "animal" lessons of reciprocity and punishment in ways that negotiated testimonies about the suspected Japanese, Rotanese, and Saipanese war criminals. Lest I be misunderstood as romanticizing native life, let it be clear that my analysis of gossip is by no means trivial. It is ontological. Taking a cue from Agamben, my reference to the ko'ko and the hilitai shows that Chamorros did not necessarily adhere to the animal/human distinction that proved so fundamental to the making of the military commission and its creation of homo sacer. Although the political function of gossip often reified the animal/human dualisms of the tribunal, as with the Guamanian racism and retribution directed against every suspected war criminal, the usage of native gossip in the court illustrated how Guamanians sought "to gain the fullest possible expression of political identity, agency, and autonomy."[81] When viewed through the broader lens of Chamorro knowledge of the material, natural, and spiritual domains, the animal/human binary does not hold up; the dichotomy remains a fiction in light of origin stories about animals and plants, on the one hand, and in the matter of familial and unknown spirit encounters with every living being, on the other.[82] As in many Chamorro clans, familial stories of the recently deceased often disclose the presence of an apparition, the smell of a fragrant flower, or even the voice and physical touch of the loved one.[83] Comparably, stories about benign and malevolent spirits—that is, the *taotaomona*—usually foreground the ghostly display of animals, humans, and other entities. As the Chamorro writer Tina Camacho Pablo observes, "Many Chamorros believe these stories of the supernatural to be true."[84]

Elsewhere, Native Hawaiian and other Pacific Islander societies view animals as playing "a more significant cosmological and political role, even though animals, as a linguistic and cultural category, are often conspicuously absent."[85] With respect to the Hawaiian notion of *kino lau*, for example, the political theorists Jonathan Goldberg-Hiller and Noenoe K. Silva explain that it "means that many plants, animals, birds, clouds, and so on are the bodies of deities, either the powerful akua nui (major akua) like Kāne, Kū, Pele, Haumea, and others, or less powerful but just as meaningful 'aumākua, family spirits."[86] As with the ko'ko and the hilitai, the animals, plants, and spirits of Hawai'i act on the world.[87] In these ways, Chamorros often view land as an animate being, if not as an extension of themselves. The land, like the people, is alive, hence the popular phrase used by Chamorros to describe themselves as *taotao tano'*, or the "people of the land." In fact, most areas throughout Guam and the Marianas are nicknamed after Chamorro clans. The hills, rivers, valleys, beaches, trees, birds, and ocean all convey their stories from the older and recent past. Historically, Chamorro mothers, godmothers, and grandmothers even buried the placentas or umbilical cords of their children in their villages, a common practice throughout the Pacific Islands to demonstrate cultural connectedness to land. As DeLisle elaborates, inafa'maolek conceptions of stewardship invoked "traditional birthing practices, like the burying of the placenta or the umbilical cord."[88] Comparably, the Chamorro attorney Michael Phillips notes that land is "literally the base of Chamorro culture. It incorporates special relationships: of clan, family, religion and beliefs."[89]

When analyzing native gossip and retribution, the ko'ko-hilitai relation, and the white racism of the court, we can then ask, how did the navy's tribunal employ Chamorro testimonies to possess *Chamorro lands* in Guam, Rota, and the wider Marianas archipelago? And how did the commission's understanding of "Japaneseness" expedite or hinder these acts? Indeed, how did the court separate man from the non-man and the animal from the human?[90]

The Threshold of Empire

In this book, I treat the military commission as the threshold from which the United States renewed or made anew its sovereignty in Guam, Rota, and the wider Marianas archipelago. How did this "lawful" process occur, and for what reasons? In the summer of 1944, the U.S. government knew that the question of sovereignty remained unsettled in light of the United States' armed conflicts with the Japanese military in the Marianas and the Asia-Pacific region. Even with Japan's surrender to the United States in August 1945, U.S. imperial claims to Guam, Rota, Tinian, Saipan, and other Pacific Islands were tenuous at best. Had American sovereignty been unequivocally true and juridically apparent, the U.S. Navy would not have issued Proclamation No. 4, titled "Exceptional Military Courts," on July 21, 1944. As I intend to demonstrate in this study, the American military created a tribunal in Guam, the first of its kind for the navy, for more than the purpose of prosecuting individuals accused of committing war crimes against U.S. citizens and nationals. Rather, Proclamation No. 4 functioned as an exceptional form of jurisprudence in its inclusive exclusion of non-American subjects: that is, the Chamorro, Chamorro-Japanese, and Japanese interpreters, police officers, and soldiers of the Japanese empire. That Guam functioned as a *military colony* of the United States—and not as a state as per domestic laws or as an independent country as per international laws—largely enabled the navy to assert its legal claims to the island. This state of exception allowed for the development of the tribunal, its selection of war criminal types, and its reassertion of the American empire—processes that occurred in Guam but that potentially could happen in other U.S. territories. As Agamben argues, the state of exception is "neither external nor internal to the juridical order, and the problem of defining it concerns precisely a threshold, or a zone of indifference, where inside and outside do not exclude each other but rather blur with each other."[91] In this respect, the tribunal "marks a state of exception—a supposed deviation from 'normal' war—and employs a set of procedural logics that have as their main goal the conceptual and material excision of the war criminal from the landscape of legitimate war-related killing."[92]

In his analysis of violence, the philosopher Walter Benjamin would describe the U.S. Navy's tribunal as the law of the "state" from which its government, military, and police sought to contain or extinguish violence from within (e.g., strikes) and violence from without (e.g., enemy militaries). As he explains, violence threatens the law not "by the ends that it may pursue but by its mere existence outside the law"; the navy's jurists thereby understood that Japan's military violence possessed what Benjamin theorized as the "lawmaking character" of the "great criminal."[93] As I show in this study, the tribunal often construed Japanese military torture, in particular, as existing outside the law so as to eradicate its lawmaking effects in Guam and elsewhere. Attempting to uphold its "law-preserving" function, the tribunal feared such torture "for its lawmaking character, being obliged to acknowledge it as lawmaking whenever external powers force it to concede them the right to conduct warfare."[94] Subsequently, the court drew from its carceral logics to suspend the separation between "lawmaking" and "law-preserving" violence. In this manner, the military police, interrogators, witnesses, and jurists participated in the carceral and security logics of the state. As Benjamin astutely observed, the "law of the police" marks the point at which "the state . . . can no longer guarantee through the legal system the empirical ends that it desires at any price to attain. Therefore the police intervene 'for security reasons' in countless cases where no clear legal situation exists."[95] That the tribunal functioned in this manner is an understatement; its unclear legal status merely reflected the paradigm of the military colony of Guam, an aporia that must be analyzed for its lawful violence.

Yet, as recent legal readings of the American military commission reveal, the tribunal only functions as an "exceptional" act of the law. This position has especially received critical purchase since the American confinement of suspected "terrorists" at the navy's prison facility in Guantánamo Bay, Cuba. Contrary to these understandings of the commission, however, I situate the tribunal in Guam as a foundational, established, and lawful exercise of colonial power *before* the War on Terror. To be clear, I do not view the military commission as a site of "justice," nor do I condone the incarceration of people at Guantánamo and other "exceptional" and secret prisons. An analysis of the U.S. carceral state, now unprecedented in its imprisonment of one in every one hundred adults, demands a robust assessment of the distinct and shared conditions that led to the disciplinary logics and tactics in Guantánamo and elsewhere.[96]

What I find equally disturbing are academic treatments of what the legal scholars Laurel E. Fletcher and Eric Stover call the "Guantánamo effect." As they rightly assert, the phrase "Guantánamo effect" describes the cumulative effect of indefinite detention, abusive interrogations, and prolonged isolation of the detainees at the U.S. naval prison in Guantánamo Bay, Cuba.[97] Yet they do not examine, let alone flag, the long histories of the military commission in the context of indigenous peoples and the American empire. What gets reproduced here and in much of the legal literature is the notion that the rule of law practiced at Guantánamo is "exceptional," an anomaly in what is otherwise the constitutionally sound rule of law. As the critic Marita Sturken asserts, Guantánamo is a "famously exceptional aberration: it is a U.S. Naval Base on the island of Cuba, yet not within the jurisdiction of Cuba, a site 'owned' by the U.S. through a perpetual lease since 1903 that the [George W.] Bush administration claimed is outside of U.S. law."[98] Studies of the American commission subsequently reify the position that these tribunals represent the weakened "rule of law," if not a breakdown in law.[99] As the legal scholars Fionnuala Ní Aoláin and Oren Gross observe, "One of the most trenchant critiques of exceptional courts in general and military courts in particular is their deviation from the ordinary process of detention, pretrial process, and the conduct of the trial."[100]

Political euphemisms such as "aberration," "deviation," and "exception" inform the scholarship on the military commission and hence restrict our understanding of the military court's relationship to U.S. empire, punishment, and race. While the tribunal has by no means served the same purpose, and while it has affected different populations for a variety of political reasons, the available legal studies on this subject have been limited by virtue of their disavowal of American Indians, Japanese Americans, Pacific Islanders, and other marginal subjects in the history of the tribunal.[101] Without a broader insight into these precedents, the current literature on the tribunal suffers from its primary focus on Guantánamo. This bias consequently inhibits our analyses of law and violence as much as it impedes our interventions against lawful violence. As the legal scholar Jace Weaver reminds us, a wider understanding of the tribunal and its relation to the principle of stare decisis allows us to analyze how every "violation of civil liberties becomes part of the next" precedent.[102]

When we place the tribunal in the context of American and Japanese colonialisms, we can therefore take stock of how the U.S. Navy transformed and normalized the laws about war in order to securitize its activities as legitimate and necessary in Guam.[103] This was precisely what the navy and other military agencies meant by "justice." As I show in this study, the navy viewed justice not as an effort to reconcile two or more aggrieved parties; rather, it took justice to mean the normalization of biopower by way of carceral and colonial logics. With the tribunal as its apparatus of normalized biopower, the navy changed Guam from a small coaling station of 1898 into a "main operating base" of 1945.[104] As a military base, the island began to conduct numerous offensive attacks under the rubric of anticommunism or humanitarian aid from World War II to the Cold War era to the present.[105] As D. C. Ramsey, vice chief of naval operations, argued in August 1, 1946, "Guam with the adjacent Marianas, and to a slightly lesser degree the other islands of the Pacific seized from the Japanese constitute the essence of the proposed naval system for control of the western Pacific and for the security of the United States. The bases now established, and being built up, are located on the islands having the largest populations."[106] By the late 1940s, Guam had effectively become a part of America's empire of bases, stretching from the Pacific to Asia and from Europe to Africa and elsewhere.[107] The island is now one of more than fifty-three hundred American military bases globally, of which an estimated one thousand are located outside the United States.[108]

Outline of the Book

This book opens with part I, "The State of Exception," in order to discuss the "passage" of colonial rule from Japan to the United States in Guam. But rather than treat the state of exception as an aberration of law, I demonstrate how the American military selectively applied various laws and regulations in its seizure of Guam and its population from Japan. Given that the American military understood this claim in terms of military necessity, I argue that the American reinvasion of the island sought to *normalize* its notion of warfare and security as true and just over anything presented in the Japanese laws of occupation in Guam and the Marianas. Whether the U.S. Navy turned to *The Penal Code of Guam*, *Naval Courts and Boards*, or the plenary doctrine in advancing this position, it construed its rule of law as morally benign and virtuous. That is why the navy issued Proclamation No. 4, titled "Exceptional Military Courts," on July 21, 1944, an act that supported the military's construction of war criminality from which its tribunal asserted whiteness as property and sovereignty.

Starting with chapter 1, "War Bodies," I examine how and why the U.S. Marine Corps and U.S. Navy created internment camps and prisoner stockades for the confinement of Chamorros, Japanese, and other subjects of the Japanese administration and military. I specifically focus on the establishment of American military and police intelligence units in the island and address how they racially classified acceptable and deviant behavior among their presumed wards, on the one hand, and their suspected war criminals, on the other. I begin to sketch, as well, the complex collusion between

American and Guamanian forms of racism and retribution, demonstrating how this biopower defined war criminality. In chapter 2, "War Crimes," I contextualize the origins of the U.S. Navy's War Crimes Tribunals Program in Guam within a longer history of the commission and within the national and international debates on war criminality at the time.

In part II, "The Bird and the Lizard," I demonstrate how native gossip, as bios, codetermined the navy's classification of acceptable and deviant behavior among the living being and the speaking being of its accused war criminals. In chapter 3, "Native Assailants," and chapter 4, "Native Murderers," I specifically take stock of the genealogy from which intranative antagonisms emerged and materialized. Whereas chapter 3 examines the assault and battery charges among the Rotanese and Saipanese men, chapter 4 accomplishes the same objective with respect to the murder charge. I explore how and why the navy's commission rendered the accused Rotanese and Saipanese as *homines sacri*, an effort that produced "test cases" and other precedents for the apprehension of Japanese nationals.

In part III, "The Military Colony," I advance Agamben's thinking on the camp with respect to the American military colony, the out-of-sight but nevertheless violent form of biopower.[109] In the last two chapters, I thus show how the navy's military commission drew from this paradigm of biopower as much as it extended its rule of law to Guam and its neighbor island, Rota. In chapter 5, "Japanese Traitors," I analyze the navy's treason trial of Samuel Takekuna Shinohara, a Japanese national and resident of Guam. Central to this discussion was how the navy portrayed Shinohara, an Issei, as violating whiteness as American property and sovereignty. In chapter 6, "Japanese Militarists," I then examine how the tribunal invoked international laws on espionage in its making of three Japanese nationals into the image of murderers and, hence, "belligerent" occupiers of Rota. I also discuss the related assault and murder charges in Guam but emphasize the significance of the Rota case in terms of the navy's efforts to expand the military colony beyond Guam. I then conclude with some reflections on law, torture, and retribution.

Part I | THE STATE OF EXCEPTION

1

WAR BODIES

During the summer and fall of 1944, the U.S. Marine Corps and U.S. Navy established several intelligence and police units in Guam. Although relatively new in their makeup and sometimes disorganized in their objectives, these agencies subjected the indigenous and settler populations of the island to the logics of the U.S. carceral state. In this chapter, I show how the American military drew from its histories of discipline and punishment in its efforts to classify the disloyal from the loyal, the criminal from the noncriminal, and the ally from the enemy among the peoples of Guam. The purpose was threefold: first, to detain and segregate the criminal, disloyal, and enemy subjects; second, to generate a public image of emasculated Japanese and Japanized subjects; and, third, to lend moral credence to the American legal apparatuses by casting suspicion and, hence, guilt upon suspected war criminals and other deviant types. Chamorros from Guam, especially individuals with backgrounds in the military and the police, likewise incarcerated anybody deemed a threat by the U.S. military. This process exacted native forms of retribution and violence; here, Guamanians often portrayed themselves and Americans as the virtuous ko'ko, thereby vilifying the Japanese, Rotanese, and Saipanese as the cunning hilitai. In doing so, the American military colluded with Guamanians to create bodies of war criminality—bodies that invoked the carceral and colonial logics of modernity in the Pacific.

Bodies of Military Intelligence

The U.S. Navy's military intelligence units partly created the juridical language, moral landscape, and racialized sphere through which indigenous and settler bodies were classified, segregated, and incarcerated in the

Mariana Islands. Unlike its more secretive, expansive, and increasingly invasive manifestations of the post-9/11 era, the U.S. Navy of the late 1930s and early 1940s lacked a structure to effectively organize "intelligence" across its war-waging campaigns in the Pacific.[1] Even the Office of Naval Intelligence (ONI), an agency responsible for negotiating legislative funds for and sharing administrative information about its intelligence apparatuses, found little support at the national level. As the military historian Alan Harris Bath reveals, "ONI lacked direct access to naval policy makers, a situation that continued throughout the Second World War. Although it was consulted from time to time, it was unable to convince leaders in the Navy Department of the need for intelligence or of its significance in decision making."[2] The demand for trained personnel, the concern to censor dissent, the uneven interpretation of military laws, and the effort to form an indoctrinated workforce plagued the rise and spread of the navy's intelligence units. The U.S. Navy ONI knew this well.

Lamenting the disorganized direction of naval intelligence, Captain Ellis M. Zacharias of the U.S. Navy reflected on this state of affairs in a letter dated January 27, 1942, to the commander in chief of the U.S. Pacific Fleet. His letter was a call to action. "The greatest single weakness of our Naval Intelligence today," he wrote, "lies in the fact that our officers are selected for reasons other than special fitness for this kind of work."[3] In his estimation, the navy assigned officers to intelligence work for "trivial and irrelevant reasons," with some individuals being recruited because "they were of foreign extraction or could speak, sometimes haltingly, in a foreign tongue."[4] As a result, Captain Zacharias opined, naval intelligence "became inferior in quality."[5] This inferiority stemmed from three factors: first, the navy's general reluctance to train officers with a rigorous academic knowledge of "foreign" societies; second, the navy's failure to indoctrinate its personnel about the importance of military intelligence; and, third, the navy's hesitation to treat seriously matters of espionage as they pertain to shore bases and establishments. He exclaimed, "Ranking officers belittle the thought of spies or the suggestion of dangerous sabotage from within, they laugh at the possibility of subversive threats to our morale, they have spoken disparagingly of the Intelligence service . . . and resent and even combat efforts aimed at effecting security."[6] While Captain Zacharias offered thin examples by way of justifying these claims, his comments still illustrated the kinds of predicaments military intelligence units faced at the onset of the war.

As a solution for addressing the "inferior" standards of military intelligence, he urged the navy to create intelligence officers whose training and objectives would make for a more capable, willing, and offensive global military. In an appendix attached to his letter, titled "The Standards of a Good Intelligence Officer," Captain Zacharias characterized the ideal intelligence officer as possessing "a mental alertness which will enable him to cope with agile and clever opposition, fortified by ample financial resources."[7] An officer must also be suspicious, aggressive, and imaginative enough to "visualize the possible plans of enemy agents and at the same time be sufficiently analytical to properly evaluate the information which comes to him."[8] Like their "foreign" intelligence counterparts, the naval officers needed to be knowledgeable about the geography, history, language, policy, and warfare of enemy countries, as much as they should be cognizant of espionage and counterespionage tactics. Captain Zacharias's suggestions thereby reflected an effort to produce knowledge about the Pacific Islands.

At the onset of the war, the navy organized all classified materials under the aegis of "Combat Intelligence" and "Radio Intelligence," military units that developed tactical information for the navy. During that period, there was no centralized agency through which military intelligence could easily be shared across the armed forces in the Pacific. The navy soon realized that a central organization was needed to transmit information across various military commands, especially since the U.S. campaign to invade Japanese-occupied territories in Guam and the Pacific demanded reliable networks of communication. On September 7, 1943, the Joint Intelligence Center Pacific Ocean Areas (JICPOA), was formed in response to these needs. Although its formation was deemed a success, the fact that its ranks consisted largely of reservists or part-time military personnel indicated that full-time military intelligence staff had yet to be realized in the then burgeoning organization. In light of these challenges, JICPOA "grew with the war until it could supply all types of the most detailed information on every phase of Japanese military, Naval, industrial, agricultural, political, and social development."[9] Reflecting a middle-class sensibility in the recruitment of intelligence officers, the reserve officers consisted of "lawyers, forest rangers, architects, newspapermen, geologists, engineers, scholars and teachers—[who became] qualified linguists and experts in the short space of two and three years."[10] As the largest producer of intelligence material, JICPOA evolved into the "only U.S. agency in which military and naval intelligence are formed into a single comprehensive organization servicing all the needs of ground, air, and naval forces of a theater commander."[11]

By intelligence, JICPOA meant "information of the enemy, his organization, equipment, capabilities, and intentions. . . . In brief, intelligence must be clarified, centralized and professionalized, and so constituted and situated in relation to the top command and to those responsible for national policy."[12] Based in Pearl Harbor (Puʻuloa), Oʻahu, JICPOA had grown to nearly five hundred officers and eight hundred enlisted personnel by 1944. Among their tasks, the most notable included the development of propaganda in the forms of leaflets and broadcasts; the creation of aerial maps and photos of Japanese civilian and military populations; the imprisonment and interrogation of Japanese prisoners of war; and the translation and interpretation of Japanese military documents. By being located in Pearl Harbor, the closest military base to the western continental United States, JICPOA stressed its reach to military units during their forays into the Pacific. As one official report noted, JICPOA's "geographical coverage for briefing was impressive. During the months of June and July 1945, members of the staff were in such widely separated places as Ie Shima, Okinawa, Iwo Jima, the Marianas, the Philippines, Hawaiian Islands, the Aleutians, and with the British Pacific Fleet in Sydney."[13]

In the summer of 1944, JICPOA claimed to have saved many lives in the Mariana Islands based on its distribution of approximately 400,000 propaganda leaflets that urged the indigenous and settler populations of the archipelago to surrender to the invading U.S. military forces. As a crucial component of these forces, JICPOA "lent assistance to the island commands in their mopping-up campaigns in Guam, Tinian [and] Saipan."[14] The U.S. Marine Corps, for example, established "Intelligence Collecting Teams" to "follow closely in the rear of assault units and gather documents and material of intelligence value. . . . All personnel were instructed to turn over intelligence material to the collection teams or to the intelligence sections, who then forwarded it to higher headquarters."[15] As the Intelligence Section of the Third Marine Division reported in May 1944, "All individuals must be impressed with the fact that no item is too insignificant to be of intelligence value. A document or article which, at first glance, may appear to have no importance whatsoever may well be the vital link in a chain of intelligence information which a higher echelon is attempting to complete."[16]

Preparing the Marine Corps for its assault in the Japanese-occupied islands, the Intelligence Section emphasized, "Every man should be made to realize that his failure to turn in immediately any intelligence information in the form of documents or material found by him could easily result in the deaths of many of his comrades due to the proper authorities not receiving the information in time."¹⁷ In addition to notebooks and other written items, these objects included automatic weapons with ammunition, communication equipment, dog tags, electronic and power plant equipment, and radar apparatuses, to name a few. With these considerations in mind, the Intelligence Section warned that the failure to heed these instructions would result in Marines "aiding the enemy and betraying their comrades"; all manner of collecting wartime "souvenirs" was likewise discouraged.¹⁸ The Joint Intelligence Center Pacific Ocean Areas thereby contributed toward the criminalization of bodies, ideas, and activities in Guam, the Mariana Islands, and other Pacific islands. In turn, the U.S. Navy's War Crimes Tribunals Program later treated such classification as lawful.

Classifying War Bodies

In *Discipline and Punish: The Birth of the Prison*, Michel Foucault argued that the spectacle of public execution, or the sovereign imposition of power onto a suffering violator of monarchial law, no longer held prominence in Europe by the late nineteenth century. The public torture of criminal bodies was on the decline; since that period, sovereign entities began to transfer punishment from the bodies of criminals to the bodies of populations. As Foucault observed, "Physical pain, the pain of the body itself, is no longer the constituent element of the penalty. From being an art of unbearable sensations punishment has become an economy of suspended rights." Referring to the white, rights-bearing body of colonial modernity, he said this of the body: "The body now serves as an instrument or intermediary: if one intervenes upon it to imprison it, or to make it work, it is in order to deprive the individual of a liberty that is regarded both as a right and as a property." He continued, "If it is still necessary for the law to reach and manipulate the body of the convict, it will be at a distance, in the proper way, according to strict rules, and with a much 'higher' aim. As a result of this new restraint, a whole army of technicians took over from the executioner, the immediate anatomist of pain."¹⁹ These technicians included chaplains, doctors, educationalists, psychiatrists, psychologists, and wardens, as well as military intelligence officers and enlisted personnel.

While Foucault's general treatment of punishment resonates with the ways in which the navy crafted its intelligence apparatuses in Guam and the wider Mariana Islands, his notion that modern punishment deprives the body of rights and property can only go so far when considering the indigenous and settler peoples of the Pacific—that is, the non-European societies of modernity. In Guam, individuals under Japan's empire became subject to the U.S. rule of law, as evidenced in the military's classification of their bodies. The intelligence briefs, administered by the military intelligence units and distributed to sailors and soldiers, are instructive in this regard. As one Marine report noted, "The military importance of Guam is great. When you capture Guam, we shall have advanced to within 1300 miles of Tokyo and shall be only some 800 miles from Japan's main bases. . . . Guam is an American territory and the people are American nationals. We will be welcomed as liberators, not as enemies."[20]

After reclaiming Guam as an "American territory," the brief identified Guamanians as Christian, peaceful, and good-natured. However, if they ignored the threats of military physical punishment, as the Marine intelligence form warned, they will, as a "law abiding" society, react favorably to the mere mention of the word "law." Even as so-called loyal natives, the threat of the law always placed Chamorros outside of it, never fully a part of the polity yet often subjected to its violence. Marines and other military personnel in Guam thus fashioned themselves as a liberating and lawmaking invading force. Of particular relevance were the ways in which the military intelligence briefs further categorized indigenous and settler bodies in Guam.

Whereas Guamanians were generally perceived as both liberated and loyal subjects of the United States, military intelligence units sometimes instructed military personnel to suspend their preconceived prejudices about the Japanese nationals, many of whom, the brief stated, were "really loyal Chamorros."[21] Clearly, the report described Chamorro-Japanese families on the island, of which there were 326 Japanese nationals who had intermarried with Chamorro clans. As the memo indicated, "This information is given to you [the Marine] in order that you may guard yourselves against hasty conclusions when a person with oriental features is found. . . . A great number of those classed as Japanese are really loyal Chamorros and it is well that you leave the screening of all these people to the Intelligence Section, which is best fitted to do it."[22] While this brief provided working definitions of indigenous and settler identities for the Marines, military police officers and military intelligence officers primarily "screened" these categories, refined the "criminal" hierarchies, and segregated the bodies. Another military police memo declared, "Our job is to give every possible aid and assistance to the loyal and to confine the disloyal. . . . This will mean that many loyal people will be confined while awaiting individual examination. All concerned must use great tact and resourcefulness. This applies particularly to

Military Police who will come in contact with the people."²³ Wary of the international implications of their tasks, the brief emphasized, "It is imperative that this be done. Failure to treat our own loyal people well would give the enemy valuable propaganda to influence the people of the Philippines against us. . . . On the other hand, it is imperative that all disloyal persons be seized and segregated from the loyal."²⁴ With the war still being waged, the American intelligence and police units knew about the legal and political stakes in repossessing Guam.

Drawing on *The Penal Code of Guam* and military proclamations, especially the laws that upheld interrogation and imprisonment, the military police became "the only police force available to see that the civilians comply with the Military Government and local laws."²⁵ As one report revealed, police personnel became "empowered to arrest violators of both type of laws."²⁶ They likewise exercised "discretion in carrying out that power."²⁷ With the military police having jurisdiction over all civilians, one of its first duties included the processing of Chamorro interpreters and police officers from Rota and Saipan. As the military police and intelligence units prepared for these investigations, the Rotanese and Saipanese sought refuge from the reinvading American forces. Sometime in July 1944, for example, nearly three hundred civilians employed by the Minseibu, the entire Kempeitai police force, and other Japanese military and police officials left Hagåtña. By that time, the American military had been bombing the island's capital for several weeks. As the Saipanese Nicholas T. Sablan recalled, "We were trying to escape danger" from the bombs of American airplanes and the shells of American ships.²⁸ The Rotanese and Saipanese interpreters, including their family members and one Guamanian prisoner, thus accompanied the Japanese contingent to seek shelter from the Americans.

At first, they traveled to the villages of Etton, Fonte, and Otdot. The Japanese officials then allowed the Rotanese and Saipanese to bring their relatives to Manengon, an area where the Japanese military had congregated most of the Guamanian population. According to Sablan, the Japanese police forces followed them to Manengon, where the group remained for two days. The remaining Japanese civilians and military personnel departed for the agricultural unit in Tai. But because the American Marines had already landed on the island and were fast approaching, the group traveled to the northern village of Upi. Once there, the Japanese civilians left the military and police forces, at which point the Japanese Imperial Army ordered the Rotanese and Saipanese to accompany the army to the coastal village of Tarague. Fearing for their lives, the Saipanese Pedro Sablan Leon Guerrero said, "We, the remaining interpreters following the Japanese police force, decided to get away from the danger that was then going around the Japanese group. We waited until our Japanese companions had left and then proceeded to Santa Rosa mountain."[29] He continued, "One of our companions had some food with him and we decided that as soon as that food was exhausted, we were to go out and surrender ourselves. At the end of five days and five nights, we decided early in the morning that because one of our Saipan boys by the name of Henry Pangelinan understood the English language and also a native of Guam going with us by the name of Pedro Zamora, that these two men go out first to where the Americans were and to inform them that we were then in the woods."[30]

Afraid of the American military, the Rotanese and Saipanese prayed among themselves and cautiously planned for their surrender, knowing that they might be tied up as a group, laid on the ground, and crushed under the weight of American tanks.[31] On August 15, 1944, Henry Pangelinan and the Guamanian prisoner Pedro Zamora left the group for the Americans, that is, the direction where the "nearest gunfire was heard."[32] "On our way to surrender," stated Pangelinan, "we prepared a white flag. While we were fixing that white flag, we heard an American whistle at us. So when we heard the whistle, we got so scared, we held up our hands and [Pedro Zamora] called out, 'Chamorros, we are Chamorros.'"[33] Pangelinan and Zamora then escorted the military police to their group. Disavowing their affiliation with the Japanese due to their fear of the Americans, the other Rotanese and Saipanese similarly approached the Marines. As Pedro Sablan Leon Guerrero explained, "As soon as we got out of the woods, one of the guards asked if anyone of us was a Japanese. We replied that we were all natives. . . . The guards went toward us and patted us on the back and told us we were already liberated."[34]

The military police then processed the Chamorro interpreters and police officers, with the exception of Luis C. Crisostomo, who was alive but missing from the group.[35] Everybody was fed as well. On the following day, August 16, 1944, the military police transferred them to a building in the village of Tomhom with other "surrendered" individuals. As Guerrero recalled, the military police "came over and gave us soap and water and told us to get out of the building, stretch ourselves, and wash our clothes but not go far."[36] He felt much relief and gratitude, especially since the military police treated him better than his stripped and handcuffed Japanese counterparts. Whatever forms of "liberation" the Rotanese and Saipanese experienced, however, were quickly diminished when the military police relocated them to the Island Command Prisoner of War Camp the next day. Attentive to the American military's racism, Saipanese Manuel Borja Tudela understood that since "the beginning we were segregated."[37]

In a joint effort to classify the indigenous and settler populations of Guam, the American military's intelligence and police units thus segregated the wartime populations along two signifying axes: the civilian and the prisoner of war. The American military "believed that interpreters (unless accompanying the Japanese armed forces), civil policemen, or wardens of jails who served the Japanese Military Government in Guam stand in the position of civilian employees of that government and should be interned as civilians."[38] Therefore, the navy interned numerous Chamorros from Rota and Saipan under the civilian subcategories of "civilian detainee" and "civilian internee." As the Marine captain and intelligence officer Nick Savage explained, "The term civilian detainee is applied to persons locked up because he or she may represent a dangerous element in society, locked up under military law against whom no formal charges have been lodged."[39] On the other hand, he stated that the "term civilian internee applies to persons who had been charged and sentenced for a crime or who had been formally recorded as representing an enemy country or holding sympathy toward an enemy country."[40] As Savage's comments reveal, the navy had wide latitude in arbitrarily determining who constituted the "dangerous" members of society.

In everyday and official discourse, the military likewise used these terms interchangeably in its screening and detaining of civilians in "protective compounds"; hence, civilians were incarcerated without any formal criminal charges levied against them. Once they were interned, the military created a census of "civilians" as per four identities: "(a) Chamorros believed loyal [to the United States] (b) Chamorros believed disloyal or whose loyalty is in doubt (c) Other civilians (d) Apprehended violators of Military Government, proclamations, orders or notices, and of local criminal laws, until such time as local jails and prisons are opened."[41] Detailing these categories further Captain Savage recalled that the "major job" of classifying civilians produced "Okinawan fishermen in one category and the Japanese women comfort troops in another category, and the Saipanese and Tinianese and the Chamorros as another category, and the allegedly disloyal half Japanese and half Chamorro Guamanians in another category."[42]

Commenting on the role of the protective compounds, Major General Roy S. Geiger of the U.S. Marines informed the interned that the compounds protected them from incurring injuries due to the ongoing conflicts on the island. "It is necessary," he said, "to remain in the compound . . . because there may be some enemy civilians among you and there may be others who sympathize with the enemy. These will be sent to the prison stockade as soon as discovered."[43] He added that the "Marines that are on guard around the compound are there to protect [civilians] as well as to prevent the disloyal from escaping. The Marines in the compound are here to assist you. They will show you how to make your shelters and have tools which you may use in making places of protection for you and your families."[44] Once interned in August 1944, the indigenous Chamorro and Asian settler populations, numbering 18,000 and 1,250, respectively, received food and medical supplies.[45] These camps were located in the villages of Hågat, Tamuning, Tutuhan, Yigo, and Yoña. Many individuals thanked the U.S. military for the much-needed assistance; Guam Chamorros felt especially relieved to witness the demise of the Japanese empire.

Yet the act of detaining these peoples represented more than a measure of population control and racialized classification. As the sociologist Orlando Patterson would put it, the camps in Guam partly invoked the "symbolic instruments" of enslavement. In fact, Patterson identifies "capture in warfare" and "punishment for crimes" as two of the eight means by which slaveholders have historically acquired slaves.[46] Slave masters all over the world, he expressed, "used special rituals of enslavement upon first acquiring slaves: the symbolism of naming, of clothing, of hairstyle, of language, and of body marks."[47] While military officials never described interned civilians as "slaves," the protective compounds nevertheless drew from the carceral history of the United States. By describing these individuals as "enemies," the American military rationalized interning them, much like how the U.S. penal state exists to shield civil society from so-called criminals and outcasts.[48]

The navy further illustrated this parallel in its incarceration of prisoners of war. Comparable to its treatment of civilian detainees and civilian internees, the military categorized prisoners of war under the vague premise that they served the Japanese armed forces in some way. According to one Marine account, the captured prisoners of war "were, or professed to be, extremely stupid, having no knowledge of any units or activity other than their own. Nearly all tactical information obtained from Prisoners of War proved to be thoroughly unreliable. With a few exceptions the documents captured were of no value to the conduct of operations."[49] On the contrary, though, the Marines tempered their dismissive and racist views of prisoner agency by stating that the "lack of information from Prisoners of War and the absence of valuable documents may reflect a growing security consciousness on the part of the enemy."[50] Japanese military officers, for example, were often less cooperative in interrogations, indicating reluctance on the part of some men to disclose information.[51] Other prisoners of war included businessmen, dentists, doctors, and teachers, as well as any Asian employed by the military. If soldiers were identified as prisoners of war, the U.S. military then transferred them to the Island Command Prisoner of War Camp, also known as the "prisoner stockade," in Hagåtña. Intelligence officers later determined if they participated in war crimes. The prisoners of war also engaged in training and disciplinary drills.[52] Their labor was utilized as well.

As with the detained civilians, the military also exploited the labor of prisoners of war, with civilians working for "any military project consistent with military security."[53] Organized by the Civilian Affairs section of the reestablished U.S. military government, the civilian laborers included "ablebodied" men over fourteen years of age, Koreans, "non-military Asiatics," and "enemy nationals."[54] The elderly, the sick, and women, including the religious, medical, and political elites, were excluded from the military's labor pool. Specifically, the military targeted individuals who could build stockades and related facilities, thereby engendering a masculine yet ultimately emasculated labor force. For this reason, interned civilians and prisoners of war, including Chamorro volunteers, sometimes participated in similar projects. As one naval memorandum declared, prisoners of war "may be used to perform work that is essential—i.e. work that would have to be done whether or not prisoners of war are available."[55]

Yet the military largely placed its "essential" labor demands on prisoners of war in construction work and, to a lesser extent, agricultural production (figure 1.1). Other forms of labor involved "handling of stores, repair of motor vehicles, laundry work, and up-keep of buildings and grounds."[56] On the other hand, the military discouraged prisoners of war from "work that directly contributes to the war effort, work that is unhealthful or dangerous, or work of a classified nature that might offer an opportunity for sabotage."[57] Otherwise, an armed guard received instructions to ensure that "all members of his detail are within sight and control"; guards were forbidden, as well, from delivering derogatory remarks to and fraternizing with the prisoners of war.[58] The military likewise informed these guards to "show a POW what is to be done, be sure they understand it, then keep them moving. An Oriental cannot be rushed. If pushed and hurried he will quit."[59]

The compounds then segregated the prisoners of war and other laborers, already racialized as loyal and disloyal subjects, by issuing cloth armbands

1.1. Japanese prisoners being searched at a POW camp on Guam. The original caption reads, "At Jap PW camp on Guam, prisoners are seen under surveyance of camp officials. Prisoners being searched at gate as they return from work" (no photo number, Rec. September 11, 1945). U.S. National Archives, College Park, Maryland.

to allow the guards to better identify and supervise their duties. As the military instructed, "Arm bands will be red for Japanese, red and white striped for Koreans, and white for all other nationalities." Further, English-speaking laborers and interpreters for the military wore a plain armband beneath their respective colored bands. In these circumstances, the color red may have signified political danger. And whereas red and white may have meant political ambivalence, white may have symbolized neutrality or loyalty to the United States. Although the military did not explain the reasons for choosing these colors, its treatment of laborers clearly followed carceral and militarized routines. These activities included attaching letters and numbers to the armbands; assigning military enlisted men as supervisors to the laborers; maintaining daily record books on laborer responsibilities; organizing eight-hour work shifts over a six-day period; and appointing armed guards to monitor Asian laborers.

Explaining the relationship between labor and imprisonment, the scholar Angela Y. Davis writes that "in the philosophical conception of the penitentiary, labor was a reforming activity. It was supposed to assist the imprisoned individual in his (and on occasion her) putative quest for religious penitence and moral re-education. Labor was a means toward a moral end."[60] For the navy, its personnel sought to reestablish a legal and political hierarchy that was temporarily usurped by the former Japanese occupational military government in Guam. Toward this goal, the navy subjected prisoners of war to "hard labor" that exceeded "the physical exertion required of troops," a process by which the navy disciplined the prisoners into subjects of U.S. colonial law.[61] As in other cases, the navy was not alone in its endeavors to punish any prisoner of war.

Chamorros who resisted the navy's demonization of the Japanese became the objects of local ridicule all the same. Silvina Charfauros-Cruz Taumomoa, for example, provided the following account of how her grandmother of the Gutgohu clan assisted the Japanese prisoners of war in the village of Hågat when the men were tasked to clean debris and collect the skeletal remains of their comrades. As Taumomoa observed, "Only my grandmother would give cold water, pull the fainting under a shade and apply cold compress." The native women of the village condemned Taumomoa, one of the few elders to help the prisoners of war, for these actions. Continued Taumomoa, "The women would then make remarks like, 'These men killed your son and ours. Why are you helping them to live? They should die as they deserved!' My grandmother would simply answer that, 'The war is over, and my son is dead. No amount of bitterness would raise him from the dead.'" Stressing solidarity for Japanese and Asian women, Taumomoa's grandmother said, "'But let me tell you, these men have mothers and wives. And somewhere in Japan, they are crying as I cried, wishing as I wished that my sons would all come home safely.'"[62]

Elsewhere, Guamanian forms of retribution complemented the web of native gossip and spite that made critiques of the navy's laws difficult and dangerous. In this respect, some members of the navy utilized native labor, racism, and violence to develop their intelligence and police units, just as some Guamanians appropriated the military's logics to their own ends. Created by the U.S. military government in November 1944, for example, the Guam Combat Patrol captured any "Japanese stragglers" who had yet to surrender to the Marine Corps and navy. Consisting of Chamorros from Guam, the native police force ranged from as few as eight men to as many as twenty-four individuals during its existence from 1944 to 1947. Describing its mission, the editors for the *Guam Gazette* reported, "'Surrender or die,' was the order given Guam's Combat Patrol to deliver to the remaining Japanese Armed Forces hiding in the hills." As Staff Sergeant Juan U. Aguon, a Chamorro, noted, "We always get them—dead or alive!"[63] Further elaborating upon their role, the editors for the Navy News disclosed that "continuous small reconnaissance patrols must be used at present to ferret out the renegades because the Japs quickly go into hiding when they encounter large searching parties."[64] As the Intelligence Section of the Third Marine Division in Guam put it, Guamanian men were chosen for their "knowledge of trails, water points, and caves . . . in hunting down small groups in hiding."[65] Describing the Japanese as stragglers or animals to be preyed upon, the Navy News thus understood them as "desperadoes [who are] shot down at sight if they attempt to resist when they are apprehended."[66] By April 1946, the American military estimated that the Guam Combat Patrol had killed "174 Japanese guerillas," with only twelve being captured and detained.[67]

In principle, the American military charged the Guam Combat Patrol to locate and arrest any remaining Japanese individuals in the island (figure 1.2). But that seldom proved the case, as illustrated in the racist coverage by the military's media and as evidenced in the racist actions by Guamanians. According to Adolf Sgambelluri, the son of the former police officer Adolfo Sgambelluri, the American military wondered why the patrol had not captured any Japanese civilians or prisoners of war three months into its operation. As Adolf Sgambelluri recalled, the Marine captain Nicholas Savage said to Adolf's father, Adolfo Sgambelluri, "What the hell? How come you haven't caught any stragglers?"[68] Suspicious of the Guam Combat Patrol's activities, Savage then instructed Adolfo Sgambelluri to investigate this case and to apprise him thereafter. The latter eventually concluded that the Guam Combat Patrol had murdered all the Japanese stragglers three months into its operations. As his son explained, the patrol "hated the Japanese so bad, they would make the [surrendered] guy run. . . . So when the guy runs down the road they shoot him in the back and kill him." He continued, "My father found out who these guys [in the Guam Combat Patrol] were, wrote the report, and it went to [Captain Nicholas Savage], and [he] took it up to the commanding general of the landing force."[69]

Knowing that murder was illegal and grounds for naval punishment, Sgambelluri's "father put in a caveat that the Chamorros have suffered for the last two years, been tortured, and they're 'getting even now.'"[70] Unsurprisingly, the American military failed to arrest the unidentified members of the Guam Combat Patrol responsible for murdering anybody they classified as "Japanese stragglers." The collusion between military classifications

1.2. The Guam Combat Patrol discussing stolen food. The original caption reads, "The Native Military Gov. patrol fighters scouring the jungles of Guam, for Japs. The day's hunting starts as members of the Native Military patrol hears a native explain that during the previous night chickens, eggs and produce had been stolen by Japs from his farm on the edge of the jungle. L-R Sgt. Juan Aguon, patrol leader, Pedro San Nicholas, Jesus Yosida, Ignacio Riverin and Antonio Manibusan, members of the patrol" (photo number 01204 CINCPAC, Rec. June 1, 1945). U.S. National Archives, College Park, Maryland.

of zoē, animal life, and native retribution coalesced here; this political nexus thrived, as well, in the circulation of native rumors and hearsay, the interrogations of suspected war criminals, the solicitation of witness testimonies, and the development of court proceedings. Rather than hold these Guamanians accountable for their actions, the military instead awarded the men of the Guam Combat Patrol, including those who perished during their missions. They received the Bronze Star Medal, the Purple Heart, and the Silver Star Medal for attempting, as one periodical noted, to "eradicate" Japanese stragglers from the island.[71]

Although the final death and capture statistics for the Guam Combat Patrol are unknown, various monthly reports indicate that numerous Japanese died under the vigilante efforts of these Chamorro men.[72] While a few Japanese survived, it is clear that the Guam Combat Patrol shored up the navy's racism in ways that supported the broader incarceration of Japanese, Rotanese, Saipanese, and other suspected individuals in Guam. As

Vicente M. Diaz and Laura Marie Torres Souder argue in their critiques of the war, providing Chamorros with limited positions of power in the form of the Guam Combat Patrol, monitoring the state of hygiene in the camps, and introducing medical aid and canned foods produced a series of cultural and historical processes. In other words, these foundational events of the war generated economies of dependence among the interned populations, reified the carceral state by which the U.S. military governed indigenous and settler subjects in the Pacific, and created Chamorro cultural systems of obligation and reciprocity to the U.S. nation that problematically persist to this day.[73]

Bodies of War Criminality

Largely unbeknownst to the indigenous and settler populations, the establishment of protective compounds and the Island Command Prisoner of War Camp merely constituted the first stage in the making of the War Crimes Tribunals Program. Although numerous Chamorro clans eventually returned to their respective villages throughout the island, and although many Asian settlers reconnected with their displaced communities, the gestures of supposed humanitarianism provided by the internment camps belied the carceral aspects of these sites. As the military commission came to fruition in December 1944, the intelligence and police units invented new bodies of war criminality that speak to Giorgio Agamben's homo sacer as the original foreclosure of political life that the sovereign claims in the name of democracy.

The making of the protective compounds in Guam thereby limited the political life, bios, of the interned Japanese settlers and indigenous Chamorros, similar to Foucault's perception of the function of prisons in modern society. As he astutely observed, these war bodies constituted "the organization of a field of prevention, the calculation of interests, the circulation of representations and signs, the constitution of a horizon of certainty and proof, the adjustment of penalties to ever more subtle variables; all this also leads to an objectification of criminals and crime."[74] As the navy attempted to control the fields of signification by which war criminality was made legally meaningful, Agamben's sacred man surfaced in the navy's calculations of criminality. As an appendage of the U.S. polity, homo sacer emerged via the navy's reinvasion of Guam because his image as an "American" law-abiding subject was suppressed during the Japanese occupation from 1941 to 1944.

That is to say, the U.S. military reduced the interned individuals to biological life, zoē, or a restricted sense of political life, bios, so as to impose its categories of war criminals and other deviant types. That Guamanians often dehumanized their Chamorro counterparts from Rota and Saipan as the proverbial hilitai reflected both indigenous notions of reciprocity and retribution as much as they illustrated the American military's erasure of Japanese political life, bios, among the Rotanese and Saipanese. The incarceration of these subjects in American-made compounds and prisoner stockades thus established a landscape wherein all things Japanese were eliminated and remade in criminal terms. As Mbembe reminds us, the "subject in the colony . . . is nothing but an appearance. He/she has a body. The colonizer can seize, harass, lock up the native, compel forced labor, make him or her pay taxes or serve as cannon fodder."[75]

As the navy understood it, war criminality involved people who committed "murders, atrocities and other violations of the laws of war against members of the armed forces of the United States or against other Americans, including the peoples of any dependency such as the Philippines."[76] With the establishment of the national War Crimes Office in December 25, 1944, Secretary of the Navy James Forrestal instructed all military units in the Pacific to "arrange for the immediate or eventual apprehension, trial and sentence of such war criminals."[77] As the War Department emphasized, "Personnel performing investigative, intelligence, police, photographic, or medical functions will during the normal course of their duties make every effort to detect and develop information regarding war crimes and to prepare and report evidence."[78] Failure to heed these orders, the War Department forewarned, could enable "many of the persons responsible for outrages against humanity . . . to go unpunished because of the failure to preserve evidence or to obtain essential information at the time of discovery and at the scene of the crime."[79] As the negotiating agency between the State and the Navy Departments, the War Department coordinated matters concerning war crimes against U.S. military personnel and "other Americans" in Asia, Europe, and the Pacific Islands. Given the navy's governance of several Pacific islands since 1898, the secretary appointed the judge advocate general of the navy with cognizance over legal issues relating to war crimes.[80]

Specifically, the secretary referred to the "Navy's Pacific" as the U.S. territory of Guam and the former Japanese-mandated islands of the western Pacific; other Pacific branches included "China, India-Burma, Japan, the Malay Section, Netherland East Indies, the Philippines, the Ryukyu Section, and the Solomon Islands Section, areas where Australia, the United States, and other allied countries conducted war crimes investigations."[81] Under its wartime jurisdiction, the navy consequently examined allegations of war crimes in the Bonin Islands, the Caroline Islands, the Gilbert Islands, the Mariana Islands, the Marshall Islands, and the Palau Islands.[82] Intelligence materials about war crimes gathered by military commands in these areas were forwarded to the judge advocate general of the navy, who furnished legal information upon request and made "recommendations with regard to procedure and personnel."[83]

Advancing the now official mandate to investigate war criminals among the interned populations in Guam's protective compounds and in the prisoner stockade, the navy also created the Advance Intelligence Center (AIC) on the island to assist the Office of the Judge Advocate General, JICPOA, the military police, and other related intelligence units in the criminalization of indigenous and settler bodies. Formed in January 1945, and based in Guam at the Advance Headquarters of the commander in chief, U.S. Pacific Fleet (CINPAC), the AIC held responsibility for "photographic reconnaissance, target selection, geography, interrogation and translation, escape and invasion, psychological warfare, flak intelligence, reference library, aviation charts and photo laboratory, and distribution."[84] Although AIC's main task was to support U.S. war efforts in Asia and the Pacific, its "interrogation and translation" section played a central role in interrogating prisoners of war in Guam.

Erecting a Quonset hut near the Island Command Prisoner of War Camp, the AIC screened and identified potential war criminals among the nearly seven hundred prisoners of war interned in the stockade. In the process, the AIC often encountered prisoners of war who said little about their wartime pasts, if not altogether resisted the agency's interrogation methods. As one intelligence report indicated, the military's "investigations are progressing slowly because of the well organized efforts being made by the Japanese involved to conceal these crimes to avoid implication."[85] "At the end of the war," the memorandum continued, "many of them were instructed as to what to say in case they were questioned by the allied forces concerning disappearances of [American] prisoners of war. At present many of them are still conspiring to keep their activities secret."[86] Whether the AIC questioned prisoners of war as to the locations of missing Americans or the manner in which they died, the intelligence unit adhered to several goals in making its evaluations.

The first purpose of the interrogations was to "perpetuate all available evidence as to permit trial of the accused at a later date"; the second objective aimed to "collect evidence which, when properly combined with evidence from other sources, may fix responsibility at levels above that of the immediate perpetrator."[87] As these parameters illustrate, the investigations employed a vertical hierarchy by which to ascertain bodies of war criminality, from the low-ranking soldiers to the high-ranking commanders of the Japanese military. If the AIC determined a war crime was committed or witnessed by a prisoner, then AIC cross-checked with administrative officers in various intelligence units to gauge if said war crime was already being investigated. If that was the case, then AIC added information to that ongoing investigation (e.g., personal statements). Otherwise, files were opened whenever new allegations of war crimes emerged. Each file identified the name(s) of the accused war criminal(s), with subheadings for the name(s) of the alleged victim(s), as in this prescribed format: "TANAKA, Juichi; alias 'The Bug-Eye"/MOTO, Taro;/1st Lt. John J. Doe—Victim."[88]

While these and other files often listed "victims" as white military men, war crimes investigating officers were also trained to imagine their "victims" as "white, female, adult, housewife."[89] Predictably, the American military gendered its victims as domestic, vulnerable, and white in its war crimes investigations, as if to signify a feminine and violated nation. The defense and prosecution teams of the military court later invoked these tropes of innocence, albeit in differently situated ways for colonial, indigenous, and settler bodies alike. Furthermore, individuals suspected of war crimes were not segregated from the wider prison population "so as to avoid disclosure that individuals are being held for future trial."[90] It was not until the military court summoned the accused prisoners for trial that their identities as war criminals were publicly exposed; they either remained in the Island Command Prisoner of War Camp in Hagåtña or were transferred to the new War Criminals Stockade in the village of Tomhom. In fact, none of the interned Japanese, Rotanese, and Saipanese individuals accused of war crimes ever received their charges until one to three months before they faced their trials. In this secretive environment, the navy's intelligence units identified their suspected war criminals among a pool of nearly 135,000 civilian and military personnel examined in Guam and the western Pacific up to the end of the War Crimes Trials Program in 1949.[91]

In these interrogations, the navy intelligence units clearly subjected interned civilians and prisoners to the surveillance mechanisms of a police state. Whereas the U.S. Constitution theoretically prevented the military from engaging in police activities without the consent of Congress or the president, as reflected in the Posse Comitatus Act of 1878, the navy had historically employed police logics in its colonization of indigenous peoples in the Pacific and elsewhere.[92] Since the act no longer applies today given its repeal during the Reagan administration's war on drugs in the 1980s, and especially due to Reagan's endorsement of military training and warfare tactics among the police, some critics now argue that the lines that distinguish the military sphere from the police sphere have altogether disappeared.[93] Those domains, however, coexisted intimately in the military colony of Guam. As a central component of the navy's carceral and intelligence apparatuses, the policing of war criminals began with the identification of individuals allegedly involved in war crimes. This was the process by which AIC, JICPOA, and others compared their respective files on war crimes. Once individuals were targeted as "war criminals," military intelligence units examined their modus operandi. As naval commander George H. Brereton explained, in "police investigation the 'M.O.' of an unknown criminal is often of considerable value in connecting him with a particular type of crime."[94]

With the identities of the accused and the victim established, and with a modus operandi on which to draw, naval intelligence units meticulously created a context to produce the "guilt" of the war criminal in question. When describing the accused beyond his or her name, for example, Commander Brereton urged investigators to "make every effort to get an accurate and complete description of the suspect, his service connections, relations, friends, prior occupation, hometown, habits and personal characteristics."[95] Second Lieutenant Ralph De Vries confirmed this tactic, as intelligence officers like himself frequently asked an accused individual when "he came to Guam, what he did here, just so we could get his life history."[96] In these cases, De Vries "investigated the people who were suspected of beatings and murder with reference to Guam citizens."[97] In the process, the phenotype of the nonwhite war criminal emerged. His age, build, and height mattered, as did his eye, hair, and skin color. Other racialized attributes—from his body amputations to his scars and from his tattoos to his gold teeth—were recorded in police notebooks.

Further reifying the body of the war criminal, intelligence officials used six interrogation techniques that charmed, forced, or intimidated the accused war criminal into providing information. The first method confronted the accused with "overwhelming evidence"; the second tactic employed a "harsh" interviewer and a "friendly" interviewer; the third style suggested immunity for the accused; the fourth approach exaggerated the offense; the fifth strategy applied hypnotism; and, finally, the six procedure utilized a polygraph.[98] For the investigators, the accused individuals revealed their guilt by their twitching hands, refusal to cooperate, declarations of innocence, sweating, changed facial skin color, or dry mouths (as indicated by their request for a drink).[99] Additionally, investigators aimed to retain the personal statements of any witnesses under oath, as prepared and written by the witnesses, the investigators, and, in some cases, the assigned interpreters. As one memorandum on war crimes interrogations asserted, "It is most desirable that the [investigator] examine under oath all witnesses who have or purport to have knowledge of such atrocity or crime."[100] Eventually, Chamorro, Chamorro-Japanese, and Japanese men and women constituted the court's witnesses not because of their knowledge of wartime events per se but because of their deep hatred of and, in a few cases, sincere sympathy for the accused war criminals in Guam. Investigators thus turned to these witnesses, notably Guamanians, to provide "personal knowledge" of criminal activities, even exploiting their antagonisms toward the accused war criminals.[101] But if said information came from another person, the investigators requested the identity and whereabouts of the individual in case their main witness could not attend the trial.[102]

Using cameras, investigators also took photos "wherever possible" of the alleged crime scene and, if possible, of the alleged victim.[103] If a body was found, which sometimes occurred, investigators photographed it, assisted a medical officer in examining any wounds, gathered evidence from the body (e.g., bullets, clothes), and searched it for any kind of personal identification. Other than using the victim's body as evidence, investigators likewise searched for fingerprints "on smooth surfaces, such as highly polished desks, window panes, light bulbs, drinking glasses, polished surfaces of weapons, glassware, cookery, etc."[104] While finding fingerprints proved difficult given the poor conditions of the investigation sites, as many homes, graves, and buildings were damaged or obliterated during the war, the related objective of creating casts and molds of footprints, tire tracks, and other physical markers seemed nearly impossible. Given these circumstances, many war crimes investigators resorted to locating written evidence, as in a diary or a memo, in order to substantiate their claims about the guilt of war criminals. These methods likewise applied to the interrogations of civilians in the protective compounds where the issue of Chamorro complicity with the Japanese empire surfaced.

Knowing that few Chamorro interpreters for the Japanese spoke English, all of whom came from the "Japanized" islands of Rota and Saipan, the navy enlisted Guamanians to translate the Chamorro and English languages. Along with personnel associated with AIC, JICPOA, and other intelligence units, the navy sought the help of Guamanians because of their intimate knowledge of the people, the island, and, above all, the suspected war criminals. The police officer Adolfo Sgambelluri was one such individual who, disguised as a civilian detainee in the camps, investigated "Chamorros that were collaborating with the enemy."[105] Another Guamanian by the name of Pedro Dueñas Camacho performed similar duties for the American military. As he recalled, "I had the position of being one of the important men . . . helping the Government and at the same time trying to locate all these natives who are Japanese collaborators, that is my job. I got their names and arrested some of them and sent them to the stockade."[106]

As a Marine who supervised the conditions of interned Chamorros in the protective compounds, Captain Charles H. Kraus praised these Guamanians for their "familiarity with the people, language and so on."[107] In his view, "the most important assistance of the native police was in the intelligence field."[108] Unlike the interrogations of prisoners of war, which immediately categorized them as disloyal subjects, the first tier of interrogations in the protective compounds attempted to segregate the disloyal from the loyal. Quite often, the disloyal civilians were described as "Japanese, Saipan natives, and natives with Japanese sympathies."[109] Commenting on the politically charged relations among the Chamorros of the Mariana Islands, Kraus noticed the "strong antagonisms that existed between Saipan and Guam Chamorros. Apparently this was caused by the fact that a large number of the Saipan civilians had been imported by the Japanese as interpreters and labor supervisors. They, doubtless, were selected because of their strong pro-Japanese feelings."[110] "Upon discovery of a questionable character," he continued, the accused "and his family, if possible, were sent to the [Hagåtña prisoner] stockade."[111] With the aid of the Guamanian police, then, the navy identified "300 civilians [who] were confined by [the navy] under charges or suspicion of being collaborators in some way."[112]

At this point, civilians accused of participating in war crimes were transferred to the Island Command Prisoner of War Camp, where they, along with their families, were segregated among the prisoner of war population. This second removal varied from camp to camp as the navy conducted its interrogations of civilians. Contrary to the prisoners who knew little or nothing about the navy's separation of war criminals among them, thereby retaining their relative anonymity as accused subjects until summoned by the military court, the civilians removed from the protective compounds to the prisoner of war stockade were immediately subjected to public exposure and humiliation. For the accused Chamorros from Rota and Saipan, they became objects of cultural ridicule and shame—what Captain Kraus called "spite"—as much as they became subjects of the military's carceral apparatuses.[113]

Guamanians affiliated with Japan's empire found themselves in a similar predicament. The American military, for example, incarcerated the Franquez family because of their wartime association with Samuel Takekuna Shinohara, a Japanese national and the senior interpreter for the Minseibu in Guam. As Rita T. Franquez recalled, her mother, Maria, was the sibling of Shinohara's wife, Carmen, by virtue of their ties to the Torres clan. The military consequently interned both families, deemed "guilty by association," in a camp "with a double barbed wire fence and machine guns placed at the corners and along the fence at regular intervals."[114] Describing the interior of the facility, Franquez said, "The crowded Japanese POW camp we were imprisoned in was flooded when the monsoon rain started. The rectangular canvas that served as a roof was strictly a rooftop cover but open on all sides which did not keep wind or rain out. The floor, of course, was dirt and flooded."[115] Rita T. Franquez, who had been a young girl at the time, also remembered how the elders and parents took turns holding their babies to keep them dry from the "the mixture of mud and feces" that sloshed beneath them.[116]

But whereas Shinohara was imprisoned for war crimes he allegedly committed, a rumor that had become widespread among the camps, the Franquez family disputed having participated in any kind of criminal activity directed against U.S. citizens and nationals. Seeking to rectify this situation, Maria T. Franquez requested to meet the unidentified commandant of the camp. Rita summarized their meeting as follows: "She finally got to see the Commandant of the prison. She demanded we be charged with: 1) a civil crime, 2) religious crime, 3) a military crime, or 4) some kind of international crime immediately as we had been prisoners for a very long time there already."[117] Maria T. Franquez "threatened that in the absense [sic] of a crime we could be charged with, we were going to climb the fence and they would have to machine gun us down."[118] Given that the interned individuals were suspects of various types, the elder Franquez utilized the military's language of war criminality as a means to clarify their legal statuses. While such efforts partly conceded to the power of the military,

1.3. Chamorro women doing laundry. The original caption reads, "Suspected Jap sympathizers interned in a prison camp on Guam" (photo number NAVAER-452A, Rec. arch 20, 1945). U.S. National Archives, College Park, Maryland.

Maria T. Franquez's attempt to climb the barbed wire fence with her family at great peril to their safety signaled a stronger opposition to colonizing forces in Guam (figure 1.3). The matter of militarized incarceration was not lost on the Chamorro mother. Explaining her insights, Rita said, "She commented no matter who our captors were, whether Japanese, Spanish or American, they had one thing in common. They all seemed to have hated the Chamorro people with a very arrogant and disparaging attitude without any respect to our humanity nor our rights as victims of super power struggles."[119] With the assistance of the Chamorro educator Agueda Iglesias Johnston and other friends and relatives, the military eventually heeded the Franquez family's request and released them from the prisoner of war camp at an undisclosed time. While a few Guamanian families escaped the military's confinement, that was not the case for the Rotanese and Saipanese.

The War Criminals Stockade

The intelligence and police units interned numerous Japanese, Rotanese, and Saipanese individuals and families, once deemed a threat to society, in the protective compounds or the Island Command Prisoner of War Camp.

But only men accused or convicted of war crimes resided in the War Criminals Stockade in the village of Tomhom, as with Tadao Igawa, Samuel T. Shinohara, Akira Tokunaga, and Juan Villagomez. Describing its environment, Rear Admiral John D. Murphy, the war crimes director, wrote, "The detention building in which the prisoners are housed are [sic] located within an area enclosed with a double fence of barbed wire. The area is lighted with flood lights, and an auxiliary generator is kept in working order and available to be put on the line in case of main power failure. Armed sentries patrol outside the barbed wire enclosure."[120] Alongside the detention building stood two barracks that sheltered the forty-eight Marine officers and enlisted men assigned to the War Criminals Stockade. Private First Class Hubert R. Brinkley, a Marine, had this to say about the incarcerated individuals: "Personally I would not trust a P. O. W. that close to me due to the fact that they had been charged with assault, cannibalism, murder, and general mistreatment of American P. O. W. Some of them had already been tried, and sentenced according to their various charges." Concerned about the welfare of the guards, he said, "I had the security of the stockade and the safety of the other guards on my mind . . . while I was on duty."[121]

Outside, the prisoners shared a pit latrine. If they wished to use the toilet or the shower, they had to run to and from each location. As part of their exercise regimen, they also cut grass, dug ditches, or performed sit-ups for up to thirty minutes each day; the military used their labor for minor construction and repair tasks as well. In terms of resources, the navy provided medical assistance, offered recreational time, screened movies, and loaned library books to the prisoners. Clergy representing the Buddhist, Christian, and Protestant faiths often visited the stockade and counseled the prisoners. Inside the detention building, the prisoners slept in cells secured by padlocks. Only basic toiletries, clothes and linens, items of worship, and reading materials were allowed in the cells. Otherwise, the military indicated that their "quarters should be devoid of unnecessary comforts, conveniences, decorations, particularly photographs and pictures of 'pin-up girls,' Japanese officials or so called heroes."[122] Without protection from mosquitoes, the navy also sprayed the toxic insecticide DDT in the cells, where, supposedly, the prisoners suffered "very little."[123] As per the navy's policy, at least one Marine guard was posted in front of the cells at all times.

With the exception of witnesses who temporarily dwelt in a separate part of the facility, the accused and convicted war criminals abided by a strict set of rules.[124] The first order required that each man "come to attention whenever an officer approaches your hut and when you are spoken to by a member of the guard."[125] Other rules demanded that the prisoners maintain clean cells, request permission to speak and use the toilet, concede to having their letters censored, and refrain from touching any part of the barbed wire gates and fences. Their only semblance of protection came in the form of a rule that forbade any guard from assaulting them; the rule "pertained to the mistreatment of Japanese and Native P.O.W."[126] If "struck or punished" by a sentry, for example, the prisoner had the right to contact a senior officer about said allegations.[127]

Sometime in May or June 1946, seven Japanese prisoners of war took advantage of this regulation by claiming that the guards had abused them during their stay in Guam (figure 1.4). Of these Japanese men, only Vice Admirals Kaoru Arima, Masashi Kobayashi, and Kunizo Mori identified their purported assailants as, respectively, Marine privates Donald W. Purcell, Raymond L. Romero, and Rocco L. Piacente. The others—all lower-ranking personnel formerly employed by the Japanese Imperial Navy—failed to identify the guards despite being able to recall their beatings. Whereas they argued that the guards had forced them to eat their meals within one minute, a few separately charged that they had extracted their gold teeth for a guard, masturbated a guard's penis, performed oral sex on a guard's penis, participated in excessive drills, or received hits and spit to the face, back, or stomach.[128]

In his statement dated July 2, 1946, Vice Admiral Kaoru Arima argued that the guards had assaulted them for having caused World War II in Asia and the Pacific Islands. As he put it, several unidentified guards approached him on May 27, 1946, and accused him of being "responsible for the happenings of the Death March of Bataan, attack on Shanghai, Hong Kong, Canton, and the attack of Pearl Harbor."[129] One sentry then hit Vice Admiral Arima "with the broom on the seat of my pants for about 15 times, slapped me about 15 or more times, and finally grabbed my head with both hands and twisted my neck several times. In doing the last act another guard helped the first guard. The others stood by and watched."[130] By physically, sexually, and verbally assaulting the prisoners, the guards conveyed ownership over them as subhuman and nonhuman bodies, zoē, that now fell under the reach of the U.S. penal state in Guam. Corporal Tsugio Asanuma relayed this sentiment when three guards demanded his four gold teeth as souvenirs on May 24, 1946. As he explained, the unidentified Marine sentries attempted to "jab" his gold teeth with a club, but failed in releasing the teeth from Asanuma's mouth. Having "no other alternative," the Japanese corporal "found and used a nail to pry loose my gold teeth."[131]

1.4. War Criminals Stockade. The original caption reads, "Japanese War Criminals Stockade Area, Guam, M. I. 1. The stockade gates. 2. The stockade guard house. 3. The emergency generator can be seen in the background" (photo number 406888, Rec. September 27, 1949). U.S. National Archives, College Park, Maryland.

In its investigation of these allegations, the navy collected statements from the guards, revealing that "no one admitted to such acts, or to seeing them performed."[132] As David N. Morris, a Marine private, claimed, "To the very best of my knowledge, there was not at any time orders given to abuse or mistreat the Nips. Neither was there ever homosexual acts imposed upon them."[133] Donald Purcell, another Marine private, stated, "I neither saw nor heard of homosexual or abusive acts."[134] Captain John N. Rentz, the commanding officer of the First Battalion, Third Marines, defended the guards. As he observed, "During the period of my command, no sentry ever spit upon a prisoner. No sentry ever forced a prisoner into a homosexual act. No prisoner was ever forcibly awakened in the middle of the night."[135] Even the American corpsman and the Japanese medical officer agreed that no Japanese prisoner had been harmed by the sentries; drawing from their daily records of "sick calls," they found no evidence of abuse at the War Criminals Stockade. As Lieutenant Tsutomu Ogawa stated, "I hereby certify that it has never been brought to my attention that any Japanese prisoners have received injury as a result of mistreatment by the guards."[136]

Taking these factors into consideration, the navy concluded its investigation of the War Criminals Stockade on July 22, 1946. It determined that the Japanese prisoners had fabricated every charge except for one regarding excessive drills. In this respect, only Private Raymond L. Romero was found guilty of forcing Vice Admiral Masashi Kobayashi "to stand at attention while holding heavy stone."[137] When asked to rationalize his actions, Romero argued that "the Jap prisoner kept bothering me all during my watch by wanting to go to the head. I took him to the head about six times, and then I told him if he bothered me once more, I'd make him stand there all night. He gave me a big smile and asked me to give him a light as he wanted to smoke, in the middle of the night. So I took him out of the cell and made him stand outside at attention [for a few minutes] with a rock in his hands."[138] By way of summary court-martial, Romero then received five days of confinement in the military's brig with bread and water. The navy deemed its investigation complete. As Captain J. A. Moriarty Jr. proclaimed, "Since this investigation, with a view to assuring proper treatment of all Japanese prisoners, Commander Marianas has directed the Commanding Officer, Marine Barracks, to make regular periodical inspections, interrogate the prisoners relative to mistreatment and take all steps necessary to prevent any violation of international law relative to persons held captive by the United States."[139]

As with Guamanian forms of retribution directed against the Japanese, Rotanese, and Saipanese, however, several Marine guards continued to assault the prisoners in the War Criminals Stockade. Like their native counterparts from Guam, the sentries rarely received punishment for their actions. At least this was the impression given by another set of Japanese prisoners. Commenting on this new round of allegations, Captain Moriarty wrote, "Well, the fat is in the fire again. The ten persons who returned to Tokyo with Lieutenant Tremayne have brought a very unfavorable report of conditions in the War Crimes Stockade at Guam since last August, 1947."[140] Unlike the previous group of Japanese men who were prisoners when the navy called for an investigation, the ten Japanese men who filed the new report were recently released prisoners at the War Criminals Stockade. That is, the military acquitted them of all charges in the summer of 1947. No longer bound by the navy's laws, these men identified fifteen Marine guards as their supposed assailants, as well as offered detailed descriptions of said abuses.

As with the case in 1946, the Japanese prisoners were reduced to objects of sexual desire and revulsion. They alleged having incurred various beatings from March 1946 to July 1947. Former prisoner Eigo Chiba, for example, witnessed the guard by the name of "Morris" order "hygiene-officer ensign Yoshizawa to get down on his hands and knees. He got on top of him and made him say 'I am a horse' while [Morris] shouted 'I'm Hirohito' and made him walk on his hands and knees."[141] Chiba himself also performed excessive drills; several guards physically attacked him as well. Elsewhere, Hideo Hataoka, a medical petty officer first class in the Japanese navy, had an unidentified sentry shove "a considerable quantity of toilet paper into my anus. As a result I suffered from constipation for about 12 days and the pain I had to endure during those days was beyond explanation."[142] On May 30, 1946, two guards then entered his cell and kicked his back and chest. As Hataoka recalled, "Being unable to stand the pain I crumbled. They urinated on my back and made me lie in the water. Then they forced me to lick the urine on the floor."[143] The next day the guards returned. "One of them held me tight," explained Hataoka, "and the other forced his penis into my mouth and emitted semen and made me drink it. After it was over they would not even let me wash my mouth."[144] Another prisoner, Mayuki Ijima, expressed this form of same-sex rape in Japanese terms. As he put it, "I was forced to carry out an act called 'Shakuhachi' (homo-sexuality using the mouth) by one of the guards. I stubbornly refused at first, but on being threatened with a pistol, I was obliged to perform the act."[145]

Indeed, the manner by which the Marine sentries exacted homoerotic control over the prisoners was widespread. As the former warrant officer mechanic Yoshio Fujino claimed, a Marine corporal by the name of "Lokey" often greeted him in the morning with the saying "hubba, hubba," a popular flirtatious phrase of the 1940s.[146] In early September 1947, Fujino described how another guard called "Choeki" then "threw dentifrice all over my head and with shaving cream he painted by [sic] eye-brows, nose, eyes and chin. He made me say 'I am a cute boy' and visit each cell in every ward."[147] Feminized in drag attire, Yoshio Fujino relented to such torture. Anybody who resisted the guards found little respite, as Shigeru Yatsuhashi realized when he refused to "lick" the testicles of Private Morris. As a result, Morris assaulted him a "dozen times," leaving Yatsuhashi with "great insult and physical pain."[148]

In light of these allegations, the navy conducted an investigation on the "three main instigators in acts against the prisoners."[149] They included an unidentified Marine sergeant and two Marine privates. Yet the navy did not pursue the investigation further for fear that the supreme commander for the Allied powers (SCAP) would reprimand the senior officers at the War

Criminals Stockade. With one case of prisoner abuse already proved in 1946, the navy appeared reluctant to make public another round of military assaults against Japanese prisoners. As Captain Moriarty elaborated, "At our request, no letter will be written through official channels regarding these incidents."[150] He emphasized that "if this bit of information reached SCAP, they too would be very unhappy. I believe it will be possible to keep the latter information from SCAP officials, providing some action is taken in Guam."[151]

The Men of Colonial Modernity

A year later, in March 1948, the War Criminals Stockade had not received any new reports regarding its prisoners. Perhaps the living conditions improved for them. Perhaps the guards ceased all forms of racial and sexual violence. But if we take seriously the comments by Captain Moriarty, we can infer that the navy censored other Japanese allegations of torture. It was as if no harm could befall the guards and prisoners of the War Criminals Stockade, a place where senior military officials often maintained the relative secrecy of their activities, if not delighted in the prisoners' moral transformations. The navy chaplain H. W. Buckingham reported in the same month, for example, that "many prisoners are reading Japanese New Testament."[152] "It is recommended," the lieutenant commander continued, "that regular visits be made by both Protestant and Catholic chaplains to administer consolations and sacraments of their faith."[153] Rear Admiral John D. Murphy, the war crimes director, similarly reveled in the ideological utility of the prison. As he expressed, "Not one single complaint or even a suggestion of a complaint was indicated.... It was obvious to the inspecting officer that the morale of the prisoners was high and that their discipline was excellent."[154] According to Rear Admiral Murphy, they never conducted "a jail break or attempted jail break"; instead, "the greatest concern to stockade personnel is the likelihood of prisoners committing suicide. Special instructions are given guards ... and all reasonable precautions are taken."[155]

That numerous military officials affirmed the War Criminals Stockade's promotion of "high" prisoner morale yet did not underscore their contradictory concern that prisoners might commit "suicide" merely illustrated the power and reach of the U.S. carceral state in Guam. By the time Rear Admiral Murphy had declared the supposedly beneficial qualities of this prison, the U.S. Navy's War Crimes Tribunals Program had already been in existence for nearly four years. But without its usage of intelligence and police units and without its reliance on Guamanian forms of retribution and violence, the military tribunal would have lacked the legal and political force to try its subjects, speak its truths, and mete out its sentences. Combined, the Marine Corps, the navy, and the Guam Combat Patrol subjected indigenous and settler peoples in Guam to the disciplinary logics and tactics of colonial modernity. In these hypermasculine, emasculated, and homoerotic spheres of racial classification and confinement, the U.S. military created and managed new bodies of war criminality, a double exclusion wherein deviant and disloyal bodies—natives and nonnatives alike—can be killed but not sacrificed by the nation.

2

WAR CRIMES

The military's racist classification of indigenous and settler peoples in Guam was not a randomly selected event, nor was it entirely unique in scale and composition. The national and international discussions on war criminality that occurred in the 1940s similarly expressed the racial hierarchies used by the military's intelligence agencies, as much as they reflected the ambivalent, contradictory, and vindictive positions of jurists, legal scholars, and military officials in the United States and elsewhere. As early as August 2, 1944, the U.S. War Department began to shape the scope and meaning of these debates with the publication of *What Shall Be Done with War Criminals?* Authored by the Harvard criminologist Sheldon Glueck, the text described the mid-twentieth-century nature of war crimes and war crimes tribunals. With the war still waging, Glueck used his association with the War Department to project a victory on the part of the United States and its allies. As he boldly asserted, the United States "will have a hand in the trial and punishment of Japanese war criminals whose offenses took place in Wake, Guam, the Philippine Islands, the Aleutians, and other Pacific areas."[1] Just how the United States would accomplish the task of incarcerating war criminals on a global scale remained unclear.

In this chapter, I reckon with this dilemma of imperial judgment as well. By examining what war criminality meant for the United States and its military agencies, I show how the U.S. Navy's War Crimes Tribunals Program developed a language of white supremacist statecraft and punishment as legitimate law in Guam. As with the incarceration of Chamorros, Japanese, and Asians in various camps, the navy turned to its rules and proclamations—all steeped in the logics of the carceral state—to make lawful its then-burgeoning military commission. National and international debates on war criminality, as much as issues of culpability, staffing, and translation, informed the making of the tribunal in Guam. With these factors in mind, I discuss how the tribunal brokered justice, expanded its jurisdiction, and fashioned its subjects.

War Criminality and the State of Exception

In Sheldon Glueck's treatment of war criminality, questions of the carceral and the colonial likewise resonated with how, if at all, U.S. federal laws on the individual "offender" would inform the prosecution of Japanese and Nazi war criminals. As he ascertained, "We regard every offender as an individual. His assets and liabilities are studied and a program is planned to make the most of his abilities . . . curb his bad habits, and gradually restore him to a useful and law-abiding place in society." But, he inquired, "Should this policy be followed for the war criminals?" Although he did not provide a definitive response, he treated individual offenders and war offenders as separate categories entitled to legally distinct forms of incarceration. As Glueck explained, ordinary offenders "can afford to experiment with the humane approach, and the public, even the victims and their families, can be made to agree to a policy of rehabilitation."[2] On the other hand, for "war offenders of the Axis type, who have committed thousands of shocking atrocities, measures of cure and rehabilitation of the individual offender according to his needs would be interpreted (especially by the surviving victims of Axis brutality) as undeserved leniency."[3]

Invoking the Moscow Declaration of 1943 as the Allied model for punishing German war criminals, Glueck offered several forms of punishment that could arise from this agreement and that could be levied against war criminals in Europe and elsewhere. The options available to the Americans, English, and Soviets included execution, imprisonment, reeducation, and rehabilitation, with the prominent offenders left alive to be "studied by psychiatric clinics . . . so that we might learn what made these men defy the laws of civilization and lead millions of their fellow countrymen to an orgy of death and destruction." Lest any of these options emasculate or humiliate offenders into "martyrs," Glueck suggested that Japanese and Nazi offenders be sentenced to "prison terms at hard labor for life, perhaps on lonely islands in distant seas, whence escape would be impossible."[4] By casting islands as sites of exile, he featured a form of punishment once employed by European governments in their transportation of convicts, lepers, and revolutionaries to islands in the Atlantic, Indian, and Pacific Oceans. As the literary critic Elizabeth M. DeLoughrey reminds us, colonial governments often perceived islands as remote locales scattered far from their metropoles and inhabited by "colonized and enslaved populations who, without access to maritime vessels, were less likely to escape."[5]

Although islands as proposed carceral sites never resurfaced in Glueck's assessment of war criminality, what must be underscored was the lack of international consensus regarding the prosecution of war criminals. Central to these discussions was the traditional definition of war criminality, broadly construed as "crimes against humanity." As Glueck opined, war criminals of this magnitude could be understood as persons who violate "(a) the laws and customs of legitimate warfare or (b) the principles of criminal law that are generally observed in civilized legal systems, or who have ordered, consented to, or conspired in the commission of such acts."[6] But as he rightly observed, the conditions of World War II spurred a series of "crimes" that were not recognized by the Geneva Convention of 1929 and its rules on "civilized" warfare between nations and their soldiers. Its laws concerning the protection of civilians, medical personnel, and prisoners proved insufficient for jurists, scholars, and tribunals that were coming to terms with the new laws on crimes against humanity.[7] Murder, rape, and theft committed by military personnel at their own initiative and not at the behest of orders constituted these crimes, as did treaty violations and acts of treason on the part of government officials. However, national courts and war crimes tribunals had yet to draft various procedures on these and other crimes of the "Axis type," an effort that other jurists realized as well.

In a speech to the American Society of International Law on April 13, 1945, Supreme Court justice Robert H. Jackson was one such jurist. In his talk, he offered a more tempered perspective on the American prosecution of war criminals than that presented by the criminologist Sheldon Glueck. As Justice Jackson proclaimed, "I have no purpose to enter into any controversy as to what shall be done with war criminals, either high or humble."[8] Yet, even with this caveat, he still offered his preference for executing war criminals on the condition that national trials refrain from participating in these acts. He said, "If it is considered good policy for the future peace of the world, if it is believed that the example will outweigh the tendency to create among their own countrymen a myth of martyrdom, then let [the war criminals] be executed. But in that case let the decision to execute them be made as a military or political decision."[9] Careful not to conflate constitutional legalism with military doctrine, Justice Jackson further cautioned, "We must not use the forms of judicial proceedings to carry out or rationalize previously settled political or military policy. Farcical judicial trials conducted by us will destroy confidence in the judicial process as quickly as those conducted by any other people."[10] By "farcical judicial trials," he meant war crimes tribunals that could wield the power of politics and militarism and not of law. "Among us," he remarked, "there are some who candidly would use courts as an instrument of power and many more who favor all of the premises of that philosophy without recognizing the conclusion. The ease with which men thoughtlessly fall into step with this philosophy is strikingly demonstrated by the attitude of many people toward the trial of war criminals."[11]

Cautious about the tendencies of courts to operate as "policy weapons," Justice Jackson defended what he believed were the fair principles of judicial review granted to individuals who faced civil courts. Addressing the attorneys, he continued, "The ultimate principle is that you must put no man on trial under the forms of judicial proceedings if you are not willing to see him freed if not proven guilty. If you are determined to execute a man in any case, there is no occasion for a trial."[12] He forewarned, "The world yields no respect to courts that are merely organized to convict."[13] As these comments indicate, Justice Jackson remained cognizant of the ways in which war crimes tribunals can leverage militarist, political, and nationalist sentiments over and beyond the rule of law. A surface reading of his remarks indicates that he viewed law, militarism, and politics as unrelated spheres of influence, a seemingly naive perspective for somebody who, on May 2, 1945, would be appointed as the U.S. chief of counsel in the prosecution of Axis war criminals. This partly explains why he guardedly welcomed the possibility of "bringing those accused of war crimes to trial."[14] As Justice Jackson emphasized, "I repeat that I am not saying there should be no trials. I merely say that our profession should see that it is understood that any trials to which lawyers worthy of their calling lend themselves will be trials in fact, not merely trails in name, to ratify a predetermined result."[15]

Having previously dissented in *Korematsu v. United States* (1944), the Supreme Court's ruling on the legality of interning Japanese Americans during World War II, Justice Jackson may have anticipated gross violations of the law wherein various court systems could "ratify a predetermined result" under the pretense of national or international law.[16] As evidenced in this case, the Supreme Court upheld the exclusion and relocation of 120,000 Japanese U.S. citizens and noncitizens from the West Coast of the United States. The majority decision endorsed the military's fear that the Japanese, as a race, conspired to spy and commit acts of sabotage against the U.S. state, especially in cities, harbors, and military bases along the coast. Recognizing the racist elements of this decision, Justice Jackson opposed the ruling on the grounds that it violated the Constitution.[17] Therefore, the legal codification of racism—what the Lumbee scholar Robert A. Williams Jr. calls the "rights-denying jurispathic power" of the law—underscored discussions of war criminality that may have troubled Justice Jackson. In this respect, Jackson knew that one court's decision could influence another's and thereby normalize racism as just. In *Korematsu v. United States*, the Supreme Court sanctioned the military curfew and exclusion orders previously decided in *Hirabayashi v. United States* (1942), thereby making legal the denial of habeas corpus to and the racial incarceration of Japanese Americans.

In legal terms, this process has been described as the doctrine of stare decisis wherein, as in U.S. courts, like cases should be decided alike.[18] For Williams, stare decisis remains a central tenet of the U.S. Supreme Court and its ongoing reliance on nineteenth-century rulings that were informed by racisms toward American Indians. By examining the landmark cases on American Indian rights by Chief Justice John Marshall, wherein American Indians became domestic "wards" of the United States in the early nineteenth century, he shows how these cases have become the precedents for denying numerous civil liberties, economic opportunities, political rights, and treaty protections to American Indians and, tellingly, to other racialized or minoritized peoples of "like cases."[19] As Williams explains, "Stare decisis, by its very nature, represents a persistent danger for the protection of minority rights in [the U.S.] legal system, threatening to expand the original principle of racial discrimination justified by a particular legal precedent to new purposes and applications."[20] Until the Supreme Court strikes down such precedents, moreover, the expansion of racial discrimination has no foreseeable limit. As he affirms, "Even without possessing a hostile intent toward any particular minority group, a judge who feels bound to enforce prior precedents because of the doctrine of stare decisis can perpetuate, in the most subtle of fashions, a system of racial inequality."[21]

Given these circumstances, Justice Jackson may have understood the emerging debates on war criminality and war crimes tribunals as crossing the lines between law, militarism, and nationalism. With the doctrine of stare decisis as a looming factor in these discussions, he alluded to the internment of Japanese Americans in his blunted criticism of the Supreme Court's failure to protect their rights to due process. Although he never identified the Japanese Americans in his speech, the allusion was discernible. As Justice Jackson indicated, "The assurance of our fundamental law that the citizen's life may not be taken without due process of law is of little avail against a foreign aggressor or against the necessities of war."[22] Implicitly referring to Executive Order 9066 and to its logic of military necessity in which the civil rights of Japanese Americans were denied, he said, "It ought to be clear by this time that personal freedom, at least the kind and degree we have known in this country, is inconsistent with the necessities of total war and incompatible with a state of militarization in readiness for one."[23] In addition to admonishing national courts that were corrupted by the "necessities of war," as in *Korematsu v. United States*, he also criticized the arrogance of "extreme nationalists" who believed that international law always worked on their side.[24]

As these sentiments illustrate, Justice Jackson engaged the postwar dangers of nationalism, retribution, and stare decisis before the American Society of International Law. He even provided a generous reading of U.S. constitutional law as redeemable despite his direct and implied critiques of its violence. So long as the military did not seek the judiciary's counsel in enforcing its decisions, Justice Jackson believed in the distinct but important roles of the judiciary and the military.[25] For this reason, he was not opposed to the making of military war crimes tribunals. In his later capacity as chief of counsel in the prosecution of Axis war criminals, for example, he expressed optimism in the justice proffered by the war crimes trials in Europe. Invoking the supposed universalism of American responsibility, he wrote, "After we entered the war, and as we expended our men and our wealth to stamp out these wrongs, it was the universal feeling of our people that out of this war should come unmistakable rules and workable machinery from which any who might contemplate another era of brigandage would know that they would be held personally responsible and would be personally punished."[26]

Ultimately, Justice Jackson called for the separation of law from policy (or law from militarism) in the defining of war criminality and in the making of war crimes tribunals, a task that, contrary to his beliefs, proved materially and politically untenable. As in the case of Guam, constitutional law, international law, and naval law, among other legal codes and doctrines, *mutually constituted* what Giorgio Agamben has theorized as the state of exception. Contrary to Justice Jackson's conviction that law operated as a fair and autonomous sphere, the law, when employed in the U.S. territory of Guam, functioned as a harbinger of militarized violence and white supremacist statecraft. When analyzed in terms of the law's historical relation to American Indians, Japanese Americans, and other "rights-denying" subjects of the United States, the conflation of law, militarism, and policy often became the norm rather than the exception. As such, Justice Jackson's treatment on war criminality was fundamentally about internationally expanding the U.S. carceral state. The dialogue on war criminality advanced by naval attorneys and officials merely reiterated the militarist and punitive character of U.S. law in the Pacific.

Take, for instance, Lieutenant Commander James J. Robinson of the Office of the Judge Advocate General of the U.S. Navy. As an attorney and military officer, he shared his views on the legal charges regarding war crimes trials before the American Bar Association and the Federal Bar Association on April 20, 1945. At a conference held in Washington, DC, the lieutenant commander recounted a series of Japanese atrocities committed against American prisoners at a labor camp located in Palawan Island, Philippines. Robinson's talk drew from media accounts and American survivor memories of the Japanese military's attempt to execute the prisoners on December 14, 1944. He summarized the plot as follows: Upon noticing that American bombers were flying above their labor camp, the Japanese soldiers ordered the prisoners to enter the air-raid shelters, at which time the soldiers proceeded to throw lighted torches, paper, and gasoline into the shelters. The Americans who tried to escape the area were immediately clubbed, bayoneted, or shot. A few Americans even ran to a nearby cliff, climbed down its face, and jumped into the ocean, thereby hoping to swim away from the camp. Only 9 of the original 150 American prisoners survived the tragedy. Recalling witness testimony of a failed escape, Robinson shared the following image: "One American who was shot in the water was dragged out through the slime and was being stabbed with bayonets as he staggered along the shore surrounded by his captors. While he was begging them to shoot him rather than burn him to death, the Japanese poured gasoline on one of his feet and set it on fire, then on the other foot and set it on fire, and then, as he collapsed, they threw gasoline over him and he was enveloped in the flames."[27] Moralizing the Americans as victims, the lieutenant commander then raised the question that dominated debates on war criminality. With the Japanese soldiers from the camp now imprisoned by the U.S. military, he asked, "What are we going to do with them?"

For the Americans who fought the Japanese or the Nazis, Lieutenant Commander Robinson surmised that these Americans would most likely respond with the phrase "shoot them." Knowing that this act would constitute a "war crime," he opposed any form of immediate violence toward individuals who were accused of war crimes. As he put it, "To shoot the perpetrator of a war crime immediately upon capture may [give] immunity to the superior officers, the master-minds or any other fellow-gangsters of the dead criminal.... Moreover, the contents of the confessions of war criminals and the court records of war crime convictions will provide information and support needed, at the peace table and elsewhere, in making appropriate provision for the prevention of future war crimes or even of future wars."[28] Lieutenant Commander Robinson thus reasoned that if the United States and its allies were to successfully prosecute soldiers and their superior officers, then the full force of the law should be applied. It is necessary, he declared, "to follow principles and rules of international law, criminal law and military law, well-established in precedent and practice among the nations."[29] As he argued, "The trials should be conducted, depending upon the circumstances of the case, in the regular national civil courts of the countries whose people have been outraged by the offenses, or in military commissions or tribunals, especially tribunals of mixed membership, that is, membership drawn from more than one nation or from more than one of the armed services or from both military and civilian personnel or from any combination of these sources."[30]

That Lieutenant Commander Robinson could casually list the ways in which hybrid, military, or national courts could extend their "outrage" toward individuals and groups accused of war crimes was indicative of at least two factors. First, several definitions of war crimes had become increasingly widespread and provisionally accepted among the United States, the United Nations, and the international community. Violations of the laws of war, an act reflecting the general elements of a "crime" (e.g., the time of the prohibited offense, the territory in which its commission is forbidden), and the crossing of an international boundary surfaced as central markers of war criminality. These definitions likewise resonated with the notions of criminality previously defined by Glueck and Jackson, as would the A, B, and C war crime classifications that later informed several tribunals. Second, the elasticity of international law enabled various court systems to selectively define war, crime, and war crimes to their own ends, if not allowed courts to violate the rules of war.[31] Despite the Fourth Hague Convention of 1907, the Geneva Convention of 1929, and other covenants on "civilized" warfare, the international law on war crimes did not adhere to a universal set of rules, let alone possess the enforcement power to ensure that countries abided by them. Hence, international law became a convenient proxy for countries that sought to broaden the scope and meaning of war crimes. As the legal scholar Gerry J. Simpson explains, "The attempt to develop a more general notion of criminality in international law has proved troublesome given the structure of the system itself." As he notes, "International law is seen simply as the contractual relations between States. When States commit wrongs they become delictually liable to other States and not to some transcendent public administrative organ."[32]

As elusive as definitions of war criminality may appear in international law, however, states and courts nevertheless invoked the foundational concept of "piracy" in their respective trials and proceedings. Discussing its etymology, the anthropologists Shannon Lee Dawdy and Joe Bonni observe that the word "piracy" originates from "the classical Greek root *'peirates'*—meaning an attempt or an attack."[33] Associated with a kind of violation, then, piracy became "the first international crime, or the first offence to give rise to universal jurisdiction" in international law.[34] With the pirate as its referent, the figure of the war criminal was "characterized as an enemy of mankind—'hostis humani generis'—operating outside the bounds of law and outside the jurisdiction of national law."[35] For this reason, Arthur G. Robinson, rear admiral of the U.S. Navy and president of the Military Commission in Guam, could declare in 1948 that war crimes were "international crimes in the sense that they are crimes against all civilized nations, like the crimes of slave trading and of piracy—and in this respect the war criminal, like the pirate . . . is an enemy of mankind . . . and as such he is justiciable by any state anywhere."[36] With the war criminal likened to the pirate and made "justiciable" by any state, it often became commonsensical for jurists, legal scholars, and military officials to levy judgment against the Japanese and Nazis accused of committing atrocities against the United States and the Allied forces.

In this respect, states frequently utilized the signifier of piracy in defining war criminality as that which disrupts "a customary flow of goods and ideas."[37] This interruption, a process often likened to conflict, deception, or theft, "frequently involves a kind of real or symbolic violence, such as the taking of a ship or hacking of a system."[38] Along these lines, courts were not merely concerned about determining the "guilt" or "innocence" of war criminals. As with piracy, war criminals were targeted for interfering in the normal state of affairs, which, for Asia and the Pacific, meant the stability of European and U.S. colonialisms. As the critic Lisa Yoneyama asserts, Japanese political and military leaders were punished and executed not for the "atrocities they committed against the people of Asia and the Pacific—that is, for Japan's 'crimes against humanity'—but for disturbing the peace and order preserved under white European and U.S. domination and for violating their colonial entitlements, properties and privileges in that region."[39] As in the case of Guam, the island became a site where the navy reasserted its hegemony over Japan, which, the naval courts held, possessed no jurisdiction over Guam and its people. As the trials examined in this book demonstrate, the navy drew from a plethora of concepts, laws, and rules in its racialized claims to justice for the injured and the dead. But what, exactly, did the navy mean by justice and jurisdiction? Given the widespread debates on war criminality, what courts did the navy eventually employ, and why? And how did the navy, alongside other military agencies, further expand the U.S. carceral state in the Pacific?

Naval Justice and Jurisdiction

In 1945, the U.S. Bureau of Naval Personnel defined naval justice as the "maintenance of naval discipline, without which the Navy cannot function as an efficient fighting organization."[40] With the waging of war as its central premise, the Bureau projected naval discipline as the "true basis of democracy, for it means adherence by the individual to the set of rules which has been found best suited to govern relations between individual members of society in order to protect the interests of the whole."[41] Contrasting criminal courts and the navy's brand of justice, Rear Admiral O. S. Colclough, judge advocate general of the navy, reiterated, almost verbatim, the definition of naval justice as disciplinary and martial in nature. He wrote, "This difference has been expressed succinctly as follows—the objective of criminal law is the protection of society; the objective of military law is the maintenance of that standard of discipline which is the *sine qua non* of an efficient fighting organization."[42] That kind of justice would be, as he put it, of global reach by the end of the war. As Rear Admiral Colclough expressed, "From a geographical standpoint, prior to the war, the administration of naval justice was roughly limited to the United States and its territories, Cuba, Iceland, and the Philippines. During the war it embraced not only Europe, the Atlantic, and the Pacific, but practically the entire world."[43] As an expanding apparatus of discipline, naval justice was achieved by exacting punishment against its disobedient ranks and its perceived enemies. For the navy, punishment was "potent but dangerous, useful but destructive; astonishingly effective when rightly used, alarmingly destructive when used wrongly." The "value of punishment lies in the object lesson it furnishes the wrongdoer, and others, that the offense must not be repeated. This is referred to as the *deterrent* theory of punishment."[44]

In accordance with the navy's deterrent theory of punishment, military tribunals became the instruments of inquiry par excellence by which naval justice was sought and attained. Reflecting on the inquiry as a relation of knowledge-power, Michel Foucault asserts that the "inquiry is precisely a political form—a form of power management and exercise that, through the judicial institution, became, in Western culture, a way of authenticating truth, of acquiring and transmitting things that would be regarded as true."[45] As per the navy's culture of discipline, military tribunals ascertained "truths" by way of punishing individuals and groups who violated the abilities of the navy to wage war. From the trial and execution of the British spy Major John André in 1780 to the arraignment and massacre of thirty-eight Dakota in Mankato, Minnesota, in 1862 during the American Civil War, military tribunals acquired, over time, the power of extreme authority, discipline, and violence.[46] Whereas civil courts have often afforded individuals the constitutional right to trials by jury and the availability of habeas corpus, military tribunals grant those under their purview neither of these rights and protections. As the legal scholar Louis Fisher observes, military tribunals have been generally "hostile to civil liberties, procedural due process, and elementary standards of justice."[47] Operating without the judicial constraint granted by the civil courts and the Constitution, military tribunals have wielded "much wider discretion as to the punishment to be imposed than is ordinarily given to civil courts."[48]

The rationale for justifying the legal power of military tribunals is explicitly expressed under article 1, section 8, of the U.S. Constitution, wherein Congress shall provide for the "common Defense" and "general Welfare" of the United States.[49] Take, for instance, clauses 13 and 14, which grant Congress and the president the license to "provide and maintain a Navy" and to "make Rules for the Government and Regulation of the land and naval Forces." These are two of several passages that provide "abundant authority" for the appointment and use of military tribunals.[50] Along these lines, the Constitution "invests the President as Commander in Chief with the power to wage war and to carry into effect all laws passed by Congress for the conduct of war and for the government and regulation of the Armed Forces, and all laws defining and punishing offences against the law of nations including those which pertain to the conduct of war."[51] The president can also appoint, as he has in the past, military tribunals and prescribe the rules under which they have to operate.[52] With its power drawn from the Constitution, Congress, and the president, military tribunals have not been, for the most part, "subject to review by the Federal Courts," including the U.S. Supreme Court.[53] At times, the Supreme Court may inquire whether a tribunal has jurisdiction over a person or an offense or whether a sentence imposed was within the scope of a tribunal.[54] But if the military tribunal "had lawful authority to hear, decide and condemn, its action is not subject to judicial review merely because it made a wrong decision on disputed facts."[55] Moreover, all errors of decision belong to the military tribunal and not to judicial courts.[56]

With respect to World War II, the United States employed three types of military tribunals, all of which were recognized as legitimate courts by the United Nations. The tribunals included, first, the courts-martial; second, the military commission or exceptional military court; and, third, military government courts and military tribunals established by the military government. The courts-martial is the most frequently used system of inquiry for the navy, having been formed to "determine if a person subject to naval law has committed a violation of the *Articles for the Government of the Navy* and, if [the court] finds him guilty, to adjudge an adequate punishment."[57] As with the Articles of War and the *Naval Courts and Boards* (1937), the *Articles for the Government of the Navy* provide the rules and procedures for determining the scope of naval law, the appropriate conduct of persons, and the criteria for discipline and punishment. These and other articles of naval law pertain to the courts-martial and to the other military tribunals, and have likewise been periodically revised. But whereas courts-martial focus solely on the prosecution of individuals under the purview of naval law, the other military tribunals have wider latitude in terms of their command structure, procedural composition, and territorial jurisdiction. Indeed, military commissions and military government courts employ naval personnel as well, as in determining the convening authority of naval officers. But these "exceptional" military tribunals differ from the courts-martial in terms of their ability to prosecute civil crimes, military violations, and war crimes, among other disruptions to military law, occupation, or warfare.[58] Such exceptional courts could likewise be administered by a convening authority, a naval governor, or a military commander, and the proceedings could occur wherever the United States asserts its claim to sovereignty as an occupier.

With the knowledge that military tribunals can assert naval justice (and political hegemony) in times of war, coupled with information gained from debates on war criminality of the "Axis type," Secretary of the Navy James Forrestal established the War Crimes Office on January 13, 1945. Located in the War Department, the War Crimes Office coordinated the administrative efforts on war crimes matters between the Navy, War, and State Departments. As his official memo to the Navy Department indicated, the national War Crimes Office aimed to "collect evidence against enemy persons who commit murders, atrocities and other violations of the laws of war against members of the armed forces of the United States or against other Americans, including the peoples of any dependency such as the Philippines, and to arrange for the immediate or eventual apprehension, trial and sentence of such war criminals."[59]

Secretary Forrestal's legal directives were especially forceful in their granting of police-like authority to naval commanders in war zones across Asia and the Pacific. As he declared, naval commanders were "directed to take necessary action" in obtaining, investigating, and forwarding information on war crimes to the judge advocate general of the navy and to the Navy Department.[60] Affirming the carceral dimension of the military, Rear Admiral Arthur G. Robinson likewise argued that it is "the duty of the victor to [punish those who violated the law and customs of war], just as it is the duty of the police and the court to apprehend, to confine, to try, and to punish those who violate domestic criminal law."[61] As he asserted, "The 'police,' the forces of law and order, must be stronger than the criminals. If not, the power of society to punish for wrongdoing would perish, for the criminal and his kin do not apply the standards of lawful society to punish the wrongdoer."[62]

Invoking what Rear Admiral Robinson eventually called the "natural and proper" authority of a victor, the War Crimes Office proceeded to sanction violent acts of intrusion, inquiry, and incarceration on an unprecedented scale across the world. In Asia and the Pacific Islands alone, these forms of policing led to the incarceration of more than three thousand individuals, with approximately another one thousand receiving death sentences.[63] While hybrid, military, and national courts from Australia to Singapore played important roles in the postwar incarceration of their respective enemies, the United States "was consistently in the forefront in the development and effectuation of the entire war crimes program."[64] In January 1945, the War Crimes Office and its affiliated branches had thus advanced a U.S. penal regime suited for the war and its aftermath, a regime the critical ethnic studies scholar Dylan Rodríguez describes as "an indispensable element of American statecraft, simultaneously a cornerstone of its militarized (local and global) ascendancy and spectacle of its extracted (or coerced) authority over targeted publics."[65]

Yet, as I revealed in the previous chapter, the U.S. Marine Corps and U.S. Navy, along with their intelligence agencies, had already begun to classify and criminalize Asians and Pacific Islanders in Guam as early as July 1944. The military's classification of such "targeted publics"—that is, the criminal, the disloyal, the enemy, and so forth—occurred at least five months

2.1. Rear Admiral John D. Murphy, director, War Crimes, U.S. Pacific Fleet (photo number 406854, Rec. September 27, 1949). U.S. National Archives, College Park, Maryland.

earlier and without the secretary's declaration to investigate war crimes. That the American military unilaterally interned and investigated these and other deviant types had much to do with how the United States viewed Guam as its colony. For this reason, the American military conducted its interrogations of Asians and Pacific Islanders without any legal or political constraints, acts that would otherwise be construed as "exceptional." As Rear Admiral John D. Murphy, director of the War Crimes Tribunals Program declared, "It goes without saying that the work of investigations was the foundation upon which all subsequent war crimes actions was [sic] based. It was the first step in the long detailed task of detection, apprehension, and preparation of evidence for cases before the military tribunals in the prosecution of the accused" (figure 2.1).[66] The navy thus interrogated anybody at any time. In this respect, the navy's legal advisers and officials argued that Japan never lawfully claimed the island and its peoples, a point emphasized in its trials of war criminals from Japan and the Mariana Islands.

Following this logic of conquest, the War Crimes Office established different war crimes tribunal branches in the European, Mediterranean, and Pacific regions.[67] In the Pacific, the General Headquarters of the Supreme Commander for the Allied Powers (SCAP) drafted the "Regulations Governing the Trials of Accused Criminals" on December 5, 1945. This policy granted any Allied nation the authority to create military courts for the trial of war criminals.[68] According to the regulations, these nations possessed jurisdiction over war crimes cases involving the waging of war and the taking of life since the "Mukden incident," also known as the Japanese military invasion of Manchuria on September 18, 1931. With a temporal frame of the 1930s to the 1940s at their disposal, the United States and its allies apprehended representatives of Japan's imperial government who were accused of war crimes. This network of inquiry relied, as well, on the integration of U.S. Army and U.S. Navy personnel into the Pacific branches. These efforts, the War Crimes Office projected, would "result in closer cooperation among all the military services, a more centralized control over activities pertaining to war crimes, and a more efficient exchange of information between war crimes officers in the field and the United States War Crimes Office in Washington, D.C."[69] While this interservice arrangement benefited the War Crimes Office, the navy eventually received sole control of the war crimes cases in the Pacific Islands, whereas the army predominated the war crimes cases covered by SCAP. For the navy, the areas that represented the Pacific Islands encompassed the Bonin Islands, the Caroline Islands, the Gilbert Islands, the Mariana Islands, the Marshall Islands, and the Palau Islands, with the army mainly focusing on Japan and the Philippines.[70]

The army, navy, SCAP, and other agencies defined war crimes as such: Class A, "crimes against peace," or the planning and initiating of a war of aggression; Class B, "conventional war crimes," or the violating of the laws or customs of war; and Class C, "crimes against humanity," or the murdering and committing of inhuman acts against civilian populations.[71] Based in Tokyo, and led by General Douglas MacArthur of the U.S. Army, SCAP primarily dealt with Class A war criminals of the International Military Tribunal of the Far East. In addition, SCAP communicated with other U.S. war crimes agencies in China (Shanghai), India (New Delhi), the Pacific Islands (Guam), and the Philippines (Manila), among others.[72] In his capacity as commander, MacArthur had the power to "(a) appoint special international military courts (*Which term shall be held to mean tribunals of any kind*) composed of military or naval officers or civilians of two or more of the United Nations, for the trial, under any applicable law, domestic or international, . . .

of Far Eastern war criminals . . . and (b) to prescribe or approve rules of procedure for such tribunals."⁷³

Unlike the courts-martial, these military tribunals wielded a triangulation of power invested in the Constitution, the Congress, and the president, not to mention an array of regulations that emanated from the War Crimes Office and its affiliated branches. For these reasons, the tribunals could "legally assume jurisdiction over all criminal offenses committed in occupied territory and over civil cases affecting the military government."⁷⁴ As noted earlier, the tribunals also held jurisdiction to try war crimes and accused war criminals without having to possess jurisdiction over the person and place of the offense. As Rear Admiral Robinson opined, "Under the familiar territorial principle of jurisdiction familiar to our domestic courts and our ordinary crimes—the convening authority is required to have jurisdiction over the person who committed the offense, and of the place where the offense was committed."⁷⁵ "This traditional concept," he argued, "is clearly inapplicable to crimes in violation of the laws and customs of war. War crimes is one of a number of exceptions to this concept. . . . The international nature of the crimes and the realistic necessity of their punishment by the injured or victor nations [are impelling reasons] for departure from the ordinary concept of territorial jurisdiction."⁷⁶ As strikingly violent as these layers of hegemony appear, though, the carceral and colonial mechanisms of naval justice and jurisdiction still hinged on another important legal principle. The U.S. Navy's War Crimes Tribunals Program would not have emerged in Guam, a military colony of the U.S. empire, without the plenary power doctrine. From this vantage point, we can analyze the navy's development of a military commission in the island, including its demarcation of "criminal" and "noncriminal" subjects among the population.

The Commission and the Colony

As disclosed in the introduction, the plenary power doctrine is a cornerstone of the U.S. empire, where it has been historically employed to uphold and protect its white citizenry, expand or fortify its national borders, and wage its protracted wars of conquest and settlement. As the legal scholar Natsu Taylor Saito argues, the plenary power doctrine remains "core U.S. law relating to American Indian nations, immigrants, and external colonies such as Puerto Rico and Guam." Wherever the United States exerts the plenary doctrine, she notes, "harsh consequences . . . are generally ignored or dismissed as aberrations, perhaps because—like the law of slavery—it is exercised over relatively powerless Others." Yet analyses of the doctrine "reveal a systematic denial of both domestic and international legal protections to those who most need them."[77]

With nonwhite peoples as its primary target, and with the acquisition of land, labor, and natural resources as its aim, the navy subsequently imposed the plenary power doctrine in Guam.[78] Reflecting on the significance of the doctrine's ties to military rule, where the law follows the flag but not necessarily the Constitution, the editors for the U.S. *Navy Report on Guam, 1899–1950* ascertained, "When the United States acquired Guam, neither the constitution nor the laws of the country were extended to the new possession. The sole administrative authority vested in the Navy, as the agent of government, was that derived from the President as Commander in Chief."[79] Naval governors then assumed control over the island much as "they had commanded naval vessels or naval establishments on previous tours of duty."[80] As expressed by the former naval commander Roy E. James, himself stationed in Guam in the 1940s, "Law and order often became 'discipline,' legislation became 'commands' or 'orders,' education became 'training,' and so on."[81] Through the plenary power doctrine, Guam became a site where "the essential elements of National Security and Local Security are inter-woven and inseparable."[82] It was this context, an island without the full application of the U.S. rule of law but nevertheless bound by its legal exceptions, that greeted Admiral C. W. Nimitz, the commander in chief of the U.S. Pacific Fleet and Pacific Ocean Areas.

On July 21, 1944, Admiral Nimitz arrived in Guam on the pretense of reclaiming the island from the Japanese government.[83] With the U.S. military invading the island on the same day, he declared, in the vein of colonial possession, Proclamation No. 4, titled "Exceptional Military Courts." Article I of the proclamation specifically stated, "Exceptional Military Courts for GUAM AND ADJACENT WATERS are hereby established. There shall be Military Commissions, Superior Provost Courts and Summary Provost Courts, the constitution and competence of which are set forth in article III."[84] As stipulated in article III of the proclamation, one or more military officers, some of whom could be appointed by a military governor, convened each court. Similarly, military officers served the dual role of judge and jury on these courts. Many of the military officers were also drawn from the naval reserve, with a few individuals coming from the air force and army. Describing the general composition of these courts, Rear Admiral Robinson stated that the conveners "were experienced trial lawyers from civil practice who had remained in the Navy under their reserve commissions. . . . They were of an unusually high caliber and were conspicuous for their marked ability as trial lawyers and their apparent devotion to the work in which they were involved."[85]

Many of the military officers received their academic training in naval law and international law. Upon their arrival in Guam, they adhered to the navy's required tour of duty; this meant that officers and enlisted personnel were compelled to reside there for at least eighteen months, the average tour of duty on the island.[86] But because of the labor shortage attributed to the war, the commission operated with fewer personnel than expected. Staff members utilized in war crimes work were even "begged, borrowed and stolen for this purpose."[87] The "technical and clerical processes of recording and filing information was in itself beyond the capacity of available personnel. However, it can definitely be said that some evidence of specific crimes was obtained and that valuable leads which formed the basis of subsequent successful investigations were obtained."[88] Highlighting the uneasy demand to fill positions but also maintain the capacity of the commission, Rear Admiral Charles A. Pownall said, "The work of all regularly assigned investigators, prosecutors and defense counsel was of an usually high character. It is hard to believe that as much work could have been accomplished with so few officers."[89]

Despite the upbeat nature of some military officials, the navy knew that its staffing shortages would hamper its ability to address unforeseen legal and political dilemmas (figure 2.2). Even with the power accorded to its tribunal in Guam, the navy still approached its claims to formerly occupied Japanese islands with caution. As Judge Advocate and Admiral Thomas Leigh Gatch expressed on April 10, 1945, "The occupation of islands in the Pacific Ocean Area is giving rise to many novel and difficult legal problems, particularly in the fields of international law, trial of war criminals and prisoners of war, and international aspects of naval justice."[90] "In many cases now arising," he said, "good precedents do not exist and when decisions are made in these cases law is actually being made. It is important that such decisions be correct, otherwise they must inevitably result in later embarrassments and difficulties."[91] Cognizant of its limitations, the military court attempted to follow legal precedents and adhere to international laws on war crimes.

In this sense, the navy sought to curtail any media coverage of racism among its staff, a premise that belied the racist foundations of the court. In light of the allegations and rulings concerning the abusive treatment of prisoners at the War Criminals Stockade, for example, military officers in

2.2. The War Criminals Stockade detachment (photo number 406877, Rec. September 27, 1949). U.S. National Archives, College Park, Maryland.

the tribunal argued that "continuous instruction and indoctrination of all ratings and ranks was essential in order to assure compliance with requirements of international law."[92] Their report continued, "This was more noticeably true as relatively new and inexperienced personnel began replacing the war time personnel. Prejudices against the Japanese appeared to be more pronounced in the seventeen to twenty year old replacements."[93] In practice, however, the navy rarely took stock of its racisms; instead, it directed its violence against anybody accused of crimes. The navy's usage of American, Chamorro, and Japanese court interpreters is a case in point.

Specifically, the tribunal understood that interpreting "between oriental and occidental languages is not comparable to coding and decoding messages, but requires a distressing amount of circumlocution and rearrangement of thought."[94] When working with interpreters, the military commission subsequently urged the prosecution and defense counsel to use "short, simple questions as free from artifice as if examining a small child."[95] The tribunal thus infantilized "oriental" languages—that is, languages spoken by Asians and Pacific Islanders—because "complicated questions," "conditional questions," "long questions," and "sarcastic questions" were purportedly beyond "comprehension" of those on trial.[96] As a result, no "criticism of an interpreter, direct or implied, was permitted to be made in

78 CHAPTER 2

open court by counsel of either side"; with English elevated as the system of signs from which all thought emanated, all translation discrepancies were resolved in court recess and with the approval of the court-appointed chief translator.[97]

With respect to the twenty-five trials concerning the Mariana Islands, the military commission provided thirteen interpreters for the prosecution and defense counsel. They included two Americans: Frederick A. Savory and Eugene F. Clark; seven Guamanians: Jorge Cristobal, Tomas A. Iglesias, Juan Manibusan, Isabel T. Perez, Joaquin C. Perez, Vicente C. Reyes, and Isabel Perez Zafra; and four Japanese: Kan Akatani, Yoshio Akatani, George Kumai, and Kimio Tsuji. Of these individuals, Jorge Cristobal, a chief steward in the navy, served as a translator in twelve cases, the most afforded to anybody. His first opportunity to work as an interpreter emerged at the behest of Admiral William Halsey, then appointed as an American naval officer in Aotearoa New Zealand in July 1944. As Cristobal recalled, the admiral said, "'I'm going to have you transferred to the Third Marine Division as an interpreter.' He told me that the Marines were about to invade Guam and take it back from the Japanese. He knew I spoke Japanese, and I could translate for the Chamorros also."[98] At the invitation of the admiral, Cristobal left his role as the officer's mess attendant in New Zealand and accompanied the Third Marine Division in its reinvasion of Guam. Later in the month, Cristobal "went in on the third wave landing at Asan Beach, and I was right there in the middle, looking like a Marine. I was wearing a helmet and everything was Marine for me! I went down that rope ladder from the ship to get into the amtrac, and I had a carbine with me. It was light to carry, and it could fire eleven shots without reloading."[99]

Excited about his newfound Marine identity but fearful of the Japanese gunfire directed at him, Jorge Cristobal landed on the shore of his homeland, only to witness two other Marines die nearby. "I couldn't explain my feeling as I went ashore, but I went right in there with the rest of them. I crawled right up there, and three or four guys followed me there in between Asan and Piti. Of course, I was very familiar with that whole area." Eventually, Cristobal reunited with his family, assisted the Marine Corps and navy as a scout, and "became a war crimes commission interrogator."[100] Having once lived in Japan as a porcelain maker in the 1930s and having worked as a steward for the U.S. Navy thereafter, he was well suited for translation services. As a result of its experiences in working with Cristobal, the tribunal decided to select other interpreters like him. On his role as a naval interpreter, he said, "A lot of people don't understand. The terminology is different. . . . Because, you know, the primary interrogator has the locations, where are they, how many people, all those things like that." Elaborating on the fear of being interrogated, Cristobal also stated, "It does make too much hard work to do that because when you talk to a person who is *very scared*, too, an enemy. Sometimes they don't answer you back, right quick. Because *they feel like they're going to be killed. I would feel the same, too, myself.*" As he explained, "The [accused war criminals] that were caught here in Guam; there were sixteen or seventeen of those guys that really know the locations of where the enemies are; but they very silent sometimes. . . . They won't talk anything at all. But common sense will tell you, if you ask them, 'Why did you kill them?' He's not going to tell why. At that time, they were pretty well stunned, too. Their mind is not clear."[101]

It is quite plausible, then, that the tribunal hired Cristobal as an interpreter for many cases because he had survived the Japanese military bombing of Pearl Harbor, his family had persevered under the Japanese military occupation of Guam, and he had "liberated" Guam as a Marine. That he assisted in many trials merely illustrated the degree to which the navy would hire biased translators to legitimize its rule of law and assert its political sovereignty. On the other hand, staff assigned to the military commission, the War Criminals Stockade, and related units did not entirely express enthusiasm in their tours of duty in Guam. Nor did everybody possess the legal and linguistic utility of men like Jorge Cristobal. In fact, numerous naval officers and attorneys resigned early or returned to the continental United States, demonstrating that the nationalist zeal often ascribed to military service was never ubiquitous. In December 1945, for example, Lieutenant Commander O'Brien desired "separation from the service"; First Lieutenant Small was not interested in "staying in the service," as were Lieutenants John K. Murphy and William Mahoney; and Lieutenant Franklin Williams simply wanted to be "released as soon as possible."[102] The dilemma of having a reliable and impartial staff of military officers was compounded further by the reality of the then reemerging apparatus of naval discipline in Guam. Because the island took several years to recover from the war, the U.S. naval court system sought to reestablish itself from the 1940s to the 1950s. To resolve this predicament, the naval government selected the military commission to handle civil crimes and Class B war crimes trials during the war and thereafter. As the chief of Naval Operations clarified, "When Military Courts are used in the administration of civil judicial matters in occupied territories and hear cases involving violations of local laws, regulations, or orders established by military government for the civil population, the words 'for Civil Affairs' shall be added to the title of such courts."[103]

As the navy understood it, the tribunal shall also "have jurisdiction over all persons in the custody of the convening authority at the time of the trial charged with war crimes committed against United States nationals and any white person whose nationality has not prior to ordering of the trial been established to the satisfaction of the convening authority."[104] Unlike the seemingly race-neutral directives issued by the War Crimes Office, the commission in Guam was more candid in its privileging of whiteness as a phenotype of injury alongside the presumed loyalty of U.S. citizens and nationals. As with the caricatured white female victim of earlier investigations conducted by American intelligence personnel, so, too, did the tribunal privilege white masculinity, property, and sovereignty in its regulations and court proceedings.

In this regard, the navy often recognized and protected white Americans (usually men) over indigenous peoples, a common pattern shared by Anglo war crimes tribunals. White privilege and protection in these tribunals often adhered to this hierarchy: first, white American citizens and military personnel; second, white Allied military personnel; third, white Allied citizens; and, fourth, indigenous and other nonwhite peoples.[105] By defining whiteness as the legal category of personhood, then, the navy's commission in Guam primarily sought to identify and safeguard white citizens and military personnel; the trope of native loyalty also upheld this racial and racist hierarchy, one that conveniently coincided with the postwar settlement of white military personnel in the island. As the historian Hal M. Friedman observes, populating the islands with "white Americans was considered one way of eradicating Japanese influence, assimilating the [indigenous] population to American rule, and consolidating U.S. control."[106]

Consequently, the military tribunal afforded its subjects "the Anglo-Saxon right of presumption of innocence until proven guilty," a rights framework that primarily benefited white heterosexual men.[107] Under the legal and political purview of SCAP, the military commission also had the power to determine, at will, the scope of its regulations. That is to say, "the proceedings of the Military Commission will be governed by the Naval Courts and Boards, except that the commission is permitted to *relax the rules* for naval courts to meet the necessities of any particular trial, and may use such rules of evidence and procedure, issued and promulgated by the Supreme Commander for the Allied Powers . . . as are necessary to obtain justice." In other words, "the commission may adopt such other rules and forms . . . as it considers appropriate."[108]

Clearly, various debates on war criminality helped to shape the making of the War Crimes Office and the international drafting of A, B, and C war crimes classifications. U.S. legal discussions on these topics forewarned the implications of linking law with militarism and politics, a process that failed to cohere nation-to-nation agreements on the treatment of war criminals other than to ensure that they be tried like "pirates" in international law. Selectively heeding these debates and measures, the United States synthesized, revised, and projected a series of federal, international, and military laws on war criminality in an unprecedented manner across the world. To this effect, the carceral and colonial regimes of the United States merged with naval notions of justice and jurisdiction in the mid-1940s, enabling military tribunals to possess nearly unchecked rules and regulations. With a history of naval governance in Guam, one that is inherently tied to the plenary power doctrine, the island was chosen to become the main site for the navy's military commission. Given its charge to try both civil and war crimes cases, the military commission drew from the authority of naval law and the four codes of law invented by the naval government in the early 1930s. These codes included the Civil Code of Guam, the Code of Civil Procedure, the Penal Code of Guam, and the Probate Code of Guam, another set of laws that coconstituted the extrajuridical threshold of the military commission. What was at stake for the navy, then, was not merely the apprehension of criminal types. Rather, the question of political sovereignty ultimately informed the making of the military commission and its efforts to reestablish order on an island and for people outside of the law.

By establishing the navy's War Crimes Tribunals Program in Guam on March 24, 1945, the United States represented itself as the claimant to the island's sovereignty.[109] As a military colony, the island—and, most vitally, Japan's possession of it—compelled the United States to reassert its sovereignty at a time when the future of U.S. colonialism in the Pacific was placed under duress and, via Japan's propaganda, anticolonial scrutiny.[110] As evidenced in its review of the international law on sovereignty, the navy asserted that "the rights of sovereignty over Guam were not lost to the United States by the Japanese occupation of the island. . . . That sovereignty had been previously exercised through the American Naval Governor of Guam. The laws promulgated by him, set forth in the Penal Code, Civil Code and Code of Civil Procedures of Guam, remained in effect during the Japanese occupation unless suspended by the Japanese under military necessity."[111]

According to the navy's War Crimes Tribunals Program, the Japanese military never suspended the codes and, as a result, Japan never eroded the sovereignty of the United States. On this matter, the judge advocate general clarified that even if the Japanese military attempted to suspend the codes, as "belligerent occupants," it lacked the authority under international law to do so. As the navy's legal advisers observed, "Belligerent occupation is 'essentially provisional' and does not transfer sovereignty over the occupied area, although the legal sovereign is not in a position, during the period of occupation, to exercise its sovereign rights. . . . The principle underlying these rules is that although the occupant in no way acquires sovereignty over occupied territory through the mere fact of having occupied it, he in fact exercises for the time being military authority over it."[112] "In the case of Guam," proclaimed the judge advocate general, "all that existed was a state of belligerent occupancy, temporary in nature, which never ripened into more."[113] By asserting the continuity of its political sovereignty, the navy, as the "protector" of its subjects, stipulated that its laws had to be obeyed in spite of Japan's imperial presence. As the navy declared, "The protection which a state owes to its inhabitants does not cease when its forces are temporarily withdrawn so that the enemy exercises the rights of any army in occupation. . . . The occupying belligerent does not become an agent of the legitimate sovereign charged with the same obligation of protection. The belligerent exercises only a temporary authority for his belligerent purposes. The laws of the legitimate sovereign continue in force. . . . [And] the inhabitants are bound to obey them."[114] Extending the procedural and jurisdictional scope of these claims, the navy's legal advisers also noted that the statute of limitations on crimes committed during the Japanese occupation had no bearing on the operation of the military commission. All violations, the navy maintained, were subjected to its "prosecution following American reoccupation."[115]

As these passages attest, the navy employed its War Crimes Tribunals Program to make certain U.S. sovereignty over Guam. Equally significant was the navy's treatment of the island's people, who, despite their respective classifications by the navy as ally, criminal, or otherwise, all fell under its "pastoral" care. In this respect, the navy's "protection" of its subjects resonated with Michel Foucault's theorization of the pastoral-shepherd-sheep as a relation of modern power and as a technology of surveillance. As Foucault argues, "The essential objective of pastoral power is the salvation (*salut*) of the flock."[116] In the navy's view, salvation partly meant the purging of "belligerent" types—what Foucault variously calls "wolfs" and "corrupted" sheep—in order to reassemble the subjects under its care. Like modern power, the power of the pastor was forceful, persuasive, and weak, as much as it was undetermined and malleable.

Regarding the issue of force, for example, the judge advocate general frequently demanded the loyalty and, hence, pastoral duty of the Chamorros of Guam. As early as March 31, 1923, the navy asserted this claim of provisional inclusion: "While a Native of the Island of Guam owes perpetual allegiance to the United States, he is not a citizen thereof nor is he an alien and there are no provisions under law under which he may become a citizen of the United States by naturalization."[117] On April 24, 1945, the navy maintained that the subject status of Guamanians as "loyal natives" persevered even during Japan's military occupation of Guam. As the navy argued, "The native Chamorros remained nationals of the United States and continued to owe allegiance to the Naval Government of Guam and to the United States. They owed to the Japanese military government only obedience and neutrality. They did not owe allegiance to Japan nor could they be legally compelled to take an oath of allegiance to Japan or to the Japanese Military government."[118] Other naval officials were more persuasive, but no less commanding and condescending in their presumptions of the island's pastorate. As Lieutenant Commander Francis Whitehair exclaimed on July 25, 1945, the "proper disposition of war criminals now . . . is essential to gain the respect, loyalty, and confidence of the civilians in the Navy's charge, as well as to establish the desired prestige."[119]

But what proves especially instructive for analyzing the navy's classes of racial inclusion and exclusion was what Foucault described as the pastor's "paradoxically distributive" power. As he states, the power is "paradoxically distributive since, of course, the necessity of saving the whole entails, if necessary, accepting the sacrifice of a sheep that could compromise the whole. The sheep that is the cause of scandal, or whose corruption is in danger of corrupting the whole flock, must be abandoned, possibly excluded, chased away, and so forth."[120] As illustrated in the protective compounds, the prisoner of war camp, and the War Criminals Stockade, Foucault's notions of the sacrificial sheep, the corrupted sheep, and wolves applied to these carceral spaces. As a result, the American military gave the interned individuals the impression that a shift had occurred not only in the pastoral care of the nation but also in the constitution of its pastorate. Rear Admiral Charles A. Pownall, a naval governor of Guam, expressed these sensibilities in a speech delivered to the island's military, political, and religious elite on May 30, 1946. Rallying them as a "team," he said, "We must re-energize

Guam as a team. In this team there is no place or position for: (a) The ex-collaborationist with the enemy, if there be any. (b) The pessimist or defeatist. (c) The crank. (d) The troublemaker. (e) The loafer" and other criminal types.[121] The attention given here to the nonpastorate is precisely the paradox to which Foucault refers. That is to say, the "salvation of a single sheep calls for as much care from the pastor as does the whole flock; there is no sheep for which he must not suspend all his other responsibilities and occupations, abandon the flock, and try to bring it back."[122]

The Final Report

In the navy's calculation of its subjects, the efforts to police individuals as markedly criminal or noncriminal were equally exhaustive endeavors. As such, each person was subjected to naval justice and jurisdiction, even though many individuals creatively and actively challenged, often under profoundly violent circumstances, the jurisprudence of the U.S. empire. As demonstrated in Foucault's theorization of the pastor, we can analyze this naval projection of power in terms of its paradoxically distributive forms of racial classification, segregation, and incarceration. As a military commission, the U.S. Navy's War Crimes Tribunals Program exemplified this form of biopower in its interrogation of 135,000 "enemy" civilians and military personnel from 1945 to 1949.[123] Including its racialized surveillance and incarceration of individuals in Guam, this number could have risen to as high as 150,000. Belauans, Chamorros, Chuukese, Japanese, Koreans, Marshallese, Okinawans, and Taiwanese were subjected to these carceral regimes. Of these groups, the navy investigated approximately 500 individuals for their supposed involvement in war crimes cases, with about one-fourth of them receiving consideration for trial.[124] These cases included allegations of cannibalism, espionage, murder, rape, sadism, and treason, among other traditional and emergent categories of war criminality.

The historian Tim Maga observed that "of the 148 Japanese nationals and Pacific islanders tried, 123 had been Japanese military personnel. Thirty of the 148 received death sentences, and several were commuted to life in prison."[125] The military commission specifically tried twenty-six war crimes cases, with the remaining cases being multiply (and sometimes contradictorily) classified as civil crimes cases or "war crime type" cases.[126] With respect to the Mariana Islands, the navy's War Crimes Tribunals Program charged two Guamanian U.S. nationals for civil crimes. Only one Guamanian U.S. national faced a war crime trial on the matter of "sexual perversion" or homosexuality. On the other hand, the military commission accused two Rotanese, eight Japanese, and eleven Saipanese men (one of whom faced two separate trials) of committing war crimes in either Guam or Rota. Other Chamorros became implicated in these cases as well, from Chamorros of Japanese ancestry to Chamorro women conscripted for the Japanese military's sex houses in wartime Guam. At the completion of the tribunal on May 21, 1949, the Japanese government owed approximately $10 million in court fees to the U.S. Navy and its affiliated agencies. With this transaction at its behest, the War Crimes Tribunals Program claimed to have purged Guam of its "war criminals," eradicated Japanese legal and political ties to the island, and reasserted a military brand of American sovereignty here and elsewhere. At least this was the impression provided by its director, Rear Admiral John D. Murphy, in his summary of the commission called *The Final Report.*

Comprising five volumes, *The Final Report* represented the culmination of what began as a series of conflicting debates on war criminality in the United States and internationally. It symbolized, as well, the navy's utilization of carceral and colonial logics in Guam. The U.S. Navy thereby employed justice as a violent project—that is, unconstitutional in its legal exceptionalisms, militarist in its seizures of nonwhite bodies and lands, and racist in its avowal of the Chamorro loyal type. For Rear Admiral Murphy, however, *The Final Report* celebrated the military commission and its pedagogical significance for training military personnel in the use of military warfare and international law. "It is essential," he wrote, "that the accumulated experience covering five years of U.S. Navy activity be summarized and recorded in brief workable form (a) for use in future planning and operations, (b) for the training and educational instruction of U.S. naval personnel, and (c) for historical reference and professional study in the field of international law."[127] Lest his critics question the commission's ability to try both civil and war crimes cases, Rear Admiral Murphy also emphasized that the tribunal "was not aimed or directed toward the objects of vengeance or retaliation. Its purpose was primarily one of deterrence."[128] His conclusion illustrated the character of imperial judgment. As he put it, "I believe the Navy military commissions convened in the Pacific have demonstrably acted in harmony with the highest traditions of judicial dignity and impartiality."[129]

Part II | THE BIRD AND THE LIZARD

3

NATIVE ASSAILANTS

As per its carceral dimensions, the military tribunal apprehended and prosecuted individuals who violated the sanctity and sovereignty of the United States. Chamorros who breached the rule of law thus became subjected to the U.S. Navy's brand of imperial judgment, as much as they became implicated in the political spectrum of the ko'ko and the hilitai. Because Chamorros were neither American nor Japanese citizens, the military tribunal also exploited their nonsubject statuses in order to justify its rulings. How the tribunal came to legally enact and morally uphold cases concerning "assault" and "assault and battery" charges is the topic of this chapter. By examining nine trials, I discuss how the commission homogenized the cultural, legal, and political differences among the accused Chamorros, remade them into "American" wards, and expunged them from the nation as nonsacrifices. Notwithstanding one assault case wherein the accused was a Guamanian, the other eight assault cases involved Rotanese and Saipanese, all of whom the Office of the Judge Advocate General deemed as having no "nationality of their own."[1] Drawing primarily from section 240 of *The Penal Code of Guam*, the tribunal defined "assault" as "an unlawful attempt, coupled with a present ability, to commit a violent injury on the person of another." The related charge, "battery," was construed as "any willful and unlawful use of force or violence upon the person of another."[2]

Establishing a Precedent

The tribunal entertained its first assault case on March 22, 1945. Miguel A. Cruz, a former *sonchō*, or Japanese-appointed commissioner, for the village of Dedidu, faced trial for allegedly assaulting Luis Cruz Camacho and

Vicente San Augustine on separate occasions in 1942. Presumably, Cruz, a Chamorro born and raised in Guam, struck Camacho on or about September 1, 1942, and choked, kicked, and abused San Augustine in the middle of 1942. As with all the cases, the tribunal never focused on a specific date; instead, the court provided the prosecution with much flexibility in determining the time of any alleged offense. As the Office of the Judge Advocate General declared, "When a date is unknown and the offense is such that it occurred at a fixed time rather than continuously over a period of time it is suggested that the date be, when possible, placed as follows: 'between the dates of about 21 December 1941 and about 15 January 1942, exact date unknown.'"[3] With respect to Miguel A. Cruz, the commission assigned Lieutenant Alexander Akerman Jr. as his legal counsel.[4] The lieutenant, a member of the U.S. Naval Reserve, argued that the court held no jurisdiction over Cruz's case because the alleged offense occurred before the issuing of Proclamation No. 4 on July 21, 1944. Further, the charge had already passed the two-year limit on the statute of limitations.

Yet the tribunal overruled these claims, leading Cruz to plead "not guilty." Given his duties as a sonchō, Miguel A. Cruz carried out the tasks administered by the Japanese civil government, the Minseibu. As the Chamorro historian Pedro C. Sanchez observed, the sonchōs and *kuchōs* (district chiefs) "had no real commitment nor dedication to their leadership position and the roles imposed upon them by what they and the people felt was a temporary government. These leaders were caught between the Japanese authorities on the one hand and the local people on the other, who were resisting them in their own way."[5] In this manner, sonchō Cruz acknowledged having assaulted Luis Cruz Camacho and Vicente San Augustine in 1942. According to sonchō Cruz, the former caused a family dispute that led to a Japanese police investigation, and the latter failed to bow to Japanese officials during a sanitation inspection. For these reasons, sonchō Cruz punished these men, both of whom contested these allegations. Luis Cruz Camacho, for instance, testified that sonchō Cruz beat him for parking his bull cart on the side of a road. Vicente San Augustine also said that the district chief had slapped him for encouraging a laborer to quit working in a field. In turn, sonchō Miguel A. Cruz disputed these counterclaims, but he did not refute the charge that he had assaulted these men for violating Japanese rules. As a sonchō, he took orders from the Japanese officials, as well as sought their advice in village matters. Because this was the first assault trial and civil crime assigned to the court, the defense and the prosecution anticipated high stakes in determining its outcome. As the national and international debates on war criminality had already revealed, the tribunal knew that its decision would set a precedent in the assault and battery war crimes cases regarding the Japanese, Rotanese, and Saipanese. As defense counsel Lieutenant Akerman warned, "The decision today will have a far reaching effect on justice on this Island, because during the Japanese occupation many people took positions under the Japanese, and as a result received orders to slap."[6] He continued, "The question which must be decided by this commission is, is it an assault, where a person, acting under orders of the Japanese officials, slaps another person? The answer will decide not only the fate of the accused, but many others, as there are a number of Guamanians in the same position as the accused."[7] Yet the prosecution, led by Judge Advocate and Lieutenant Colonel Teller Ammons, stated that this question held no bearing in the court. He surmised that if the tribunal were to excuse Cruz for the reason that he followed Japanese orders, then "it would be impossible to bring anyone charged in a like manner to trial."[8]

Heeding the prosecution's position, the court found Miguel A. Cruz guilty of all charges on March 26, 1945, thereby sentencing him to a one-year prison term in the Guam civil jail. But unlike the war crimes cases on assault that followed, Cruz did not petition the court to afford him the rights of a prisoner of war. As a U.S. national and Chamorro from Guam, he fell under the sovereignty of the tribunal even though he was considered an official for the Japanese government because of his previous duties as a sonchō. In the succeeding cases, however, the tribunal dismissed every attempt on the part of Chamorros from Rota and Saipan to categorize themselves as prisoners of war. During the span of their trials from March 1945 to October 1945, a majority of the Rotanese and Saipanese requested to be treated as personnel formerly affiliated with Japanese civil and military units in Guam.[9]

In refuting these petitions for prisoner of war status, the tribunal did not engage the Geneva Conventions (humanitarian laws of combat) or the Hague Conventions (laws of warfare) in ways that could have offered greater protections for the accused.[10] Nor did the U.S. government seek Japan's legal assistance for the Chamorros and Japanese located in Guam at that time.[11] The Marine Corps captain Nicholas Savage, an intelligence officer, expressed this uncertainty. As he observed, "It is my understanding that in the case of an internee as well as a prisoner of war, the Japanese Imperial Government or protecting power has been notified, but that is carried out by [the U.S. Army Provost Marshal General's Office] who took their information from us and acted upon it. I am not positive of that, but we may assume they did."[12] Although Japan eventually became involved in the tribunals, especially regarding Japanese atrocities toward American military personnel, Japan did not know that its colonial subjects were being tried for war crimes in the early months of 1945. This is not to say that the court did not take seriously the principle of discrimination between combatants (e.g., prisoners of war) and noncombatants (e.g., civilians).[13] It very much did.[14] For the tribunal, the Rotanese and Saipanese were not combatants. They were noncombatant "civilian detainees" and "civilian internees," classifications developed by military personnel in August 1944.

Captain Savage clarified the principle of discrimination as such: "Chamorros from Saipan or Rota, who do not wear uniforms, who were not officially members of the Japanese police but were acting as interpreters and informally as investigators, those individuals have been classified as civilian detainees."[15] As he emphasized, they were "wards of the Japanese Government and not citizens and they were certainly not theologically Japanese."[16] By characterizing Rotanese and Saipanese as not having "uniforms," Savage represented them as noncombatants in the classical sense of the term. Yet this definition does not account for indigenous laborers and soldiers, among other roles assigned to or forced upon them, in the colonial militaries of World War II.[17] Despite Savage's failure to acknowledge Chamorros as having comparable "combat" statuses to segregated Japanese American battalions in the U.S. Army or Navajo code-talker units in the Marine Corps, he nevertheless portrayed the Chamorros as having militarized positions in the Japanese empire. As he surmised, Chamorros from Rota and Saipan "were employed or paid by the civil administration, assigned miscellaneous jobs, sometimes to the police department, civil police, sometimes to the military police, sometimes in unloading or loading ships at Piti and Sumay, and sometimes as civilian construction workers at Agana or Oroto airfield."[18] But the adjective "military" was not the same as the phrases "military conscription" or "military employment," positions no Chamorro could confirm as having, since they had lost all relevant documents during the American reinvasion of Guam.

Being classified as civilian detainees and civilian internees also served other purposes rather than simply rejecting the prisoner of war status afforded to combatants. As Savage implied, the law of armed conflict is gendered so as to construct masculinity in terms of the "male warrior, the defender of the security of the State."[19] Those who do not subscribe to this broad notion, as with noncombatants, are equated with "the female."[20] By rendering Chamorros from Rota and Saipan as civilian detainees or civilian internees, the military tribunal thus treated them as feminine and female, a material and symbolic process that rendered them as nonmale properties of the U.S. state. Signified as such, these Chamorro men could be made into bare life—that is, feminized natives without politics—in the racial hierarchy of the combatant/noncombatant distinction.[21]

As the cases in this and other chapters reveal, the Rotanese and Saipanese became bare life, "morphing" from political subjects to biological objects "that can be enslaved, tortured or killed with impunity."[22] As the theorist Helen M. Kinsella argues, "When the difference of combatant and civilian is legitimated by reference to putatively biological differences of men and women, sexual difference is established not only as a natural fact but as an ontological basis for political and social differences as well. In other words, discourses of gender *produce* the distinctions of sex and sex difference we are now accustomed to identifying as the *ground* of those differences."[23] The categories of civilian detainees and civilian internees had little to do, then, with drawing distinct lines about who could be judged for assaulting or killing on the basis of what actions they committed in the past.[24] Instead, the gendered, ontological, and racialized connotations of the "civilian" feminized the Chamorro men as biological objects, zoē, and as newly acquired properties of the United States.

Of Thieves and Rapists, Liars and Slackers

With the civil crime trial of the Guamanian Miguel A. Cruz established as a precedent, the military tribunal proceeded to address four assault cases from March 30, 1945, to September 26, 1945. The accused individuals, all of whom were Saipanese, were Jose C. Cabrera, Pedro Sablan Leon Guerrero, Henry S. Pangelinan, and Nicholas T. Sablan. The first person up for trial was Nicholas T. Sablan. Described by a military report as "notoriously cruel," Sablan arrived on Guam on January 23, 1942, to work for Kaigon Keibeita, a naval unit, in the village of Sumay.[25] In the island, he married Antonia Taitingfong and had one child. Sablan then received orders to transfer to a Japanese police station in Sinajaña. Occasionally, he served as an interpreter for other police officials, including the Kempeitai (military police), in the villages of Dedidu, Hagåtña, and Piti. As he explained, "During all the Japanese time I was under the Minseibu; I was placed to help the Navy but was getting paid by the Minseibu."[26] On March 30, 1945, Sablan faced the tribunal's charges of four specifications of assault, all against men, and two specifications of assault with intent to commit rape, all against women.

As in the majority of war crimes trials concerning Rotanese and Saipanese, the Chamorro men and women who pleaded as "victims" came from Guam. Jesus B. Rodriguez, a police officer previously employed by the Minseibu and a former colleague of Sablan, was one such person. Accused by Sablan and police chief Kedira of locking up a "certain Japanese" and throwing away the key at the Sinajaña jail, Rodriguez claimed that they tortured him. Recalling an evening in 1942 when Sablan arrested him, Rodriguez said, "When we got to the office, he hit me, kicked me and made me kneel down."[27] Disputing the accusation, Rodriguez reported that he "did not lock any Japanese." At that point, Sablan placed a tangantangan stick—that is, a local wood branch—on top of Rodriguez's calves. As Rodriguez noted, "He stepped on the two ends and kept working it until my legs were swollen."[28] "After he did that he ordered me to go outside and kneel. Later on he called me in, took some twine, tied my hands in the back, and had the twine run up my neck. He took me out and tied me against the flagpole all night. The next morning around nine o'clock he took me to jail and I was locked up."[29]

Whether or not Jesus B. Rodriguez participated in the locking up of a "certain Japanese," the mere possibility of this event warranted punishment so as to suppress any form of native resistance against Japan's empire. As such, it was not a coincidence that Sablan tied Rodriguez to a flagpole for one evening, an act that severely bruised his arms and neck. Although Rodriguez did not confess to committing a crime, the confession was a central node of inquiry for Sablan and other interpreters and police officers.[30] This was the case for Jose G. Salas, the second Chamorro in the trial who accused Sablan of assault. Salas recalled that, in January 1942, Sablan approached him, tied him to a *camachile* tree, and beat him for no reason. Afterward, Sablan asked Salas if he broke into Maria Brunton's home, which was located near the camachile tree, and stole unspecified items. Salas remarked, "In order to stop the punishment, I said, 'I did.' After that the accused took me to Sinajana and turned me over to the Japanese chief by the name of Kedira."[31] According to Salas, Kedira investigated him, released him that evening, and ordered him to return the following day.

As instructed, Salas returned to the Japanese police station in Sinajaña, only to be escorted by Chief Kedira to Maria Brunton's house, where Sablan again tied him to the camachile tree and beat him for a second time. As a bystander to the assault and as a witness for the prosecution, Brunton took the stand and relayed that neither Kedira nor Sablan allowed her to give Salas a cup of water and that Salas was innocent of any accusations of theft.

As Brunton explained, "I knew that he did not steal at all for he referred to many items which were not included among the missing things in my house."³² But she kept these thoughts to herself at the time of the interrogation for fear of not knowing how Sablan and Kedira would respond. Eventually, they released Salas, the confessor of guilt.

Jose L. Mangloña, the third person presumably assaulted by Nicholas Sablan, likewise experienced a "slapping" by him. Like Rodriguez, sometime in 1942, he, too, had a tangantangan branch placed on his legs, with Sablan pressing his weight against it. But unlike the previous testimonies, Mangloña did not share much information other than to state that Sablan let him go when the police believed Mangloña did not commit a crime. His comments were very brief, as if to signal his hesitation in retelling the past. In contrast, the last Chamorro man from Guam to testify as a victim had more to say. Pedro Dueñas Camacho, another resident of Sinajaña, detailed the reason for his punishment, ensuring that the "Saipanese" be labeled as responsible for the assault. Camacho informed the court that Sablan arrested him in September 1942 on the suspicion that he was hiding two Americans, Radioman First Class A. J. Tyson and Machinist First Class C. B. Johnson. Given the high-profile nature of this case, the Japanese police drove Camacho to the police jail in Hagåtña, where, as Camacho put it, there "were five Saipan natives at this time."³³ Once there, Camacho refused to admit sheltering the American men, even though he purportedly helped them. But upon hearing his refusal to reveal their whereabouts, Camacho said, "everyone started to strike me, kick me, slap me. Nicholas Sablan came over with a lash made of No. 8 steel flexible wire and told me to get down on the floor with only my hands and feet touching the floor. He began striking me with . . . forty or fifty lashes. At this time my body was bleeding all over."³⁴ Sablan and other police officers then placed Camacho, unconscious and unable to speak, in a "dark cell." Not able to cull information from him, Sablan discharged Camacho. As for Tyson and Johnson, the police found them a month later at Mount Machanao, where they were "shot on the spot."³⁵

Another person placed within a violent context was Dolores Santos Cruz, the first woman to testify against Nicholas Sablan regarding the intent to commit rape specification. Section 220 of *The Penal Code of Guam* defined the charge as such: "Every person who assaults with intent to rape, an infamous crime against nature, mayhem, robbery, or grand larceny, is punishable by imprisonment in the Island prison for not less than one nor more than fourteen years."³⁶ As part of their investigation concerning stolen goods from Maria Brunton's residence, Sablan and police chief Kedira approached Cruz at her home. They met early in the morning sometime in January 1942. When Cruz denied stealing anything from Brunton's house, Sablan and Kedira warned her about the potential consequences for lying. But Sablan had other intentions, even asking Cruz when her siblings would return home from work. Satisfied with her response, Sablan and Kedira left. At ten o'clock, Sablan then returned by himself, declined Cruz's invitation to eat lunch in the outside kitchen, and walked to the second floor of her home. From there, he called Cruz to follow him. As she observed, "When I got upstairs he had already taken off his shirt, undershirt, and his pants were open. After that the accused told me to sit down and not to leave the house. When he stretched himself down on the floor, I got up from the chair and went over to the house of my other brother, Juan."[37] Sablan then rushed after her, finding her on the second floor of Juan's home. According to Cruz, "He held me with his two hands and pulled me down to the floor. I ran away from him. When I did not want to comply with his wishes, he slapped me on the face and knocked me down the stairs."[38]

Fearful that she might get killed if she did not have "sexual intercourse" with him, Dolores Santos Cruz yelled for her brother, who, upon entering the home, noticed Sablan. Acknowledging his presence as a figure of authority, Juan Cruz then asked Sablan to "take good care" of his sister and to not harm her. Sablan replied, "I'll take care of her better than you can," a reference to how Cruz, a brother and a man, had been emasculated by a Japanese-appointed interpreter and police officer. As the feminist scholar Zillah Eisenstein asserts, women and men are feminized in the process of rape; everyone is shamed.[39] Without any physical resistance, Sablan then escorted Dolores Santos Cruz to the police headquarters in Sinajaña, but let her return home. Later that day, Kedira and Sablan investigated Cruz once more about Burton's stolen goods. They chose not to incarcerate her.

Whereas Dolores Santos Cruz did not receive any jail time, the second woman to testify against Nicholas Sablan did so as a "civilian detainee" in the Island Command Prisoner of War Camp. Presumably incarcerated for "keeping house" with a Japanese police chief by the name of Shimada, Agueda Dueñas Diego discussed how Sablan nearly raped her.[40] Although she knew Sablan "like a brother," given their mutual interactions with the Japanese police, she supported the prosecution's interrogation of him for reasons not disclosed to the court.[41] On the stand, Diego, also known as Ida, recounted an evening in April 1944 when she was sleeping at the home of Tomas Oka in the village of Sinajaña. As she expressed, "The accused came around at 12:30 midnight and woke me up. He called my name. . . . I got up, put on my dress and went to the door."[42] When Sablan explained that Chief Shimada wanted her for something "important," Diego grudgingly put on her wooden clogs and left with him on a bicycle, even though her stomach ached. On the way to the police station in Tutujan, Sablan took a detour to an uninhabited ranch. Realizing that they were not headed to meet the police chief, Diego tried to get off the bicycle, but Sablan restrained her. When they parked, Diego scolded Sablan, saying, "I don't want to get in the ranch and why are you telling a lie? You told me that I was wanted at the jail and why did you bring me to this place?"[43]

Adjusting his rationale, Sablan told Diego to enter the ranch house and wait for Chief Shimada, who was scheduled to arrive soon. In her testimony, Diego recounted, "When I refused to get in he held me and tried to carry me into the ranch. I struggled with him and tried to get away. He held me and threw me down on the grass among some rocks. My back got hurt from that fall."[44] Diego continued with her testimony: "When I asked him why he was doing this to me, he replied that he wanted to have sexual intercourse with me because he had always wanted. I said, 'No.'" Sablan then repeatedly assaulted Diego, even choking her and attempting to lift her dress. Diego described how she defended herself: "I pulled his hair with one hand and his ear with the other and pushing him at the same time so I could get up. . . . I kicked him and he kicked me. He got on top of me again and lifted my skirt. At this time he opened his pants and had his organ out. . . . All during the struggle I had my legs crossed in order not to give him any chance to do anything."[45] Reminding Sablan that he had a wife and a child, Diego admonished him for his actions, at which point Sablan became enraged. At that point, she informed Sablan that she was going to tell Chief Shimada about the assault. Immediately, Sablan "calmed down and apologized."[46] Diego then agreed to not say anything if Sablan would let her return home, and he agreed. On the next day, Diego reported Sablan's attempted rape to Chief Shimada.

Satisfied with Diego's testimony, army Lieutenant Colonel Teller Ammons of the prosecution excused her from the stand. With sufficient evidence to portray Nicholas Sablan as an assailant and attempted rapist, the prosecution sought no further information about how Chief Shimada responded to Sablan's violence. The defense counsel's sole witness, Grace Taitano Flores, briefly appeared next, only to confirm that Sablan knew Diego. Nor did Lieutenant Alexander Akerman Jr., the defense attorney, ask Flores if she could vouch in any way for Sablan's innocence. All the defense could muster was that Sablan was under "duress" during said beatings; with respect to the two specifications on assault with the intent to rape, Lieutenant Akerman claimed that Sablan never assaulted Dolores Santos Cruz. As for the second specification, he informed the court that Sablan had a sexual relationship with Diego. In his court statement, for example, Sablan wrote, "I admit, I asked her to have sexual intercourse with me. Before this time, Ida and myself were very friendly and having sexual intercourse. . . . The night Ida stated that she refused to have sexual intercourse with me, her reason for which was that she did not want Shimada to know about it, but I did not force her to have sexual intercourse with me."[47] Following this premise, Lieutenant Akerman attempted to defend Sablan with a logic akin to the act of rape itself. As he reasoned, Sablan was innocent because "there is a presentation of law that when a man has had sexual intercourse with a woman on one occasion, that on a subsequent occasion it will not be his intent to rape but merely to renew this relationship."[48] Not heeding these positions, the military tribunal sentenced Nicholas Sablan to ten years' imprisonment on April 5, 1945.

Nearly two months later, on May 23, 1945, the commission entertained the trial of Henry S. Pangelinan. Although Pangelinan was born and raised in Saipan, his parents were originally from Guam. For nine months in 1930, he even visited the island, where he learned the English language; in 1932, he then left for Yokohama, Japan, where he pursued an elementary education, worked at the Helms Corporation, and met his wife, Hideko Koyama. They returned to Saipan in 1937. On January 13, 1942, Pangelinan received an order to work in Guam. Educated in Guam, Saipan, and Yokohama, he earned the position of master at arms at the Japanese jail in Hagåtña. Despite his affiliation with the Japanese police, however, he befriended prominent Guam Chamorros and informed them of impending danger during the war period. The Chamorro educator Agueda I. Johnston, for example, favorably portrayed Pangelinan as somebody who "had been friendly to the Johnston family, telling them of the times when the Japs intended to raid the natives for American money or radios, or reporting news favorable to the Americans that he had heard over Japanese radios."[49] His relationship with relatives in Guam and Saipan, coupled with his educational and travel experiences, may have led Pangelinan to move beyond the racialized polarities of the war and to assist Agueda Johnston and others.

Despite Pangelinan's extensive educational background for the time, his responsibilities may have been more mundane than expected. As he recalled, "My duties were to look after the prisoners in the main cell. Whatever the prisoners need I had to report to the authorities. When the prisoners went out to work I had to check them, and when they came back I did the same."⁵⁰ He continued, "I was also in charge of sanitation. I had the prisoners go out on trucks. I took them to collect garbage and trash. That is about all I did every day."⁵¹ Given his relatively high status, perhaps Pangelinan chose to supervise the prisoners; he may have even been relieved, as well, from having to torture others. As he expressed, "Other kinds of work were handled by other members of the force."⁵² Consequently, only one resident accused Pangelinan of assaulting him.

The other men who purportedly received beatings from Pangelinan were three prisoners who were previously incarcerated by the U.S. Naval Government for burglary or theft. After the establishment of the Minseibu, they continued their sentences under the Japanese police of Hagåtña. Because the Japanese government recognized their sentences, the tribunal assumed that "the Japanese acknowledged the Penal Code of Guam as being in effect."⁵³ The commission likewise detailed how these men became "trusties" for the Japanese police, otherwise known as individuals who had "free rein" in assisting the interpreters and officers with daily tasks.⁵⁴ For the court, what mattered was proving what constituted Pangelinan's reputation for being "viciously cruel to the inmates of the prison," an image that tainted the trust between him and the four Chamorro men.⁵⁵ Facing one assault charge and one assault and battery charge, Henry Pangelinan reengaged them not as three prisoners and one civilian. Instead, he met them as newly employed people under the U.S. Naval Government in Guam.

Antonio Toves Atoigue, a driver and the first witness for the prosecution, characterized Pangelinan as insensitive to the labor involved in finding, cutting, and transporting firewood. During one trip to the jungle in February 1943, Atoigue asked Pangelinan to find another person to help him carry a large log, but Pangelinan refused. Not able to transport the "very heavy" log, Atoigue returned to the Hagåtña jail only to realize that Pangelinan had reported him to the Japanese police for disobeying work orders. As Atoigue recalled, "After I was questioned the accused tied my hands behind me with a rope backwards and the rope was run across my neck holding my hands up and a piece of wood was run through my back and the accused started kicking it and the other Japanese did the same."⁵⁶ Already imprisoned by the Japanese police, Atoigue returned to a "dark cell," where his hands remained "tightly tied" behind his back for twenty-four hours.

Another former "trusty" and a newly commissioned patrol sergeant by the name of Juan Blas Manibusan entered the court next to cast suspicion on Pangelinan's wartime conduct. Of all the men in the trial, though, Manibusan viewed Pangelinan and his family with high regard. On the stand, he said that Pangelinan "was, and always" is a friend.[57] Pangelinan also saw Manibusan as a "very good man," even convincing the Japanese authorities to grant him parole on April 8, 1942.[58] He then invited Manibusan to live, as a farm hand, with his family at his ranch in Maite. As Pangelinan expressed, "I treated him like my son."[59] Why, then, did Manibusan suddenly turn on Pangelinan? Perhaps Manibusan's postwar role as a police officer under the U.S. Navy compelled him to express gratitude to a "liberator" by way of criminalizing a Saipanese. To this effect, Manibusan described an incident from sometime in October 1942 when Pangelinan punished him for "stealing clothes and sugar from his ranch."[60] As he stated, "He started beating me with his closed fist and clubbed me with a material used in fencing, which lasted for about half an hour. Then the accused went to the kitchen in his ranch, took out a kitchen knife and started towards me and his wife intervened and spared me."[61]

Juan Flores Flores, another former prisoner and a chauffeur, alleged that Henry Pangelinan tortured him sometime in July 1942. As Flores put it, "He wanted to exchange his old clothes for my good clothes and when I didn't want to, he punished me."[62] Flores then received beatings from Pangelinan for one week. The last person to testify was Jose Diaz Cruz, the only civilian and another police officer under the navy. As with the previous testimonies, Cruz briefly recounted his encounter with Pangelinan. For him, punishment came as the result of his of ignorance rather than disobedience. Sometime in March 1942, he met Pangelinan in one of the prison rooms at the request of an unidentified Chamorro police sergeant. When Cruz failed to explain the purpose of his summons, Pangelinan assaulted him. As Cruz explained, Pangelinan "said that when a man comes there he should know why he came there and then he started slapping me with the palm of his hand and after several slaps told me to kneel down." Not afforded the opportunity to refute these allegations, Henry Pangelinan was found guilty on May 29, 1945. The tribunal sentenced him to two years in prison.

On July 2, 1945, the court then entertained its fourth case on assault and battery. Confined for allegedly beating eleven individuals, Pedro Sablan Leon Guerrero, a Saipanese, originally arrived in Guam on January 23, 1942. Although he occasionally assisted the Japanese police in Hagåtña, he primarily investigated crimes with naval officials based in Yoña. Recalling his assignment, Leon Guerrero stated "that any order given by a superior officer to me must be considered by me as an order and must be complied with, otherwise it will be too bad for me."⁶³ Kanzo Kawachi, a former assistant chief of police in Guam and a prisoner in one of the island's stockades, explained the purpose of orders in his capacity as a defense witness for Guerrero. As he said, "The interpreters received orders from the higher authority as to whether they will punish the accused or not, unless the interpreter has some bitter argument with the accused, then the interpreter usually uses his own discretion in punishing the accused, without the orders of the higher authority."⁶⁴ One order concerned the interrogation and torture of Chamorros suspected of harboring American military personnel or engaging in U.S.-related activities.

Joaquin A. Limtiaco, a farmer, came forward as the first witness for the prosecution. From August 26, 1942, to October 20, 1942, he stated, Leon Guerrero had assaulted him on the suspicion of sheltering U.S. Navy enlisted men. To this accusation, Limtiaco remarked, "I was asked whether I had some Americans in hiding and I replied in the negative."⁶⁵ Unconvinced by Limtiaco's response, Leon Guerrero and four other police officials beat Limtiaco at least three times a week during his nearly three-month imprisonment at the Hagåtña jail. As Limtiaco recalled, Leon Guerrero "said to me, 'I have never punished any Chamorro but this time I will come near killing you,' and he started beating me with a bull whip after he made me take the position of crawling with the tips of my toes and the palms of my hands touching the floor."⁶⁶ Limtiaco continued, "After they got through beating me up, they took me over to the bathroom, wet a towel over my face, took off my pants, and started pouring water over my nose."⁶⁷ Unable to cull any "truth" from Limtiaco, a Japanese naval officer by the name of Kimura then allowed Limtiaco to leave the jail on two conditions. They included searching for the missing Americans and providing updates to the police in Hagåtña once every three days.

While it is not clear if Joaquin Limtiaco played a role in the arrest of Chamorros suspected of knowing the whereabouts of Americans in Guam, the court transcripts reveal that the sonchō of Yoña, Jose Salas Terlaje, identified the men and escorted them to the village police station. They included Ramon S. Baza, Juan B. Cruz, Juan L. G. Mesa, and Jesus P. Quitugua, all of whom recalled being assaulted by Pedro Sablan Leon Guerrero and Japanese naval officials on October 16, 1942. During the beatings, sonchō Jose Salas Terlaje was "told to sit on the side and listen to the answers given by the people." Afterward, the men stood before Terlaje and informed him "that they were not going to commit the acts that they had already committed and that from thereon they will abide with all the rules and regulations."⁶⁸

A month later, Manuel B. Cruz and Jesus C. Borja separately reported to the Hagåtña police station, where Leon Guerrero questioned them. For failing to confess their knowledge of the missing Americans, Leon Guerrero beat them on two different occasions. Cruz described his torture as such: Leon Guerrero "tied my two hands with an electric wiring and then tied me up to the beam of the building and then he took the whip, commonly called Chilin Guaka, and started striking me. . . . When I felt the handle being struck against my face and was about to be unconscious, Pedro, the accused, said, 'Probably he is dead,' and then the accused loosened the electric wire and he pushed me to the left hand side."[69] As a witness for the prosecution, Cruz then indicated how he received more lashings from Leon Guerrero, a form of punishment also imposed upon Jesus Borja and others from Yoña. After their beatings, they were released.

The three remaining Chamorro men who testified against Pedro Sablan Leon Guerrero were Ramon S. N. Camacho, Jose E. Espinosa, and Arturo C. Hines. They argued that Leon Guerrero falsely accused them of stealing a chicken owned by Francisco Taitano, a resident of the San Ramon district in Hagåtña sometime in December 1943. Inocencio Aflague, the sonchō of San Ramon, informed the men of this allegation, as well as accompanied them to the Hagåtña jail for further questioning. Upon arrival, Camacho, Espinosa, and Hines insisted that they were cooking pork earlier that evening, even claiming that Inocencio Aflague found no "chicken feathers around" their residence.[70] As Ramon Camacho noted, "I found the accused sitting on his desk. He called me over and . . . asked me whether I stole the chickens and I told him I did not. He told me that he will beat me up. He made me take the crawling position and started beating me up. After the 13th time that he struck me, I fainted and that was all I remember."[71] Jose Espinosa and Arturo Hines were also tortured in this manner.

As with the previous investigation in 1942, sonchō Inocencio Aflague—like sonchō Jose Salas Terlaje of Yoña—witnessed the beatings and forced confessions of Camacho, Espinosa, and Hines. Knowing that Espinosa was "sickly," Aflague, when called to the stand, even said that he tried to prevent Leon Guerrero from lashing the young man.[72] Yet he failed in his attempt, a risky intervention that may have represented him as an American man of courage and innocence before the tribunal. On the other hand, Leon Guerrero testified to the contrary in describing what may have been Inocencio Aflague's undesirable position as a sonchō. When examined by the judge advocate, Leon Guerrero claimed that sonchō Aflague urged "me to punish them a little so that they can have something to fear."[73] After the two-hour lashing session, Leon Guerrero released the men from the jail. Whether or not sonchō Aflague participated in these violent acts, his attendance—coupled with the awe and fear expressed by the incarcerated men—had already established the sanctity and sovereignty of imperial Japan. As the legal theorist Paul W. Kahn explains, torture is a "form of sacrifice that inscribes on the body a sacred presence. Faith, politics, and torture were conjoined in a spectacle of sacrifice designed to produce in the audience a kind of terror—a combination of dread and awe before the sacred mystery of sovereign power." As he asserts, "Political power was stabilized by the transformation of torture from mere fear of violent injury to awe before the sacred character of the sovereign."[74]

But now under the reins of the U.S. Navy, Pedro Sablan Leon Guerrero had lost his symbolic and material association with the Japanese empire. Stripped of his ties to Japan, he was constructed by the tribunal as zoē, a feminized war criminal whose pleas lacked any legal basis. For one thing, the court dismissed the defense's use of a Chamorro translation of Japanese police orders from December 27, 1941, as well as failed to locate Japanese-language equivalents of this and other regulations. Further, the tribunal did not entertain his request to contact Spain as his "protecting power," the only such inquiry made by any of the Rotanese and Saipanese interpreters and police officers. In response to these actions, Leon Guerrero called the court "highly prejudicial." Seeking legal support to address this bias and consequently delaying the proceedings for nearly a month, he argued that "the test of what petitioner should know, and what was proper for him to do in carrying out his assigned duties, must be what he had learned under Japanese rule."[75] Denied these requests, Leon Guerrero admitted to having punished seven of the men. But he did not assault four individuals, specifically Juan B. Cruz, Manuel B. Cruz, Pedro D. Perez, and Jesus C. Borja. On July 24, 1945, the tribunal sentenced Pedro Sablan Leon Guerrero to a prison term of five years and six months.[76] Judge Advocate and Lieutenant Colonel Teller Ammons described him as an assailant who followed a "custom of cruelty."

Two months later, on September 26, 1945, the military commission entertained its fifth case on assault. But unlike the previous Chamorro defendants, who were born on Guam or Saipan, Jose C. Cabrera, though Saipanese, was initially raised in Palau. As a series of atolls and islands located south of Guam, the capital of Palau, Koror, served as the location for Japan's civil administration. Cabrera lived there since 1916, later moving to Saipan at the age of eleven. He then became a manager at a soap factory. And, on December 8, 1941, the Japanese police ordered him to invade

Guam. For the next three years, he served as an interpreter and police investigator for Japanese officials in the village of Talo'fo'fo, often with the assistance of Miguel Quitugua, the kuchō, or district chief. Now faced with eleven specifications of assault and battery, Cabrera pleaded "not guilty" to the charges.

The first witnesses for the prosecution—Jose Delgado and Juan S. Salas—portrayed Jose Cabrera as a man who did not follow the rule of the law, American or Japanese. They separately argued that Cabrera tortured them for "singing" around six o'clock in the evening, nearly three hours before the curfew time of nine o'clock.[77] They alleged that this incident occurred sometime in January or February 1944 prior to fetching tuba, an alcoholic beverage or vinegar made from fermented coconut sap. As they noted, Cabrera apprehended them, took them to his ranch, and instructed them to kneel on the ground; Cabrera then slapped Salas and scorched Delgado. As Delgado remembered, "The accused took a piece of wood [from Cabrera's kitchen fire] which was glowing and burned me on the stomach."[78] In his defense, Cabrera testified that these men were drunk rather than sober, perhaps having left an evening tuba-drinking session in early January 1944. He also clarified that Delgado and Salas were singing "an indecent song," one that should not have been shared "on the street." As Cabrera explained, "I told them that it was all right to drink and sing but there was a certain place where that kind of song should be sung."[79] Although the court did not inquire as to the nature of the song, Cabrera stated that he warned them about its indecency. He emphasized, as well, that punishment was not warranted on account that the men were walking outside, before curfew, around seven thirty in the evening. But a few days later, Cabrera found the men singing the same song in the same place after nine o'clock at night. Taken aback by their failure to recognize his authority, he recalled the encounter in these terms: "I spoke to Juan Salas and said, 'Have you forgotten that about two or three nights ago I warned you something similar to this and why are you repeating it?' He said, 'I am happy.' I said, 'Didn't I tell you not to be out after nine o'clock and not to sing indecent songs?'"[80] Cabrera then acknowledged having slapped the men for being "fresh" and for violating the curfew, but he refuted the claim that he burned Jose Delgado; as Cabrera expressed, "I only meant to scare him."[81]

As in this episode of vulgar songs and singers, other witnesses similarly represented Jose Cabrera as a police officer who had no patience for "slackers." Six specifications of assault allegedly stemmed from what was Cabrera's disregard for easygoing, irresponsible, and lazy individuals. Vicente R.

Ulloa, a farmer from Talo'fo'fo, testified that Cabrera assaulted him in September 1943 for "being a slacker."[82] Ulloa argued that this attack occurred at a Japanese ranch, Kaigon Tai, at a time when Ulloa was plowing the land with his water buffalo in preparation for the planting of seeds. Another witness, Juan R. Mesa, said that Cabrera slapped his face for missing a meeting with the Seinendan, the Chamorro Young Men's Association. Others like Pedro S. N. Chargualaf, Albert T. Meno, Juan Tedtaotao, and Jesus A. Unpingco received beatings for, respectively, failing to send a message, "fooling too much," reporting late to work, and forgetting to repay a loan.[83] It was then alleged that Cabrera assaulted the remaining two witnesses—Theresa Pablo Reyes and Jose A. Pablo—for stealing items.

For these reasons, the Judge Advocate and Lieutenant Colonel Ammons characterized Cabrera as a "sadistic" person who subjugated the people of Guam "into slavery by fear and force and to break their will to resist."[84] Acknowledging Cabrera as a mere creature of U.S. law without the rights of a citizen or prisoner of war, Ammons continued, "None of these people had a trial and it appeared as though the accused had unlimited power to deal with these American subjects according to his own dictates and that the accused's attitude was an absolute disregard for the right of the people and for the existing laws of Guam."[85] In response to these allegations, the defense counsel, Lieutenant Henry P. Bakewell of the U.S. Naval Reserve, noted that Cabrera was "a nice appearing fellow, and there is nothing wrong with him that a little education will not fix."[86] The first American "educational" session began with the court's sentencing of Jose Cabrera to five years and six months' imprisonment, effective September 28, 1945.

"They Treated Me There Just as They Treated Me Here—Like an Animal"

As these war crimes trials demonstrate, the tribunal treated the Rotanese and Saipanese interpreters and police officers as homines sacri, animals without any legal or political rights. On the other hand, Guamanian testimonies of "loyalty" to the American state upheld the tribunal's prosecution and eventual incarceration of the remaining four individuals accused of assault and battery, namely, Fritz Angocio Mendiola, Domingo S. Quintanilla, Francisco P. Sablan, and Jose P. Villagomez. This was also the context that compelled the military tribunal to ask the first defendant, Domingo Quintanilla, if the Japanese government in Rota and Saipan was "nice" to him during the war. To this question, Quintanilla responded, "No. They treated me there just as [the U.S. Naval Government] treated me here—like an animal."[87]

Originally from Rota, Quintanilla arrived in Guam on April 31, 1942, and had been employed at a charcoal plant, a papaya business, and a military airstrip. As with many of the interpreters and police officers, he was forced into militarized labor for the Japanese. As Quintanilla expressed, "I didn't leave voluntarily. A Japanese policeman came over and notified me that I was going to leave."[88] As one of the four remaining trials on assault and battery, his case involved eight specifications, many of which involved disputes in labor. In this regard, Quintanilla claimed that he tortured individuals who did not meet the labor expectations of the Japanese government. As he opined, "I was only told to see that they worked hard. . . . Sometimes the Japanese decide and sometimes they punish the people themselves. If I informed them that some natives were ill and couldn't perform any work, they would tell me that I was siding with the Chamorros" from Guam.[89] Quintanilla's trial commenced on October 15, 1945. Eight witnesses—mostly farmers and laborers from the villages of Dedidu, Inahålan, and Malesso'—testified as to how he supported the Japanese empire.

Jose P. Aguon and Juan B. Rosario alleged, for example, that Quintanilla assaulted them, respectively, for being sarcastic to a laborer and for seeking monetary compensation. These separate incidents occurred at the charcoal plant in Dedidu sometime in January and April 1944. The Hagåtña airfield was another site where, in the summer of 1944, four men—Juan C. Benavente, Jose R. Gomez, Jesus A. Quinata, and Jose Espinosa Tedpago—each received beatings from Quintanilla for, according to Quintanilla, the infractions of laughing and joking, arriving late to work, arguing with laborers, and providing wrong work schedules. Yet none of these men incurred a sentence in one of the island's Japanese jails. As this and related cases on militarized labor illustrate, punishment was often swift, as the Japanese officials needed men to hastily construct airfields, bunkers, and gun placements in 1944. But while the tribunal focused on the violence of Quintanilla's physical beatings, the court sidestepped the question of his sexual assaults—that is, his "crime against nature"—in two allegations. The *Penal Code of Guam*, section 286, defined "crime against nature" as a person who commits same-sex activities with mankind or with any animal that "is punishable by imprisonment not less than one nor more than ten years."[90] Unlike the related charge, "sexual perversion," which targeted the "mouth" as a site of same-sex deviance, crime against nature construed "any sexual penetration, however slight."[91]

While neither of the prosecution's two witnesses revealed anything that could have resembled "sexual penetration," they offered seemingly matter-of-fact testimonies of same-sex intimacies that could have likewise criminalized them had it not been for their "loyal" struggles in the imperial presence of Domingo Quintanilla. The first witness, Ricardo T. Mantanona, explained, "One day I was sick and the accused came over to our camp. He went directly to my cot and sat beside me. He started fingering my testicles. Then he began rubbing it for a matter of 20 minutes."[92] With no reference as to how they may have pleasured or displeasured each other, he simply described how Quintanilla punished him for not working at the Hagåtña airfield in May 1944. As Mantanona said, "After that he started hitting me, combined with kicking. What I received as a result of this beating were blood coming out of my mouth and my face was all swollen."[93] Refusing to labor further for Japan's empire, Mantanona accepted the beating by Quintanilla even though his "sickness became worse." His loyalty and resistance were self-evident; after all, he "never reported to work" until the Americans had reoccupied Guam.[94] The second witness, Ramon C. Garrido, was less candid. As he noted, "In June 1944, I was sick. The accused, Domingo Quintanilla, came over to my tent to find out why I didn't report to work. I told him I was sick. The accused said, 'Let me feel you.' When he touched me he said I had a fever. He told me however to go to work."[95] When Garrido disobeyed Quintanilla's order to work, Quintanilla then hit him with a stick below the waist while Garrido was "lying in bed."[96]

Comparable to how naval officials would later censor Japanese prisoner allegations of same-sex rape at the War Criminals Stockade in 1946 and 1947, the tribunal remained silent in 1945 on how these homoerotic assaults or exchanges could be construed as "crimes against nature." This was a telling omission given that the U.S. military had already begun to incarcerate individuals accused of homosexual acts during World War II.[97] Nevertheless, the court's refusal to acknowledge same-sex intimacies supported its juxtaposition of native "sacred men" against their native "American" counterparts in Guam. As expected, Judge Advocate and Lieutenant Colonel Ammons drew on this carceral logic to characterize Quintanilla's actions as "slave labor tactics" and his duties as "contrary to the laws of civilization."[98] The defense counsel, led by Lieutenant Commander Henry P. Bakewell, then represented Quintanilla as a "child" who knew nothing about the politics of law, American or Japanese. As Bakewell exclaimed, "While ignorance of the law is normally no defense, it is a defense in the case of children. While the accused is not a child, he had no more opportunity to learn of the laws of Guam than would a child. . . . He was not a free agent. He was himself a victim."[99] The court then sentenced Domingo Quintanilla to four years imprisonment.

In the next trial, another Chamorro interpreter, Fritz Angocio Mendiola, confronted fourteen specifications of assault and battery on October 18, 1945. Originally raised in Rota, Mendiola received four years of elementary schooling there, as well as drove a truck for a Japanese sugar mill called Nanyo Kohatsu Kabushiki Kaisha. He then arrived in Guam primarily to assist the Japanese police on February 19, 1942. But, as Mendiola recounted, his duties shifted to supervising Chamorro laborers at the Piti navy yard and the Sumay air base, two important military sites for the Japanese government. Linking authority with punishment, he described his role as such: "I was told that I could punish anyone that was fooling during working time or left the place without asking. The boss told us, Japanese and interpreters from Rota, that we were to boss the laborers and that if anything that was disobeyed we were to go ahead and punish them."[100] Jose Santos Sablan, a former laborer and witness for the prosecution, stated that farmers and previously enlisted U.S. Navy personnel constituted the workforce of these areas. The men came from the villages of Asan, Barrigada, Mongmong, Piti, and Sumay, among others. Whereas most laborers were paid with modest food rations, Sablan claimed that U.S. military personnel earned one yen and twenty-five sen for performing fourteen to sixteen hours of work per day. As a steward's mate first class for the U.S. Navy, he said that the Japanese military treated him as a "prisoner of war." His partially embellished claim attempted to bolster his masculine image as a loyal American native before the tribunal. But Sablan's comment lacked official endorsement, as the Japanese transported white American prisoners of war to Japan in January 10, 1942. Chamorro enlisted men like Sablan were left with their families in Guam and were not interned in prisoner of war camps in Japan or elsewhere.

Jose Santos Sablan believed that Fritz Angocio Mendiola should be punished for having tortured him, an American military man, in March 1943. Another witness even said that Mendiola delighted in his punishments, at times "laughing" at the injuries and insults he inflicted upon others.[101] Recalling having been assaulted by Mendiola from November 1942 to December 1943, a total of twelve witnesses for the prosecution affirmed the violent nature of this young man from Rota. With no witnesses to complicate this one-sided characterization of Mendiola, the tribunal featured the testimonies of Vincent Aflleje, Rafael C. Crisostomo, Jose B. Cruz, Nicolas

Cruz, Celestine B. Damian, Francisco S. Dueñas, Fecundo B. D. Garrido, Francisco Manibusan, Joaquin M. Muña, Jose Santos Sablan, Jesus M. San Nicolas, and Francisco M. Tajalle over a two-day period. These men variously claimed that Mendiola had assaulted them for these and other reasons: attending a Catholic mass; breaking the handle of a pick (a digging tool); disobeying a work order; drinking water during a rest session; failing to perform a strenuous task; stealing a rice ration; and welcoming a newborn baby.

Jesus M. San Nicolas, for example, argued that Mendiola instructed him to lift a heavy item at the navy yard in Piti sometime in November 1942. Not having the strength to fulfill this objective, San Nicolas refused to follow Mendiola's order. As San Nicolas noted, "The accused ordered me to pick up a box which was very heavy. I told him I couldn't do it because it weighed somewhere around 350 pounds. He said, 'What happened to all the nourishment you have been eating?' I told him it was too heavy for one person to carry. He got angry and took a piece of board, 1" by 6" about three feet long and hit me four times; then with closed fist he hit me twice on the jaw. He told me I could not perform my work well because I was still waiting for the Americans."[102] As in this and other instances, the signifier "American" demonstrated disloyalty to Japan or loyalty to the United States. Taking advantage of this politicized dualism, Judge Advocate and Lieutenant Colonel Ammons revealed that the Guamanians "never gave up hope . . . that American justice would return."[103] In response, the defense counsel repeated the tired trope of Rotanese and Saipanese ignorance, equating their presumed legal naïveté with childlike appearances and tendencies.[104] As for Mendiola, he admitted punishing the laborers but only because Joya, Sasak, and Wada—three partially identified Japanese officials—had ordered him to do so. With another poor defense, the tribunal found Fritz Angocio Mendiola guilty of all charges on October 19, 1945. As a result, he received five years and six months' imprisonment in the island stockade.

Three days later, on October 22, 1945, the Saipanese Jose P. Villagomez came before the military commission on account of seven specifications of assault and battery. Originally found guilty of murder in an earlier trial on March 15, 1945, a topic explored in the next chapter, he appeared before the court once again. Having worked in Saipan as a police officer since 1935, he had acquired extensive experience in conducting interrogations for the Japanese government before coming to Guam. Cognizant of his subordinate but authoritative position, Villagomez understood his responsibilities as a police officer. As he expressed, "The punishment was according to the orders given. If my superior told me to slap, then I slap, if to whip, then I whip."[105] When Villagomez arrived in Guam in December 8, 1941, he abided by these rules in his capacity as "a civilian, army, or navy man."[106] As an interpreter and police officer stationed at the Hagåtña jail, Villagomez sometimes dealt with offenses committed in the neighboring villages of Anigua and Sinajaña. These included accusations of espionage and theft, as well as suspicions of assisting the American military. Assaulted for being a spy, for example, Felipe Aguon Unpingco testified that Villagomez periodically clubbed him with a baseball bat at the Hagåtña jail over a period of five days in October 1942.

At the trial, Unpingco, a farmer, stressed the long-term effects of these torture sessions: "I have continuous pain on the neck and I cannot raise my arms."[107] The remaining witnesses for the prosecution—that is, Juan Flores Flores, Jesus Mantanona Chiguina, Luis Cruz Camacho, and Joaquin Aflague Limtiaco—similarly testified about having been assaulted by Villagomez in 1942. Among these men, Luis Cruz Camacho indicated having the longest sentence at the Hagåtña jail. Imprisoned for eighteen days, he described one of Villagomez's most favored forms of punishment. As Camacho revealed, "The accused took two benches and then made me stretch my hands on one bench and my feet on the other forming a bridge. Then he got on my back and started jumping. When I fell, he made me take the same position; then he took a club about 4 feet long by one inch diameter and started hitting me with it until it broke. After that he took a whip and whipped me from my legs all the way up to my neck until I was numb."[108] When asked by the tribunal if he punished Camacho in these ways, Villagomez replied, on the stand: "No. I saw him for the first time this morning."[109] In fact, he said, he never met Felipe Aguon Unpingco nor did he punish any of the men, claims eventually dismissed by the commission. As such, the tribunal found Jose Villagomez guilty of all the charges and sentenced him to three years' imprisonment on October 22, 1945, the first and only day of his trial.

The last case regarding the Saipanese Francisco P. Sablan differed no less in terms of how the military commission repeatedly espoused its notion of "justice"—that is, white supremacist punishment and statecraft—as morally superior to its Japanese counterpart. With Pearl Harbor as his national reference for American valor and triumph, Judge Advocate and Lieutenant Colonel Ammons proclaimed, "As the world knows, there is a difference in the concept of justice between the Americans and the Japanese; that has been fully demonstrated before and since the 7th of December 1941."[110]

With twenty-four specifications of assault and battery, seventeen witnesses for the prosecution, and two witnesses for the defense, Francisco Sablan may have very well understood "American justice" as heavily favoring the views of the prosecution, if not the majority. Or he may have drawn parallels between the military tribunal and the Japanese police system, viewing both as equally authoritative, masculine, and punitive. These are the kinds of issues the Rotanese and Saipanese men may have contemplated.

In Sablan's trial on October 29, 1945, three separate parties came forward to incriminate him for his role as a police officer at the Hagåtña jail. The first, Juan Santos Tenorio, alleged that Sablan had assaulted him sometime in October 1942 for stealing a *fusinos* (hoe). He was then released after one day of questioning. Whereas this incident involved only one person, the other two events involved larger groups in the fall of 1943. Yet nobody testified as to Sablan's supposed violent character from his arrival in Guam on December 8, 1941, to his arrest by the U.S. Navy in August 1944, a point lost on the part of his defense counsel. And notwithstanding the testimonies of Tenorio and one police officer, the remaining witnesses identified themselves as former prisoners of the Hagåtña jail. These witnesses were thus taken as legitimate sources of evidence in such trials, with little criticism as to the composition of their character. For this reason, attempts to escape prison and play dice—activities deemed illegal by the American and Japanese penal codes—were valorized as heroic efforts to subvert the authority of the Japanese police.

In October 1943, for example, Jose A. Concepcion, Jose Mafnas Mendiola, and Enrique Rabago left the Hagåtña jail for an undisclosed location in the nearby village of Otdot. As Mendiola explained, "We ran away from jail because we were hungry."[111] As the second party to accuse Francisco Sablan for his violence, these men claimed that Sablan had tortured them over a three-day period. With little focus on why they were imprisoned in the first place, they diverted attention to Sablan's cruelty. As Concepcion put it, the "accused took the three of us upstairs and lashed me with a bull whip and clubbed me with a baseball bat."[112] Afterward, they remained imprisoned. The third and final group to levy allegations against Sablan consisted of one Guamanian police officer, Felix Wusstig, and thirteen prisoners: Juan Borja, Ignacio T. Castro, Vicente R. Cruz, Vicente Sablan Cruz, Jose M. Eclevea, Juan F. Flores, Miguel Garrido, Ignacio Nededog, Vicente Pangelinan, Juan N. Perez, Manuel L. Rosario, Juan C. Tedtaotao, and Dorotheo Zamora. With the exceptions of Eclevea and Rosario, all of them were released from the Hagåtña jail under the American occupation. The men then took on responsibilities as farmers and laborers, with a few becoming bartenders, commissioners, or nurses. As a group, they pleaded their innocence for playing dice on the evening of December 31, 1943, an activity that many thought was legal under the Japanese occupation. Only Jose Eclevea and Juan Tedtaotao—individuals who were originally sentenced by the U.S. Navy for their respective crimes of theft and attempt to commit rape—admitted that gambling was illegal under the American government. As Eclevea announced, "Before the Japanese time, we knew [gambling] was against the law, but not during the Japanese time. We were not informed about it."[113] Gambling and any "banking or percentage game played with cards, dice, or any device, for money, checks, credit, or other representative of value" were considered misdemeanors under *The Penal Code of Guam*.[114]

Exaggerating their ignorance about the laws on gambling, a few of the prisoners implicated Sablan for supporting the New Year's celebration. As Vicente Reyes Cruz clarified, the "accused lined up the boys and told them they were going to have a happy time" on the eve before January 1, 1944. By "happy time," the prisoners assumed that Sablan had condoned the act of playing dice. They also observed that Sablan may have used this moment to remind them of their "right" to be Japanese and to celebrate their newfound identity over anything American. As the Guamanian police officer Felix Wusstig recounted, "There were about 60 inmates and the accused made us get in line and questioned us if we were still thinking of the Americans and then he said that up to that time we were still thinking of bacon and ham and there isn't one single American ship to help us."[115] He continued, "Then he said that he still could not understand why we had that American feeling, American hearts, and that we should be by right, Japanese."[116] But rather than take this cue as a warning, the Guamanian prisoners and lone police officer embraced the "happy time" of playing dice. They were wrong.

As Juan Tedtaotao observed, "On the night of December 31, 1943, we thought we would have a nice time, so we decided to shoot craps. We were in the toilet shooting craps when the accused came and found us. I was the first one he slapped. Then we all managed to run to the main cell. He followed us and started slapping and whipping in there."[117] The other prisoners claimed that Sablan, branding a machete by his side, had entered the jail drunk, after having consumed sake with the other police officers at a nearby building. In his defense, Sablan said that gambling was illegal under Japanese laws, a point reiterated by Henry S. Pangelinan, a defense witness and former interpreter for the Japanese.[118] And while Francisco Sablan acknowledged having assaulted many of the men, he denied hurting seven of them. All actions emanated from orders given by his Japanese supervisors, Churoka and Shinaga. As with all of the cases on assault, Sablan faced a vengeful court. He was a child, if not property, before U.S. law. As Judge Advocate and Lieutenant Colonel Teller Ammons opined, any "child knows it is wrong to assault his playmate, and each adult knows that he is not permitted to assault his fellow men without justifiable cause. I do not believe the accused's mind was perverted to such a degree that he could not distinguish between what was right and what was wrong."[119] As a sacred man of the war, Francisco Sablan received the guilty sentence of six years' imprisonment, with all charges proved. On October 30, 1945, he became a native war criminal.

Guaho Lokue Chamorro Yo

In becoming "war criminals," the Rotanese and Saipanese may not have fully comprehended their role in the making and remaking of U.S. colonial law in Guam. Without having the legal and political resources to mediate the court's allegations, let alone not having the capacity to understand the English language, many of them apologized for their actions. Utilizing the refrain of cultural solidarity, "Guaho lokue Chamorro yo," as in "I am also Chamorro," they urged the tribunal to reduce or dismiss their sentences. As Henry S. Pangelinan remarked, "Gentlemen, I, myself, am a Chamorro. And had in mind the betterment and welfare of the people of Guam and the constant desire to save my own people from falling into the pitfall which the Japanese had in store."[120] Jose P. Villagomez similarly expressed, "Even though I had an official position and order, I have considerations and sympathies toward humans since I am a Chamorro and a Catholic."[121] Others did not know the Americans. As Nicholas Sablan pleaded, "I pray that the court consider that I am a humble Chamorro and ever since my birth was under the Japanese Government and for that matter I do not understand the Americans and its customs."[122]

A few interpreters and police officers also emphasized the restrictive conditions under which they performed their duties in colonizing the Guam Chamorros. As Domingo S. Quintanilla disclosed, "I am sorry it happened. I was ordered to do it. If disobeyed I would be punished. In fact, I myself was punished for not driving them hard enough. . . . I heard it was wrong, and asked Boss. The Boss said it was Japanese time, not American time. . . . I promise it will never happen again."[123] Should a Rotanese or Saipanese refuse an order, he was tortured by a Japanese police supervisor. Describing this environment where violence begets violence, Fritz Angocio Mendiola said, "I was more than once threatened with a sword. I was beaten many times for refusing to oppress the Guam Chamorros. . . . I always tried to avoid striking the Guam Chamorros, and did so only after I was ordered and threatened. I was beaten so many times myself that I honestly believe that I felt worse than the Guam natives did."[124] Himself apologetic for his actions, Francisco P. Sablan clarified what may have been a shared view among the men. As he stated, "In 1941, I came to Guam under orders of the Governor of Saipan. I never was instructed on Guam law and acted at all times under orders of my superiors. I did not know I was doing wrong. . . . I am sorry this happened, and it will never happen again."[125] As Henry S. Pangelinan put it, "It is difficult for you to understand what one must do when they have to serve under Japanese masters. I ask that you take that into consideration in judging my case."[126]

As their cases reveal, the military commission found every Chamorro man from Rota and Saipan guilty of "assault and battery." Following the civil crime trial of Miguel A. Cruz, a former sonchō, the court set a precedent in determining what constituted this crime and its various specifications in the context of Japanese-occupied Guam. That the tribunal began with this Guamanian sonchō is telling not only because Cruz had the shortest sentence of one year's imprisonment among the nine men accused of these charges. As the making of the U.S. Navy's War Crimes Program had already demonstrated, cases such as these were meant to renew and "test" the thresholds of constitutional, military, and international law in Guam. While Cruz may not have fully taken on the dimensions of a "sacred man," given that he was an American national and subject to U.S. laws, his trial showed the degree to which the tribunal practiced impartiality. His case represented the military commission as nonpartisan in its apprehension and prosecution of any violator—Guamanian, Rotanese, or otherwise—of U.S. laws.

Remade into "civilian detainees" and "civilian internees," the Rotanese and Saipanese men lost any right to prisoner of war statuses under international law, as well as any protection afforded by the U.S. Constitution. As homines sacri, their bodies now constituted the thresholds of the state and its laws on crime in Guam. As Michel Foucault would argue, their cases represented the modern shift in punishment from being a public spectacle of mutilation and death to an institutional "economy of suspended rights."[127] This erasure of rights pertained, moreover, not simply to the sacred men in question. Rather, the carceral and colonial character of the tribunal was further revealed in its disregard for American crimes presumably committed by Guam Chamorros during the Japanese occupation. That the court failed to address other charges—notably, the stealing of clothes, hens, money, and sugar and the playing of dice—illustrated the tribunal's selective application of The Penal Code of Guam and the careful construction of acceptable and deviant native types. Neither the defense nor the prosecution addressed these blatant omissions; at the very least, these efforts can be read as the tribunal's reshaping of its laws so as to accommodate its political objectives in expunging any Japanese threat from the nation. Instead, the tribunal portrayed Rotanese and Saipanese as criminals of the state, whereas the court affirmed Guamanians as noncriminal and loyal wards.

By also referring to Rotanese and Saipanese "war criminals" as harbingers of "slavery," the tribunal appropriated the "world's master trope for imperial forms of domination."[128] Not even the apologies and lamentations on the part of the men could alleviate the navy's use of this metaphor, one that was likewise imposed upon Rotanese and Saipanese accused of committing murders in Guam. As with the condemnation of "blackness" in early twentieth-century America, wherein black criminality became a tool to measure black fitness for citizenship, the court's treatment of Rotanese and Saipanese "customs" as being akin to "slavery" excluded these Chamorros from the nation, on the one hand, and protected the tribunal's jurists from the charge of racism in the colony, on the other.[129] The tribunal had constructed a brand of native criminality that made its laws appear as benign and lawful rather than as racist and unlawful.

4

NATIVE MURDERERS

As in the nine trials concerning native assault and battery, the U.S. Navy's War Crimes Tribunals Program similarly apprehended individuals accused of committing murders in Japanese-occupied Guam. Notwithstanding the first murder case against a Guam Chamorro and U.S. national, Juan Muña Dueñas, the six Saipanese men tried for this war crime were reduced to bare life. They included Antonio Camacho, Luis C. Crisostomo, Juan Reyes, Manuel Borja Tudela, Jose P. Villagomez, and Juan Villagomez. Of these men, only Jose P. Villagomez faced two separate trials, one for assault and battery and one for murder. In this chapter, I examine these cases, all of which invoked the court's definitions of murder as per the *Naval Courts and Boards* and *The Penal Code of Guam*, both of which understood murder, verbatim, as "the unlawful killing of a human being with malice afterthought."[1] Malice "may be express or implied. It is expressed when there is a manifested or a deliberate intention unlawfully to take away the life of a fellow creature. It is implied, when no considerable provocation appears, or when the circumstances attending the killing show an abandoned and malignant heart."[2] Depending on the degree of murder, the punishment entailed either death or imprisonment. As section 190 of *The Penal Code of Guam* noted, "Every person guilty of murder in the first degree shall suffer death, or confinement in prison for life; and every person guilty of murder in the second degree is punishable by imprisonment in prison from five years to life."[3] As per the systematic inclusive exclusion of particular types of natives from the U.S. nation, the military tribunal entertained its first civil crime case in ways that extended its racism and retribution.[4]

Establishing Another Legal Precedent

Comparable to the case of the Guamanian Miguel A. Cruz, the commission began its murder proceedings with another Guamanian by the name of Juan Muña Dueñas, an elderly farmer from the village of Talo'fo'fo. But unlike other trials wherein the naval intelligence personnel searched for suspected war criminals, Dueñas approached military officials and confessed to murdering Manuel Pablo Mantanona, a former kuchō from Talo'fo'fo, on October 26, 1944. As he recalled, "After that I took my gun and hand it to the Marines. . . . I didn't go."[5] But when Dueñas's trial commenced two months later on December 28, 1944, he changed his mind and pleaded "not guilty" for reasons not disclosed to the court.

When Juan Muña Dueñas was detained, the chief of the police, Lieutenant Commander Jon Wiig, requested that he give a statement. But because Dueñas did not comprehend the English language, Chief Wiig enlisted the translation services of Juan Manibusan. When Chief Wiig was called to the stand as a witness for the prosecution, the tribunal asked him if he had apprised Dueñas of his "constitutional rights" as an American national under military guard. Illustrating the court's disregard for the rights of its subjects, Dueñas responded, "I did not give the warning in exact accordance with Naval Courts and Boards. I think he was fully informed of his constitutional rights and he wanted to make a statement after receiving the warning."[6] Based on the statement, then, Dueñas shot Manuel Pablo Mantanona because of a dispute concerning the distribution of corn. According to Dueñas, Mantanona and his godfather, the sonchō Vicente C. Castro, conspired to deprive Dueñas of his share of fifteen out of thirty-five baskets of harvested corn. As Dueñas exclaimed, "The Commissioner [Vicente C. Castro] and Manuel Mantanona were cheating me of my corn harvest, meaning that when I ask the Commissioner about it, he will tell me to see Manuel Mantanona and when I ask Mantanona, he will tell me to see the Commissioner."[7]

In the statement gathered by Chief Wiig and in corresponding testimonies, Dueñas argued that the Kaikuntai, the Japanese agricultural unit, designated his land as one of several areas in Guam to grow produce for the Japanese military. As the Chamorro historian Pedro C. Sanchez explained, the Kaikuntai "set up headquarters in Tai, between Chalan Pago and Mangilao. . . . It recruited all Minseibu officials, teachers and police in the villages, and ordered them to mobilize as field hands all able-bodied women and all children over twelve years old. . . . They cultivated sweet potato, corn, taro, yam, tapioca and other food crops."[8] With his land divided into two lots, one for the Kaikuntai and one for his family, the respective clans of Castro, Dueñas, and Mantanona planted and harvested corn. Dueñas was supposed to receive half of the produce, which, he revealed, was fair. But, in practice, Dueñas claimed that Manuel Pablo Mantanona repeatedly cheated his family from his share of the corn during and after the war.

According to Dueñas, the Castro, Pablo, and Mantanona clans of Talo'fo'fo also ridiculed the elderly farmer and his sons on several occasions. And, yet, Dueñas continuously sought a peaceful resolution even though these families had threatened to destroy his life, children, and land. Clearly, their strained relationship had little to do with corn and more to do with power. In fact, several testimonies revealed that these clans worked closely with and benefited greatly from their ties to both the American and the Japanese military police. This arrangement partly explained why American and Japanese investigators failed to settle their conflict. As a result, Juan Muña Dueñas used his U.S. military–issued carbine to murder Manuel Pablo Mantanona on October 26, 1944. Whereas the prosecution enlisted ten witnesses to confirm the accusation, the defense counsel provided no witness whatsoever. The tribunal then sentenced Dueñas to life imprisonment for voluntary manslaughter, as much as it created a precedent for its proceedings on murder.[9]

From Striking a Father to Watching a Baseball Game

What was at stake in these murder trials? As described in the previous chapter, Chamorros accused of assault and battery received prison sentences of various durations. Yet the tribunal did not levy the death penalty. As section 246 of *The Penal Code of Guam* makes clear, prisoners who serve "life sentences" can incur the death penalty if they are found guilty of inflicting "great bodily injury" upon others.[10] Otherwise, *The Penal Code of Guam* indicates that only persons found guilty of murder in the first degree can "suffer death."[11] With respect to sentences not requiring the death penalty, then, the commission possessed the ability to judge such decisions.

Now faced with Chamorros accused of murdering others, the military court deferred its final judgments to the secretary of the navy whenever sentences required the death penalty. As Judge Advocate General and Rear Admiral T. L. Gatch explained, "Except where a sentence of death is imposed, the officer ordering the trial is the authority taking final action thereon."[12] In making this point, the judge advocate general specifically focused on the murder trial of Jose P. Villagomez, a case that raised "complex questions of the status of Villagomez, of what law he violated and what court can properly try him."[13] Was he a Japanese national? Did he infringe upon the U.S. laws of Guam? Did the Hague Regulations and its Articles of War afford any protections to civilians like Villagomez? Judge Advocate General and Rear Admiral Gatch raised these questions in March 1945, a month after Villagomez's murder trial in February and several months before his assault trial and battery trial in October of that year. As the senior naval officer reasoned, "Because it is the first case of this nature to be tried by a military commission, and because the action taken may have an effect upon the Japanese treatment of American prisoners; it is recommended that the Military Governor of Guam be instructed to send the record to the Secretary of the Navy for examination."

With Jose Villagomez and other Saipanese up for their murder trials, the tribunal inscribed its power over these sacred men so as to incorporate them into the nation only to be punished and expunged as nonsacrifices. With the death penalty looming as one potential sentence, the court thus reinforced the "civilian" status positions of men like Villagomez and the penal codes of the United States. As the judge advocate for his trial, Lieutenant Colonel Teller Ammons, surmised, "He lived as a civilian and worked as a civilian. He has been classified as a civilian internee or civilian detainee since first being taken into custody by the armed forces of the United States on or about the 10th day of August, 1944."[14] Downplaying Villagomez's genealogy as a Chamorro from Saipan and disregarding his legal and political ties to Japan, the lieutenant colonel remade Villagomez into an "inhabitant" of Guam, a euphemism for an American colonial subject. As the military officer exclaimed, "The story of how or why he came to the Island of Guam is not impressive or material. From the first day he set foot on Guam and at all times since, he has been subject to the penal laws of Guam and upon violations thereof his status is now and has been the same as any other civilian inhabitant and no different."[15]

With the assistance of the Judge Advocate and Lieutenant Colonel Teller Ammons, the prosecution began its trial of Jose P. Villagomez on February 26, 1945. He was accused of murdering Vicente Sahagon Babauta in August 1942. Immediately, the prosecution refuted any claim that Babauta had cut his father sometime in that year, the alleged assault that led to Villagomez's arrest of the young man from the village of Dedidu. As a farmer, Babauta produced copra and pastured cows, among other tasks. He was also innocent, emphasized Hector C. Sgambelluri, the former sonchō of Dedidu and a witness for the prosecution. As a Japanese-appointed official, Sgambelluri witnessed the torturing of Babauta at the Hagåtña jail, as well as recalled Babauta's denial of having harmed his father. At the same time, the sonchō acknowledged that Babauta's parents were involved in a dispute, and that his father had a fresh cut on his face. But Sgambelluri never revealed the sources of the family's conflict or his father's injury. Nor did the defense counsel and the prosecution identify the father's name or solicit his testimony. What concerned the prosecution was how Jose Villagomez arrested, tortured, and killed Vicente Sahagon Babauta without due process.

On the first point, the prosecution enlisted the testimonies of three Chamorro police officers formerly employed by the Minseibu and the Japanese navy. They included Pedro Sablan Leon Guerrero, Juan A. Roberto, and Juan Villagomez. The latter two were cousins. Only Roberto was from Guam, whereas Leon Guerrero and Juan Villagomez were from Saipan. Claiming to be a low-ranking police investigator, Roberto informed the tribunal that he took orders from "all Japanese police officers and also from Saipanese police officers."[16] As with every Guamanian police officer, he attempted to absolve himself of any crime associated with the Japanese empire. That no Guamanian police officer faced the tribunal for any charge demonstrated the efficacy of such evasive strategies, if not illustrated the power of the "loyal native" trope in the legal imagination of the court. On the other hand, Leon Guerrero and Juan Villagomez remained interned as civilian detainees, facing, respectively, assault and murder charges. As a group, they identified Jose Villagomez as a member of the search party for Vicente Sahagon Babauta.

With Shimada as the senior police officer, the police argued that Jose Villagomez and the search party arrested Babauta later that evening. Roberto, the lone Guamanian, stated that he only saw Babauta whenever he took him to the hospital for treatment. As if to demonstrate his care for the prisoners and his noninvolvement in the interrogations, Roberto said, "I had to help this man several times because he can't hardly stand up."[17] Whereas Roberto disavowed any violence on his part, the Saipanese officer Pedro Sablan Leon Guerrero acknowledged being present during the investigation. Leon Guerrero admitted, for example, that Jose Villagomez whipped Babauta with "three or four lashes."[18] Juan Villagomez, the other Saipanese officer, claimed to have little knowledge of the case, stating only that Shimada and Jose Villagomez hurt Babauta. With nothing to lose, however, one Guamanian witness for the prosecution described the assaults on Babauta. As the former "office boy" for the Hagåtña jail, Jose Miner Eclevea observed the interrogation.

Initially imprisoned by the Japanese for theft in December 1944, Eclevea, aged seventeen, quickly gained the trust of the officers. Assigned to "take care" of the interpreters' rooms, he had access to every part of the police facility. Eclevea indicated that at least five men—Antonio Camacho, Juan Reyes, Shimada, Ungawa, and Jose Villagomez—tortured Babauta on the evening of his arrest. The punishment began when Ungawa, a Japanese police officer, instructed Babauta to lie on the deck, stomach down. As Eclevea recounted, "Shimada asked him to tell the truth, and while being questioned he was whipped. When Shimada was tired whipping he will pass it on to Ungawa and from Ungawa to the rest of the Saipanese, Juan Reyes, Jose Villagomez, Antonio Camacho. . . . The five of them took turns; every time one of them got tired, he passed [the bullwhip] on to the others; Babauta was punished from 10 o'clock in the night to 4 o'clock in the morning continuously."[19] Afterward, Babauta was allowed to rest in a cell until nine o'clock, when Jose Villagomez resumed the investigation. Villagomez then used a bullwhip to solicit the truth from Babauta.[20]

Refusing to confess to a crime after undergoing more than six hours of torture, Babauta persisted in claiming his innocence. Yet the torture had already converted Babauta into a subject of Japan. As the literary critic Elaine Scarry expounds, torture is a "process which not only converts but announces the conversion of every conceivable aspect of the event and the environment into an agent of pain."[21] As a representative of "pain," Babauta's bodily injuries served as a stark reminder of the power of the Japanese police force. Sonchō Sgambelluri, officer Leon Guerrero, and "office boy" Eclevea variously witnessed the conversion of Babauta from a "farmer" to a "criminal" through the respective lenses of a village official, an interpreter, and a domestic worker. But the conversion and extension of pain were not complete, as Babauta's body was circulated, first, at the hospital and, second, throughout the village of Dedidu. As if to signify Japan's imperial reach into every crevice of society in Guam, his body had to be seen, touched, and handled by multiple individuals across public, official, and private spaces. Take, for instance, the actions of Juan Roberto, the Guamanian police officer who repeatedly escorted the "very sick" man to the hospital over a course of several days.[22]

While it is not known how many times Babauta sought care at the hospital, the nurses implied that he had more than three trips. On one occasion, native nurse Rosa C. Farfan said that Babauta's body was "shaking," though he was able to walk. The second visit was worse. As nurse Farfan observed, "When he came by the hospital by stretcher I looked at his back and he had contusions, black and blue marks from his buttocks up to his neck; black and blue and swollen."[23] During a different visit, Maria Quintanilla Matanane, another native nurse, applied "red medicine (mercurochrome)" across Babauta's bruised and lacerated back.[24] Rita Gogue James, the senior nurse and the native liaison between the jail and the hospital, summarized the context. As she remarked, "When he was brought over to the hospital, I found out something was wrong with his neck and all the left side body was somewhat like paralyzed. He could not sit straight, and he had bruises on his body which appeared as though he had been beaten by a club."[25] Nurse James thus described a man who became increasingly ill over time.

As every torture session demonstrated, one did not have to be present to witness the power of Japan. When the Japanese police finally released Babauta from the Hagåtña jail, he returned to his family in the village of Dedidu. Taken by car, his mother greeted him when he arrived home. As Ana Sahagon Babauta recalled, "When he was brought over to the ranch he could not get out of the car because he was shaking." Regarding his overall appearance, she noted, "He was yellow in color and his breath had a bad odor. . . . I saw black and blue marks and he had a gaseous stomach."[26] Babauta's neighbor, Ramon Cruz Santos, and his godmother, Maria Arriola Uson, likewise confirmed the young man's ailing condition. As Uson observed, "He looked very grave; he could not urinate, could not move his bowels." Babauta only said, "I am going to die. I know I am going to die."[27] He then passed away at his family's ranch in Dedidu sometime in November 1942. His relatives laid him to rest at the Pigo cemetery, an area located far south of Dedidu. As with the other graves, his burial site faced the beach.

In response to these allegations, Jose Villagomez emphasized that he "never whipped" Vicente Sahagon Babauta.[28] Instead, Villagomez portrayed himself as an inexperienced police officer and interpreter, if not as a subordinate of the Guamanians and the Japanese. As he expressed, "No interpreter could go through any investigation unless it was ordered by Shimada. Unless I was ordered to conduct an investigation, I will not do so, but on those days I was new on the Island and I was following Adolfo Sgambelluri according to the way he carried out things."[29] Like the Guamanian police officer Juan Roberto, Villagomez deflected any responsibility on his part. It is rather telling, as well, that the Guamanian police officer Adolfo Sgambelluri did not testify in this case, as Villagomez identified him as an investigator from which to learn policing techniques. When they searched for Babauta, for example, Villagomez offered to find the area in Dedidu where Babauta assaulted his father with a machete. To this proposition,

Sgambelluri purportedly said, "You don't have to inquire any more since we know the district."[30] In this respect, Villagomez implied that Sgambelluri and other Guamanians might have played more active roles—that is to say, knowing places, arresting suspects, and torturing people—in such interrogations. Yet these matters never surfaced in the trials.

Supporting Jose Villagomez's testimony, the defense counsel attacked the credibility of the prosecution's witnesses. The counsel noted that nobody could agree as to when Vicente Sahagon Babauta entered the Hagåtña jail. As Lieutenant Alexander Akerman Jr. and Vicente C. Reyes argued, "We have evidence of 3 or 4 witnesses that he was brought to jail on August 1942; others in October 1942."[31] The same logic applied to the number of individuals who were accused of assaulting Babauta; some said two, a few said five, and one said six. That more than one person tortured Babauta was enough reason to question the prosecution's claim that Jose Villagomez murdered him. As the defense counsel asserted, there "was not one iota of evidence that the injuries described by some of the witnesses as having been inflicted by the accused caused the death of the deceased."[32] Not heeding these criticisms, the court proclaimed that Jose Villagomez assaulted Babauta twice—once on the evening of his arrest and again on the morning of his detainment. For the tribunal, such beatings caused Babauta's death.

For these actions, the commission found Jose Villagomez guilty of second-degree murder, thereby sentencing him to ten years of hard labor. But the court was not satisfied with this outcome. Although the tribunal did not apprehend all the individuals accused of assaulting Babauta, the commission targeted Juan Villagomez, a Saipanese police officer, as similarly responsible for causing the farmer's death. Himself a witness for the prosecution in the trial of Jose Villagomez, Juan Villagomez later faced the murder charge on October 31, 1945. But whereas the former's trial lasted twelve days in February and March 1945, proceedings for the latter took two days to complete. The difference in duration had much to do with the court's interest in establishing Jose Villagomez as the primary murderer of Babauta; hence, little attention was placed on Juan Villagomez with respect to the murder charge. Juan Villagomez's shorter trial reflected this sensibility, as the tribunal spent more effort in finding him guilty on four specifications of assault and battery. In addition to being accused of murdering Babauta, Juan Villagomez was alleged to have separately attacked the following four men in Guam: Gonzalo Ecleva, Jose C. Guerrero, Jose M. Martinez, and Blas T. Taimanglo.

With respect to the murder charge, Juan Villagomez provided partial statements as to his involvement in the interrogation of Vicente Sahagon Babauta. As a witness for the prosecution in Jose Villagomez's trial, Juan Villagomez described himself as an aloof bystander. As he put it, "When that case was brought to the jail, I was not there. I was out. When I went to the jail that night I was very sleepy; it was around 8 o'clock. As I entered the jail I heard some weeping going on. The guard's duty was to check people coming in. I saw on the table a piece of paper and on it was the name Vicente Sahagon Babauta."[33] At that point, Juan Villagomez walked upstairs, where he noticed Shimada whipping Babauta in an interrogation room; Villagomez then went to bed. Shortly thereafter, Shimada called for Juan Villagomez. When he did not respond, Shimada approached him in his bedroom, presumably saying, "What is the matter with you? You are the only interpreter that does not work after working hours. You just went out after working hours, while the others [were] working."[34] At Shimada's request, Juan Villagomez then entered the interrogation room where he witnessed Jose Villagomez, his relative, assaulting Babauta.

But when he approached the stand in his murder case, Juan Villagomez admitted to having "slapped" Babauta "about six or eight times."[35] Maintaining his position as an outsider to the investigation, Villagomez said that he spent no more than fifteen minutes in the interrogation room. However, two of the prosecution's witnesses, Jose Villagomez and sonchō Hector C. Sgambelluri, disputed the type of punishment used by Juan Villagomez. While they agreed that Juan Villagomez briefly interacted with Babauta, they argued that Villagomez whipped him at the request of Shimada and Ogawa, another Japanese police officer.[36] With Juan Villagomez implicated in the death of Babauta, the tribunal then summoned the four men who claimed to have been victimized by Villagomez. Jose C. Guerrero and Gonzalo Eclevea separately testified to having been struck by Villagomez sometime in March or April 1942. As they recounted, they were traveling along a road in the village of Barrigada around six o'clock in the evening. Guerrero rode a bull cart, and Eclevea peddled a bicycle, with approximately twenty feet between the men. According to Guerrero, Juan Villagomez first met him on the path, at which time he ordered Guerrero to dismount from the wagon. Villagomez then punched and kicked Guerrero for being "an American," even threatening his life with a gun.[37] After recording his name, Villagomez let Guerrero return to his bull cart.

A few minutes later, Villagomez asked Gonzalo Eclevea if he, too, was an American. Eclevea responded, "No, I was still a Chamorro."[38] But rather than go along with Villagomez, Eclevea briskly questioned Villagomez's use of a flashlight. As he noted, "As I was going along Barrigada road someone flashed a light right in my face. It was the accused that did it. I asked him who he was and what authority he had to flash his light in my face.... Then he came over to me and told me I was acting fresh and started hitting me. After he had hit me, my lips began to bleed. He broke my false teeth and cut my lips and for two days I could not eat."[39] Eclevea was then released. As for the third specification of assault and battery, Jose M. Martinez argued that he was beaten for stealing bananas from Juan Combado, a farmer from the village of Talo'fo'fo, sometime in June 1943. According to Martinez, Juan Villagomez beat him with a club "over 60 times."[40] The last witness and alleged victim of Villagomez, Blas T. Taimanglo, spent barely one minute on the stand. Although he stated that Villagomez punished him, he could not identify him before the court. When asked by the prosecution to "look" at the accused, for example, Taimanglo simply muttered, "I do not know this man."[41] As with the murder trial of Jose Villagomez, the tribunal welcomed these convoluted testimonies as evidence. Likening Juan Villagomez to a slaveholder who broke the "will" to resist among the Guam Chamorros, the tribunal found him guilty of all the charges and sentenced him to life imprisonment.

In the fourth and joint murder trial concerning Antonio Camacho and Juan Reyes, the court likewise imposed its regime of violence on the defendants, who were charged with murdering Pedro Gogue Sablan, a Guamanian, in early 1942. But unlike the Rotanese and Saipanese men who were already imprisoned in Guam's stockades, the court did not extract Camacho and Reyes from these "American" locales. With the assistance of military intelligence and police personnel, the tribunal identified, detained, and transferred these men from Saipan, a nearby "Japanese" island, to Guam on January 19, 1945. With respect to Antonio Camacho, the U.S. military initially mistook him for a civilian without any ties to wartime Guam; the military even employed him as a "policeman" to guard an internment camp in Saipan.[42] But upon recognizing his identity as a former interpreter and police officer for the Japanese government in Guam, the military placed Camacho in a prisoner of war camp in Saipan on November 14, 1944. Juan Reyes suffered the same predicament, though the U.S. military did not hire him in any capacity.

The tribunal then established the "civilian" statuses of Antonio Camacho and Juan Reyes, opening their trial on April 27, 1945. Pleading "not guilty" to the charge of murder, Camacho and Reyes heard the prosecution's witnesses recount the capture and punishment of Pedro Gogue Sablan. Jose Quidachay Villagomez, a garbage collector and a friend of Sablan, recalled the arrest in March or April 1942. He said, "Three of us were taken at the same time. Pedro Sablan, Juan G. Rivera and myself."[43] Villagomez identified Antonio Camacho and the Japanese officer Shimada as the individuals who arrested them in the village of Otdot. Accused of theft, they were escorted to the Hagåtña jail and held in separate cells for a three-day period. Prior to their imprisonment, Villagomez noted that Pedro Gogue Sablan was "in good health."[44] The prosecution then attempted to establish Antonio Camacho and Juan Reyes as the primary assailants of Sablan. In the confines of his cell, for example, Jose Quidachay Villagomez "heard Sablan yelling" from an area located above him. Specifically, he claimed that Sablan screamed "Ay, Nana!" ("Mother!") every time "he was whipped."[45]

Whereas Villagomez heard somebody beat Sablan, his friend and fellow inmate Juan G. Rivera saw Camacho and Reyes attack Sablan. Rivera was one of three eyewitnesses. Called from his cell for questioning, he went upstairs and found Juan Reyes "hitting Pedro Sablan with his fist, against the wall, then tripped him and when he was down started kicking him."[46] These beatings occurred on a Friday. But what proved especially disturbing was the testimony of the third eyewitness, the nurse Rita Gogue James. As a key witness for the tribunal, James often accused the Rotanese and Saipanese of torturing Guamanians. In Sablan's trial, however, she also sketched how medicine served the punitive goals of these police officers.

As the senior native nurse, James explained that the Japanese, Rotanese, and Saipanese police officers occasionally asked her to inject "one quarter grain of morphine sulphate and 1/150 grain of atropine sulphate" into the bodies of some prisoners (figure 4.1).[47] At other times, only the Japanese doctors at the hospital prescribed these medications. But these narcotics were not used to help the prisoners in any way. As James emphasized, "These were not injections for the purpose of curing them, but rather to calm them down."[48] By relaxing certain inmates, the police officers reduced the "noise" in the jail, prepared said prisoners for future punishment, and created a better sleeping environment for the officers and inmates alike. As the nurse observed, "They always had me inject those that were punished as to relieve them from making so much noise." Reflecting on the official policy of the medications, James stated that the police officers did not "take care of them in case they had the intention of punishing and beating a person to the extent of death."[49] She thus detailed how the punitive measures enacted at the Hagåtña jail caused the injuries and deaths of the Guamanian prisoners.

4.1. Chamorro nurses and Japanese medical staff, Hagåtña, Guam, ca. early 1940s (photo number AH5-111, Rec. August 2, 1945). U.S. National Archives, College Park, Maryland.

With respect to Pedro Gogue Sablan, nurse James sought the assistance of an unidentified Japanese doctor and requested to administer the medicine to the inmate. After the third request, she received permission to visit the jail and provide the shots. James described how, at the jail, she and the doctor waited outside an interrogation room "because the door was locked while Pedro was inside being punished. Then a prisoner came and opened the door and I entered the room with the doctor and found Pedro being punished by the two accused." After the beating, she and the doctor followed Sablan to a "dark cell," where they gave him the drugs to stop his "groaning."[50] The following day James met Juan Reyes at the hospital. She carefully broached the topic of assisting Sablan, who was her nephew. Emphasizing her kindness to Reyes as an entry point into this discussion, James stated, "I told him that I had been very good to him; I gave him medicine and everything he needed and then I mentioned about the punishment inflicted upon my nephew." In response, Reyes purportedly said, "That is all right, never mind."[51] That Juan Reyes rejected nurse James's plea to help her dying nephew was as unsettling as the beatings themselves.

Two individuals then discussed the effects of these assaults on Pedro Gogue Sablan. Manuel, his brother, said that Pedro "was badly injured. He had bruises all the way from his head down his back to his heels and arms. He could not lie flat on his back. He had to sleep flat on his chest and about a week later, he could not take any position but a sitting position. He remained in a sitting position and even slept in that position."[52] Former inmate Jose Quidachay Villagomez agreed, saying that Sablan "could not work" after the torture sessions.[53] In early June 1942, Sablan passed away at the age of thirty-five.

With no consensus on the alleged time of Sablan's detainment, the defense attorneys, Lieutenant Alexander Akerman Jr. and Vicente C. Reyes, requested that such testimonies be discredited. They likewise questioned whether Pedro Gogue Sablan had any injuries in the first place. One of their witnesses, for example, claimed that Sablan did visit the Hagåtña jail but left the facility unscathed. The defense counsel then called on Commander Ralph C. Smith of the Medical Corps. A licensed doctor from Texas and a U.S. Navy reservist, Smith argued that Sablan might have passed away from having "tuberculosis," an illness common among Chamorros at that time.[54] While Smith refrained from declaring the cause of death, his testimony sought to cast doubt on the prosecution's allegations.

But in the defense counsel's enlistment of the witnesses Jose Q. Quinata and Joaquina M. Ishizaki, it floundered in portraying the innocence of the Saipanese Antonio Camacho and Juan Reyes. As per its strategy, the defense utilized the testimonies of Quinata, a store owner, and Ishizaki, a weaver, to place Reyes as solely assigned to the village of Humåtac. The purpose was to show that Reyes never had the time to visit the Hagåtña jail, as he translated for Humåtac's Japanese-language adult school "six days a week, none on Sundays."[55] If the prosecution alleged that Pedgro Gogue Sablan was detailed over a three-day period, then it was inconceivable for Juan Reyes to have participated in said interrogation given his weeklong duties in Humåtac. Yet this defense tactic failed for two reasons: first, the witnesses never discussed Antonio Camacho and how he, too, was far removed from the activities of the Hagåtña jail; second, the defense counsel never attempted to rectify Juan Reyes's earlier testimony that he had, in fact, worked as an interpreter and officer in the villages of Hågat, Hagåtña, Humåtac, Machananao, and Piti.

In his closing remarks as the judge advocate and prosecutor, Lieutenant Colonel Ammons did not entertain these contradictory statements. As he announced, "No untruths were evident in the testimony of any witnesses

```
                        INDIVIDUAL RECORD
Case No.: 7             WAR CRIMES TRIAL
File: A17-10,CAMACHO, et al

Name:      REYES, Juan

Rank or Rate:   Civilian

Branch of Service:

Nationality:    Saipanese

Address:        Saipan

Duty Assignment:   Interpreter, Civil Jail, Agana, Guam

Nature of Offense:  MURDER - 1 spec

Place & Date of Offense:  Civil Jail, Agana, Guam - early 1942 *

Date of Trial:  27 April 1947

Sentence of Commission:  Death by hanging

Date of Sentence:  5 May 1947

Action of Convening Authority:  Approved 14 June 1945

Action of Reviewing Authority:  Approved 21 August 1945

Action of Confirming Authority:  Commuted to life imprisonment 3 January

Sentence Executed:   14 June 1945

Remarks:  Confined Civil Jail, Agana, Guam.


    *As a result of repeated beatings, the victim died at his home about
     after.
```

4.2. The death sentence of Juan Reyes, Guam, May 5, 1945. U.S. National Archives, College Park, Maryland.

for the prosecution in the record of this case." Trumping the efforts of the defense counsel, he said that they "cannot alter, modify or change the testimony contained in the record nor can the counsel for the accused, in his argument, re-enact the case by imagination or supposition contrary to the evidence presented and contained in the record of the case."[56] Dismissing the defense counsel's "imaginary" premises, the judge advocate found

Antonio Camacho and Juan Reyes guilty of first-degree murder on May 5, 1945 (figure 4.2). The tribunal then sentenced these Saipanese men "to death, to be executed by hanging," with "two-thirds (2/3) of the members of the Commission concurring."[57]

The Captain of Liars

The two last murder trials, involving Manuel Borja Tudela and Luis C. Crisostomo, proved no less violent in the tribunal's adjudication of the defendants. In Tudela's case, the court charged him for assaulting Antonio M. Babauta on or about March 19, 1942, as well as accused him of murdering Francisco Cruz Salas on or about August 7, 1943. On the first specification, for example, the prosecution called the sixteen-year-old Babauta, a Guamanian, to take the stand and to describe how Tudela punished him. Knowing that Inalåhan's village feast of Saint Joseph occurred in March, Babauta had no difficulty in recalling when Tudela summoned him to the home of sonchō Francisco C. Sablan. On the morning of this celebration, Babauta claimed that sonchō Sablan, kuchō Antonio B. Carbullido, and an unidentified Saipanese woman witnessed Tudela beat him and a Saipanese boy, Joaquin. Giving no reason for why the police officer interrogated him, Babauta simply portrayed Tudela as an assailant of innocent children. With the native officials and fellow villagers in attendance, Babauta mentioned that Tudela "took off my pants and he took a whip and started whipping me."[58] Although Babauta could not remember Joaquin's surname or state if Tudela punished him as well, Babauta hinted at something involving him and the other boy. As Babauta mentioned, "I told [Tudela] that I was not with a certain boy."[59] Claiming that his punishment lasted from nine to eleven o'clock in the morning, Babauta then described how his nose and ears bled, how his left thigh became scarred, and how his right leg became numb in the months after the interrogation.

The next witness for the prosecution and a previous kuchō, Antonio P. Carbullido, saw Manuel Borja Tudela assault Antonio Babauta at the sonchō's residence in Hågat. Given that Babauta resided at Carbullido's ranch, the elderly farmer attended the interrogation. According to Carbullido, Tudela questioned Babauta as to the whereabouts of Carbullido's lost *galaide*, also known as an outrigger canoe, used for travel and work within the island's reef areas. To this inquiry, Babauta answered that he had no idea what happened to the canoe. Instead, Carbullido described a chain of responsibility that led to the arrests of Babauta and the Saipanese boy,

Joaquin: first, Carbullido owned the canoe; second, Carbullido tasked Cecilio Sablan, another villager, to manage the canoe; third, Sablan "lost" the canoe; fourth, Carbullido requested payment for the lost canoe; fifth, Sablan refused to offer any monies since, he alleged, the two boys—Antonio and Joaquin—lost the canoe; and sixth, Tudela apprehended Antonio and Joaquin on the suspicion that they were guilty of these actions. But rather than treat the boys fairly as per Japanese police standards, Carbullido explained that the Saipan boy Joaquin received "not much" whipping.[60] The farmer even claimed that Joaquin blamed Babauta, a Guamanian, for unmooring the canoe from the shoreline and presumably causing it to drift away. On the other hand, Babauta incurred severe abuse. As Carbullido remarked, he "was crying while the whipping was going on. He hollered, 'I am dead,' every now and then when the whip landed. The accused said, 'As young as you are you know how to tell a lie. If you grow up you will be the captain of liars; so it makes no difference if you die.'"[61]

When Manuel Borja Tudela took the stand, he admitted to having punished the boys Antonio and Joaquin. But he refuted any allegations of favoring Joaquin, the Saipanese boy, because the boys were equally responsible for losing the galaide. As Tudela recounted, "I questioned Antonio Babauta and [Joaquin] as they were suspected by Cecilio of letting [the canoe] loose. They, the two boys, at the beginning started blaming each other, but later on during the course of the investigation admitted that they did it." To emphasize the parity in his punishment of Antonio and Joaquin, he continued, "I took a whip and whipped each boy about six or seven times."[62] Likening his interrogation to the punishment accorded to younger siblings, Tudela explained that he beat the boys "in the same manner as I whip my sisters and brothers whenever they do something wrong."[63] For the prosecution, however, Tudela represented a person who had no regard for the lives of the Guamanians, young and old alike.

Having portrayed Manuel Borja Tudela as an assailant of American subjects and a violator of U.S. laws, the prosecution then presented witnesses who accused him of murdering Francisco Cruz Salas on or about August 7, 1943. As the principal witness, former sonchō Francisco C. Sablan of Hågat detailed how he arrested Salas around two o'clock in the afternoon of August 6, 1943.[64] As per Tudela's orders, sonchō Sablan summoned Salas to the Hågat police station on the suspicion of possessing dynamite, one of several Japanese violations in line with possessing firearms and radios.[65] When Sablan arrived at the jail, he noticed that two unidentified men were being investigated; afterward, Tudela brought in Salas, a laborer at a Japanese rice field in Hågat. As sonchō Sablan recounted, "I saw Francisco C. Salas while he was being questioned about the dynamite and I also saw him being whipped."[66] In his recollection, the village commissioner identified Tudela and Takabana, a Japanese police officer, as the assailants. But Sablan provided no reason as to why Tudela and Takabana accused Salas of owning dynamite. However, two witnesses, Rosa Aquiningnoc Salas and Maria U. Torres, only saw Tudela punish Salas with a "tangantangan stick."[67] Rosa Aquiningnoc Salas, the daughter of Francisco Cruz Salas, described how she witnessed the torture session unfold from the nearby home of Maria Torres. According to Salas, the two-story Hågat police station was "about 20 yards" from Torres's porch, where she, Torres, and two other women viewed Tudela beating Francisco Cruz Salas with a wooden club between seven and nine o'clock on the evening of August 6.[68] Given the porch's proximity to the interrogation room on the first floor, both Salas and Torres then placed Tudela and the deceased Salas in the same area and time period. After nine o'clock, Rosa Aquiningnoc Salas stated, somebody shut the door and prevented them from peering into the room.

By foregrounding these testimonies, Lieutenant Colonel Teller Ammons of the prosecution represented Francisco Cruz Salas as having been tortured for at least four hours on August 6, 1943. During this time, the prosecution alleged, Manuel Borja Tudela was present at the Hågat jail from the early afternoon to the late evening. In assessing Salas's death sometime thereafter, the crucial questions remained. That is, did Salas eventually die by hanging himself voluntarily? Or did Tudela and Takabana execute Salas by hanging? Or did Salas pass away as a result of the beatings, with Tudela and Takabana staging his hanging? Witnesses for the prosecution implied that the latter had occurred. When he was called to the stand, for example, sonchō Francisco C. Sablan confirmed Salas's passing on August 7, as well as questioned the origins of his injuries. He first recalled Manuel Borja Tudela's visit to his home, wherein the interpreter notified him about Salas's death. Around six o'clock in the morning of August 7, the two men left for the Hågat police station. As Sablan noted, "I ate my breakfast and then went with Manuel Tudela for the police headquarters. When I opened the door I saw the body of Francisco C. Salas hanging on the hinge of the door. A fishline was twined three times around his neck, and his feet were about three inches from the floor." Two other unidentified men were hanged as well, with, as Sablan put it, marks around their necks "which showed signs of struggle but on the body of Salas, there were no marks and his tongue was not hanging out."[69] Kuchō Antonio P. Carbullido arrived later at the jail, where he, too, saw the dead men. With respect to the unknown men, he said, "One of them had a rope and was hanged to a fir tree, the other one had a fiber around his neck and suspended from an extension in the ranch."[70] Like Sablan's testimony, Carbullido questioned if Salas had indeed died by hanging. As Carbullido observed, "The bodies that I saw hanged, their faces were swollen and black and the tongues were out. Francisco Salas' face was not swollen and his tongue was not out. It looked as if he died a natural death."[71]

Another witness for the prosecution, Jesus C. Okiyama, informed the tribunal that he encountered the hangings as well. At the request of sonchō Francisco C. Sablan, villagers Okiyama and Jesus B. Charfauros removed the noose from Salas's neck. Given that Charfauros had passed away during the war, only Okiyama testified as to how this process took place. As Okiyama related, "When the commissioner ushered me in, he told me to come inside and when I got inside I found some Japanese officials. They told me to untie the string that was suspending Salas' neck. I could not untie the string right away. . . . I held Francisco Salas by the shoulder and [Jesus B. Charfauros] cut off the string. . . . I held Francisco Cruz Salas by the shoulder and [Charfauros] held him by the legs and we carried him and placed him down on the floor, the head facing the Japanese officials."[72] The Japanese officials included Takabana, the Hågat police supervisor, as well as the governor's aide, the chief of police, and Dr. Isoda. The last three men represented, respectively, the Minseibu, the Hagåtña police station, and the hospital. Sonchō Sablan then described how Dr. Isoda stripped Salas of his trousers, revealed his groin area, and examined his buttocks and penis. As a bystander, the commissioner stated that "when the pants were pulled down, I saw black and blue marks and bruises in the region around his penis and on the front part of the hips."[73] Supporting the prosecution, Sablan emphasized that Salas evidenced no neck trauma that might have suggested death by hanging.

Later, at around eight o'clock in the morning, sonchō Francisco C. Sablan and police officer Manuel Borja Tudela brought the body of Francisco Cruz Salas to his family. His wife, Joaquin Aquiningoc Salas, received him at the home of their relative, Maria C. Aguigui. As in the previous testimonies, she disclosed nothing that implied her husband had been hanged. As Joaquin Aquiningoc Salas noted, "He had bruises on his forehead, cheek and nose. His back had black and blue marks and was swollen. One hand was also swollen. There were marks on his wrist which showed that he had been tied. His testicles were enlarged and ants were crawling on his back."[74] On the matter of her husband's death, Salas then discussed how Tudela and the Japanese officials requested "to be pardoned for the mistake they had done." Recalling her conversation with Tudela, she said, "When he asked for forgiveness I told him he did not do anything to me. I told him if you did something to any person to go that person and ask that person for forgiveness because you did not do anything to me."[75] Her husband's pleas for forgiveness were also absent from the discussion, an issue previously raised by their daughter and witness, Rosa. Nor did Joaquin Aquiningoc Salas believe that her husband's death was a "mistake." The spiritual guilt and shame rested on Tudela and not on the Salas family.

In his defense, Manuel Borja Tudela testified that he had no role whatsoever in the hanging of Francisco Cruz Salas. He merely interpreted for Takabana, the police supervisor, and whipped Salas "not more than eight times." Following Takabana's orders, Tudela then hit Salas with a wooden club "about five or six times."[76] In contrast to the prosecution's allegation that he punished Salas for at least four hours, Tudela's beatings may have lasted for as little as fifteen minutes or as long as several hours. Whatever the case, he assured the tribunal that he did not use his "whole force" in whipping Salas, portraying the torture session as matter-of-fact in character. While he may have intended to downplay the violence of such interrogations, he unwittingly conveyed the converse by describing the spatial politics of the Hågat precinct. In this manner, his contrasting of the first-floor police room and the second-floor family room disturbingly revealed the worlds in which the police officers dwelt. As he explained, "Takabana told me to stay with Salas in the [first-floor] room where this incident took place, and he went upstairs to clean up and have dinner with his family. When he was through with his dinner, he came down and relieved me. I went upstairs also and cleaned myself up."[77] With no separation between the imperial realm of the police and the domestic realm of the family, Tudela's portrayal of the Hågat police station illustrated the intimate spaces by which the police maintained power. As with other police sites scattered across the island, the Hågat location exemplified what the anthropologist Ann Laura Stoler calls the tense and tender ties of empire, where "macropolitics are not lodged in abstract institutions but in their management of meanings, their construction of social categories, and their microsites of rule."[78] With the Hågat police station functioning in these terms, Tudela then narrated how Takabana tied Salas's hands to a bench, thereby restraining him. At that point, Salas "was still alive and was sitting up";[79] he also "looked sad."[80] "Then Takabana told me," continued Tudela, "that I could leave now because there was no extra bunk or bed in the quarters for me to sleep on and being a single man he probably considered that, and he told me to go home."[81]

As per his recollection, Tudela left the Hågat jail around 7:45 PM, visited the residence of his aunt Maria Pangelinan until 9:00 PM, and went to the home of his friend Baltazar Carbullido to sleep until 5:30 the next morning. When he returned to the police station at 6:00 AM, Takabana shared "not very good news" with him.[82] As Tudela expressed, "Takabana told me that Salas hanged himself. I doubted his words and I went in to see the man. I asked him if I could see the body and Takabana replied that it was all right but I was not to open the door. I opened the door slightly and took a peep. I saw [Francisco Cruz Salas] hanging and he was very stiff."[83] With only Tudela claiming that Salas had hanged himself, the defense attorneys Lieutenant Alexander Akerman and Vicente C. Reyes attempted to dismiss the murder charge.[84] As they opined, "It is submitted that there was no evidence or no facts on which can be inferred any premeditation or malice aforethought in this case, and for lack of evidence, the charge of murder or homicide has not been proved beyond a reasonable doubt."[85]

The prosecution then relied on a medical expert, Lieutenant Commander Harry M. Zimmerman, to establish what caused the death of Francisco Cruz Salas. Attached to Medical Research Unit No. 2 and the Guam Civil Affairs Hospital, the Yale-trained doctor argued that Salas "did not die of hanging or strangulation," despite the fact Zimmerman did not examine Salas's body.[86] Given Zimmerman's selective use of the evidence, Judge Advocate and Lieutenant Colonel Teller Ammons concluded that "the deceased was beaten by the accused and there is one thing sure, Salas did not die as a result of hanging or strangulation."[87] "Now as to malice or premeditation," the prosecutor continued, "I think the accused demonstrated a wanton disregard for the rights and feelings of the deceased . . . and caused the death by going much farther than an ordinary man in like circumstances would have gone, and in doing so, demonstrated an abandoned and malignant heart."[88] As Ammons speculated, Tudela, "in an attempt to cover up the crime committed against Francisco C. Salas, placed the cord around the neck of Salas after he was dead and suspended his body from the door hinge. This must have been done after he, Salas, had been dead for at least five hours."[89] Finding Manuel Borja Tudela guilty of assault and battery and first-degree murder, the tribunal transformed him into a sacred man of the war. He was sentenced to death by hanging on May 17, 1945, with two-thirds of the court members concurring.

The last murder trial focused on Luis C. Crisostomo, a twenty-five-year-old Saipanese accused of murdering two men and assaulting thirteen individuals in Guam. Among the interpreters and police officers, he was the last to surrender to the U.S. military, on January 1, 1945. Other men had yielded earlier to the navy, in August and November 1944. Crisostomo had hidden in Guam's jungles since the American reinvasion of the island in July 1944, moving from the villages of Fena and Hågat in the south to the coastal area of Litekyan in the north. Upon his capture, the navy detained him at the Island Command Prisoner of War Camp. When Crisostomo appeared before the tribunal on June 4, 1945, the first murder charge specified that he killed Joaquin Mafnas, a bull cart driver, sometime in March 1944. The second murder charge alleged that he killed Pedro G. Dumanal, a suspected rebel against the Japanese military, sometime in February 1944. Both men had resided in the village of Hågat, as did most of the people who came forward as victims of Crisostomo's violence. Others lived in the nearby districts of Apla and Atantano.

With respect to the assault and battery charges, one witness claimed that Luis Crisostomo beat the farmer Antonio Reyes in September 1943 without providing any corroborated evidence whatsoever. Whereas this allegation might have been another instance of outright vengeance, other Guam Chamorros argued that Crisostomo variously punished them for requesting to visit an expectant mother, spreading rumors about a downed Japanese aircraft, and stealing cigarettes and money from their neighbors. A wide range of people testified along these lines, such as the farmers Joaquin A. Barcinas and Jose C. Guzman, the housewife Flora C. Cruz, and the timekeeper Juan Muña Salas. Others, such as Juan C. Babauta, Ramon Lizama Cruz, and Jose Cruz Reyes, asserted that Crisostomo had mistakenly accused them of stealing and slaughtering a carabao for their consumption sometime in October 1943. But rather than interrogate them in one place at the same time, Crisostomo questioned them separately at his home in Hågat and at the police station. He beat them all.[90] Yet the crux of the Crisostomo's trial was his apprehension of Guamanians suspected of planning an armed rebellion against the Japanese police and military units in March 1944. With the Americans having begun their bombardment of Guam in February 1944, the possibility of a native revolt occurring was not a matter for conjecture. With the fear of an invasion, the Japanese police and military sought to suppress any form of resistance.[91] This subtext informed Crisostomo's interrogation of two Chamorro men and two Chamorro women accused of possessing weapons.

As the prosecution's first witness in this matter, the laundress Catalina Degracia Cruz explained that Crisostomo tortured her in Hågat and Atantano sometime in March and April 1944. Two assaults occurred in one day at the ranch of Rosa Aguigui in Atantano, whereas the third series of beatings happened at the Hågat jail over a span of five weeks. As she recalled, Crisostomo "kept asking me where was the machine gun. And every time I told him I didn't know about that, he told me that I was telling a lie and kept on beating me. The accused said that he was going to kill me because I was not telling the truth."[92] During the initial beatings, a few Chamorro villagers and Japanese officials witnessed the interrogations. The Chamorro farmer Gervacio Ignacio Santos was one such individual. Testifying for the prosecution, he said, "Every time the accused asked her about the machine gun and the rifle, Catalina said that she did not know, and that God knows there was no machine gun and rifle; the accused said that there is no God but the Emperor."[93] Shortly thereafter, Santos noted that several unidentified Japanese officials had brought Catalina Degracia Cruz's son, Inecto, from a work site in Otdot to the ranch area. With his mother lying on the ground and urging him to confess, Inecto Degracia Santos faced his torturer. Crisostomo then clubbed the young man and, as Santos put it, made his "bowels move." "Then the accused clubbed the boy again about 6 times until the boy collapsed and then picked him up and threw him into the river and was told to clean himself up."[94] As with his mother Catalina, Inecto Degracia Santos was interrogated as to the whereabouts of dynamite, a machine gun, and a rifle. When he confessed to seeing a machine gun, he abided by his mother's wishes in a vain attempt to halt the beatings. But rather than acknowledge the young man, Crisostomo clubbed him "until he was unconscious."[95]

Catalina Degracia Cruz then testified that her son had died, though she did not fault Luis Crisostomo in any direct way. Based on the testimonies provided by her and other witnesses for the prosecution, the Japanese Imperial Army may have executed Inecto Degracia Santos sometime in March 1944.[96] As such, the tribunal did not hold Crisostomo responsible for these killings. Nevertheless, the severe ways by which the Japanese and Saipanese punished Guamanians suspected of harboring weapons demonstrated the fatal circumstances that accompanied said allegations. This was also the context in which the court charged Crisostomo for murdering the forty-eight-year-old bull cart driver Joaquin Mafnas. First, the prosecution established that two Japanese-appointed village officials, sonchō Felix Torres Pangelinan and kuchō Vicente D. Lizama of the Apla district, apprehended Mafnas in April 1944.[97] At the request of the Japanese police supervisor Takabana, sonchō Pangelinan and kuchō Lizama then escorted Mafnas to the Hågat police station.

Second, the prosecution featured witnesses who claimed to have buried the dead body of Joaquin Mafnas at the Hågat cemetery. According to Cerilo Reyes Barcinas, Juan Taijito Reyes, and Vicente Blanco Terlaje, Luis Crisostomo ordered them to disregard their duties at an airfield and to transport Mafnas from the police station to the cemetery. When the men arrived at the Hågat precinct, they found Mafnas behind the building. As Terlaje observed, "The body was lying flat on the stomach and one leg was bent, the other stretched out and his clothes were all wet. The body was stiff, and his skin appeared tight, maybe because he had been dead for quite a while."[98] Emphasizing that Mafnas perhaps died from drowning, Barcinas said that "while picking up the body and putting it on the cart, water was dripping . . . from the mouth and nostrils."[99] Once the men had placed Mafnas on the cart, they covered him with banana and coconut leaves, took him to the Hågat cemetery, and buried him in an unmarked grave. Crisostomo then warned the men to not spread any rumors about their activities. Otherwise, recalled Terlaje, "the same thing would happen to us."[100]

Third, approximately one year after the passing of Mafnas and three months before the onset of the trial, several naval officials, prison guards, and village leaders brought Luis Crisostomo, now a prisoner, to the Hågat cemetery on March 12, 1945. Among them were the same individuals who helped to bury Mafnas. Their goal was to locate his remains. But the task proved onerous given that the cemetery was "torn up by fox holes."[101] Reflecting on their predicament, Second Lieutenant Ralph De Vries stated that the "three men could not quite decide where the body was located."[102] Although Crisostomo also dug several holes and provided some direction, nobody could positively identify Mafnas among the bodies recovered. As an officer for the military police and a witness for the prosecution, De Vries even speculated that Crisostomo may have been trying to "mislead" the search party.[103] One hour into their digging, De Vries then asked Jose Iglesias Leon Guerrero, a plainclothes police officer, to solicit a statement from Crisostomo.

Initially, Crisostomo expressed no apprehension in responding to the request from Leon Guerrero, a man disguised as a fellow Chamorro villager. As the police officer explained, "Luis said, 'I am going to tell the truth, and no matter where I go, I will tell the truth and I don't care who hears it.'"[104] But as the conversation progressed, Crisostomo realized, perhaps for the first time, the role reversal occurring before him. That is to say, the hollowed sections of the earth, the exposed remains of unidentified bodies, the presence of three armed soldiers, the lingering smell of human rot and gunpowder, and the usage of the Chamorro and English languages imbued his confession with a "proper relation to the sovereign."[105] As one witness described, he transformed from a "loud-talking" interrogator for Japan into a "pale" and "frightened" prisoner of the United States.[106] Once an extension of the Japanese empire, his new voice as a "civilian detainee" helped to sustain the faith of the American empire and its laws among the subjects of Guam.[107] As the legal theorist Paul W. Kahn put it, "Before there is a theory of law, there is a belief that law is the word of the sovereign."[108] The police officers did not offer any protections to Crisostomo under U.S. and international laws other than the right to "be quiet."[109] As the officer Jose Iglesias Leon Guerrero disclosed, "I said, 'Luis, do you wish to state how Mafnas was punished? If you want to make a statement about it, it is your privilege to do so, but if you don't care to make any, you don't have to. . . . If I am through with the statement according to the way you say it, are you willing to sign it?' And he said, 'Yes.'"[110]

As another witness to Crisostomo's confession, Second Lieutenant Ralph De Vries "saw him sign the paper," as did the three men who buried the middle-aged bull cart driver at the Hågat cemetery.[111] Not satisfied with Crisostomo's signature, the naval officials consequently compelled Cerilo Reyes Barcinas, Juan Taijito Reyes, and Vicente Blanco Terlaje to "sign a paper which said that Luis and Takabana killed Joaquin Mafnas."[112] By submitting their signatures to the naval authorities, they, like Crisostomo, acknowledged the murder of Mafnas, if not illustrated some degree of complicity. Their signatures thus represented what the literary critic Scott Richard Lyons calls "x-marks." As he argues, an "x-mark is a contaminated and coerced sign of consent made under conditions that are not of one's making. It signifies power and a lack of power, agency and a lack of agency. It is a decision one makes when something has already been decided for you, but it is still a decision."[113] Titled "Confession in the killing of Joaquin Mafnas," Luis Crisostomo's statement revealed the ways by which birds and lizards engaged the Japanese past and the American present. For Crisostomo and his supervisor Takabana, Mafnas represented a military threat, given his suspected ties to Pedro G. Dumanal and his possession of dynamite and weapons. As per the contents of the confession, both Crisostomo and Takabana clubbed, punched, and whipped Mafnas when he was splayed on the porch of the Hågat police station, when he was tied to a *pugua'* (betel nut) tree, and when he was fastened to a water pipe.

Indeed, what proved central in the prosecution's usage of this statement was not merely Crisostomo's avowal of his violence per se. What mattered was the kind of violence attributed to the interpreter and not to the American members of the court. As with the tribunal's treatment of the Japanese, Rotanese, and Saipanese as harbingers of "slavery," the court similarly focused on Crisostomo's and Takabana's employment of the "water cure" as another exemplary instance of native barbarism and Japanese savagery. As a result, neither the defense nor the prosecution referenced the water cure as America's "most notorious form of torture" against its enemies in North America and the Philippines.[114] Only Japan and its colonial subjects, it seemed, endorsed this truth-telling practice. As Crisostomo related, "Takabana and I took Joaquin to the backyard of the office. Immediately, Takabana said to me, 'Bring me one end of the water hose.' I turned on the valve and Takabana placed the end of the hose, where the water was coming from, at the mouth of Joaquin for about a minute, and on his nose too for about a minute. After that, Takabana told me to drown him, but I said to him, 'What are we waiting for? The man kept saying that [Pedro G. Dumanal] never came.' About two or three times we have investigated and we get the same reasons. But Takabana said, 'Drown him and I will be responsible.' That was the time when I drown him from the mouth about one minute."[115] According to Crisostomo, Mafnas was "still alive" at eleven o'clock that evening, but the torture had already taken a toll on his body. As the native police officer from Saipan confessed, "At about 4:00 o'clock in the morning, Takabana came and said, 'Get up, Joaquin has died.'"[116]

With the murder of Joaquin Mafnas rehearsed by Luis Crisostomo, the prosecution turned to its second murder charge, regarding the death of Pedro G. Dumanal, another symbol of indigenous resistance to the Japanese military and police. Among villagers, Dumanal was known as a "free spirit" who did not respect the American and Japanese colonial administrations; as such, he often confronted individuals from their governments who threatened his family.[117] As the source of Crisostomo's and Takabana's fears, he especially represented an impending native revolt, given the allegations that he held and circulated weapons among the Guam Chamorros. The key witness for the prosecution, a carpenter named Jose Rivera Camacho, took the stand first. He described how Crisostomo attacked Dumanal with a machete in the midmorning of February 23, 1944. From atop a coconut tree, Camacho saw the men approach each other at the base of a hill in the village of Apla. Whereas Crisostomo was alone, Dumanal was with a friend, Lorenzo Punciano. Recalled Camacho, "Pedro was talking in Chamorro and he said, 'You are looking for me. Here I am,'" to which Crisostomo replied, "'Yes, I was looking for you.'"[118] "I saw the two close together," continued Camacho, "then I saw Luis raise his machete. He swung the machete, but I did not know exactly where it landed. After that I saw the two rush at each other; then I saw the machete again thrusted. . . . Then Pedro fell to the ground."[119] Both Crisostomo and Punciano then fled the area. Afterward, Camacho descended from the tree and approached the lifeless Dumanal, where he found Dumanal's revolver "placed on the safe," meaning that the weapon could not be fired.[120]

Jose Rivera Camacho then returned home quickly, hitched a carriage to his horse, and caught up with Crisostomo on his way to Hågat. Along the bull cart path, they met Japanese military and police officials. As Camacho noted, "I turned the carriage and picked them up. I took them back to the place where the killing took place. They carried on conversation there, then people started coming. Shortly after that quite a number of Japanese navy men came with weapons, machine guns, pistols and rifles. . . . They even touched the body and turned it over. They were even kicking the body."[121] Camacho and other men then dug a grave for Dumanal about sixteen feet from the road. Later that day, an unidentified villager informed Maria Dumanal Blas that her father had been killed. Living nearby, Blas then visited the makeshift gravesite to confirm the death of her father. As a witness for the prosecution, she described how she removed dirt from the grave and came across one of her father's hands. As Blas remarked, "I knew my father's hand. . . . He had quite a bit of hair on his hand and his hands resembled my hands a little. No one can fool me about my father's hands."[122]

Based on the recollections provided by three witnesses, the prosecution represented the Saipanese Luis C. Crisostomo, armed with a machete, as the aggressor and the Guamanian Pedro G. Dumanal, armed with a locked revolver, as the victim. On the other hand, the defense team of Lieutenant Alexander Akerman and Vicente C. Reyes provided three witnesses whose testimonies demonstrated otherwise. Juan Sarmiento, a poultry farmer, said that Dumanal often paraded around the village of Apla, claiming that he was "the commissioner."[123] Another witness for the defense, Manuel M. Borja, alleged that Dumanal assaulted him in the early morning of February 23, 1944, the day of his passing. Finally, the third witness and bystander, Nicholas Concepcion Grey, saw the fight unfold between Crisostomo and Dumanal. In fact, even the prosecution's lead witness, Jose Rivera Camacho, placed Grey in the vicinity.[124] But unlike Camacho, who, atop a coconut tree, only heard the two acknowledge each other, Grey caught more of their conversation given that he stood approximately twenty-five feet behind Crisostomo. As Grey explained, "I heard Pedro Dumanal say that he was going to settle up the matter for all the time he stayed in the woods and all the sufferings that he went through. Pedro Dumanal further said, 'It was not so much for the sufferings I went through, but it is for the sufferings my family went through.'"[125]

But contrary to the prosecution's portrayal of a defensive Dumanal, Grey argued that Dumanal initiated the attack on Crisostomo. As he stated, "Before they got together, I saw Pedro Dumanal draw out his revolver from his pocket. Then I saw the accused rush toward Pedro Dumanal. . . . During the struggle, I saw the machete in the hands of the accused. I saw him swing it towards Pedro Dumanal's hand. After the accused cut Pedro's hand, the revolver fell from the hands of Pedro Dumanal, then Dumanal fell to the ground. After Dumanal fell to the ground, I saw the accused on top of him."[126] Lorenzo Punciano, Dumanal's partner, then reached for the revolver while Dumanal attempted to choke Crisostomo. Glancing over to Punciano, Crisostomo purportedly said, "'Oh, I see you, too, are in this. If that is in your mind, something will happen to you that you haven't been expecting.'" Realizing the potential consequence of his actions, Punciano dropped the revolver and ran away. Crisostomo then stabbed Dumanal in the chest, as Dumanal pleaded, "'Let me go, let me get up.'"[127] According to Grey, the entire struggle lasted barely five minutes.

In their closing remarks, the defense counsel asserted that Luis C. Crisostomo "acted in self-defense," meaning that his first-degree murder charged should be dropped in favor of the nonpunitive specification "justifiable homicide."[128] On the matter of Joaquin Mafnas's death, Lieutenant Akerman and Vicente Reyes disputed the admission of the "confession" as evidence, first during the halfway point of the trial and again at its conclusion. As they asserted, "In the case before this commission, it is uncontradicted and not denied that a foreigner was placed between two guns and this purported statement was obtained in this manner. Not only has the prosecution failed to prove beyond a reasonable doubt that it was voluntarily given, but it has been proven beyond a reasonable doubt that this purported confession was not voluntarily made."[129] Further, the defense counsel questioned the prosecution's claim that Joaquin Mafnas died by "drowning through the nose," given that none of their witnesses could corroborate this allegation.[130] They only confirmed Crisostomo's role in the burial of the bull cart driver and supposed conspirator of weapons at the Hågat cemetery. That Crisostomo was a "foreigner" caught between the interplay of orders and war, duty and right, mattered little to the tribunal. The court subjected him, as homo sacer, to U.S. law and, in the violent seizure of his body, renewed the law's force in its treatment of "foreign" subjects. He was remade in the image of his new sovereign as an inhabitant of Guam, treated as a war criminal, found guilty of first-degree murder, and expunged from the nation as a nonsacrifice. On June 22, 1945, two-thirds of the commission voted to execute Luis C. Crisostomo by hanging by the "neck until he is dead."[131] The transformation was complete.

The Merciful U.S. Government

As in the trials concerning assault and battery, the U.S. Navy's military commission represented the Saipanese men accused of murder as "war criminals" of the native type. The court found six of them guilty of first- or second-degree murder, with Jose P. Villagomez and Juan Villagomez receiving, respectively, sentences of a ten-year period of hard labor and a lifetime term in prison. On the other hand, the tribunal condemned Antonio Camacho, Luis C. Crisostomo, Juan Reyes, and Manuel Borja Tudela to death by hanging by the neck. Initially at stake for the latter was the death sentence (figure 4.3). Upon a closer review of their cases, however, Acting Secretary of the Navy John L. Sullivan reduced their sentences to lifetime imprisonment at hard labor. Writing for the *Guam Gazette*, editor Juan B. Manibusan relayed the news to his local readership. In an article titled "Three Obnoxious Saipanese Escape Death," he communicated, "Three loyal subjects of the Land of the Rising Sun escaped death sentence when the Acting Secretary of the Navy on 3 January 1946 commuted the sentence of death to imprisonment at hard labor for the term of their natural life. They were Antonio Camacho, aged 28, Luis C. Crisostomo, aged 26, and Juan Reyes, aged 23, all natives of Saipan."[132] The fourth Saipanese, Manuel Borja Tudela, likewise received the same reduced sentence. As with the Rotanese and Saipanese men who requested clemency in the assault and battery trials, these four Saipanese men petitioned naval officials to reconsider their sentences. They hoped to achieve even lesser sentences.

Take, for instance, a letter written by Jose P. Villagomez on July 19, 1951. In this letter, addressed to the secretary of the navy, he confessed to the wrongs he had committed. As Villagomez remarked, "I have completed almost six years of my original sentence, and during this period of my confinement I have been brought to realize the sheer folly of adhering to the fanatical and barbarous policies and brutal practices of the Japanese Mili-

4.3. The War Criminals Stockade, Guam (photo number 406885, Rec. September 27, 1949). U.S. National Archives, College Park, Maryland.

tary Government." Fanatical? Barbarous? Brutal? The American conversion of Jose Villagomez seemed apparent, as he never used these terms to describe the Japanese empire in his trials. Because of his confinement, he was "brought in close contact with the benevolent and democratic principles of the great liberty loving, and mighty United States of America." Villagomez then decried Saipan's previous subjugation under Germany and Japan. As he stated, "It is an unfortunate fact that we Saipanese during the past half century have been subject to the cruel and inhumane treatment of both the German and Japanese Military Government."[133] Apologizing for his "evil" practices, Villagomez pleaded for another reduced sentence so he could reunite with his family in Saipan.

In October of that year, Antonio Camacho, Luis C. Crisostomo, and Juan Reyes also drafted a letter for the secretary of the navy. They wrote, "It is true that we were used, by force, by the Japanese authorities, as instruments in some of the atrocities they perpetrated. There was no choice left for us. Either we slapped people at their command or we were threatened with execution." More vitally, they apologized to the clans whose family members they assaulted or murdered during the war. As Camacho, Crisostomo, and Reyes revealed, "We have contacted all the family of the people we offended during the war and the victims of our forced cruelty and they are all willing to forgive us, and they understand why we, contrary to our reasoning and will, were forced to act the way we did." With their families living in "poverty" and bearing the shame of their wartime atrocities, these men asked the secretary of the navy to grant them the "lenient and merciful" ways of the U.S. government.[134] Even the warden of the Guam Penitentiary, A. A. Jackson, vouched for the change in their attitude as "model prisoners" of the U.S. military. "They have been obedient," he said, "cheerful and very industrious at all times. It is recommended that favorable action be given the attached petitions for clemency."[135] In response, the Office of the Secretary of the Navy reduced each of their sentences once again, this time to imprisonment at hard labor for forty-five years.

Part III | THE MILITARY COLONY

5

JAPANESE TRAITORS

Drawing from its pool of accused war criminals, the tribunal interrogated and tried numerous Japanese men for committing crimes against U.S. citizens and nationals. As with its feminization of Rotanese and Saipanese men as noncombatants without politics, the commission similarly racialized suspected Japanese war criminals. Knowing that they represented an enemy and rival nation, however, the court recognized the Japanese as citizens in domestic and international laws. In this way, the tribunal held a related but decidedly different position when addressing the matter of Japanese war criminality in the military colony of Guam. One crucial distinction between natives and nonnatives resided in the tribunal's acknowledgment of Japanese political life, *bios*. Japanese citizenship, Japanese martial and combatant traditions, and Japanese territorial claims over Guam—all legible markers of imperial governance—mattered to the commission and its legal interpretations of sovereignty.

In this chapter, I analyze the treason trial of Samuel Takekuna Shinohara, a Japanese national and resident of Guam, in an effort to demonstrate how the tribunal viewed him as a sacred man integral to the eradication of Japanese sovereignty in the island. Central to this discussion was how the U.S. Navy portrayed Shinohara, an enemy Issei, as violating whiteness as American property and sovereignty. For this reason, the treason charges and other specifications accused him as an assailant, thief, and organizer of military brothels. But the commission simultaneously represented Shinohara as a "residential alien" who owed allegiance to the United States, an act that signaled the then-emerging shifts in American perceptions of Japanese and Japanese American subjectivities from external threats and subversive elements to budding Cold War partners with the United States.[1] How and why the commission constructed him as a sacred man whose criminality signified alien and traitor, enemy and conspirator, is thus the subject of this chapter. I then conclude with Shinohara's responses to these allegations.

Spy, Traitor, and Other Allegations

Samuel Takekuna Shinohara migrated from Japan to Guam in 1905 and married into a prominent Chamorro family, the Torreses of Hagåtña. His wife was Carmen, and together they had two children, Cecilia and Gil. He later became a successful entrepreneur, owning the Hagåtña Gas Kitchen, the Rooster Bar, and a small taxi operation. These businesses catered to the residents of Hagåtña and the personnel of the U.S. Naval Government.[2] Shinohara was also the president of the Japanese Society of Guam, as well as a fluent speaker of the Chamorro, English, and Japanese languages. When the Japanese military attacked the island on December 8, 1941, Shinohara then became involved in a war of profit and privilege because of his business background and fluency in several languages. These characteristics, however, proved troubling for the naval governor of Guam, George J. McMillin, who ordered the immediate arrest of Shinohara and other influential Japanese citizens.[3] The Japanese bombing of Pearl Harbor (Pu'uloa) and Guam on the same day led McMillin to racialize the Japanese business community as potentially suspicious and threatening and, in his view, deserving of incarceration. Two days later, though, McMillin surrendered to the Japanese invading forces, at which time Shinohara and the other Japanese civilians were released from the jail. In a moment of role reversals, the Japanese military then incarcerated McMillin and other American military personnel in the same prison that had housed Shinohara. A month later, on January 10, 1942, the Japanese military transported McMillin and other white American prisoners of war to Japan.

As for Shinohara, he remained in Guam, where he extended his services to the Japanese military and the Minseibu. Along these lines, the Guam historian Robert F. Rogers describes Shinohara as a "Japanese loyalist," whereas the American historian Tim Maga depicts him as an "advisor and part-time 'justice investigator' for the new government."[4] One of his peers, a teacher named Kyomon Miwa, portrayed Shinohara in comparable terms. Recalled Miwa, "I arrived in Guam in September, 1942, as a school teacher. We were told that, as the island of Guam was one of the first places to be conquered by Japan, Japanese policies and installations were to be tried out here, and the experience gained was to be applied in the occupation of other areas. When I first came to Agana I found that Mr. Shinohara was a prominent and influential person and it seemed that he was looking after the welfare of many Japanese families."[5] Another acquaintance, Hirose Hisashi of the 54th Naval Guard Unit, commended Shinohara for having a "brilliant mind and personal magnetism."[6]

Whereas members of the Japanese government and military often portrayed Shinohara in favorable terms, several prominent individuals in Guam felt otherwise. After the war, they specifically accused him of spying for Japan before its occupation of the island. For example, Ignacia Bordallo Butler, a Guamanian entrepreneur, had a conversation with Shinohara in 1942 in which he supposedly remarked, "I was a spy for the Japanese Government during the American time."[7] Providing more details to these allegations, the Guamanian educator Agueda Iglesias Johnston explained, "All of us suspicioned Shinohara. Every time the Japanese schooner came into port, the captain of it, a Jap named Okno, would come to visit Shinohara at this home. This schooner always seemed to time its visits to coincide with the times when the Pan American clippers were in."[8] When the Japanese military invaded the island, she said, a captain by the name of "Owata" visited Shinohara's house and assisted in releasing him from the jail.

Gonzalo R. Eclevea, another Guamanian, discussed how Shinohara once spied on American naval facilities at the harbor in the village of Sumay. Sometime before the war, Eclevea witnessed Shinohara drive his car, an Essex sedan, near the work site. Seated in his vehicle for three to four minutes, Shinohara saw "all of our installations."[9] These buildings included "gasoline storage tanks, pipe lines, and fuel lines which were to refuel the submarines and destroyers as they came along side."[10] Adding to these suspicions, the Japanese resident Shintaro Okada alleged that Shinohara engaged the Japanese military on several occasions. As he stated, "I went on a trip to Japan on the Gold Star about 1932. Shinohara also went on this trip. While we were in Tokyo, Shinohara told me he had an appointment with the Taigunsho (Japanese Naval Dept.). He went there two or three times. I could not understand why he would be going there."[11]

While neither these individuals nor the tribunal furnished any documentary evidence of Samuel T. Shinohara's role as an alleged spy for Japan, the recollections featured here demonstrate the kind of gossip and racism directed against him (figure 5.1). With Shinohara construed as a disloyal and traitorous subject, his personhood represented a militarized brand of the "yellow peril" that the United States criminalized in its courts. As with the treason cases of Iva Toguri d'Aquino, the so-called Tokyo Rose, and

5.1. Carmen Shinohara and Samuel Shinohara, Guam. Reproduced with permission from the Shinohara family. Photo by Dr. Austin Shelton, University of Guam.

Tomoya Kawakita, among others, Shinohara's wartime activities similarly came under suspicion. As the historian Naoko Shibusawa explains, "The Cold-War-era treason trials, as well as the Red scare espionage trials of the period, allowed the federal government to pillory disloyal individuals."[12] In addressing these cases, the United States sought to "prove, by the testimony of two witnesses to the same act, (1) that there was an overt act of aid and comfort to the enemy, (2) performed with the intention of betraying the United States, (3) which has the actual effect of providing aid and comfort to the enemy."[13] If a civil court shows that two individuals witnessed a person or group conduct the same "overt act" that provided aid and comfort to the enemy, then said individual(s) could be found guilty of treason and potentially sentenced to death. As per U.S. constitutional and statute law, only U.S. citizens and nationals could be put on trial and only in the context of a civil court.

In its consideration of the treason charge in Guam in 1945, the U.S. Navy's War Crimes Tribunals program selectively interpreted the meaning of this crime. That is, the court disregarded the principle that only American citizens and nationals could be tried for treason. Initially, moreover, the tribunal accused four traitors to the U.S. government: one American national; one Japanese national; one colonial subject of Japan; and one person whose political identity remained ambiguous. These four men were, respectively, Pedro Mantanoña, Samuel T. Shinohara, Jose P. Villagomez, and Juan S. Onedera. Take, for instance, the Saipanese Villagomez, who was convicted of murder in February 1945. In a memo to the judge advocate general of the navy in April 1945, the commission considered trying him for treason.[14]

The court likewise accused Juan S. Onedera, a Chamorro-Japanese man, in June 1945, even providing Guamanian testimonies that he "put on a Japanese soldier's uniform."[15] One witness, Geronimo Mendiola, said that Onedera "was completely equipped with Japanese field equipment including a cartridge belt and rifle. . . . He told us how big the American soldiers were, showed us some American cigarettes he had and told us how he had killed some Americans with his rifle."[16] Another witness, Jose T. Gutierrez, claimed that Onedera "had already killed three American soldiers. He said he was going back to fight some more [in the coastal and village area of Asan]."[17] The Guamanian Pedro Mantanoña, the only U.S. national identified by the court, faced similar accusations, but unlike Onedera and Villagomez, who never received any charges, the tribunal had drafted three specifications of treason for Mantanoña on January 23, 1945. The specifications alleged that he disarmed three Guamanian men and prevented them from joining "a group of armed natives who intended to help the armed forces of the Government of the United States in battle against the enemy" in July 1944.[18] Because it did not find evidence to support its claim, however, the commission dropped the charge against Pedro Mantanoña and upheld its portrayal of Guamanians as loyal wards.

Ultimately, the tribunal tried Samuel T. Shinohara only for treason. The original charges, dated May 12, 1945, began with treason and read in part, "In that Samuel T. Shinohara, an inhabitant and resident of Guam . . . did . . . on or about December 16, 1941, willfully, knowingly and treasonably adhere to Japan, an enemy of the United States, and give aid and comfort to Japan." The commission categorized Shinohara's "overt act" in terms of theft, an act wherein he assisted the Japanese military in procuring "the property of the Naval Government of Guam."[19] As per the court's definition, the property amounted to $8,300 in U.S. currency and $1,000 in U.S. checks. With Shinohara classified as an American subject who failed to adhere to his allegiance to the United States, the commission outlined the other charges and specifications.[20] They included charge II, theft; charge III, assault and battery; and charge IV, taking a female for the purpose of prostitution, with two specifications on coercion. Yet these charges painted Shinohara as an enemy Issei who had the ability to steal one American vehicle, assault one American citizen, and prostitute two American nationals. Further, on July 20, 1945, the commission released additional charges and specifications on treason, assault and battery, and the desecration of the flag.[21] The additional treason charge contained three specifications, which focused on three overt acts—two in December 1941 and one in April 1942—believed to have aided the Japanese military. The first specification alleged that Shinohara removed an electric generator from Ignacia Bordallo Butler, an inhabitant of Guam; the second alleged that he organized the making of a Japanese labor organization, Dai Nisei. The third and final specification alleged that Shinohara offered provisions for the Japanese military and naval forces in Guam.

On July 28, 1945, the military commission assembled over these allegations, as did Shinohara's defense counsel, which was led by Lieutenant Emory L. Morris, U.S. Naval Reserve. Vicente C. Reyes, a Chamorro attorney, acted as the interpreter and assistant for Morris. Initially, Lieutenant Morris dismissed the jurisdiction of the commission. He argued that Shinohara was a "citizen and national of Japan" who "owes no allegiance to the Naval Government of Guam and the United States of America, or either of them, during the time Guam was occupied by the military forces of Japan."[22] On July 31, 1945, for example, the defense counsel called on its first witness, Francisco T. Flores, an employee of the naval government's Department of Records and Accounts. Referring to Shinohara's cedula record of 1920, Flores explained, "On page 36, under column 640, the name Takekuma Shinohara, native—Japan; district, state or country—Tagoshima; sex—Male; age—29; civil status—single; occupation—salesman; actual residence—Lot No. 57, San Ignacio Street. Tagoshima as I understand it is somewhere in Japan, and San Ignacio Street was a street in Agana, Guam."[23] By bringing Flores to the stand, the defense counsel hoped to confirm Shinohara's allegiance to Japan, thereby challenging the military commission's jurisdiction. In response, the tribunal asserted that Shinohara was a subject of the U.S. Naval Government because his cedula record was registered in Guam and not in Japan. As a result, Shinohara pleaded "not guilty" in spite of the allegations that he was in breach of his allegiance to the naval government and the United States. How, then, did the commission create this seemingly extralegal position? If civil courts are the venues for discussing the constitutional clauses on treason, how does one analyze their uneven application in a military tribunal, their racialized usage in a military colony, and their exceptional treatment of a Japanese citizen? What do we make, as well, of the additional charges, the ones that focused on U.S. "property" claims to bodies and objects in Guam?

Properties of the Colonial State

In its judgment of Samuel T. Shinohara, the military commission did not begin with the original and additional treason charges directed against him. Convened by Lieutenant Colonel and Judge Advocate Teller Ammons, the tribunal commenced by engaging the lesser charges and specifications on theft, assault and battery, desecration of the U.S. flag, and prostitution. The prosecution—also led by Ammons—aimed to accomplish four goals: first, to reestablish the property claims of the U.S. Naval Government as per the laws of possession; second, to find Shinohara guilty of violating these property claims; third, to fault Shinohara for treason; and, fourth, to accord him the death sentence.

In its understanding of "property," the navy drew from the U.S. law on property rights, a law historically premised on the enslavement of blacks and the dispossession of Native Americans in North America. The legal scholar Cheryl I. Harris theorizes this racially entangled but lawful process as the white investment in property. As she asserts, "The origins of property rights in the United States are rooted in racial domination. Even in the early years of the country, it was not the concept of race alone that operated to oppress Blacks and Indians; rather, it was the interaction between conceptions of race and property that played a critical role in establishing and maintaining racial and economic subordination."[24] For Harris, the institutional slavery of blacks as property to be assigned or inherited, and the erasure of first possession rights among Native Americans led to the legal conflation of whiteness, privilege, and property. As she explains, "This racist formulation embedded the fact of white privilege into the very definition of property, marking another stage in the evolution of the property interest in whiteness. Possession—the act necessary to lay the basis for rights in property—was defined to include only the cultural practices of whites. This definition laid the foundation for the idea that whiteness—as that which whites alone possess—is valuable and is property."[25]

With its white-oriented ideology, the tribunal claimed that the United States owned, as its possessions, the bodies and lands of Guam. Shinohara's wartime abuse of an American military officer, two American nationals, an American flag, and an American car—properties said to belong to the United States—thus violated the sanctity of whiteness as property and sovereignty, for which he had to be punished. In this section, I discuss how the tribunal treated Shinohara as the manifestation of the Japanese empire in Guam. I begin with an examination of the theft and assault and battery charges, detailing how naval officials like Lieutenant James E. Davis and Captain George J. McMillin informed the carceral imagination of the court and its Guamanian witnesses. I then close this section with an analysis of Shinohara's brothels and demonstrate how the Guamanian "prostitutes" Alfonsina Flores and Nicholasa P. Mendiola negotiated the Japanese *ianjo* system and the American military commission.

Original charge II regarding theft, for example, alleged that Shinohara stole James E. Davis's Chevrolet automobile, valued at $1,200, "in and about the month of February 1942, in the City of Agana, Guam."[26] If convicted of grand theft, an act resulting in the seizure of items worth more than $100, Shinohara faced, as per *The Penal Code of Guam*, section 489, "imprisonment for not less than one nor more than five years."[27] During the third day of the trial, the commission inquired as to the owner of the Chevrolet vehicle, seeking the testimony of the defense witness Francisco T. Flores. Under oath, he said, "According to the records of application for automobile registration I have here, it shows that Lieutenant James Edward Davis registered in the year 1940 in the Department of Records and Accounts."[28] When the judge advocate asked what kind of vehicle Davis owned, Flores replied, "Plymouth, practically brand new, with a light green color."[29] The court then established the responsibilities Davis held as an American naval officer, a navy chaplain, and the head of the Department of Education in Guam. Flores and other Guamanian witnesses also claimed that, subsequent to the Japanese invasion of the island on December 8, 1941, the Japanese military had detained Davis and, a month later, had transported him to an unidentified prisoner of war camp in Japan.

The crucial question was whether Shinohara indeed stole the vehicle, an allegation neither confirmed nor denied by Flores. He argued that although Shinohara rode in the automobile during the war period, he never knew if Shinohara claimed ownership over the vehicle. He was simply a passenger.[30] On the other hand, the prosecution enlisted five Guamanian witnesses who, collectively, presented three points: first, Davis never sold the car to anybody after December 8, 1941, as the government offices were closed; second, Shinohara or his son, Gil, drove the car on various occasions; and, third, several individuals chauffeured Shinohara or his family in public view. These witnesses also implied that Davis's American automobile signified whiteness. The vehicle symbolized slogans like "Plymouth's Got It!—more value, beauty, luxury than any other low-priced car in history," works contained in a 1939 advertisement that sought to attract white American consumers in the post-Depression era of the late 1930s.[31] As a vehicle for working- and middle-class white families, the Plymouth was created for urban lifestyles. Knowing that the Plymouth symbolized America's industrial resilience, the prosecution's witnesses thus conveyed what may have been appalling to the commission: that is, that Shinohara transformed Davis's American-made automobile into a vehicle of imperial Japan.

Vicente P. Herrero, the second witness for the prosecution, hinted at these scenarios, saying that Shinohara might have attached a Japanese license plate to the Plymouth. As he surmised, "There must be a license plate by the Japanese but what number and flower, I could not recall. . . . I could not make out who is who from any of the plates, the cherry blossom, or the anchor."[32] Yet Herrero did not disclose whether Davis's vehicle was registered for Japanese civilian use, as per the symbol of the "cherry blossom," or for Japanese naval use, as per the symbol of the "anchor." The witness Jose P. Crisostomo was more forthcoming, stating that the Plymouth had a cherry blossom license plate, marked "number '2.'"[33]

On August 2, 1945, the fifth day of the trial, the commission opened the floor to the third original charge and the second additional charge on "assault and battery." The former charge asserted that Samuel T. Shinohara struck Captain George J. McMillin, then governor of the U.S. Naval Government, on or about January 20, 1942, in Hagåtña, Guam.[34] The latter charge, differing only with respect to the time of the assaults, alleged that Shinohara slapped McMillin in the face. Whereas the original charge indicated a period around January 20, 1942, the additional charge stipulated that other assaults occurred around December 10, 1941, and January 1, 1942. In each case, the prosecution turned to *The Penal Code of Guam* and to five Guamanian witnesses in arguing that Shinohara attacked the "official" embodiment of U.S. property in Guam, Captain and Naval Governor George J. McMillin. Section 240 of *The Penal Code of Guam* clarified assault as "an unlawful attempt, coupled with present ability, to commit a violent injury on the person of another."[35] Section 242 also defined "battery" as "any willful and unlawful use of force or violence upon the person of another."[36]

The first witness, Felix Q. Nauta, was a seaman second class of the Insular Force, U.S. Navy. He recalled the incident as occurring before 7:00 AM on December 10, 1941, the time of McMillin's surrender to the Japanese military. Nauta stated that "while we were already captured by the Japanese, we were sitting in the plaza with other native enlisted personnel facing towards the east. Then I turned to my right . . . and I saw Shinohara slap the Governor of Guam." When the judge advocate asked Nauta to explain where the assault happened, Nauta responded, "Right in front of the Governor's palace."[37] As per Hagåtña's topography, the naval governor resided at the Plaza de España, the site of sovereignty first established by Spain in the 1700s and later appropriated by the United States in 1898 and the Menseibu of Japan in 1941.[38]

Two other witnesses, Francisco Santos Aguon and Eugenio B. Borja, then recalled another assault on McMillin, which was said to occur between 9:45 and 10:00 AM on a day in late December 1941. As for the location, they identified a golf course in Agaña Heights where, among a gathering of Japanese military personnel and Chamorro laborers, Aguon "saw Shinohara slap the Governor."[39] But unlike the previous testimony, Aguon and Borja embellished the past with a patriotic lamentation for the United States. Aguon had this to say about the scene in Agaña Heights, a hill overlooking the city of Hagåtña and its adjacent shoreline: "There was a national flag, stars and stripes, planted on a buoy [in the bay] which made a target for a kind of heavy artillery, most likely 3-inch guns. I do not know definitely but it was a heavy gun."[40] Borja similarly noted that "we were standing up there facing the ocean and the [U.S.] flag was on the ocean. The Governor and Shinohara passed in front of us and the Governor told Shinohara, he said, 'Will you tell the Japanese to be nice to the Chamorros because they will be nice to them?,' and after Shinohara heard this he slapped the Governor and said, 'You are no Governor.'"[41]

Based on these testimonies alone, the prosecution's Guamanian witnesses portrayed McMillin as a vulnerable and defeated white figure of colonial authority. In keeping with this theme of a violated "America," the prosecution then entered additional charge III, desecration of the flag, into the court record on August 4, 1945, the seventh day of the trial. The charge alleged that Shinohara "did, in or about the month of February or March 1942, in or near Agana, Guam, publicly defile and cast contempt upon the flag of the United States of America by using a flag of the United States of America for the purpose of wiping off a bar."[42] Section 310a of *The Penal Code of Guam* defined the desecration of flags and the terms for punishment as follows: "Whoever, in any manner for exhibition or display . . . publicly mutilates, defaces, defiles, tramples upon or casts contempt by word or act upon any such flag, is guilty of a misdemeanor, and shall be punished by a fine not exceeding fifty dollars or by imprisonment not exceeding thirty days."[43]

Herbert Johnston, a civilian administrative assistant employed by the Military Government Labor Department, opened the floor by indicating the location of the said charge. He described how the Elks Club, an exclusive joint for American military officers, transformed into Omiya Kaikan, a social space for Japanese military officers, during the war. The desecration of the U.S. flag, Johnston asserted, occurred on this property, then managed by Shinohara. As he remembered, "On one occasion there was a party . . . [where] they had dinner and when I got to the place, they were clearing the hall for dancing. A lot of liquid was spilled on the floor. When the dancing was about to start, I saw [Shinohara] wipe the floor with an American flag. . . . I turned away and coughed and I did not see what happened after that." Johnston then described the flag as "navy standard size 9, about four feet long," so as not to conflate bunting, or cloth decorated with patriotic colors, with the U.S. flag.[44] Two former "waitresses" of Omiya Kaikan, Beatrice Santos Rios and Olita T. Santos, confirmed these allegations, as did the former bartender, Jesus L. Fernandez.[45]

With Shinohara represented as both devious and violent, the tribunal turned to its claim that Chamorro women in Guam belonged, as property, to the United States. The eighth day of the trial, August 6, 1945, illustrated these sensibilities in the fourth original charge, "taking a female for the purpose of prostitution." The two specifications noted, respectively, that Shinohara "in and about the month of February 1942" unlawfully took Alfonsina Flores and Nicholasa P. Mendiola "for the purpose of prostitution." The specifications accused him of procuring the consent of Flores "by misrepresentation" and soliciting the consent of Mendiola "against her will," key distinctions that informed how the women and others understood prostitution.[46] In *The Penal Code of Guam*, the chapter titled "Rape, Abduction, Carnal Abuse of Children, and Seduction" outlined several definitions of prostitution and prostitution-related crimes. Section 265, "Abduction of Women," and section 267, "Abduction," provide a useful context for understanding how *The Penal Code of Guam* codified prostitution as a crime and the role of coercion therein. As section 265 emphasized, "Every person who takes any woman unlawfully, against her will, and by force, menace, or duress, compels her to marry him, or to marry any other person, or to be defiled, is punishable by imprisonment not less than two nor more than fourteen years."[47] Similarly, section 267 read, "Every person who takes away any female under the age of eighteen years from her father, mother, guardian, or other person having the legal charge of her person, without her consent, for the purpose of prostitution or for lewd purposes, is punishable by imprisonment not exceeding five years, and a fine not exceeding one thousand dollars."[48]

As these sections demonstrate, the phrases "against her will" and "without her consent" provided some degree of protection for girls and women. The phrases offered the prosecution some relief in its efforts to address the charge of prostitution and to seek justice for Alfonsina Flores and Nicholasa P. Mendiola. At the same time, sections 265 and 267 assumed that women belonged to their husbands, their parents, or their guardians; such heteronormative language portrayed women as properties bestowed with meaning vis-à-vis heterosexual marriage or heterosexual genealogy, or both. Read in these terms, *The Penal Code of Guam* interpreted the abduction of women and abduction generally as criminal processes that violated the property claims of husbands, parents, or guardians. This terminology likewise resonated with international laws on rape and sexual assault, where such crimes have been "categorized as an outrage upon personal dignity, or as crimes against honor" rather than as violence against any person.[49]

Thus, the testimonies provided by Flores and Mendiola mattered insofar as they upheld the prosecution's notion that they were properties of the American government. Rape and sexual assault were secondary to the primary charge that Shinohara abused American properties for the purpose of establishing at least two prostitution rings. The first alleged brothel catered to two Japanese military officers, Governor Hiroshi Hayashi and the governor aide-de-camp Sakai, both of whom resided in the "Kerners' house" of San Antonio, Hagåtña.[50] Owned by Albert and Mercedes T. Kerner, the Kerners' house resembled what the anthropologist C. Sarah Soh calls a "concessionary" ianjo, or comfort facility.[51] As she notes, the concessionary ianjo is "divided into two subtypes: the 'house of entertainment,' which served primarily officers, and the 'house of prostitution,' which catered to the rank and file." Because the Kerners' house served military officers, and because Shinohara, a civilian, leased and managed the place, the site can be described as a concessionary ianjo with one exception. Unlike other ianjo that housed many military officers, the Kerners' home remained a brothel for only two officers in 1942. According to the prosecution, Alfonsina Flores was misled as to her exact role at the home, hence the specification of "misrepresentation." Such misrepresentation began with an unexpected visit to the Flores ranch in the village of Malojloj. In February 1942, Juan C. Mesa, a chauffeur, Shinohara, and Sakai arrived at the Flores home, where they greeted Jose Dueñas Flores, the father of Alfonsina. As a witness for the prosecution, Jose Dueñas Flores recounted, "The accused came to my ranch with the Japanese officer and a driver and the accused said, 'We come here to ask for your 17 year old daughter to be a service girl.'" To this request, Flores responded, "My daughter is not capable to do that kind of work."[52]

The mother of Alfonsina, Rafaela San Nicholas Flores, then confronted Shinohara. She inquired, "I asked him how did he know [Alfonsina] was 17 years old. I said to him, 'Who told you about it?' I further said to the accused, 'You came from [Hagåtña] up to this place. You passed many other girls, why did you come directly to this ranch? You did that on purpose.'" Her husband, Jose, then argued that he was "ready to fight and kill because [prostitution] is not the custom out here," to which Rafaela Flores countered, "there is nothing we can say or else we will get killed."[53] With Alfonsina crying in the background, her parents complied with Shinohara's forceful demands. But Rafaela Flores persisted in her critique of patriarchy and prostitution, requesting that she accompany her daughter to Hagåtña and pressing Shinohara in other ways. Upon arriving in the city, she referred to Cecilia, Shinohara's daughter, asking him, "Now what are you going to do about it? How would you like to have this done to your daughter?"[54] Berating the Japanese empire, she said, "'Even if you turned the Kingdom of Japan over to me, it will never satisfy me. I would rather have my daughter back." Refusing to implicate his daughter, Shinohara assured Rafaela Flores that Alfonsina would be cleaning a house, with her family receiving help in the future. As her final appeal, Rafaela Flores then requested that the governor aide-de-camp Sakai marry Alfonsina.

Although Alfonsina was already engaged to a Chamorro man, Vicente Flores Blanco, her mother insisted that she marry Sakai. If a wedding was pursued, Alfonsina and Sakai would have participated in *mamaisan saina*, otherwise known as "requesting the permission of elders."[55] In the 1940s, this process required the groom's parents to meet at the bride's home, where they, along with elders, requested the consent of the bride's family. Families would then exchange items of cultural significance, such as *pugua* (betel nut), so as to link their children and clans.[56] For Shinohara, though, marriage was not an option. Already crying, Alfonsina Flores recalled, "Then Shinohara said that I must listen and obey or else I will be beheaded." She then recounted moving to the Kerners' house, where she "was made to sleep with Sakai."[57]

According to Alfonsina Flores, for six months she was "forced to stay" in the Kerners' home, where Shinohara, as the "boss," promised her 20 yen per month for her labor.[58] In the end, she collected 50 yen of the 120 yen promised. Her value, as property, also amounted to five pounds of tobacco, the only compensation Shinohara provided to the Flores family. During this period, however, Rafaela Flores visited her daughter several times a week, demonstrating the accessible nature of the residence. Further, Alfonsina Flores frequently left the Kerners' house at her own volition, often traveling to her family's ranch and the homes of other relatives. Neither the Japanese soldiers in the area nor Shinohara tortured her for these actions, perhaps because of her newfound political relationship with governor aide-de-camp Sakai. At most, Shinohara could only say "cuss words" against Alfonsina Flores, an indication of her rise in status as an indigenous woman and colonial subject of the Japanese military.[59] She then quit when Sakai left Guam for an undisclosed location in the summer of 1942, at which time she returned to her family.

Another undeveloped account in this narrative concerned her older sister, Alice, who was already living in the Kerners' home upon Alfonsina's arrival. Based on the testimonies of Alfonsina and her parents, Alice Flores may have performed "domestic" services for the other Japanese officer of the house, Governor Hiroshi Hayashi. Interestingly, neither the defense counsel nor the prosecution addressed the role of Alice Flores other than to describe her duties as a house cleaner and to identify her as Alfonsina's sibling. Was Alice Flores a prostitute, already assisting Shinohara during the war? Why, as well, did the Flores family reveal little about her presence in the Kerners' house? And what led Alfonsina Flores to becoming the source of contestation in this narrative of wartime prostitution and indigenous survival? Or was she a prostitute who accused Shinohara for failing to keep his promises and payments?

Despite the fact that these questions remained unanswered by the court, Alfonsina Flores and her family recounted several points that stressed Shinohara's ties to prostitution: first, Shinohara seized Alfonsina Flores as property of the Japanese military; second, Shinohara threatened to kill the Flores family; third, Alfonsina Flores resided in the Kerners' home against her will; and, fourth, Sakai may have raped her. On the latter point, Alfonsina Flores never mentioned the term "rape." As such, she may have had a sexual or nonsexual relationship with Sakai, something akin to what the sociologist Seungsook Moon describes as "cohabitating prostitution," where intimate liaisons can lead to long-term partnerships.[60] Indeed, several kinds of prostitution may describe Alfonsina Flores's relationship with Sakai and Shinohara. At the same time, she knew better, saying, "They were not going to make a good girl out of me."[61]

The specification regarding Nicholasa P. Mendiola conveyed a comparable pattern of abduction and coercion, but with some fundamental differences. Whereas the prosecution portrayed Shinohara as transforming Alfonsina Flores into a prostitute, the prosecution characterized Nicholasa Mendiola as a prostitute manipulated to work in the second prostitution ring operated by Shinohara. Unlike the Kerners' house that accommodated only two Japanese military officers, the other concessionary ianjo, located in the village of Piti, favored military officers and enlisted personnel in greater numbers. It is quite probable that Shinohara may have been linked to these and other brothels, but the prosecution did not pursue this inquiry. It instead focused on proving that Shinohara forced Mendiola, against her will, into one prostitution ring from February or March 1942 to June or July 1942. In doing so, the prosecution may not have represented Mendiola as a "good girl," but it certainly acknowledged her indigenous agency as a "modern girl."[62] As the historian Sarah Kovner argues, the "modern girl" in Japan and its colonies was an ideal of femininity variously embraced and resisted by women across the empire in bars, cafes, dance halls, and restaurants.[63] This ideal blurred the eroticized roles between nonsexual labor, rape, and sexual labor in these sites. Waitresses, for example, could have assisted bar customers, as much as they could have labored as prostitutes. A Guamanian police officer and witness for the prosecution, Adolfo C. Sgambelluri, confirmed the flexible identity and negotiating power Mendiola yielded as a modern, single girl in Guam.

In early 1942, a chauffeur, Samuel T. Shinohara, Jesusa Taitano, two Japanese navy personnel, and a female prostitute sought the assistance of Sgambelluri, who was then working for the Japanese police department. As a group, they drove to the district of Anigua, an area adjacent to Hagåtña, where Nicholasa Mendiola resided. As Sgambelluri stated, "Upon arrival there, [Shinohara] sent me in to call Nicolasa [sic] to the car as he would like to talk to her. Nicholasa was rather reluctant to come out. She made excuses. Finally she came out and while at the car, Shinohara asked her to come down with him to Piti and work at a whore house where Japanese enlisted personnel were being entertained. She answered that she would later on if she can get clothes to wear as she had on only rags."[64] According to Sgambelluri, Shinohara offered to provide Mendiola with clothes and "anything else she wanted."[65] When the prosecution called her to the stand, she reiterated these details but emphasized the importance of her two children. As she recalled, "Then [Shinohara] asked me if I wanted to work at the whore house. I told the accused that I could not do it on account of my children. He insisted and said, 'Come and try it at least for three days and see how you like it,' and I said, 'No.'"[66] Failing to persuade Nicholasa Mendiola, Shinohara threatened to punish her. At that point, she relented and accompanied everybody to the ianjo in Piti. But because the manager was not there, they dropped off Mendiola at her home in Anigua.

Two weeks later, she met Shinohara, who offered her a new position at a "saloon" where she, as a "bar maid," would serve drinks. As Nicholasa Mendiola recalled, "I was willing to do that." After agreeing to pursue this job, she remembered being taken "to the hospital to have my physical examination and after I had passed physically, I was given my paper."[67] Having undergone tests that may have assessed venereal diseases, both under the U.S. Naval Government and then under the Japanese military, she described the most recent examination as if it was routine. When the defense asked her to define the purpose of these exams, she observed, "I do not want to answer that question. It lowers my reputation, but if I must answer it then I will."[68] Before the defense could reply, the military commission instructed Mendiola to not answer the question. But she did respond to Shinohara, who, two days after her physical examination, returned to her home. Without any explanation as to how their negotiations unfolded, Shinohara then took her to the ianjo in Piti. During the trial, Mendiola only shared what she experienced upon entering the brothel. As she noted, "I found rooms in that building. There was a boy. I stayed there and it was either the first or second night when the accused came and brought an officer. . . . [Shinohara] brought in two Japanese officers and then the accused said, 'Take care of these men,' and I said, 'What for?' and he said, 'Well, your line of work.'" She refused, with Shinohara threatening to punish her. Mendiola recounted that she soon complied, saying that she and an officer "went into the room and slept together because that was what we were supposed to do."[69] Clarifying what she meant by "sleeping," she said, "We had sexual intercourse."[70]

For the prosecution and the court, Nicholasa P. Mendiola demonstrated that Samuel T. Shinohara coerced her into working as a prostitute for the Japanese military. While she did not discuss the role of the "boy" in the Piti brothel, she illustrated her intimate familiarity with the various "whore houses" in Guam and indicated that she had the same level of autonomy as that afforded to Alfonsina Flores. Once charged with "vagrancy" under the naval government, then becoming a "reformed" person before the war broke out, Mendiola assumed the position of a "modern girl" for four to five months.[71] She also had sexual relations with at least one Japanese military officer, providing evidence of an existing prostitution ring in Piti where she, like Flores, became the sexual property of Shinohara and Japan. As Judge Advocate Teller Ammons declared, "The accused not only forced these women to cohabit with the enemy Japanese, but he went further; by fear of death and punishment, he forced these two women to subject themselves to the bestial desires of men of the accused's own selection, who were members of the enemy invasion forces. They were Japanese. No lower trait of character can be found in any man."[72]

As implied in Ammon's racist and sexist comments, however, we should not read too much into the legal rhetoric of coercion, abduction, and consent as providing relief to Flores and Mendiola. In the last instance, The Penal Code of Guam, like the commission and prosecution, did not attempt to remedy the violence of prostitution inflicted upon these women. Several reasons explain this rationale where the women were paradoxically cast as unwanted "aliens" but valuable properties of the U.S. state. First, section 175 of The Penal Code of Guam, "Importation and Deportation of Undesirable Aliens," identified prostitutes as one of several "classes of aliens" that are not allowed entry into Guam. The so-called aliens included "anarchists," "feeble-minded persons," "idiots," "imbeciles," the "mentally or physically defective," "paupers," "polygamists," and "professional beggars," among others.[73] Should such an individual arrive on the island, section 175 stated that he should be "deported to the country whence he came at any time within three years after the date of his entry into the island."[74] In other words, The Penal Code of Guam defined prostitutes as an undesirable class of people. Confounding this position was the reality that American brothels existed in Guam before the war. In official terms, the U.S. military rarely suppressed prostitution here or elsewhere; if laws were passed to this effect, they mainly addressed control of venereal disease.[75] Second, the tribunal never accused Shinohara of providing the conditions that led to the possibility of Flores and Mendiola being raped, a subtext occurring throughout the trial but never made clear by the prosecution or defense. If rape was entered as a war crime in the trial, then the terms of punishment would have set a precedent in naval law and thereby offer a fuller sense of justice for the women. Third, and finally, the prosecution punished Shinohara for possessing Alfonsina Flores and Nicholasa P. Mendiola as U.S. nationals and properties of the naval government.

By arguing that Shinohara transformed an American car into a Japanese military vehicle, assaulted an American military officer and governor, desecrated the American flag, and prostituted two American nationals, the prosecution therefore asserted that Shinohara had violated the sanctity of whiteness as property and sovereignty in Guam. In these ways, the commission represented him as bearing the martial and material markers of the Japanese empire. But how did the lesser charges—allegations that placed Shinohara outside the zone of Japanese sovereignty—render him as a "residential alien" who owed allegiance to the United States?

The Residential Alien as Homo Sacer

In this section, I discuss how the tribunal construed Shinohara's inclusive exclusion with the American nation as per his four "overt acts" of treason. These acts included organizing a youth group called Dai Nisei, seizing an electric generator, stealing American monies from a bank, and supplying provisions for the Japanese military. These activities presumably aided the Japanese enemy. I then show how the court and other naval officials began to shift Shinohara's national identity from an enemy and foreigner of Japan to an ethnic minority and resident of an American military colony.[76] For instance, the four treason charges afforded him the political rights of a residential alien, a legal category whose loyalty was bound to the United States. Specifically, he was an Issei who betrayed his allegiance to America, even though the United States had considered the Issei as "enemy aliens" during the war.[77] Drawing on section 37 of *The Penal Code of Guam*, "Treason, Who Only Can Commit," the court stated that "every person, resident in the island of Guam" owes allegiance to the Naval Government of Guam or the United States.[78] *The Penal Code of Guam* likewise required the constitutional rule of an "overt act," verified by two witnesses, only differing in its understanding of punishment and attainders. In this respect, the death sentence applied, as did the option of imprisonment "at hard labor for not less than five years."[79]

On the other hand, neither *The Penal Code of Guam* nor the military commission invoked anything resembling attainders, meaning that the court could extend, as it did, punitive measures against the "properties" of Shinohara. Without the protection of the Constitution's second clause on attainders, the commission held the authority to seize related assets that belonged to Shinohara and his family, assuming, of course, that he perished as a result of receiving a death sentence. Indeed, Shinohara was still a sacred man in Agamben's sense of the term, and not only because he was deprived of what the court construed as his Japanese personhood. Shinohara remained a homo sacer because of his crossing into the zone of indistinction that comprised both American and Japanese sovereignties in Guam. To be clear, this "crossing" entailed a process that constituted an inclusive exclusion not with one "city" as per Agamben's theories on bare life and political existence but with two "cities"—Japan and the United States—claiming power over Guam. Crossing over into the United States thus required that Shinohara become a residential alien, but one condemned, as Judge Advocate Teller Ammons put it, as a "traitor."[80]

On the tenth day of the trial, August 8, 1945, the commission opened with additional treason charge I, specification 2, regarding the making of Dai Nisei, what the prosecution described as a Japanese labor organization in Guam.[81] A total of seven men for the prosecution testified, six of whom came from Chamorro-Japanese families: Jose Caesarius Blas, Jesus Cruz Hara, Juan Santos Okada, Jesus Carbullido Okiyama, Felix Flores Sakai, and Jesus Baza Sayama. The lone police officer and perhaps the only non-Japanese person was Juan R. Rivera. In his testimony, Rivera recalled how this group emerged as a labor organization for the Japanese military in February 1942. He said, "I was inside the office of the Menseibu when Mr. Shinohara came in talking to Juan Castro, the native in charge of the native policemen. Suddenly Castro called me over and directed me to inform the bunch of persons listed in a paper to appear at Shinohara's residence."[82] Castro then instructed Rivera to track the individuals, instructing them to meet at Shinohara's restaurant at 8 o'clock in the morning.

Jesus Carbullido Okiyama, one of the witnesses, filled in the details. At the first meeting with twenty to thirty Nisei present, he said, Shinohara "told us that the United States of America and the Imperial Government of Japan were in a state of war, and that the Americans had been pushing the Japs around for a considerable length of time and the Japanese could not stand it any longer and finally came to a show-down."[83] Okiyama then relayed how Shinohara categorized American racism as the grounds for localizing Japanese anticolonialism in Guam, saying that "the Nisei, the half-caste of Guam, had been pushed around by the Americans and the time has come when we shall do everything possible to help the Japs win the war."[84] The "act," as Okiyama remembered it, concerned Dai Nisei's role in providing "services to any of the established Japanese military units here."[85] With Shinohara identified as the founder and leader of Dai Nisei, Okiyama recounted that members of Dai Nisei helped "to build air fields" and other military facilities.

Although nobody agreed on the exact date of its formation, they confirmed Dai Nisei's existence from early 1942 to the summer of 1944 when the U.S. military invaded the island. Therefore, military conscription appropriately characterizes the kind of labor Dai Nisei performed for Samuel T. Shinohara. Member Jesus Baza Sayama, for example, worked at an "air base" and "dug tunnels for air raid shelters."[86] Others made "tunnels" at the district of San Ramon, built "air base transmission lines from Agana to the Agana Air Base," and performed biweekly "drills" at the San Antonio Plaza, among other tasks.[87]

On the thirteenth day of the trial, August 11, 1945, the prosecution entertained additional charge I, specification 1, wherein Shinohara allegedly assisted the Japanese military in taking Ignacia Bordallo Butler's electric generator. This "act" occurred in or about December 1941, an event not clearly verified by three witnesses employed by the prosecution. The owner of the generator, Butler, testified first and provided the most details. She asserted that Shinohara, an unidentified Saipanese interpreter, and three unnamed Japanese military personnel arrived at her residence in Hagåtña in early December 1941. One of the Japanese men was an officer who wanted her generator, kept in her basement, for unknown reasons. Fearing for the safety of her family and her husband, Chester Butler, who was an American prisoner of war in Japan, Ignacia Bordallo Butler did not resist the men's seizure of her generator. When the prosecution asked her to identify the U.S. manufacturer of the generator, she simply replied, "The Onan brand."[88] But the matter of theft was not established, as she recalled receiving "a slip of paper written in Japanese" from the group, which could have been a promissory note.[89] Yet Butler could not furnish the document for the court, as it was lost.

The ambivalence continued with the two last witnesses for the prosecution. Carlos Bordallo, the younger brother of Ignacia Bordallo Butler, mentioned having been present at her home during Shinohara's visit. At the request of his sister, he led Shinohara and the other men to the basement, opening its lock and witnessing the men load the generator onto a truck and leave the residence for an unidentified location. In support of the prosecution, Carlos Bordallo identified the three Japanese men as belonging to the "military," but he failed to make explicit the generator's role in advancing Japan's war efforts. As he noted, "I do not know where they were going to use [the generator] but it was going to be used."[90] Jose S. Okada, the final witness, clarified the generator's usage. As a former electrician for the Japanese navy, he claimed that the military transported the generator to a naval ship, where it powered film equipment to "show drama, news reels, and comics."[91] Yet Okada's argument was equally flawed. As the defense demonstrated, he never witnessed the "act" wherein Shinohara allegedly stole the generator in Hagåtña. Nor did Okada identify Butler as the owner of the generator, Onan as its manufacturer, or an unknown Japanese military officer as its heir apparent.

Undeterred by these contradictions and inconsistencies, the prosecution solicited the testimony of Galo Lujan Salas, a Chamorro cashier for the U.S. Military Government of Guam, to address the third case of treason on August 13, 1945. On the fourteenth day of the trial, Salas affirmed Shinohara's "act," original charge I, as the theft of "about" $9,300 on or about December 16, 1941, said monies being the property of the naval government of Guam. As one of two witnesses, he recalled the event occurring at the naval government's Records and Accounts Office, in Hagåtña, in the early afternoon of December 19, 1941. As the former cashier for the naval government, he confirmed that monies and records were stored separately in two vaults at this office. At that time, Salas alleged that Shinohara, two Japanese military officers, and four Japanese armed guards escorted him to the office, then housed in the R. E. Coontz building. As Salas recalled, "Shinohara stated that it is better for me to open the safe than to refuse or else I will be killed and then the accused told me he is one of the officials of the Japanese Imperial Government. Then I put my right hand up to my head still thinking what was I to do whether to open the combination or refuse."[92] While Salas was pondering his next course of action, Shinohara conversed with the Japanese soldiers, but Salas did not know what they were saying. Soon thereafter and without any warning, Salas said at the trial, "one of the Japanese soldiers tore my shirt under my right hand by his bayonet. I stated to Shinohara I did not expect those things to be done to me, but Shinohara insisted that I open the safe, so then I opened the combination for they were forcing me to do so or else I will be killed."[93]

Salas then recounted how Shinohara "opened the door of the safe," at which point "one of the Japanese officers came along and took all the money and papers in the safe that belonged to the Naval Government."[94] He estimated that the Japanese officer stole $7,639.41, a difference of $1,660.59 when one considers the commission's allegation that Shinohara assisted in the theft of $9,300. Despite this gross discrepancy, Salas emphasized repeatedly that Shinohara and the Japanese military officers "forced" him to open the safe containing the monies that belonged to three groups. They included the naval government, which owned $5,100 in cash; the Bank of Guam, which possessed $1,300 in cash; and several residents of the island, whose combined checks totaled $1,239.41. After opening the safe containing these monies, Salas then unlocked the combination for the vault holding the government records. The paper monies, he said, were placed in a white canvas bag, held by an officer, with Shinohara carrying the loose coins in another pack. Another Japanese officer took possession of the government records. Afterward, Salas described how he, along with Shinohara and the Japanese military personnel, left the Coontz building and walked to the former U.S. Marine Barracks. On his way, Salas recalled, he saw Vicente Zafra, the chief commissioner of Guam, standing beside the road. Although Galo Lujan Salas did not identify the person or individuals who stored the monies in the Marine Barracks, another building occupied by the Japanese military, he offered ample evidence to suggest that Shinohara participated in the theft of funds variously owned by the Bank of Guam, local residents, and the naval government. However, the second witness, Vicente Zafra, failed to describe anything resembling theft.

The prosecution then presented additional charge I, specification 3, to conclude its fourth and final case on treason. The tribunal alleged that Shinohara on or about April 1942 supplied the Japanese military and naval forces with provisions and refreshments, an "overt act" whose legitimacy rested on the testimony of five Guamanian witnesses. The first person on the stand, Vicente M. Taimanglo, a truck driver, acknowledged Shinohara's role in opening the bar, Omiya Kaikan, on February 16, 1942. As the former bartender and cashier for the officer-only club, Taimanglo stated that Shinohara often organized several parties for Japanese naval officers. As he explained, "In case an officer came, he would go to the list [of priced food and drinks] and pick out what he wanted in the list, then that was prepared and served to him by one of the girls, then a bill will be ready for him and he pays one of the girls and then the girl turned over the money to me."[95] According to Taimanglo, Shinohara coordinated an "opening party," a "farewell party" for the governor, and "only by invitation" parties with Chamorro "girls."[96]

The last and fifth witness for the prosecution, Steward First Class Jorge E. Cristobal, then translated the bar's name, Omiya Kaikan, in an effort to define the club as a government locale. He claimed, "Omiya, the word literally translated means shrine, temple or a place of worship. Kaikan is a hall not necessarily a small building, but it is considered an assembly hall. Those two words together I would say: Omiya Kaikan is an assembly hall for either a church, court officials or nobles."[97] If one believed, as Cristobal presumably did, that the offering of provisions to the Japanese military in an "assembly hall" counted as an "overt act" of treason, then Samuel T. Shinohara clearly betrayed the United States. How did the defense counsel refute such allegations? In the next section, I address this question by further exploring the racisms and technical contradictions of the court.

In Defense of Shinohara

In the remaining days of the trial, Lieutenant Emory L. Morris of the defense counsel featured eight witnesses to counter these charges alleged by the commission. In addition to his first witness, Francisco T. Flores, he employed nine witnesses in the last five days of the trial, whereas the prosecution utilized thirty-six witnesses, nearly a 300 percent difference in number, over an eighteen-day period. But rather than address each charge and specification, the defense counsel focused on only a few allegations. For reasons not explained to the commission, the defense did not compel its witnesses to appraise two treason allegations—original charge I and additional charge I, specification 1—and the prostitution allegation, original charge IV, specifications 1 and 2. This is not to say, though, that the defense counsel did not entertain these issues in the closing argument. Regarding additional charge I, specification 3, for example, the defense counsel argued that Shinohara never furnished drinks and food (e.g., beef, cake, ice cream, soda, whiskey) for the Japanese military. Jesus S. Sayama, one witness for the defense, also stated that Omiya Kaikan was not, as the prosecution argued, an "assembly hall" for strictly government or religious purposes. In fact, Sayama troubled the notion that Shinohara organized parties for the Japanese military, since the Japanese Society of Guam, with Shinohara as its president, held events for Governor George J. McMillin and the U.S. Navy before the war.

With the "overt act" of provisions placed in doubt, Sayama then testified against another treason allegation, additional charge I, specification 2, which stipulated that Shinohara created Dai Nisei for the purpose of aiding the Japanese military. He explained that several groups were formed during this period, all with various ties to the Chamorro public, the Japanese community, and the Japanese military. Confounding the prosecution's position that Dai Nisei was the only group to assist the Japanese military, Sayama listed Kohatsu (a Japanese organization from Saipan), Nihon Jin Kai (Japanese Society of Guam), and Seinendan (Chamorro Young Men's Association) as having comparable ties to the military. Further, Sayama argued that Dai Nisei was not a militarist organization but was rather a group where young, mixed-race Japanese learned the Japanese language, including drills that would prepare them for fires and typhoons.[98] He also explained that one should not conflate the meanings of Dai Nisei as second-generation Japanese and Dai Nisei as an organization for second-generation Japanese. Addressing this vital distinction, Jesus S. Sayama mentioned having known some of the prosecution's witnesses, such as Jesus Carbullido Okiyama and Felix Flores Sakai, saying that they were, indeed, "Dai Nisei," second-generation Japanese.[99] Yet he hesitated to conjoin the double meaning of the term by assuming that these men participated in the Dai Nisei organizations.

After exhausting their witness testimonies on two treason charges, the defense counsel temporarily ignored the other treason allegations and proceeded to address the lesser charges. Two of their witnesses, Lourdes Anderson and Margaret Anderson, came forward with respect to additional charge III, the desecration of the U.S. flag. Their point was simple: Shinohara never placed the U.S. flag on the floor of Omiya Kaikan. Nor did Shinohara steal an American vehicle owned by Lieutenant James E. Davis. Refuting the property claims of the prosecution, the defense counsel even called on Bishop Miguel Angel Olano to testify against this charge.[100] On the contrary, they argued that the Japanese military had seized all vehicles in early December 1941 and not two months later, into the new year. As Bishop Olano stressed, "After two days of occupation, all cars were confiscated by the Japanese Government."[101]

On the charges concerning the assault and battery of Governor George J. McMillin, the defense counsel did not directly ask its witnesses if these acts occurred. These allegations emphasized that Shinohara "slapped" McMillin on three separate occasions: December 10, 1941; January 1, 1942; and January 20, 1942. The defense counsel instead drew from the testimony of Shinohara's wife, Carmen Torres Shinohara, and his daughter, Cecilia Torres Shinohara. Yet they did not fully examine the chronological and topographical contradictions previously outlined by the prosecution and its witnesses. The closest approximation to this effort came when the defense counsel stressed that the prosecution's Chamorro witnesses could not have seen the assaults that allegedly took place in Hagåtña. If they did, they offered vastly different accounts of the time and place. The court also erred in identifying January 20, 1942, as one of these dates when McMillin, along with other prisoners of war, had already departed for Japan ten days earlier.[102] The defense counsel maintained its skepticism with respect to the other dates, knowing that the men of the Insular Force, segregated as a group across the Plaza de España, were among a large crowd of six hundred

American and Japanese military personnel and were located far from the vicinity where Shinohara allegedly slapped McMillin.[103]

In his closing argument, Lieutenant Morris reiterated these fictions. He likewise insisted on the innocence of Samuel T. Shinohara, whose actions, following the 1907 Hague Regulations, adhered to the international laws on occupation and property. Take, for instance, the commonly cited English version of article 43, wherein the occupant is obligated to "take all measures in his power to restore and ensure, as far as possible, public order and [civil life]."[104] When the law was originally debated at the Brussels Declaration of 1874, the authors of the article sought ways to protect local inhabitants, thereby compelling the occupant to restore their daily life as quickly as possible. But by the mid-twentieth century, occupants often read this duty as the "authority to prescribe and create changes in a wide spectrum of affairs."[105] In either case, the occupant, like Japan, had the right to conduct itself as per international law. The expansive meaning attributed to "public order" and "civil life" in article 43 was no less ambiguous than article 53 and its clause on "property." In countering the prosecution's charges on theft and treason, the defense counsel specifically invoked the second section of article 53, which read, "All appliances, whether on land, at sea, or in the air, adapted for the transport of persons or things, exclusive of cases governed by naval law may be *seized*, even if they belong to private individuals, but must be restored and compensation fixed when peace is made."[106] As Lieutenant Morris expressed, "The evidence is clear and complete to the effect that the Japanese authorities, as the occupant power, had the right to seize all automobiles in Guam; and did seize them on 10 December 1941, and within the next few days following that date."[107] As with article 43, there exists wide latitude in the meaning attached to article 53, whose first section stipulates that "an army of occupation" can take possession of properties belonging to the enemy state.[108] Yet, as evidenced in its second clause, the occupant can take the properties of "private individuals" as well, provided that such properties are either restored or compensated upon the declaration of peace. With this broad sense of ownership, the defense counsel asserted that the Japanese authorities possessed the "right of requisition" (1) to confiscate all automobiles; (2) to take the money and checks belonging to the U.S. and the naval government; and (3) to remove Ignacia Bordallo Butler's electric generator.[109]

But when it came to the prostitution charges, the defense counsel floundered in its attempts to absolve Shinohara. With respect to Alfonsina Flores, for example, the defense counsel revoked the specification of "misrepresentation," stating that her case was one of "duress" in light of her fear of being killed or punished by the Japanese military. Lieutenant Morris then blamed the Flores family and not Shinohara. As he put it, "This girl's older sister, Alice, had been at the Kerner home one or two weeks. She apparently liked it there and arranged for her younger sister to come and join her. Gentlemen, the proper people to be charged of this crime are the father, the mother and the other people involved, and not [Shinohara]."[110] Although the defense counsel hinted at a complex web of prostitution among the Flores family and others, Morris did not pursue this angle any further. He instead discussed the specification concerning Nicholasa P. Mendiola as having no grounds for duress. Because of Mendiola's statuses as a "vagrant" and an unmarried woman, the defense counsel argued that she entered into prostitution "voluntarily."[111] Further, Shinohara should not have been charged with treason as the "two witness" rule was not uniformly applied in the specifications. With regard to the charges concerning the Dai Nisei organization, the defense counsel simply asserted that Dai Nisei never functioned as a group of laborers for the Japanese military.

In lieu of these arguments posed by the defense counsel, the military commission and judge advocate convened and determined their findings. With no precedent in U.S. law on the matter of charging a residential alien with treason, they turned to the English case of *De Jager v. Attorney General of Natal* (1907) as an international authority on treason. Specifically, the commission cited the Crown's successful prosecution of De Jager, a citizen of the South African Republic who lived in a British territory. During the Boer War, De Jager accepted an official position in the South African Republic forces.[112] After the war, the Crown read his act as high treason, eventually convicting De Jager of this charge for failing to maintain his allegiance to the Crown. For the tribunal, this English case provided an international precedent to justify the court's proceedings. Along these lines, the commission issued its statement on the twenty-third and last day of the trial, August 27, 1945. It found Shinohara guilty of every treason charge and the lesser specifications, except original charge II regarding the theft of an American vehicle and additional charge II concerning the desecration of the U.S. flag. As Judge Advocate Teller Ammons said, "The Commission, therefore, sentences him, Samuel T. Shinohara, a civilian, to death, to be executed by hanging the said Samuel T. Shinohara by the neck until he is dead, two-thirds (2/3) of the members of the Commission concurring."[113]

As homo sacer, the military commission included Shinohara within the fold of the U.S. nation, only to be cast out and sentenced to death as a nonsacrifice. As per naval law, the U.S. secretary of the navy, the Office of the Judge Advocate General, and other legal experts then determined if Shinohara's death sentence was fully justified. As he awaited the review of his death sentence, Shinohara dwelt in solitary confinement at the War Criminals Stockade in Guam. In the next section, I discuss how he reflected upon his future despite having remained silent during the entire trial. As a person charged with the highest crime against the state, Shinohara saved a few words for its highest figure of naval authority, its secretary.

To the Honorable Secretary of the Navy

Almost a year later, on July 4, 1946, Colonel James Snedeker of the Military Law Division evaluated the legal merits and flaws of Samuel Shinohara's trial. In a memo addressed to the navy's Office of the Judge Advocate General, he found no fault in the lesser charges. But Colonel Snedeker disputed the commission's findings on treason. For instance, he observed that "nothing in the laws of the United States warrants the conclusion reached, and international law, as such, is equally devoid of justification for this holding."[114] Given the potential implications of this case, Colonel Snedeker reasoned that the judge advocate general "may be in order to re-examine the pre-trial opinion and to reconsider whether or not Shinohara is properly chargeable with treason."[115] His concern partly hinged on the U.S. failure to protect Shinohara, as a resident alien in Guam, from the Japanese occupation; without such protection, the United States had no basis to try Shinohara.[116] Additionally, Shinohara's status as a Japanese citizen "was compellable to perform acts for his sovereign state when that state completely occupied and controlled Guam."[117] As a subject "duty bound" to Japan, he should not have been charged with treason in the first place. Based on his internal assessment of the trial, Colonel Snedeker recommended that the original and additional charges on treason "be set aside."[118] But should these charges on treason remain, he recommended that Shinohara "be afforded the opportunity of having the Supreme Court pass upon the principle involved."[119]

Unbeknownst to Shinohara, though, the Office of the Judge Advocate General would not address Colonel Snedeker's memo until spring 1948, almost three years after he received the death sentence. In the meantime, Shinohara solicited the legal assistance of Fredrick T. Suss, a lieutenant in the U.S. Naval Reserves. Their first course of action concerned the preparation of affidavits in an effort to appeal the court's judgment. On October 18 and 19, 1946, for example, Lieutenant Suss compiled affidavits from four individuals, two of whom had previously assisted the prosecution.[120] One of these, Kyomon Miwa, took responsibility for forming the Dai Nisei Young Men's Association, whereas another man, Juan Santos Okada, disavowed his affiliation with the same organization. Shinohara then submitted a five-page affidavit on November 3, 1946, which raised several issues.[121] One concerned his imprisonment by the U.S. Navy: first, from December 8 to 10, 1941, and, second, from August 23, 1944, to the time of his trial and postsentence confinement. In the former case, the navy never informed Shinohara as to why he was incarcerated; in the latter, the navy offered no explanation until July 20, 1945, eight days before his court case began. At that time, Shinohara received only two thirty-minute consultation periods from a defense counsel not of his choosing.

Moreover, the defense counsel refused to call on eight of his recommended witnesses, a group of Chamorro and Japanese men. Likewise, Shinohara encouraged Lieutenant Morris and Vicente Reyes to contact former naval governor George J. McMillin, knowing that he survived the war and could be available for the trial. Yet the defense counsel rejected this request as well, as much as it refused to entertain Shinohara's disagreements with the translation of Chamorro and Japanese terms during the trial. And when he pleaded with the defense counsel to speak as a witness, Lieutenant Morris and Reyes ignored him. Speaking in the third person, Shinohara wrote, "That he desired to take the stand in his own defense and requested this of his counsel who told him that his word had no weight before the court and though he urgently desired to deny the charges brought against him and to testify in great detail, he was thwarted in this regard."[122] Once the findings were issued, however, Lieutenant Morris asked Shinohara if he would like to testify in mitigation. But before Shinohara could respond, Reyes, a Guamanian, silenced him. As Shinohara recalled, "Reyes stated in words to the effect that Japan had lost the war and there was nothing to say."[123] But there was much to say in his petition to "The Honorable Secretary of the Navy," James Forrestal, on January 2, 1947.

With the guidance of Lieutenant Fredrick T. Suss, Shinohara authored a forty-four-page petition that highlighted the critiques expressed in his personal affidavit, a military lawyer's review of his trial, and the defense counsel's closing argument. These issues included the commission's lack of due process, its disavowal of international laws on property, and its selective interpretation of the "two witness" rule. At the same time, some topics appeared in his petition that were not addressed by his defense counsel. These included the ambiguity in the wording of the charges and in the everyday cross-examinations among the witnesses, as in the conflating of Shinohara with unidentified officers (e.g., "they") rather than isolating Shinohara as the accused person (e.g., "he").[124] Comparably, Shinohara noted how the periodization of "in and about" in the charges enabled the prosecution to broadly determine the timing of said charges.[125]

He also opposed biases of the commission, as demonstrated in the court's overruling of the defense counsel's attempt to strike any testimonies on the Japanese shooting of the U.S. flag across the Hagåtña harbor. As Shinohara observed, he had nothing to do with these events. But with the war still raging between Japan and the United States, he correctly surmised as to how the image of a damaged U.S. flag replaced "considerate judgment with unreasonable passion for it kindled the flame of outraged patriotism which was already aglow in the heart of each American officer on the Commission. That the court had in fact abandoned cool, considerate judgment in favor of passion and prejudice is shown by the fact that it failed to strike out such improper evidence on the motion of the accused."[126] Although he revealed nothing about the passion and prejudice of the Japanese empire, Shinohara astutely unpacked the American and Chamorro racisms and technical and legal contradictions of the court.

With respect to the Chamorro-Japanese and Japanese witnesses, many of whom had families incarcerated by the Americans, he described how their fear of an unknown future dictated the content of their testimonies more than any search for justice. As Shinohara ascertained, "Many of the witnesses against the petitioner were of Japanese blood and had parents confined by the American forces in the local stockade. They were fearful of being momentarily seized by the Americans and thrown into prison because of their ancestry."[127] As for the Guamanian witnesses, he argued that those who testified against him were "fearful of the troubled times and were most anxious to impress the Americans with their own loyalty by condemning him whom the Americans accused of being a traitor."[128] As he rightly noted, "A fair trial under such circumstances is well nigh impossible."[129] But contrary to his efforts to remain impartial, Shinohara infantilized the "Chamorro people, who, as witnesses, have proven to be as unreliable as children, telling the court what they think it wishes to hear and with no regard for the truth of their oaths."[130] He gave the example of the five Guamanian men who accused him of slapping the former naval governor George J. McMillin, the same McMillin who was now "willing to testify on behalf of the petitioner" in an attempt to disprove these charges.[131]

In his petition to Secretary Forrestal, Shinohara shared these and other views as a residential alien in Guam, his preferred status after the war. Taking this position, he accepted the sovereignty of the United States, always remaining "complete and sincere" in his allegiance to the nation.[132] As if to subvert the zones of indistinction, he decried what was perhaps the most fundamental legal issue of the case, a point alluded to in his affidavit but altogether suppressed in the trial. That is to say, Shinohara argued that the tribunal held no jurisdiction to prosecute him, as the protection owed to him by the United States was removed when he was incarcerated on December 8, 1941. As he noted, the "Naval Government did in fact withdraw this protection . . . by the evidence which showed that soon after war was declared, the petitioner was seized by the government and thrown into prison with other Japanese nationals. Thus the government unmistakably indicated by its action that it chose not to accept the temporary allegiance which the petitioner owed to it, but instead regarded the petitioner as an enemy from whom no allegiance was expected."[133] The absence of an arrest record, the lack of witness testimony about his alleged crime, and the government's silence on the role of the Enemy Alien Act in Guam led Shinohara to believe that the United States "had terminated whatever allegiance was owed to it by the petitioner by removing the protection upon which it was founded."[134]

On April 28, 1948, the Office of the Judge Advocate General finally reviewed Shinohara's trial, but it did not reference his petition in its report. Overall, its assessment paralleled the initial critique offered by Colonel James Snedeker, USMC, of the Military Law Division. But the opinion of the Office of the Judge Advocate General differed in its view that the United States could legally try Shinohara and in its recommendation to set aside specific charges. Whereas Snedeker urged that all treason charges be removed, the Office of the Judge Advocate General still found Shinohara guilty of treason with respect to additional charge I, specifications 1 and 2, regarding, respectively, the theft of a generator and the mobilization of Dai Nisei. The other shift in the navy's internal purview of the case concerned former naval governor and Captain George J. McMillin. In a statement addressed to the Office of the Judge Advocate General, McMillin "unequivocally denied that the accused struck him in the face or otherwise on the dates specified or on any other date."[135] As Shinohara had been trying to say all along, he never assaulted the naval officer. As a result, the Office of the Judge Advocate General dismissed all charges related to assault and battery. On July 8, 1948, John Nicholas Brown, acting secretary of the navy, addressed these reports, to which he said: "[It] is not clear in my mind that the offenses actually constituted treason. This point of view is not taken on legal grounds, but is based purely on a lay reaction to the circumstances as I presently see them. I would appreciate an explanation which would clarify this point and establish the offenses as war crimes."[136]

After having analyzed the acting secretary's memo and the other internal reports, G. L. Russell, judge advocate general of the navy, issued the following recommendation eighteen days later: "In view of the foregoing, it is the opinion of the Judge Advocate General that a sentence of fifteen years at hard labor to be executed in Japan is commensurate with fairness and consistent with the law and existing regulations."[137] On August 24, 1948, Acting Secretary Brown, replied in kind. Concurring with the judge advocate general's conclusion, Brown proclaimed that "the sentence of death, to be executed by hanging by the neck until dead, is hereby commuted to imprisonment at hard labor for a period of fifteen (15) years. Time served in confinement by Shinohara since the thirteenth day of October 1945, shall be regarded as time served with respect to the sentence commuted."[138] Shortly thereafter, the navy transported Shinohara to the Sugamo prison in Japan, where he completed his sentence, after which time he returned to Guam to live with his family.[139] But because the navy upheld additional charge I, specifications 1 and 2, Shinohara, as homo sacer, remained a traitor to the United States, guilty of high treason, and symbolically expunged from the nation. The navy likewise sustained the lesser and original charge IV, prostitution, with specifications 1 and 2, demonstrating its commitment to protect its "properties" in Guam.

Reforming the Japanese American in the Military Colony

As this treason case and precedent reveal, the U.S. Navy's War Crimes Tribunals Program incarcerated Samuel Takekuna Shinohara to demonstrate the reach and violence of its rule of law. The navy's racialization of him as a Japanese enemy and foreigner signaled a militarized brand of the "yellow peril" that had to be expunged from the nation so as to frame the United States as a virtuous country.[140] The Guamanian and Chamorro-Japanese testimonies about innocence, patriotism, and victimization consequently provided the foil from which these legal determinations of Japanese war criminality drew their moral and political legitimacy. Once again, we witness here the political life of indigenous knowledge and retribution—the proverbial ko'ko of Guam—in codetermining the direction and force of the court and its proceedings. But because the commission and senior naval officials commuted Shinohara's death sentence, he was remade into a model Japanese American of Guam. By way of gossip, statecraft, and theater, his trial publicly informed the Issei and Nisei that they, too, could rid themselves of any criminal tendencies, absolve their imperial pasts with Japan, and become reformed residential aliens of the military colony. Although the shifts in national and geopolitical perceptions of Japanese and Japanese Americans would take fuller shape in the 1950s, Shinohara's contentious war crimes case foreshadowed popular American convictions that Japan had transformed from an external enemy and subversive threat to a democratic partner in the Cold War era of empire.[141]

6

JAPANESE MILITARISTS

With Samuel T. Shinohara represented as a traitor to the United States, punished as a nonsacrifice to the nation, and reformed as an ethnic minority in Guam, the tribunal addressed the remaining seven trials concerning allegations of Japanese atrocities in the islands of Guam and Rota. The cases involved only Japanese defendants, as the court never jointly prosecuted Chamorros and Japanese from the police and military units. Instead, the tribunal segregated them because of their perceived national, political, and racial identifications. In this chapter, I examine seven trials wherein the court understood the accused Japanese as treacherous and violent, akin to its systematic portrayal of Rotanese and Saipanese as practitioners of modern slavery and torture. This is especially notable in the first four cases on assault and battery, wherein the wartime actions of Akiyoshi Hosokawa, Kanzo Kawachi, Kyomon Miwa, and Hirose Ogawa came under the judgment of white American jurists and native Guamanian witnesses alike. In the next two trials, the court accused Tadao Igawa and Matsukichi Kobayashi of murdering Chamorros in Guam. At stake for these Japanese nationals was whether or not they assaulted or murdered Guamanians believed to have known or assisted George Tweed, the last surviving American sailor on the island. The Japanese military and police viewed Tweed, a radioman, as a threat to their daily operations. Matters of espionage and the possession of weapons—allegations said to have challenged the authority of the Japanese empire—also came under consideration. In these respects, these six cases on assault, battery, and murder demonstrate how white supremacist punishment and statecraft colluded with native retribution in the shaping of the military colony in Guam.[1]

In the seventh and final murder case, the tribunal addressed the question of Japanese military violence in Rota, an island under the sovereignty of Japan. Despite the fact that American laws did not apply there, the tribunal prosecuted three Japanese men accused of murder. Faced with potential death sentences, Shigeo Koyama, Yoshio Takahashi, and Akira Tokunaga confronted the commission's allegation that they organized the executions of five men in Rota, an island located north of Guam and another home to Chamorro clans. But unlike the previous rulings that focused solely on Guam, the court defined these men's war criminality as a militarized brand of the "yellow peril" that had to be eliminated from the territory of Rota.

Japanese Militarism in Guam

With the exception of Samuel T. Shinohara, the tribunal uniformly treated the Japanese nationals as "prisoners of war," a classification that accorded them the agency of male combatants. At the same time, every Japanese national was made into "an inhabitant of Guam," as if to demonstrate their familiarity with *The Guam Penal Code* and other U.S. laws. In this sense, the court employed the principle of discrimination between combatants and noncombatants in seemingly paradoxical terms. By codifying and making punishable native and Japanese war criminality, the tribunal thus upheld the political order of the military colony.[2]

In the four assault and battery cases that follow, Kyomon Miwa was a teacher and the only man to plead guilty. On the other hand, Akiyoshi Hosokawa, Kanzo Kawachi, and Hirose Ogawa were officers and enlisted men in the Japanese Imperial Army or Japanese Imperial Navy who asserted their innocence. They likewise refuted the jurisdiction of the United States in Guam. Whatever their rank, the military personnel also saw their authority as superseding decisions made by civilian officials during the U.S. invasion of Guam in the summer of 1944.[3] How the tribunal perceived this chain of responsibility amid a collective and among individuals likewise mattered in these trials.

In the first case on assault and battery, for example, the tribunal revoked Sergeant Major Akiyoshi Hosokawa's claim that his superior officer Tosin Koda was responsible for torturing the Guamanians Manuel Q. Lizama and Joaquin Santos Salas in early June 1944. Opined Hosokawa, "The orders that I received from the lieutenant in charge of the military police [Tosin Koda] were that to question these fellows, and also to stress punishment if necessary if I find them telling a false statement."[4] Despite his efforts, the prosecution maintained that Hosokawa, a member of the Military Police and the Twenty-Ninth Infantry Division, had unjustly punished these two men.

When he was called to the stand, Manuel Q. Lizama, a gardener, argued that Sergeant Major Hosokawa arrested him on June 7, 1944, for possessing a rifle and knowing the whereabouts of George Tweed, the last American sailor in hiding. Lizama denied both accusations. Not believing him, the military police officer beat Lizama on two separate occasions at the Kempeitai headquarters in Tutuhan, a small mountain located directly above the capital of Hagåtña. On the day of his arrest and first interrogation session, Lizama recalled, "the accused started whipping me with an automobile fan belt and then started hitting my head with a book and also he hit me with his closed fists."[5] Two days later, Sergeant Major Hosokawa jumped on the thighs of Lizama while he was in a kneeling position; the military officer also threatened to take his life with a sword. Afterward, Hosokawa detained Lizama in the Hagåtña jail. On June 13, 1944, the American military then bombed and destroyed parts of the police facility, thereby allowing Lizama to escape the prison. Ultimately holding Akiyoshi Hosokawa responsible for said assault, the tribunal eventually found him guilty on September 13, 1945, and sentenced him to one year in prison.

The second trial began shortly thereafter, on September 17, 1945. Charged with fourteen specifications of assault and battery, the forty-year-old naval police officer Kanzo Kawachi reconnected with his alleged victims in the space of the courtroom. They included the Guamanians Baltazar J. Bordallo, Pedro Dueñas Camacho, Isabel Taitano Cruz, and Joaquin Limtiaco. Of these witnesses, only Joaquin Limtiaco appeared in the earlier cases concerning the Rotanese and Saipanese police officers and interpreters.[6] In the trial, he accused Kanzo Kawachi of arresting him on the suspicion of assisting Americans during Japan's occupation of Guam. Recalling his beating at the Hagåtña jail in April 1944, Limtiaco said, "The accused questioned me about Americans. I told him I did not know anything about the Americans so he told me to open my mouth and he took his revolver and pointed it to my mouth and then he started pulling the trigger. After that he commenced kicking me, then he took his revolver again and placed it to my ear."[7]

Another witness for the prosecution, Pedro Dueñas Camacho, confirmed Kawachi's history of torturing individuals associated with the missing American sailor. After being summoned, Camacho and his wife, Mabel, arrived at the Hagåtña jail, where they were instructed to sit and wait for Kawachi. It was a Sunday in April 1944. Two hours later, they met Kawachi and the Saipanese interpreter Pedro Sablan Leon Guerrero. Aware of the new allegations against him, Camacho immediately confessed to having assisted other Americans in September 1942, a crime for which he had already been punished. Camacho also insisted on having no relationship whatsoever with George Tweed. Along these lines, he recalled, perhaps with some irony, how the naval police officer used an "American made" gun as a way to extract information about the American.[8] As Camacho observed, "I told him I did not know anything about Tweed; then . . . he kicked me, hit me with his pistol and finally he stopped and told me that he would take me to the Army Military Police to be killed because I was telling a lie."[9] Given that military executions emerged after the American bombing of Guam in February 1944, Kawachi's threat was legitimate. But before the naval police officer could continue, Mabel Camacho intervened. "I got up," she remarked, "and told the accused that my husband didn't know anything about Tweed and that if he kept on [beating my husband with the pistol] that I will report him over to the military police. Then the accused told me that my husband was telling a lie and that he knew about the Americans but would not say it."[10] Now standing, she continued with her account: "Then I said to him that he did not know anything about it and made him understand that I knew some of the officers in those days and that if he kept on with the punishment, I will report him."[11] In response to this counterthreat, Kanzo Kawachi "quit" the interrogation.[12]

Whereas Mabel Camacho protected her husband, Pedro, from further punishment, other Chamorro women lacked the political capital to challenge the authority of the naval police officer. Isabel Taitano Cruz was one such person. On June 3, 1944, Kanzo Kawachi arrested her for wearing a hat that supposedly belonged to George Tweed. Initially, Cruz asserted that she never knew anything about Tweed, at which time Kawachi tortured her with a bullwhip and a ruler over a three-day period, causing bruises to Cruz's back, legs, and shoulders. Kawachi also sexually assaulted Cruz in the presence of other police officers. As she noted at the trial, "He asked me if I was pregnant and I said, 'No,' then he said, 'Come over here' and so I went over to him and he was feeling me over my breast, pressed my stomach and feeling my—I can't say that—and so he was laughing with the others. There was Pedro Leon Guerrero and a couple more Japs. All acted as if they were having lots of fun."[13]

Perhaps fearing rape or death, Cruz relented to Kawachi's interrogation. Admitting her knowledge of Tweed's hat, she confessed, "A lady friend of mine gave me a hat. The sun was hot and she asked me if I would like to wear Tweed's hat and I said, 'I don't care if it's anybody's hat, it was so hot, and I will wear it.' So I took the hat home and threw it away. It was worn out."[14] Afterward, Kawachi showed a picture of "Mr. and Mrs. Tweed and baby" to ascertain if Cruz truly knew the man. She did. As Cruz admitted, "He had been around my place and . . . I cannot help knowing him, because I was around his house," indicating a potential relationship between the two.[15] Whatever the case, she promised to help the Japanese civilian and military police locate the missing American sailor. If she had succeeded, she would have received an award in the amount of two hundred yen and government support for her family. She would have never had to work another day in her life.

It is doubtful, of course, if Kanzo Kawachi would have rewarded Isabel Taitano Cruz or others for locating George Tweed. Instead, the converse proved true. That is to say, such interrogation tactics culled what the sociologist Lisa Hajjar describes as "forward-looking information of security value" from various individuals.[16] In this way, the logics of security and insecurity orchestrated everyday life in the Japanese colony. The last witness for the prosecution and a prominent Chamorro politician affirmed this truism. Baltazar Jerome Bordallo, also known as "B.J." among Guamanians, testified that Kanzo Kawachi and two unidentified Saipanese men kidnapped him on August 17, 1943. Taken from his residence around one o'clock in the morning, he was led to the Hagåtña jail, where Kawachi and other police officers tortured him for five days. As Bordallo recounted, "The routine was to ask me questions about the whereabouts of Tweed; and I would answer every question that I did not know where Tweed was, and then the beatings begins. Sometimes they beat me up standing, and sometimes the two Japanese would tell me to get down on my fours and hit me on my back. I remember the last beating I received and that was to tie both my limbs and hang me to a beam, and I received . . . at least 40 lashes on my back."[17]

When he could no longer bear the pain, he thought about the safety of his wife and their thirteen children, at which point he made an agreement with Kawachi.[18] "The essence of the contract," said Bordallo, "was that if I don't find Tweed within 20 days I was to turn myself over to the Japanese authorities and forfeit my life. The contract was written in Japanese."[19] Yet neither Kawachi nor other Japanese officials executed Baltazar Jerome Bordallo after he failed to locate the American sailor nearly three weeks later. Because Bordallo did "not break under torture," Kawachi believed he was innocent.[20] The defense attorney Lieutenant Henry P. Bakewell hoped that the tribunal would feel the same way about his client.

In his case, the naval police officer blamed "Kimura," the chief of the Naval Police, for ordering Kawachi to abuse the Chamorro men and women suspected of knowing George Tweed. Further, Kawachi knew nothing about two of his purported victims, Pedro Dueñas Camacho and Joaquin

Limtiaco, let alone Mabel Camacho's story of wartime resistance. As his defense counsel asserted, the "accused maintains unshakenly that he has never seen them before."[21] Nor did the naval police officer strike Isabel Taitano Cruz, the Chamorro woman accused of wearing a hat owned by an American. As Kawachi put it, "I did not have anything to do with the punishment of Isabel Taitano Cruz."[22] He also assured the court that no sexual molestation took place. "Since I noticed that lots of these women in Guam have big stomach, I think I asked her whether she was conceived or not."[23] Kawachi merely followed orders.

As evidenced in other trials, the U.S. Navy's War Crimes Tribunals Program rejected efforts on the part of the defense to levy responsibility on higher-ranking Japanese officials. By denying Lieutenant Bakewell the opportunity to question Kanzo Kawachi's chain of command, the tribunal found Kawachi guilty of assault and battery, except for one specification concerning Baltazar Jerome Bordallo. The court then sentenced Kawachi to a prison term of six years and six months at the Island Command Stockade in Guam. These carceral logics also applied to Japanese nationals who expressed remorse (figure 6.1). As the only person to plead guilty, for example, Kyomon Miwa accepted the consequences for hitting Maria C. Siguenza in November 1942.

As the defendant in the third trial on assault and battery, Miwa explained how he deeply regretted punishing Siguenza for failing to follow his instructions as a teacher. The incident took place outside the classroom, in the village of Asan. As he stated at the trial, "We were out in the rice paddies cleaning up the parasites. So during working hours, I told half of the children to go on the right and the other half to the left side. Work had started already, and I happened to notice that they were not doing their work. Some of them were giggling, some were talking and doing some eating."[24] After repeating his orders four times, he turned to Maria C. Siguenza, a child who happened to be near his side. As Miwa remarked, "I told her twice to stop eating. I think she was eating a mangoe [sic], but she did not take my word. So I hit her on the head lightly, then I asked her whether that would make her listen to my orders. Much to my surprise I saw that her head was bleeding."[25] He then brought Siguenza to the hospital, where she received medical treatment; afterward, he returned her home. Miwa also reported his actions immediately to the education superintendent at the Menseibu. Seven days later, the Army Medical Department reprimanded him for beating a child, an act that violated the rules and regulations of teachers.[26] As such, an unidentified soldier then struck the back of Miwa's head, causing

6.1. Japan's surrender to the United States. The original caption reads, "Japanese POW at Guam, with bowed heads after hearing Emperor Hirohito make announcement of Japan's unconditional surrender" (photo number 490313, Rec. August 15, 1945). U.S. National Archives, College Park, Maryland.

it to bleed. Now under trial with the military tribunal, he continued to share his guilt and accept whatever consequences may come his way. Because of his frank confessions under both regimes of rule, the court sentenced Kyomon Miwa to six months imprisonment at the Island Command Stockade in Guam. His trial began and ended on September 20, 1945.

The fourth and last case on assault and battery was just as brief. At the end of a trial held on October 12 and 13, 1942, the tribunal found another Japanese national guilty of torturing seven Guamanians: Joaquin A. Charfauros, Manuel B. Cruz, Joaquin Limtiaco, Pedro Q. Sanchez, Vicente S. Sanchez, Jose F. Topasna, and Jose Q. Topasna. As witnesses for the prosecution, the men variously claimed that Hirose Ogawa, a naval police officer, clubbed, kicked, punched, or whipped them at the Hagåtña or Humåtac jail in September 1942, October 1942, or September 1943. In each allegation, very little context was provided with regard to how the naval police officer investigated these cases. The court represented him as a Japanese militarist, a racialized caricature that complemented its native Rotanese and Saipanese counterparts. Now subjected to the American empire, Japanese nationals like Hirose Ogawa became "American" by federal,

JAPANESE MILITARISTS 187

international, and military laws that recognized them as threats to society, on the one hand, and by court rulings that banned them from political life in the colony, on the other.

Executing the Ko'ko of Guam

The last three murder trials focused on the Japanese military executions of Chamorros in Guam and Rota. In this section, I examine the military commission's separate treatments of Tadao Igawa and Matsukichi Kobayashi, two Japanese nationals charged with murdering, respectively, the Guamanians Vicente Lizama and Vicente Sablan Baza in June 1944. Although the court addressed related atrocities in subsequent years, its rulings on Igawa and Kobayashi concluded its assessment of Japanese militarism in Guam. That the court ended with the spectacle of execution demonstrated its efforts to present a range of Japanese war criminalities across the tribunal's threshold of zoē and bios. In the construction of these deviant types, Japanese war criminality meant alien, traitor, and minority, as with Samuel T. Shinohara; it also signified a militarized brand of the "yellow peril" that was to be expunged from the nation.[27]

On April 10, 1945, the tribunal began its proceedings with Matsukichi Kobayashi, a cook and mechanic for the Kempeitai.[28] The court accused him of executing the Guamanian farmer Vicente Sablan Baza in June 1944. Along these lines, the prosecution called on Baza's daughter, Beatrice, to explain how Matsukichi Kobayashi came to murder him. She said, "My father was taken by the Japanese twice. The first time he was taken, I went to find out because I understood he was going to be locked up."[29] After receiving information from the Saipanese Nicolas T. Sablan, Beatrice Cepeda Baza found out that her father was imprisoned at the Hagåtña jail on suspicion of possessing a gun. She then requested to bring food to her father every day, which she did at the discretion of the Japanese police. But when the American bombings increased in June 1944, Baza noted that her "father escaped from jail because the jail had been bombed already."[30] "On that same day," she continued, "the Japanese came to get him."[31] Yet neither Beatrice Cepeda Baza nor her mother, Teresa, knew what happened to Vicente Sablan Baza. Whether this was a genuine or staged observation, Teresa Baza could only say, "I do not know."[32]

The testimony provided by the Saipanese Jose P. Villagomez may have been a surprise for the Baza family. On behalf of the prosecution, he said that Matsukichi Kobayashi and other members of the Kempeitai arrested

Vicente Sablan Baza at his home in Yoña. They then returned to the Kempeitai headquarters at Tutuhan. Around six o'clock in the evening, they departed for Fonte, a nearby valley. The police officers and interpreters also dug two graves. One was for Baza, another was for Vicente Lizama, a fellow escapee. Initially, the Japanese police officer Kamitani intended to execute Baza, but Kobayashi intervened. As the witness Nicolas T. Sablan observed, "Kamitani held his sword with his two hands and said to the accused, 'Let me strike him because my sword is new; it has not been used.' Then the accused asked to do it himself and he used the sword of Kamitani. Vicente Baza was the man who was beheaded at this time."[33] Kobayashi said, "Let me kill him."[34] Remembering the execution, Jose P. Villagomez concurred, explaining, "The accused was facing north and raised up his hands like this. Baza was kneeling like this and sort of stooping forward facing the hole, when he was struck. The head was not entirely separated from the body.... [The sword] went through his throat completely except for the skin of the front part of the throat."[35] The execution party then covered the bodies with dirt.

When he had the opportunity to speak, Matsukichi Kobayashi admitted to murdering Baza but only because he was ordered to do so. Rather than express a willingness to kill the fifty-nine-year-old farmer, he revealed his commitment to upholding "an order to decapitate" given by First Lieutenant Koda of the Kempeitai.[36] Kobayashi understood his interaction with Kamitani at the execution site as such: "On the way out, I said to Kamitani, 'Please, lend me your sword,' Kamitani said, 'My sword is new, I do not know whether it will cut or not,' then Kamitani said, 'This is my sword so I will like to try it,' then I said to Kamitani, 'Since I have been ordered to do this execution, I will do it.'"[37] Now feeling remorse for his actions, Kobayashi stressed that he did not work for the Kempeitai at his "own request."[38]

In his defense, Lieutenant Alexander Akerman did very little to examine the chain of command responsibility in the murder of Vicente Sablan Baza. Simply urging the commission to "vote for acquittal," the defense attorney claimed that Matsukichi Kobayashi showed "no malice aforethought."[39] He was not guilty for this reason, a position refuted by the prosecution. Eventually found guilty of murder, Kobayashi was sentenced to imprisonment for life.[40] But whereas Kobayashi received a relatively quick trial, one that disclosed few details about the execution of Vicente Sablan Baza and Vicente Lizama at Fonte, the case regarding Tadao Igawa proved otherwise. Unlike Baza, who had no ties to the American military, Lizama previously worked for the U.S. Navy, a fact not lost on the American members of the tribunal, who saw him as "property" of the United States. Hence, more attention was accorded to Lizama's trial. On February 8, 1946, the military court consequently addressed Igawa's violation of American sovereignty by charging him with the murder of Vicente Lizama sometime in June 1944. Originally employed as a police officer for Japan's South Seas Government in Tinian, Igawa received orders from the Japanese navy to work in Guam. He arrived at the island on September 9, 1942, where he assumed the responsibilities of an officer in the Kaigon Kebetai or the Naval Intelligence Police. With an impending American invasion in June 1944, police officers like Tadao Igawa then fell under the jurisdiction of the Kempeitai headquarters in Tutuhan.

At the time, the Guamanian Vicente Lizama was imprisoned at the Hagåtña jail because of his affiliation with the U.S. Navy. The Japanese police believed that Lizama, a former enlisted man with twenty-five years of service, posed a security threat to them. As his wife, Vicenta Q. Lizama, explained, "He was suspected of being a spy for being a long time in the U.S. Naval service and that because he had a gun. The gun, however, was turned over to the Japanese during the early occupation."[41] Testifying for the prosecution, she said that her husband had fled the jail when the American military bombed and destroyed parts of the building. When Vicente Lizama returned to his family in the village of Yoña, he did not fear the Japanese police. As his wife disclosed, "He told me this: 'I do not have to hide because I have done nothing wrong.'"[42] This reassuring remark provided only temporary comfort for Lizama's family, as the Kempeitai search party, led by inspector Tadao Igawa, found him in June 1944. The Saipanese interpreter Jose P. Villagomez made the arrest.[43]

The search party then met another group of civilian and military police officers, who had recently captured Vicente Sablan Baza. The two cases merged here. The group then delivered the Chamorro prisoners to Sergeant Major Akiyoshi Hosokawa at the Kempeitai headquarters in Tutuhan. According to Villagomez, he left the police station to have lunch around eleven o'clock in the morning. When he returned at around five o'clock, he found Vicente Lizama and Vicente Sablan Baza tied to a camachile tree. The Kempeitai then released them, at which point the execution party was formed. The thirteen-member squad consistent of Antonio Camacho, Antonio R. Camacho, Vicente Camacho, Pedro Sablan Leon Guerrero, Hirata, Akiyoshi Hosokawa, Tadao Igawa, Kamitani, Kato, Matsukichi Kobayashi, Kowachi, Nicolas T. Sablan, and Jose P. Villagomez, all of them personnel assigned to police units in the army and navy. A few were instructed to carry picks and shovels. All were preparing to walk to Fonte, a valley located approximately five hundred meters from the Kempeitai headquarters.

As a member of the execution party and as a witness for the prosecution, Sergeant Major Akiyoshi Hosokawa argued that Lieutenant General Takeshi Takashina ordered Tadao Igawa to behead Vicente Lizama.[44] With Igawa designated as the executioner for Lizama, the thirteen-man squad left for Fonte. Once there, several of the Chamorro and Japanese police officers dug two graves, one for Lizama and one for Vicente Sablan Baza. Two meters apart from each other, Lizama's grave lay north-south, whereas Baza's grave lay east-west. The men stood above their graves. A coconut tree separated them, with a mango tree nearby as another marker of the site. Igawa adorned a formal Japanese naval uniform, with a sword dangling by his side, whereas Lizama wore the navy dungaree shirt and pants of an enlisted man. The contrast between authority and subjugation could not have been more stark: while Vicente Lizama appeared haggard and rankless with his older American navy attire and slippers, Tadao Igawa dressed in a naval uniform with his rating of one star and one anchor attached to his collar.

At the trial, Sergeant Major Akiyoshi Hosokawa described the moments leading to the execution. As he recalled, "We just dug the grave and asked the deceased if he had anything to say. He said, 'I would like to have a cigarette.' That is all."[45] But Vicente Lizama, now blindfolded, did have something to say for the Saipanese. As the interpreter and witness Nicholas T. Sablan noted, "Before he was made to kneel, Lizama said these words: 'Farewell, Saipanese . . . we will meet in front of God.'"[46] By not faulting the American or the Japanese colonial governments for his execution, Lizama implied that Chamorros from Rota and Saipan were responsible for his death, an action that only Yu'us, or God, could forgive or condemn. The naval police officer Tadao Igawa then swung his sword at the neck of Vicente Lizama, severing it in one stroke. Matsukichi Kobayashi also executed Vicente Sablan Baza, but because this trial focused solely on the murder of Lizama, the court only confirmed the death of the two men. The Japanese officers then ordered the Saipanese interpreters to straighten the bodies of Baza and Lizama. The men filled the graves with dirt and said a prayer. Afterward, the group returned to the Kempeitai headquarters, where Tadao Igawa reported to their supervisor, Lieutenant Koda, and informed him of the successful execution.[47]

More than a year later, in October 1945, eight members of Vicente Lizama's family, the Guamanian police officer Juan Fejeran, and the Saipanese interpreter Nicolas T. Sablan arrived at the grave site in Fonte. After Lizama's body was exhumed, his wife, Vicenta, identified the false teeth and clothing as belonging to him. At the trial, their daughter, Soledad Lizama Concepcion, also related, "We first found the skull, next the upper limbs, then the back bones and the lower limbs, and a pair of home made sandals."[48] "I recognized," she said, "the false tooth, the gold tooth and the initials [V.L.] on the sandals which the deceased was wearing."[49] With the death of Vicente Lizama established and with the four men claiming to have witnessed his execution, the military tribunal then called Tadao Igawa to the stand. When asked if he knew the name of Vicente Lizama, he replied, "I have forgotten the name of the person but I think that was the man I killed."[50] Expressing amnesia about his violence, Igawa simply sketched a scene of military order and obedience in the colony. Stressing that the execution was "legal," he said, "The reason why I believed it was a legal execution was because it was a general's order, and I was told also by our company commander [Lieutenant Koda]."[51] Igawa commented, "In my mind this is not murder."[52] Further, Igawa observed that Lizama had to be killed because he posed a security threat to the Japanese military. For this reason, Lieutenant Koda was "rather happy" with Igawa's arrest and execution of Lizama.[53] But a few minutes into his cross-examination by the prosecution, Igawa expressed remorse: "Since this was the first execution I had known I never heard of any objection or anything said of not doing the thing as told. . . . Not that I wanted to decapitate the native but the orders came from the higher authorities and I had to do it."[54]

Tadao Igawa's defense counsel, consisting of Second Lieutenant Edmund S. Carpenter and Sergeant Calvin W. Dunbar, similarly asserted that Igawa received orders to kill Vicente Lizama. As homo sacer, Igawa ultimately represented the bios of Japanese militarism and war criminality, acts that existed outside the "civilized" laws of war. As the defense counsel stated, "It is difficult for the western mind to understand the exact position of the Kempetai [sic] because we have never had a similar unit in our armed forces."[55] They concluded that "although the method of execution may first appear both frightful and unpleasant to the English mind, yet that is not true of the Oriental who sees in it a religious and cultural significance."[56] Comparable to the tribunal's portrayal of the Rotanese and Saipanese as masters of slavery, water torture, and other atrocities, the court similarly recognized nationals like Tadao Igawa as "Orientals" whose capacities for violence exceeded anything familiar to the United States.[57]

Tadao Igawa's criminality only mattered to the court insofar as his execution of Vicente Lizama constituted what the judge advocate called a "cruel and dastardly act" to be punished and expunged from the nation.[58] As Judge Advocate and Lieutenant William A. Buckles queried, "Could any civilized man, as we know a civilized man, draw back a large sword with both hands and then viciously, brutally, cruelly, with one powerful and crashing blow slash down on the helpless and defenseless figure before him with such force and violence as to completely sever the head from the body, without having enmity of heart?"[59] On Igawa's premeditation, the judge advocate asserted that Igawa apprehended Lizama, submitted the prisoner to his superiors, wore a formal naval uniform, traveled with the execution party, and used a sword to kill Lizama. With his superiors Lieutenant General Takeshi Takashina and Lieutenant Koda believed to have passed away, on February 18, 1946, the tribunal sentenced the sixty-year-old naval officer Tadao Igawa to hanging by the neck "until dead."

Imprisoned at the War Criminals Stockade, Igawa was allowed to smoke cigarettes, write letters, and meet a Buddhist priest. The prison guards also inspected his cell in case he possessed an instrument with which he could "take his life."[60] On July 23, 1947, the acting secretary of the navy approved his death sentence. The tribunal then prepared his execution at the Joint Communications Activity Area in the village of Finegayan. On September 23, 1947, Marine Corps and U.S. Navy security officers informed Igawa that he was to be hanged the following day. When asked if he had any final words to share, Igawa replied, "I will speak here. I know no English, and during my trial I did not know what was said. My lawyer hardly talked to me. I have not so far received a copy of my trial. Due to these facts I cannot reconcile my self with the sentence of the court."[61] The Marine Corps officer in charge of the execution, Lieutenant Colonel George R. Newton, described Igawa's face as having a "worried, puzzled look" upon receiving notice of his execution. "After returning to his cell," wrote the lieutenant colonel, "IGAWA chewed his fingernails, picked at his arms and rubbed his legs. He conversed with the Priest fifteen (15) to twenty (20) minutes, showing excitement at this time. At 1600 he began to write, tore up his letter several times before finishing. From 2000 until 2230, when he retired, he read his prayer book and paced in his cell. He slept well, occasionally talking in his sleep, and was awaken at 0500."[62] In the afternoon and evening, Tadao Igawa wrote a few letters to his family and friends. To his father and mother, he said, "I would like to thank you for what you did for me while I was living and ask for your care for the others."[63]

To his wife, Yukiko, he remarked, "Since our marriage I have troubled you all the time without a moment of happiness and now with the ending of this day I am to climb the steps to be hanged. I greatly appreciate your service to me. Please take good care of our parents and children. This is all I ask of you." Regretful, he apologized to his partner, "I am very sorry to make you bear this great responsibility, but please think this is our fate and take care of yourself. Please give my best regards to our relatives and to the mother of Miyamoto. The weather is very good this morning. The leaves of the palm trees are shaken by the cool breeze that is blowing." To his children, Hiromi, Kohiko, and Ryuhide, Igawa stated, "Your father will be back home before you get this letter. But the life at home is very hard; so the 3 of you please help your mother and take good care of your grandmother and grandfather."[64] Refusing to submit to the tyranny of the tribunal, Igawa concluded with a poem:

> Being a person to be sacrificed
> I have nothing to say,
> I will ride the wind of the God
> And be purified today

Here, Igawa understood himself as a sacrifice for Japan, a telling contrast in terms of how the American military commission judged him as a war criminal and nonsacrifice.

In an act that resembled the execution of the U.S. Navy sailor Vicente Lizama, the tribunal then stripped Tadao Igawa of his military uniform, dressed him in a plain shirt and trousers, and handcuffed him at six o'clock on the evening of September 24, 1947. The Officer in Charge of Executions, Lieutenant Colonel George R. Newton, summarized Igawa's last steps as follows: "Accompanied by the Buddhist Priest IGAWA was led past the witnesses to the foot of the gallows. Immediately thereafter he mounted the scaffold; leg shackles, hood, and noose were placed, and IGAWA was dropped through the trap at 1951. Prayers were said by the Buddhist Priest. He was declared dead by the two (2) official Medical Observers at 2002, 24 September, 1947."[65] The official hangman was First Lieutenant Charles C. Rexroad of the U.S. Army.[66] But, according to the son of the Guamanian police officer Adolfo Sgambelluri, three police officers pulled the lever for the trapdoor (figure 6.2). Whereas one hangman was usually an American official like First Lieutenant Rexroad, the two other hangmen were often Guamanians like Adolfo Sgambelluri and Joe Gutierrez.[67] As the younger Sgambelluri explained, "All three would pull simultaneously the trap [to hang the accused], but nobody knew who really pulled to release the trap door."[68] Thus, these Guamanians may have executed Tadao Igawa. Whoever

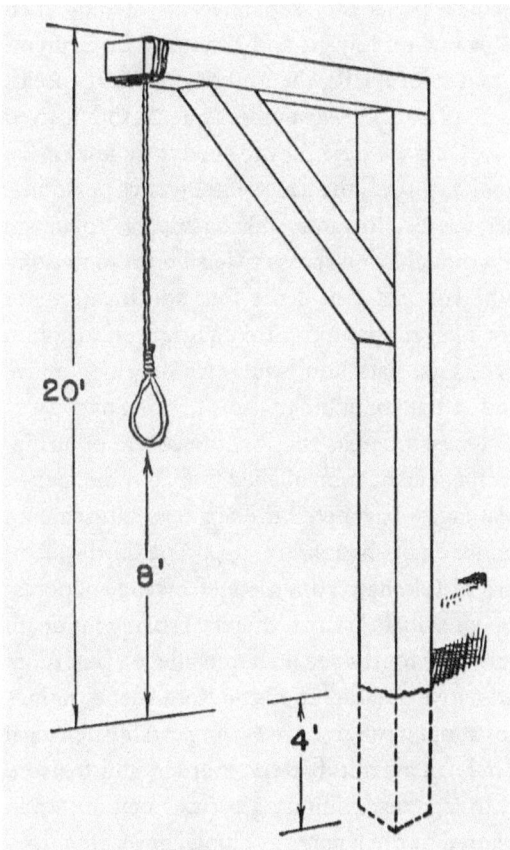

6.2. Diagram of equipment for execution by hanging. Image from Record Group 125, Records of the Office of the Judge Advocate General, War Crimes Branch.

committed the act is irrelevant. Their participation in the gallows merely illustrated the nexus of law, torture, and retribution.

The American Military Colony in Rota

In the final trial, on January 26, 1949, the tribunal accused three Japanese military personnel of murdering four Chamorros and one Spanish national in Rota, an island located immediately north of Guam. The Japanese nationals were Shigeo Koyama, Yoshio Takahashi, and Akira Tokunaga, former soldiers of the Imperial Japanese Army. Originally demobilized in October 1946, these men returned to their homes in Japan and found employment there. Whereas Tokunaga worked at a construction company in Kumamoto prefecture, Koyama and Takahashi labored, respectively, at a family farm and a public health center in Tokyo. Without the issuing of warrants and the disclosing of charges, the Japanese police then separately arrested the men in 1948: Takashi on May 2, Koyama on July 31, and Tokunaga on September 25. After processing the men at local jails, the American military police turned them over to the Sugamo prison. On November 17, 1948, they arrived at the War Criminals Stockade, Guam, where they resided in solitary cells. Nearly a month later on December 7, 1948, the navy's intelligence personnel at the War Criminals Stockade coerced Koyama, Takahashi, and Tokunaga into providing "statements" without having access to legal representation.

On December 10, 1948, the tribunal issued the four specifications of murder. The first specification alleged that Akira Tokunaga, then a captain and commanding officer of the First Battalion, shot "two unarmed native inhabitants of said Rota Island" on or about June 25, 1944.[69] One native was presumed to be Bonifacio Estebes, whereas the identity of the other native was "unknown." The second specification alleged that all three men—Koyama, Takahashi, and Tokunaga—bayoneted the Spanish national and Catholic brother Miguel Timoner on or about July 5, 1944. The third specification alleged that Takahashi and Tokunaga administered cyanide of potassium to a native believed to be Ignacio de la Cruz, thereby causing his death on or about July 5, 1944. Finally, the fourth specification alleged that Akira Tokunaga shot "one unarmed native inhabitant of said Rota Island, names to the relator unknown," on or about July 8, 1944.[70] Having established legal precedents in the previous trials on assault, battery, murder, and treason, the prosecution now turned to Japanese military atrocities committed in Rota, an island once administered by the Japanese colonial government.

As with the American occupation of Japan and its former colonies, the U.S. Navy's War Crimes Tribunals Program addressed the Japanese execution of five individuals in Rota not because of its supposed altruism for the Chamorro victims. Rather, as the historian Yukiko Koshiro asserts, the United States utilized its postwar regimes of governmentality to "make the Japanese comply with the American victors in the remaking of Japan and Asia."[71] At stake for the military tribunal was the sovereign future of Rota, a geographic, moral, and political template from which the court sought to assert American laws in Asia and the Pacific. As with the neighboring islands of Guam and Tinian, the U.S. military had seized these sites for the purpose of launching aerial assaults on Japan, with the atomic bombings of Hiroshima and Nagasaki in August 1945 being the most notable.[72] With Rota, the Japanese killing of one foreigner and four natives suggested that the Japanese government failed in its "civilized" efforts to rule its subjects and lands. Hence, the trial aimed to eliminate Japanese governance, on the

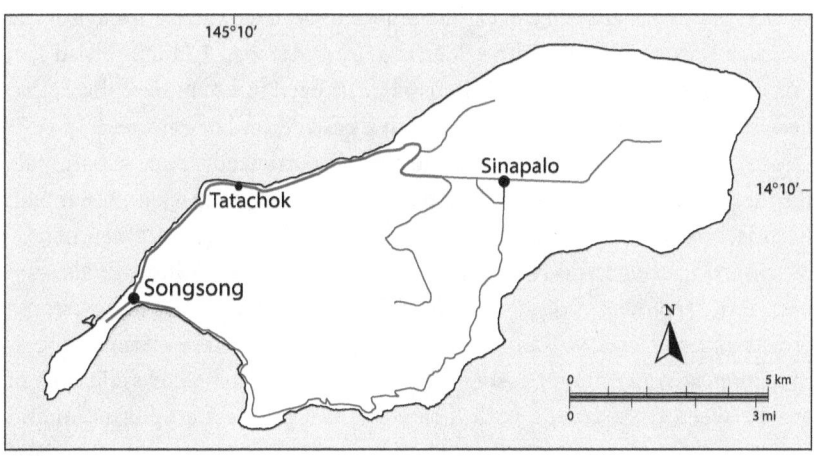

Map 6.1. Rota

one hand, and to assert white American claims to property, on the other.[73] As the political theorist Carl Schmitt explained, "In every case, land-appropriation, both internally and externally, is the primary legal title that underlies all subsequent law."[74]

In defending the Americans' right to jurisdiction and land appropriation in Rota, the prosecution cited a memo authored by Rear Admiral Charles A. Pownall on January 19, 1949. Reiterating the legal reach of the tribunal originally outlined by Admiral C. W. Nimitz's Proclamation No. 4 on July 21, 1944, the prosecution argued that the commission "shall have jurisdiction over all Japanese nationals and others who worked with, were employed by or served in connection with the former Japanese Imperial Government, in the custody of the convening authority at the time of trial, charged with offenses committed against United States nationals . . . and white persons whose nationality has not prior to ordering of the trial been established."[75] In this manner, the tribunal appropriated international laws of conquest and possession. The establishment of the Trust Territory of the Pacific Islands (TTPI) in 1947, for example, demonstrated the "lawful" ways by which American sovereignty extended into former Japanese colonies like Rota. As a charter of the United Nations, the TTPI terminated Japan's sovereign rule over its colonies in favor of the American construction of military bases and the American development of wage economies in these sites.[76] As the historian David Hanlon argues, "The veil of legitimization provided by internationally sanctioned treaties or arrangements often can be used to hide or even help promote the subordination of others. The 1947 Trusteeship Agreement between the United States and the United Nations over the postwar status of the Caroline, Mariana, and Marshall Islands served just this purpose."[77] In short, the United States utilized the TTPI to replace Japanese militarization in these islands with its own brand of empire.

Moreover, by 1949 the tribunal had already sentenced Japanese nationals for murdering Americans and Pacific Islanders in the Chuuk and Marshall Islands, areas once administered by the Japanese South Seas Government.[78] By asserting that various Japanese nationals murdered individuals suspected of "espionage" or spying, the court relied on the laws and customs of war as per the Hague Convention of 1907. Under these circumstances, the Japanese execution of suspected spies in Rota constituted violations of war between combatants, with little legal and political emphasis on and protection for civilians.[79] Knowing that the U.S. Constitution, the *Naval Courts and Boards*, and *The Penal Code of Guam* lacked judicial force in Rota, the prosecution therefore selectively applied Proclamation No. 4, the TTPI, and the Hague Convention to justify its jurisdiction over the accused Shigeo Koyama, Yoshio Takahashi, and Akira Tokunaga.

But the defense counsel differed on these matters of personhood and property. Consisting of Commander Martin E. Carlson, Junjiro Takano, and Sadamu Sanagi, the defense argued that the United States held no jurisdiction over the foreign, national, and native inhabitants of Rota. Citing the League of Nations' mandate that granted Japan's establishment of laws over the island, the defense counsel reasoned that Rota was an "integral part of the Japanese Empire."[80] As such, every person was subjected to the laws of Japan from 1914 to 1944, with the laws of the Japanese Imperial Army taking effect in the summer of 1944. These laws included the Criminal Code, an Ordinance for the Treatment of Judicial Affairs, Japanese Army Regulations, Law for Criminal Procedure, Law Relating to the Application of the Criminal Code, and Regulations Governing the Security of Military Secrets in the South Sea Islands, among others.[81]

In response, Judge Advocate and Lieutenant Commander Joseph A. Regan objected to the introduction of these "foreign laws" because they lacked relevance.[82] The military commission concurred. The defense counsel then urged the tribunal on January 20, 1949, to consider separate trials for Shigeo Koyama, Yoshio Takahashi, and Akira Tokunaga. They realized that because the defendants had provided statements to American intelligence personnel on December 7, 1948, these materials would have incriminated one or all of them. Take, for instance, the petition by Yoshio Takahashi, a surgeon in the army and a graduate of the Medical Department at the Kyoto

Imperial University. As he expressed, "These affidavits made at the request of American Naval Officers while I was being held in confinement without charge being preferred against me and without benefit of Counsel, if offered into evidence and proved, will if accepted, tend to implicate my co-defendants, one of whom was my superior and the other a subordinate."[83] Shigeo Koyama and Akira Tokunaga provided similar remarks to the court.

Further, the defense counsel motioned for a change of venue because "the action is brought in the wrong place or district, and because a military court here on Guam cannot legally try them for the offenses charged and alleged to have been committed on Rota Island."[84] On January 20, 1949, six days before the onset of the trial, Commander Martin E. Carlson asserted, "We are of the opinion that Rota Island is not a part of the military command of Commander Naval Forces Marianas. There is no inherent authority in the convening authority, a commander of naval forces only, to appoint this military commission to try three Japanese civilians for alleged offenses said to have been committed on Rota Island during the period from June 25, 1944 to July 8, 1944."[85] In lieu of holding their trial in Guam, the defense counsel preferred "a change of venue to Tokyo, Japan, Rota Island, or Honolulu, Territory of Hawaii."[86]

While the defense counsel did not fully elaborate on why it chose Honolulu, Rota, and Tokyo as potential venues for the cases, its rationale proved futile given that the military commission had conceded to the prosecution's claims and counterclaims. Yet in each case, the defense counsel and prosecution erased Chamorro land stewardship and political power in Rota. This treatment became apparent in their disagreements over jurisdiction and in their avowal of the Rotanese as noncitizen subjects of Japan. For example, the prosecution understood them as a "tranquil, and presumably obedient" population.[87] On the other hand, the defense utilized euphemisms to conceal the exclusion of Chamorros from the national polity. As the defense stated, the "Native inhabitants of Rota Island were not foreigners according to domestic laws of Japan. They were generally treated in the same manner as Japanese nationals."[88] Equally problematic, two of the accused Japanese nationals—Akira Tokunaga and Yoshio Takahashi—remembered the Rotanese as if they were mutual friends and partners in the Japanese empire. As Tokunaga explained, "The native population of Rota Island was approximately 800. . . . Their intelligence surpassed those of the resident Koreans and Okinawans, and they willingly volunteered to cooperate with the Japanese Forces."[89] Stressing that he had formed a "strong bond of friendship" with the Chamorros, he expressed, "I was overwhelmed with gratitude whenever I observed these people in my tours of inspection working side by side with the soldiers with sweat streaming down their muddy faces."[90] Yoshio Takahashi similarly observed, "As our relationship became closer, I came to know that they were like the Japanese who were willing to do their best for their country without knowing the tragic destiny awaiting them."[91]

As these comments reveal, Takahashi and Tokunaga subscribed to what the anthropologist Renato Rosaldo calls "imperialist nostalgia," or "a mood of nostalgia that makes racial domination appear innocent and pure."[92] By underscoring their supposed amicable relations with the Rotanese, they attempted to demonstrate their generosity and innocence to the military tribunal. As Rosaldo asserts, much of "imperialist nostalgia's force resides in its association with (indeed, its disguise as) more genuinely innocent, tender recollections of what is at once an earlier epoch and a previous phase of life."[93] Contrary to the romanticized memories of Rota, then, the Rotanese recalled a different set of circumstances than those described by the Japanese. Manuel M. Ogo, for example, labored for the Japanese military at a time "when friendships between Japanese soldiers and Chamorros were illegal and severely punished, even by beheading."[94]

With rumors circulating about their impending deaths at the hands of either the Americans or the Japanese, many Rotanese thus feared for their lives. With food shortages and the conscription of male laborers, they suffered greatly. As Ogo put it, "We all lost weight . . . even the Japanese who, of course, had first claim to the food that was produced."[95] Albert Toves, another Rotanese, likewise experienced the hardships of war, but from the lens of a native intermediary. Identified by his Japanese name of "Kondo Akira," he worked as a supervisor for a company that cultivated castor beans from 1936 to 1944. He also advised Chamorro, Korean, and Taiwanese harvesting crews in Rota and received a salary that "conformed to the standard salary for high-grade Japanese supervisors."[96] That status then changed dramatically when the American military began bombing Rota on June 11, 1944.

With the imposition of military law, Toves lost his job as a supervisor and became a cook for the Japanese Imperial Army. In the process, he witnessed the forced relocation of Chamorros from the village of Songsong to the village of Tatachuk. As a privileged person, however, Toves remained in Songsong with his family because of his culinary responsibilities for the army. But that was not the case for most Chamorros. As he stated, "Other

Chamorros had previously been evicted from Songsong and sent to live in [Tatachuk], a newly-created, apartheid-type village."[97] Toves then interacted closely with nineteen field commanders on a daily basis as he was their primary cook. At one meeting, he overheard them talking about how the war "was failing on all sides of us."[98] As he revealed, "I didn't have to listen very closely to what they were saying, for just looking at their faces told me all I needed to know. . . . It made me remember the signs that Japanese war-protestors used to put up along the highways in Japan that showed a ferocious fighting cock (America) shaking a baby chick (Japan) to death, and that had a sign printed under it that said 'a chick must not attack a rooster.'"[99]

As the remarks by Ogo and Toves demonstrate, Chamorros from Rota interpreted the war as disruptive and destructive. As a result, neither the defense counsel nor the prosecution took seriously the collective and contradictory notions of "America" held by the Rotanese. Unlike their portrayal of "loyal" Chamorros who often welcomed the return of the Americans to Guam, the court possessed no comparable caricature from which to present Americans as "liberators" in Rota. The Rotanese notions of Americans were too anticolonial, racially charged, or politically subversive. As Ogo disclosed, he and many native men were prepared to resist the American military: "Each one was ordered to equip himself with a sharp bamboo spear which he must keep constantly by his side so that when invasion occurred he could join in a banzai charge that would repel the American invaders."[100]

Casting the Americans as imperial aggressors, he added, "Under the direction of our honchos, we practiced our attack on imaginary hordes of American barbarians coming through the surf, who, if we failed, would surely cut off our ears and tongues and who knows what else, for that was their purpose in coming to Rota!"[101] To entertain these volatile memories of the war would have thus questioned what Aileen Moreton-Robinson theorizes as the "moral high ground" of national and international laws on possession.[102] By not including these Rota Chamorro narratives of place and by adhering to international laws on jurisdiction and land acquisition, the tribunal thereby presented itself as a virtuous and morally legitimate apparatus of wartime justice. How, then, did the final murder trial manifest the court's application of domestic laws on jurisdiction and international laws on espionage and land possession? In the next section, I discuss how the commission imposed these laws on three soldiers of the Imperial Japanese Army in Rota without knowing who, exactly, they executed.

The Five Unknown Victims of the War

In his opening statement on January 26, 1949, Judge Advocate and Lieutenant Commander Joseph A. Regan summarized the four specifications of murder levied against Shigeo Koyama, Yoshio Takahashi, and Akira Tokunaga. He explained that "while there were five individuals killed, there were three different incidents."[103] Representing the prosecution, Lieutenant Commander Regan said, "The killing of two natives on the 25th of June 1944 for which in this trial Tokunaga, alone, is being held responsible. On the 5th of July the Spanish brother Miguel Timoner was killed as a result of the activity of all three of the accused. On the same date, Ignacio de la Cruz was executed and for this Tokunaga and Takahashi, but not Koyama are accused. A few days later, namely on the 8th of July the fifth person was executed and for this Tokunaga alone is accused."[104] Yet the prosecution did not discern the identities of the men who died, that is, the four Chamorros and the one Spanish national. With the exception of the priest Miguel Timoner, the tribunal's charges did not divulge the names and occupations of the victims. At best, the Chamorros were "believed to be" Bonifacio Estabes and Ignacio de la Cruz; the "exact names" of the other two men were "unknown." Unofficially, however, American investigators contemplated whether anybody actually murdered Miguel Timoner. As one intelligence report revealed, American military personnel "have been unable to get a single Japanese to admit that he knows about the execution of the priest on Rota. . . . The Japanese insist all the people executed were natives."[105]

For these reasons, none of the accused Japanese soldiers ever claimed to have murdered Miguel Timoner, let alone a Spanish national. Nor did any of the Japanese witnesses recall or document the names of the Chamorro men. Without disclosing the names of the five victims, the tribunal then premised its proceedings on the dubious nature of their identities. This questionable position was likewise compounded by the court's failure to attract a large pool of Chamorro witnesses from Rota. Lacking the conflicts of the birds and lizards in Guam, the commission found no "loyal" Chamorros from which to merge their white racisms with native vengeance and retribution. And because the Rotanese could have levied criticisms against the Americans and Japanese, therefore jeopardizing the court's legitimacy, the tribunal remained relatively silent on the matter of native testimonies from Rota. With a few exceptions, the trial mainly focused on the knowledge and experiences of Japanese soldiers in the Imperial Army.

For the prosecution, establishing the role of espionage proved vital given the court's reliance on international laws of war and land possession. One of its key witnesses, Major Shigeo Imagawa, emphasized how the militarized environment of Rota created the conditions for spying. As he expressed, "After the U.S. forces landed on Saipan on June 15th [1944], what affected the Japanese Army and residents on Rota was the approaching of U.S. ships and there were frequent false reports which were spread around the island saying that the United States forces had landed on Rota and this resulted in confusion."[106] Anybody accused of spying was thus arrested by the military police. In Imagawa's estimation, espionage meant "a person detecting military secrets and disclosing them to the enemy, and who commits subversive activities."[107] Although he did not know the number of people detained and executed by the military police, he did indicate how Chamorro gossip informed the Kempeitai in its apprehension of spies among the native population.

What especially troubled the Japanese military was the Chamorro rumor that "in the event of a landing by the United States forces, they would at once run over to them and ask for their protection, by disclosing information of the Japanese units, and persuade and incite others to follow them."[108] With respect to the five unknown men, Major Shigeo Imagawa believed they were killed for possessing a notebook of army positions, "waving flags at planes or spreading cloths on the ground during daytime in an attempt to signal to the American planes."[109] As this soldier's testimony revealed, the Japanese military and police sought to suppress any form of native espionage. The circulation of anti-Japanese rumors—that is, marginal and covert perspectives—likewise demonstrated the range by which Chamorros variously understood the Japanese military occupation. But because the prosecution argued that the five men were killed as spies without trials, the prosecution determined that the court was obligated to evaluate the actions of Shigeo Koyama, Yoshio Takahashi, and Akira Tokunaga.

Regarding the first specification, the prosecution relied on its first witness, Yukio Yasui, to discuss the execution of two natives on or about June 25, 1944. As a former warrant officer and platoon commander stationed in Rota, he identified Captain Akira Tokunaga as the person responsible for delivering the order to shoot these men, one of whom was believed to be Bonifacio Estebes. As Yasui stated, Captain Tokunaga instructed him to "execute" two natives accused of espionage. In explaining how he attempted to refuse the order, Yasui remarked, "As I had no experience in executions by firing squad, I requested the battalion commander on receipt of this order, that he, the battalion commander take the natives elsewhere."[110] But Tokunaga dismissed Yasui's request on the grounds that the execution should occur immediately for he feared being bombarded by another American air raid. Eventually, Warrant Officer Yasui conceded to Captain Tokunaga's wishes and organized the execution in the village of Tatachuk. "I ordered six men," he said, "to be members of the firing squad. . . . After the preparations had been completed at the scene of the execution the battalion commander brought two natives to the scene and read to them their sentences of execution."[111] As with every Japanese witness, Yasui did not know the names of the men; he only recalled that they were handcuffed.[112] He continued, "I received the two prisoners and blindfolding them I stood them in front of the hole, ordering the three men on the firing squad on the right-hand side to aim at the victim on the right hand side and the three on the left to aim at the victim on the left side. I gave the order to fire."[113]

Other soldiers offered more intimate accounts of their roles as executors. For example, army Superior Private Kenichi Hosoya remarked, "No matter what kind of crimes these two men had committed, in my heart I thought it very sad to imagine the surprise and sorrow of the wife [sic], children, and aged parents who would be left behind when the families heard that these two men had been shot and had died." As a soldier lacking "the power to control these things," Kenichi Hosoya then said, "Up to that time there hadn't been a moment during which the gun I held felt heavy. I closed my eyes, and from the bottom of my heart I fervently prayed for the repose of their souls. . . . I vaguely remember the voice of Platoon Leader YASUI giving the order to shoot and the fact that my arms, hands, and fingers were all trembling."[114] Corporal Yoshimaro Sato, another member of the firing squad, observed, "We could not bear to execute those holding the same citizenship as ourselves and carried it out in a very solemn manner."[115] Taken from investigative records, these statements did not enter the court records as evidence. Yet the American intelligence officials presumed that Hosoya and Sato participated in the murder of two Chamorros, a point verified by their affidavits. But because the court had apprehended their commanding officers, Hosoya and Sato did not incur any charges.

With regard to the second and third specifications of murder, the prosecution enlisted the support of the only two Rotanese witnesses available to the tribunal. They included the former field laborers Ramon B. Blanco and Tomas Cruz Manglona, both of whom worked as messengers for the Kempeitai headquarters in the village of Tatgua. Along with other Japanese witnesses, they detailed the arrest and execution of Ignacio de la Cruz, a

Chamorro, and Miguel Timoner, a Spanish priest, on or about July 5, 1944. According to Tomas Cruz Manglona, the Kempeitai police ordered him to summon Timoner and de la Cruz. Although he did not know where the order originated, he acknowledged having seized the fifty-year-old Spanish brother and the seventy-year-old Chamorro artisan. Whereas Manglona characterized Timoner as "on the whole, white," he said nothing about the physical appearance of de la Cruz.[116] But he did note that the priest was an "energetic" Spaniard "always dressed in that habit."[117] On the other hand, Manglona described de la Cruz as a "man of many trades. He could make shoes and he could also make rings."[118]

The Kempeitai then escorted Igancio de la Cruz and Miguel Timoner to two execution sites, with the former being led to a jungle area beside the headquarters and the latter being directed to a nearby shelter with chairs and tables. Approximately 150 meters separated the two locations. What linked the second and third specifications of murder, then, was not only the simultaneous arrest of de la Cruz and Timoner but the manner in which they were meant to die. Following Captain Akira Tokunaga's order to execute these men, Second Lieutenant and surgeon Yoshio Takahashi attempted to kill them with poison. A witness for the prosecution and a former staff member of the medical unit, Yoshizaki Tokuichi identified the poison as "potassium cyanide."[119] He also saw Takahashi place the poison in coffee cups at the execution sites. Another witness, Corpsman Sergeant Major Takashi, recalled, "I left my work and went to the scene of the execution. There were one native and several soldiers. The native was made to sit down and Second Lieutenant Takahashi was saying something to him. In a little while some coffee was poured in a cup and a small portion of some kind of powder was put into the coffee and mixed."[120] Identifying Takahashi as the person who placed powder in the coffee, Corpsman Sergeant Major Takashi then stated, "This native drank this coffee but he spilled some from his mouth and he didn't drink very much. The native who drank this coffee pressed his stomach with his hand and fell backwards. In a little while this native who fell down got up and seemed to be in agony and the native was in this condition for a little while."[121]

Realizing that the "native" did not immediately die from the poison, Second Lieutenant Yoshio Takahashi sent a runner to Captain Tokunaga, requesting directions for the botched execution. When the messenger returned, the surgeon was informed to order Private Shigeo Koyama, one of the accused, to stab the native. The tribunal thus charged the soldier Koyama, the surgeon Takahashi, and the commander Tokunawa with murdering, by "bayonet," the priest Miguel Timoner. Several Japanese suspects and witnesses in Guam and Tokyo confirmed that these three Japanese nationals killed a man. Yet none of them referenced a foreigner. The second and final Rotanese witness, Ramon B. Blanco, then argued that Koyama "stabbed" Ignacio de la Cruz, a Chamorro who did not initially die from the poison.[122] But specification 3 insisted that de la Cruz expired from potassium cyanide poisoning and not from a bayonet wound. Despite the convoluted nature of these charges and testimonies, the prosecution ultimately asserted that Second Lieutenant Yoshio Takahashi staged the two murders of Ignacio de la Cruz and Miguel Timoner on or about July 5, 1944.

Shortly thereafter, Tokunaga ordered the execution of the last unknown native and suspected spy on July 8, 1944. As per specification 4, only Tokunaga was charged with killing this man at Tatgua. Suekichi Yoshimura, a former engineering warrant officer with the Imperial Japanese Army, followed the order. Now testifying for the prosecution, Yoshimura said, "I was ordered to execute a native by the company commander."[123] A clearing was then made in the jungle near the Kempeitai headquarters. After forming a firing squad of two men, Yoshimura instructed them to shoot the unknown native. The Kempeitai officers then buried the three men in unmarked graves near their headquarters.

As the only Japanese national accused of all five specifications of murder, former battalion commander Akira Tokunaga approached the stand first. In discussing his history as a military officer, he explained that he received his training at army military academies in 1936 and 1939, after which he was transferred to the First Regiment, First Division, in Manchuria. In March 1944, he then moved to Rota, where he led the First Battalion, Tenth Independent Mixed Regiment. At the young age of twenty-six, he supervised the operations of the army unit from March 1944 to September 1945, the latter date signifying his surrender to the Americans. But by June 1944, Tokunaga noted, Rota had become a "field of battle," with its civil administration barely operating because of the American assaults in Rota and Saipan.[124] As a result, he said, "There was no other way but for the army to take over the maintenance of peace and order of the civilians because Saipan Branch Office of the South Seas Government Office had ceased to function and the branch office on Rota had been demolished by bombing and it was almost impossible for it to function."[125] Given the collapse of the civil administration, Captain Tokunaga became the senior official among the civilians and military personnel in Rota. Reflecting on his challenges, he said, "It was my first experience since I entered the army in which I was placed in contact with the navy as well as the civilians. I felt that I was unequal to carry such an enormous burden of responsibility when I realized that I had to stand above all and direct matters concerning defense, liaison, and coordination work of the whole island, but I exerted all my efforts in that direction."[126]

In his new role as the military commander of Rota, Captain Akira Tokunaga then convened the island's leadership on June 14 to 15, 1944, to discuss this shift in governance. At these meetings, he emphasized that everybody had to follow military laws, natives had to provide laborers for the construction of fortifications, and nonmilitary personnel had to reside in newly created "safety zones" designated for the Chamorro and non-Chamorro populations.[127] Another stipulation concerned the matter of "subversive acts." As Tokunaga disclosed, the civil administrators and village representatives "were cautioned to be on the alert for subversive acts and acts of treason and spreading rumors, because such acts were prevalent."[128] Lookouts and patrols were thus formed, with each group scanning the island for individual acts of "treason," a term that placed the discussion in the realm of Japanese laws. By framing the discussion along these lines, Tokunaga resisted the prosecution's claim that the five unknown victims were "spies" whose murderers could only be judged within the context of international law. In Rota, only Japanese military laws applied during the time when these men died, that is, from June 1944 to July 1944. For the army, every order was lawful in its hierarchy of command responsibility.

Under these circumstances, individuals accused of treason suffered the penalties of imprisonment or death. As Captain Tokunaga reasoned, five natives were executed for violating the articles on treason in the Military Secrets Security Law and the Army Criminal Code. Although espionage constituted one of these acts, itself a treasonous crime, the criminal codes explicitly aligned with domestic military laws. On these matters, no reference whatsoever was made to international laws, including the Hague laws of war. Take, for instance, article 27 of the Army Criminal Code: "Those who have done the actions described in the following shall be condemned to death: 2.—To spy for the benefit of the hostile powers, or help hostile powers in espionage. 3.—To convey military secrets to the enemy powers."[129] Tokunaga then assigned several soldiers in the Kempeitai to separately arrest and interrogate five Chamorro men sometime in June and July 1944. Referring to several letters, secret notebooks, and bottles and clothes used for signaling purposes, the lower-ranking soldiers found that "these five men had conspired in their efforts to detect and gather military secrets, the conditions of the air field, the disposition of troops and armament of the military forces, and had passed this information on to the enemy and these five had been constantly engaged in this work."[130]

Other acts of treason included their efforts to "cut telephone wires and thereby [obstruct] operational movements." Continued Captain Tokunaga, "They signaled to enemy planes and ships by various methods and disclosed the position of the airdrome and of troop concentrations and guided the enemy in bombing and naval bombardment. They spread unfounded rumors and worked to break down the morale behind the lines and they planned to contact and to guide the American forces in the event of an invasion."[131] Shigeo Koyama, one of the three accused Japanese nationals, also claimed to have seen three incidents of treason unfold in Rota. Although Koyama failed to identify any individuals, he said, "When I was on the lookout duty from eleven o'clock in the night till three in the morning I frequently witnessed flash signals which seemed to be from a flash light."[132] On the second example of treason, he "frequently saw signal lights which went alternately from green to red. When a signal flare would go up from the land then rocket flares could be seen out at sea and it seemed as though they were signaling with each other."[133] Whereas he witnessed these two events from afar, he described the third and final instance of treason as occurring only a few moments before his arrival. In one patrol, Koyama noticed that burning charcoal "had been laid out in the form of an arrow pointing toward the [Sinapalu] air field in the day and when I saw this again it was all white in ashes. . . . I was able to observe that this form of signal could be used both in the day and the night."[134]

As these comments reveal, Captain Akira Tokunaga, Private Shigeo Koyama, and the investigating officers in the Kempeitai believed that the five Chamorro men had shared information with the American military, a point previously disputed by the prosecution and by the lack of any corresponding evidence. And when the court asked Captain Tokunaga to submit the bottles, clothes, and letters used in these acts of treason, he mentioned that all the materials were lost after the war. Nor did he organize a trial for the accused Chamorros on the premise that they lacked the facilities, as well as the capacity to transfer the men to Guam for further judgment.[135] Instead, he wired the commanding general of the Twenty-Ninth Division in Guam and sought his counsel. According to Captain Tokunaga, the unidentified commanding general ordered him to execute the five men because they had already been found guilty of the crime of treason. As he stressed, "We executed them because the Japanese Forces had to defend Rota Island

and punished these traitors in accordance with the laws which demanded the penalty of death for acts of treason."[136] Yet the matter of treason did not apply solely to the acts of five men, as Captain Tokunaga may have feared most the growing discontent among the wider population of Rota had he refrained from murdering the men. As he tellingly noted, "If this was left uncontrolled the number of such cases would have increased and would only go to accentuate and perpetuate these acts. The very character of this crime imperiled the defense of Rota and, ultimately, the fate of all the armed forces and residents on Rota."[137]

Every defendant, then, admitted to having murdered these unknown men, as Tokunaga, Takahashi, and Koyama did not dispute the nature of their charges. They merely challenged the authority of the military tribunal, its notion of espionage, and its reliance on international laws. As defense attorney and naval commander Martin E. Carlson insisted, "It is our contention that the five persons punished in June and July of 1944 on Rota were punished as traitors. International law does not apply in this instance."[138] Adamant that only Japanese domestic laws can address treason, he turned to American and English case laws as providing examples of owing allegiance to the country in which one resides. As Carlson asserted, "So we see that both English cases and United States federal cases hold that even aliens can commit treason against the country in which they are domiciled. All five persons described as having been killed in the specifications owed a duty of allegiance to Japan. The proof is clear and strong that all of these five persons had resided in Rota for many years and were bound to obey all the laws of Japan."[139] He even invoked American treason law in defending the right of Japanese laws in governing native "aliens." As Carlson concluded, the "persons killed were not spies but were traitors and saboteurs who committed overt acts openly as well as by stealth with the intent to give comfort and aid to the enemy, the American invasion force threatening to invade all the Mariana Islands including Rota Island."[140]

Attorney Junjiro Takano concurred with Commander Carlson's references to treason laws. But rather than call the Rotanese "aliens," a legal term familiar to American members of the tribunal, Takano used the phrase "quasi-Japanese subjects."[141] As he explained, "It is true that the natives of Rota Island of the South Seas Mandated Territory did not automatically assume the nationality of the Mandatory, Japan, but if they desired to become naturalized subjects of Japan, they were qualified to do so."[142] Takano asserted, "The natives of Rota Island stood in a peculiar relation to Japan. Thus, although they did not possess all the identical rights and duties of

Japanese nationals . . . they were treated in the same manner in many respects as Japanese nationals."[143] Comparable to the bare life of the Chamorros and Japanese in the tribunal, the Rotanese also came under the laws of Japan but were not entitled to its citizenship. The five men executed in Rota were thus expunged from Japan as nonsacrifices.

With the tribunal's claims to jurisdiction and land acquisition in Rota now at stake, Judge Advocate and Lieutenant Commander Joseph A. Regan defended the court's right to evaluate the actions of Chamorros and Japanese who never subscribed to the U.S. rule of law. On the matter of treason, he referenced the previous case of Samuel T. Shinohara, a subtext raised by the defense counsel. Refuting the implications this trial may have for the murder charges at hand, Lieutenant Commander Regan said, "I am not going into the argument by the defense about the Shinohara case and the case here. Shinohara was a Japanese who came to Guam and lived on Guam for many years. I know that Shinohara was tried for treason, or for acts which were called treason, back in about July 1945."[144] Disavowing Shinohara's position as a Japanese national and treating him as a residential alien who owed allegiance to the U.S. Navy and the United States, the judge advocate argued that his treason charge stemmed from having gathered "information for the Japanese." His abuse of American "properties" constituted acts of treason that aided the Japanese military in Guam.[145] For these reasons, Regan asserted that "the Shinohara case does not compare with the present one because here you have natives who presumably actively engaged in the business of spying."[146]

Judge Advocate and Lieutenant Commander Regan then remarked, "Let me say this, it is no part of the prosecution's case to prove that these men were in fact spies. All we have to show, and I am sure we have shown it, is that the Japanese who had the handling of them believed them to be spies."[147] Confirming his ignorance of the victims' identities and motives, he continued, "We don't know nor can any of us know whether Miguel Timoner, fifty some odd years old, or Ignacio de la Cruz, in his late seventies, went sneaking around Rota seeking information to pass along to the Americans. We'll never know that, but we do know from the evidence before this court that Tokunaga thought they did these things and thought they were spies."[148] As the trial concluded on February 16, 1949, the commission reviewed these arguments, including petitions for clemency. One petition illustrated Tokunaga's "good and righteous" character.[149] Another petition for Takahashi, the surgeon, described him as "humane, diligent, honest."¹⁵⁰ As for Private Koyama, his relatives begged to not lose their "prop and beam" of the family.¹⁵¹

In the end, the tribunal found Tokunaga, Takahashi, and Koyama guilty, sentencing them, respectively, to seven years, five years, and one year of imprisonment at the Sugamo prison in Japan. Cast as Japanese militarists, their punishment as war criminals and their expulsion as nonsacrifices from the nation came on the heels of a particular American appropriation of international laws on espionage and land possession. Making international law as its own, the tribunal extended its jurisdiction into Rota, the Marianas, and other non-American lands in the former Japanese empire of Micronesia. As the legal scholar Natsu Taylor Saito argues, American leaders often "rely upon the international law and legal institutions that justify their control over the lands, peoples, natural resources, and markets which allow them to maintain their hegemonic status."¹⁵² Had the court addressed the testimonies of more than two Rotanese witnesses, however, it would have further complicated the logics concerning espionage and treason, if not altogether questioned the imperial claims of both Japan and the United States. This is not to say, though, that the court entirely suppressed Rotanese agencies, as evidenced in the prosecution's brief disclosure that one victim "wore upon his body a tattooed American flag."¹⁵³ As the only reference to an American tattoo, it appeared as if the tribunal refused to entertain Rotanese affinities with the Americans.

In this regard, the language of spies not only invoked international laws for the purpose of suspending American domestic laws so that the American rule of law could be expanded beyond its national borders. Rather, spies meant that one aided an enemy without having a fixed notion of loyalty, as spies could represent an indefinite range of citizenships and nationalities in international law. Whatever the case, the fleeting mention of an "American tattoo" suggested that the tribunal had encountered a subaltern native memory that existed outside its domain of influence. Albert Toves, the Rotanese who went by the Japanese name of Kondo Akira, recalled that two Chamorros had this tattoo. One was Ignacio Manglona and another was Ignacio Cruz (or potentially Ignacio de la Cruz, one of the natives "believed to be" killed). According to Toves, Manglona was "eighty four years old, mild mannered and kindly, and maybe a little senile. He had once worked on a whaling ship and had gotten a favorite whaler's designed tatooed [sic] across his chest: a large heart containing an American flag."¹⁵⁴ The Kempeitai killed him for having the American tattoo. As Toves suggested, "So far as I know that was his only crime, but that was enough to get him tied to a tree up near where the Rota Hospital now stands, right out in the sun with a Japanese soldier standing near by in the shade to see that no one brought him food or water, and in about a week he was dead."[155]

Although Toves did not explain how Ignacio Maglona died, he revealed his frustration in not having the ability to assist the elderly man. As he mentioned, "It was hard on me to walk by him and hear him beg me for a cup of water, 'Albert, Albert,' he would plead, 'for Christ's sweet sake bring me water, for the sake of Christ on his cross, for the sake of our ancestors.'"[156] Fearful of how the soldier might respond to their interaction, Toves did not help Manglona. He instead imagined a response that reflected the colonization of all Chamorros—ko'ko and hilitai alike—across the archipelago. "There was nothing I could do," Toves said, "but explain to myself that this was the way things were and had to be accepted, just like you don't argue with earthquakes or typhoons—you just try to live through them."[157] Ignacio Cruz, "a light-skinned Chamorro and a former seaman," likewise died from bearing the same tattoo. He was accused of being a spy, as was Brother Miguel Timoner. As per Toves's memory, the Kempeitai beheaded Timoner for "waving a handkerchief at an American plane."[158] Another person executed by the Kempeitai was Bonifacio Estebes. But whereas the first specification of murder claimed that he was killed by a firing squad, Toves said that the Japanese military beheaded Estebes for pretending to read a Japanese newspaper. Yet the issue of reading was not a charge per se, as the Japanese military only levied the death sentence to any Chamorro "who was caught informing himself of the war's failure."[159] But Estebes was innocent of this crime, given that he "was retarded and could read nothing."[160] Based on Albert Toves's observations, the Japanese military executed at least three Chamorros and one Spanish national. Whether or not these or other men died by bayonet, beheading, firing squad, or poison, the tribunal had clearly established one fact: American jurists now viewed Rota as the property and possession of the United States.

The Japanese Militarists of the Mariana Islands

The tribunal's criminalization and racialization of Japanese nationals in Guam and Rota revealed the historical imbrication between white supremacist punishment and statecraft and native retribution and violence. In its treatment of seven trials on assault, battery, and murder, the military court transformed these Japanese men into militarists, enemies who were included in the nation only to be excluded as war criminals and violators of international law. Part of that metamorphosis entailed the questioning of one's faith in the Japanese empire. Take, for instance, the comments shared by Hirose Ogawa, a naval police officer who was found guilty of assaulting seven Chamorros. As he professed, "I was a naval military civilian of the Guam Civil Affairs during the Japanese period. I had to obey the orders of my superiors in the Japanese period. At the order of my superiors, I beat natives. Now, under the American government, this has become a bad thing."[161] Acknowledging his conversion, he said, "Hereafter, I absolutely will not do this kind of thing."[162] The naval officer Kanzo Kawachi likewise discussed how he shifted from "openly" torturing people to suppressing these beliefs and learning another brand of imperial justice. He appeared to embrace his faith in the American empire, claiming, "From now on I will study the democratic system of America and will devote myself according to the orders of America which is the world's leading power."[163]

In these court-induced confessions, these and other Japanese nationals not only revealed a change in their attitudes about Japan and the United States. That they explicitly marginalized the agencies of all Chamorros—Guamanians, Rotanese, Saipanese, and others—demonstrated that the birds and lizards never fully inhabited any nation. This disavowal was revealed in their absence of apologies directed to the Chamorro clans affected by their violence, as well as in their failure to grant Japanese citizenship to Chamorros. And if the "people of the land" (*taotao tano*) could be removed from their islands as political agents, then any colonial law could seize a territory devoid of native peoples, if not strip all semblances of them. To this effect, the military tribunal prosecuted Japanese nationals in Rota not only for their perceived war criminality but also for their purported claims to indigenous lands. By criminalizing their roles as belligerent occupiers and soldiers of the Japanese empire, the court rendered Japan's sovereignty in Rota as unlawful, uncivilized, and ultimately in need of a new political order.[164] As the historian Takashi Fujitani astutely argues, the biopolitical sphere of modern power finds significance in a person "insofar as she or he affects the strength of the state, either positively or negatively."[165]

Conclusion

As the trials in the U.S. Navy's War Crimes Tribunals Program reveal, the logics and tactics of incarceration, militarization, and possession manifested as the U.S. rule of law in Guam.[1] At least two points matter here. First, the military commission established itself to reclaim what Japan had illegally seized, namely, the *white American property* of Guam. White supremacist punishment and colonial statecraft emanated from this juridical claim and moral desire. As the critical ethnic studies scholar Dylan Rodríguez explains, the sanctity of whiteness must be projected and protected for fear of nonwhite incursions. As he argues, "Conceptualizing whiteness as a form of property, and white civic identity as a collective entitlement to ownership (of property, Others, and propertied Others), implies that when 'nonwhites' threaten, attack, or steal the common property of white civil society, they are actually violating the sanctified materiality, and the vicarious and deeply valued collective bodily integrity, of whiteness."[2]

Given that the U.S. Navy viewed the bodies and lands of Guam as its own, whiteness signaled a collectivity to be protected, a property to manage, and a virtue to aver and defend. The navy's prosecution of Japanese war criminals as per the history of anti-Japanese immigration in the United States, on the one hand, and as per the global shift to more inclusive regimes of governmentality, on the other, attested to these logics of white possession.[3] As with the Tokyo war crimes tribunal, its proceedings assessed Japanese war criminality in ways that "helped Americans understand at the same time what was good about the Japanese."[4] The wartime ideology of Japanese soldiers running amok and killing others with no regard for life underscored much of the white American and Chamorro racisms toward the Japanese as a vilified, monolithic society. But because the military commission viewed Japan as a rival nation, the tribunal dehumanized the Japanese in a manner that nevertheless accorded them a stronger degree of politics, that is, bios or political life. That is why the court treated the Japanese as "belligerent" occupiers of Guam and Rota and not only as "war criminals" who had to be reformed or eradicated from these islands. And yet the navy knew, like the broader American government, that "the continued exclusion of Japanese Americans from the national community threatened to undermine America's ability to win the war and the peace that would follow."[5]

For these reasons, the navy's tribunal represented its counsels, witnesses, and proceedings as humane and virtuous.[6] A reporter for the *Navy News*, a popular periodical in wartime Guam, celebrated this sensibility on October 26, 1947, stating, "The bringing to trial and meting out of justice to military criminals who over-stepped recognized bounds in World War II is in itself a great accomplishment. Under the jurisdiction of the United States Navy, military courts have successfully prosecuted and punished hundreds of the enemy who committed atrocious crimes against our countrymen."[7] In construing the personhood of homo sacer, the commission thereby relied on the logics of white possession and property. But whereas the court generally viewed the Japanese as "combatants," the tribunal judged the Rotanese and Saipanese as "noncombatants." The former were bios, people with politics; the latter were zoē, animals without politics. The crucial point is that the laws on war recognized combatants as the only legitimate category of personhood in the 1940s, thereby rendering the Rotanese and Saipanese men as the animals, the hilitai, and, as such, the most abject bare life of the court.[8]

As demonstrated in the more than one hundred Guamanian and Chamorro-Japanese testimonies featured in the trials, the tribunal relied heavily on the ko'ko-hilitai relation. This cultural and political process both collapsed and hardened the distinctions between animals and humans; for Chamorros, all lives—animal and human—are intertwined. But when lives are codified by the U.S. rule of law, native rumors determined which lives were more animal or more human than others. The ko'ko-hilitai relation, as testimony, thus gained relevance, meaning, and force in the law. Central to this indigenous network of power was the matter of torture. As Guamanians and Chamorro-Japanese witnesses drew on their memories of being tortured by the Japanese police in Guam, they collectively harnessed the lessons and power of native reciprocity and retribution. As the second and most vital part of my argument, the ko'ko-hilitai relation subsequently upheld the logics and tactics of U.S. incarceration, militarization, and possession as true and just.

Of Torture and Testimony

As many witnesses disclosed, Chamorros in Guam frequently recognized the subordinated positions of their faith and their families under the Japanese regime whenever they, under torture, used the refrains "Ay Yu'us!" (Oh, God!) and "Ay nåna!" (Oh, mother!). That they employed these phrases in separate interrogations and over a three-year period illustrated their indigenous collectivity as Guamanians as much as demonstrating Japan's incomplete project of colonizing them from "American" to "Japanese" subjects.[9] Very seldom did a person fail to confess; if he did not, he was killed. But one's submission or resistance to a confession did not guarantee one's safety. For these reasons, many people, mainly men, died from execution by bayonet, dynamite, firing squad, hanging, poison, starvation, and water torture. Japanese-appointed Guamanian commissioners called kuchōs and sonchōs often assisted in their arrests. As witnesses to these torture-induced interrogations, they affirmed the power of Japan's empire in Guam only to later testify about Japan's demise in the navy's tribunal.

That the Japanese, Rotanese, and Saipanese interpreters and police officers tortured many individuals in Guam demonstrated the degree to which an ideology of hate, a diminished legal and moral inhibition for violence, and a culture of legitimate violence against an "enemy" had congealed along the axis of a militarized masculinity.[10] As the anthropologist Alexander Laban Hinton elaborates, killing another person "tends to become easier when perpetrators are desensitized to violence, internalize violent ideologies, dehumanize their victims, undergo moral restructuring so that violence becomes morally justified, use euphemistic language that masks their deeds, and displace responsibility onto figures of authority."[11] For the Chamorro men from Rota and Saipan, they clearly embodied a militarized masculinity that served "two essentialized master binaries," that is, the colonized/colonizer and the man/woman.[12] As young men, they were expected to follow their obligations with one or more clans and especially with their elder relatives. In fact, all of the Rotanese and Saipanese men had relations in Guam. Their labor, construed as *che'cho lahi* (men's work), was used to farm the land or fish the sea. Yet they required every accused Guamanian—old and young alike—to submit their bodies and thoughts to the Japanese empire. Indeed, torture and the fear of torture increased their social status as proper men of the colony, but their overall failure to engage in a reciprocal network of power with Guamanians resulted in the severance of clan and kin.

With their newfound masculinity under the Japanese empire, they often tortured and murdered others with relative impunity. Their positions as police officers shielded them from Guamanian retaliations that may have occurred from such an outright violation of inafa'maolek. At the same time, the Rotanese and Saipanese men had further transformed the popular meanings of boys and men, fathers and sons, and cousins and uncles under the regime. While their actions were by no means totalizing, their marginalization of alternative masculinities under Japan's empire shaped their manhood as hegemonic.[13] This brand of militarized masculinity required one to be tough, independent (outside of one's obligations to a clan), without emotion, and especially arrogant.[14] In the public sphere, for example, they flaunted their authority and commanded the obedience of their peers. Only a few men resisted this image of themselves, yet every interpreter and police officer became a modern man of empire in the space of the interrogation room. Some Rotanese and Saipanese even subscribed to a promiscuous heterosexuality that allowed them to pleasure, with little constraint, in women from the villages. That they received frequent injections from the Japanese hospital for gonorrhea and syphilis revealed not only their violence against native women but also their collusion with the Japanese "comfort" system that coerced or employed women from Asia and the Pacific Islands. But unlike their Japanese supervisors and other authorities who saw themselves as the rightful occupants of the Mariana Islands, the Rotanese and Saipanese found in torture a militarized masculinity "apposite to its context, not an indigenous subject replete with power."[15]

In other words, the police did not have to utilize torture to exhibit Japan's sovereignty; that was an order given to and obeyed by their Rotanese and Saipanese colonial subjects. Torture thus had many lives: it existed in the Japanese military and police orders to colonize Guamanians; in Rotanese and Saipanese imaginations of militarized manhood; in the broken teeth and bones of native prisoners; in the marked and unmarked graves of the murdered; in survivor testimonies of Japanese, Rotanese, and Saipanese violence; in American trial proceedings about Japanese military "barbarism" and native "slavery"; in American military and political claims to the properties of Guam and Rota; in Chamorro, English, and Japanese translations of everyday and official discourses; and, above all, in Chamorro proverbs about reciprocity and retribution. Torture likewise enhanced or challenged a nation by producing an "enemy" from which the disciplinary logics of power and paranoia operated. As the critic Anne McClintock elaborates, torture produces "the bodies of 'the enemy' and make[s] the prisoners legible as enemies, thereby putatively 'legitimizing' the occupation."[16]

Testimonies of torture, however, did not result in the mass incarceration of Chamorro men from Rota and Saipan after the war. For although the U.S. Navy construed "blackness" as a "stable racial category in opposition to whiteness," its criminalization of Rotanese and Saipanese interpreters and police officers did not result in a carceral apparatus that racialized them as "black" and privy to criminal acts.[17] What ensued in the aftermath of the tribunal was not the construction of prisons for "deviant" Rotanese and Saipanese men.[18] Instead, Guamanian gossip and retribution acted like the claws of the *ayuyu* (coconut crab) in their attacks against Rotanese and Saipanese men from the 1940s to the 1970s. The purpose was to insult and injure males who represented Rota and Saipan. The father of David Sablan, for example, once served as a Saipanese interpreter in Japanese-occupied Guam. In the late 1940s, David Sablan then pursued his education in Guam, where, to his surprise, numerous Guamanians called him "pro-Japanese" and "Japanese lover." As a young man, Sablan did not understand why Guamanians hated him. As he explained, "I was always being threatened and had to run away to keep from being beaten up. . . . I never stopped to fight; I always ran."[19] Antonio Shimabukuro Borja, a Chamorro-Okinawan from Rota, confirmed these Guamanian animosities toward the Rotanese and Saipanese. As Borja noted, he "didn't go out much" whenever he visited his relatives in Guam after the war. "I was still scared and Guamanians didn't like the Chamorros from Rota and Saipan because of the things they did on Guam."[20]

The Men of the Military Colony

With the Rotanese and Saipanese men now portrayed as deviant types, the U.S. Navy's War Crimes Tribunals Program turned to its exemplars of acceptable manhood in the colony. As with the awards given to the Guam Combat Patrol for its racist killings of "Japanese stragglers," Guamanian police officers also received accolades for their service to the military commission (figure C.1). The *Guam Gazette*, a local periodical, identified two Guamanian police officers and former assistants of the Japanese police in particular: Desk Sergeant Juan A. Roberto and Staff Sergeant Adolfo C. Sgambelluri. Written by Judge Advocate and Lieutenant Colonel Teller Ammons, the letters expressed his gratitude. With respect to Juan Roberto, for example, the lead prosecutor of the tribunal claimed, "Now that the cases

C.1. The Guam Combat Patrol's murder count of 128 "Japanese stragglers." The original caption reads, "Record board of Japanese stragglers killed by police patrols" (no photo number, Rec. April 16, 1945). U.S. National Archives, College Park, Maryland.

before the Military Commission involving war crimes on Guam have been finished, I wish to express to you my personal appreciation for all the assistance you have given me in bringing to trial those accused of crimes on Guam." Regarding Adolfo Sgambelluri, the lieutenant colonel said, "You have played a very important part in compiling information upon which to prove the charges. . . . I personally appreciate all the assistance you have given, and you have rendered an exceedingly patriotic service to your people on Guam and the Government of the United States."[21]

Even some of the emasculated Rotanese and Saipanese interpreters and police officers of Japan's receding empire later transformed their statuses from sacred men to proper men of the American colony. Although the navy initially sentenced them to death, confinement for various years, or hard labor for their natural life, it commuted the death sentences to forty-five years of hard labor in 1951. After these men were imprisoned for eight years, the navy paroled everyone so they could reunite with their families in Rota and Saipan.[22] In the 1960s, for instance, Jose P. Villagomez became a security guard for an abandoned American military base in Saipan.[23] Luis C.

Crisostomo also found employment as a sentry for the Central Intelligence Agency, likewise located in Saipan.[24] Another interpreter, Elias Parong Sablan, had worked for the Japanese police in Guam for a month but did not incur any criminal charges from the tribunal. He subsequently became the chief of police in Saipan.[25] Whether they worked as unarmed guards for the native police, temporary security personnel, or armed members of the Constabulary Force, several men became indoctrinated into another sphere of militarized masculinities.[26]

As with the treason trial of Samuel T. Shinohara, the navy eventually reformed some of the Rotanese and Saipanese into low-ranking police officers of its regime. Given their statuses as formerly convicted war criminals and as non-U.S. citizens, they effectively entered a zone of violence comparable to the one they previously experienced, as interrogators and torturers, under the Japanese empire. By becoming police officers for the navy and its agencies, they likewise renewed the force of law in Guam, Rota, and Saipan, where "male dominance, heterosexism, whiteness, violence, and ruthless competition" are valued.[27] While not every Rotanese and Saipanese male subscribed to this militarized masculinity, as a few pursued other careers or simply returned to their farms, the processes by which the American military transformed them from nonsacrificial subjects to potentially sacrificial police officers demonstrated that they, too, could have become torturers again.[28] Of course, the navy's War Crimes Tribunals Program and its jurists never conceded to their histories of torture, let alone slavery.

It appeared as if only the Japanese, Rotanese, and Saipanese knew the political significance of torture and the violence it wielded in exerting the power of an empire. Stressing its virtuous high ground, the military tribunal subsequently targeted numerous Japanese nationals for committing atrocities and injuries in the Mariana Islands that stemmed "from cold and criminal calculation, committed in total disregard of the elementary consideration of human rights as well as in defiance of the well-established rules of international law."[29] Disregarding its racist interpretations of laws, the commission heralded its elimination of the internal and external threats posed by the Japanese government. The tribunal then increasingly viewed Japanese nationals and Japanese Americans as nonmilitarists, if not as new partners in America's Cold War order. As its director, Rear Admiral John D. Murphy, stated, "I desire to affirmatively point out that all Japanese did not subscribe to the sinister purposes and practices." Contrary to the court's homogenization of the Japanese as belligerents, militarists, or traitors, Murphy emphasized that they can be welcomed through their service to the U.S. rule of law. As he noted, "Among them there are untold members who believe in right and the principles which we ourselves support, as evidenced by those who came forward without expectation of individual gain to lend assistance in furtherance of our objectives."[30]

As the following native confession comparably illustrates, the threshold of the tribunal allowed for the elimination of Japan's empire and for the renewal of the U.S. rule of law in Guam. At the center of this inclusive exclusion resided the accused war criminal and the confluence of native and white hegemonies. In this interrogation, the unidentified American intelligence officer confirms this nexus of biopower by asking if the Saipanese interpreter and police officer Antonio Camacho can differentiate between good and bad behavior, between the American and Japanese empires, and between his faith in family and in God. The former interrogator had now become the interrogated. Camacho, a sacred man, confessed to an American intelligence officer representing the new empire:

Q: *Do you believe in God?*
A: Yes.
Q: *Do you believe lying is a sin for which you must answer?*
A: Yes. My mother and the priest have both taught me since childhood that to lie is a sin, and must be repaid.
Q: *Do you realize that in beating people as you did in Guam was wrong?*
A: Yes. I knew it was wrong all the time, but since I was ordered to do so by the Japanese, I knew they would punish me if I failed to obey those orders.
Q: *Do you want to admit your sins and wrongs to me and ask for mercy?*
A: I have already done so. The extent of my wrong-doing was given to you the other day. This is all I have done; I have no more to tell you.[31]

....

Confession and conversion. Torture and retribution. Indeed, the navy's War Crimes Tribunals Program would have not asserted the U.S. rule of law without the active participation of its Guamanian and Chamorro-Japanese witnesses. With its reliance on native gossip and vengeance and white supremacist statecraft and punishment, the military tribunal established the American empire in Guam, Rota, and the Mariana Islands. In the process, the commission never perceived Chamorros as citizens of Japan or the United States. Nor did the tribunal seek to address their noncitizenship statuses in any way. For each empire, the ko'ko and the hilitai remained as animals without politics, zoē, even though Guamanians, Japanese, Rotanese, and Saipanese all found in torture *political reasons* to extend or extinguish American or Japanese rule. Even today, the U.S. rule of law operates in seemingly "exceptional" ways wherein indigenous and settler communities are made and remade into homines sacri in Guam and the entire Mariana Islands. As the theorist Cary Wolfe warns, to live "under biopolitics is to live in a situation in which we are all always already (potential) 'animals' before the law—not just nonhuman animals according to zoological classification, but any group of living beings that is so framed."[32] But by decolonizing this paradigm of biopower, we can utilize gossip and law for reconciliation and healing rather than for discipline and punishment.[33]

From this vantage point, we can also examine the making of biopower in terms of the military colony, a paradigm that enabled American and Japanese colonialisms and militarisms to operate as legitimate law in the Mariana Islands. Homines sacri thus emerged on the threshold of the navy's tribunal not as a singular, universal, and passive subject of law; rather, they surfaced as the court's nonsacrificial assailants, belligerents, militarists, murderers, perverts, and traitors. This is precisely why we must turn to Guam as a paradigm of the military colony if we are to address Giorgio Agamben's philosophy of zoē and bios in colonial and indigenous settings. Such efforts can refute claims of American exceptionalism from Germany to South Korea and from Iraq to Guantánamo, demonstrating that military bases—and their courts—can function as integral parts of American empire building from the mid-twentieth century to the present.[34]

Notes

Abbreviations

MARC   Micronesian Area Research Center, University of Guam, Mangilao, Guam
NACP   U.S. National Archives at College Park, College Park, MD
NARA-PAC   U.S. National Archives and Records Administration—Pacific Region (San Francisco), San Bruno, CA
RG   Record Group
WCSC   War Crimes Studies Center, University of California, Berkeley, Berkeley, CA

Introduction

1 Marikita Palacios Crisostomo, "The Interpreter's Wife," in *Saipan: Oral Histories of the Pacific War*, ed. Bruce M. Petty (Jefferson, NC: McFarland, 2002), 83.

2 I seldom use the term "Guamanian" because of its current usage in the U.S. Census to mean both indigenous Chamorros and "residents" of Guam (e.g., Chinese, Filipino, Korean). But because Chamorros from Guam and others involved in the U.S. Navy's War Crimes Tribunals Program frequently utilized "Guamanian" in their proceedings, I will respect their preference. In this study, the term "Guamanians" thus refers to Chamorros and mixed-race Chamorros from Guam. Lastly, I employ "Chamorro" over other comparable spellings like "Chamoru" and "CHamoru" because the former is used widely in the Commonwealth of the Northern Mariana Islands and Guam.

    According to the naval officer and assistant chief of police Kanzo Kawachi, the Japanese military administered this order in Guam. Refer to the Kanzo Kawachi Court Transcript, September 17, 1945, p. 32 (hereafter cited as Kanzo Kawachi Court Transcript), World War II Document Archive, Pacific Theater, U.S. Navy Trials (microfilm reel no. 144575), WCSC.

3 Ty P. Kāwika Tengan, "Re-membering Panalāʻau: Masculinities, Nation,

and Empire in Hawai'i and the Pacific, *Contemporary Pacific* 20, no. 1 (Spring 2008): 29.
4 Crisostomo, "The Interpreter's Wife," 85.
5 Giorgio Agamben, *Homo Sacer: Sovereign Power and Bare Life*, trans. Daniel Heller-Roazen (Stanford, CA: Stanford University Press, 1998), 83.
6 Agamben, *Homo Sacer*, 82.
7 Kevin Attell, *Giorgio Agamben: Beyond the Threshold of Deconstruction* (New York: Fordham University Press, 2015), 129.
8 Barak Kushner, *Men to Devils, Devils to Men: Japanese War Crimes and Chinese Justice* (Cambridge, MA: Harvard University Press, 2015), 8.
9 Giorgio Agamben, *State of Exception*, trans. Kevin Attell (Chicago: University of Chicago Press, 2005), 23.
10 Agamben, *State of Exception*, 50.
11 Agamben, *State of Exception*, 2.
12 Agamben, *State of Exception*, 2–3.
13 Agamben, *Homo Sacer*, 8.
14 Agamben, *Homo Sacer*, 8.
15 Tom Frost, "The *Dispositif* between Foucault and Agamben," *Law, Culture and the Humanities* 15, no. 1 (2015): 156.
16 Frost, "The *Dispositif* between Foucault and Agamben," 156.
17 Frost, "The *Dispositif* between Foucault and Agamben," 157.
18 At the same time, the anthropologist Akhil Gupta reminds us that Agamben's notion of biopower often lacks application in the study of structural violence in non-Western settings, areas that do not have unified state apparatuses, and sites where the poor are actively included in projects of national sovereignty and humanitarian care. Refer to Gupta, *Red Tape: Bureaucracy, Structural Violence, and Poverty in India* (Durham, NC: Duke University Press, 2012).
19 Catherine Mills, *The Philosophy of Agamben* (Stocksfield, UK: Acumen, 2008), 69.
20 Mills, *The Philosophy of Agamben*, 77.
21 Paul Havemann, "Denial, Modernity and Exclusion: Indigenous Placelessness in Australia," *Macquarie Law Journal* 5 (2005): 60. Homines sacri is the plural of *homo sacer*.
22 Havemann, "Denial, Modernity and Exclusion," 60–61.
23 Elizabeth A. Povinelli, *The Cunning of Recognition: Indigenous Alterities and the Making of Australian Multiculturalism* (Durham, NC: Duke University Press, 2002), 180.
24 Jodi A. Byrd, *Transit of Empire: Indigenous Critiques of Colonialism* (Minneapolis: University of Minnesota Press, 2011), xx.
25 Simone Bignall and Marcelo Svirsky, "Introduction: Agamben and Colonialism," in *Agamben and Colonialism*, ed. Marcelo Svirsky and Simone Bignall (Edinburgh: Edinburgh University Press, 2012), 3.
26 Bignall and Svirsky, "Introduction," 3.
27 Agamben, *Homo Sacer*, 171.

28 Mark Rifkin, "On the (Geo)Politics of Belonging: Agamben and the UN Declaration on the Rights of Indigenous People," *Settler Colonial Studies* (2015): 3, accessed June 14, 2016, doi: 10.1080/2201473X.2015.1090527.
29 Lisa Yoneyama, "Liberation under Siege: U.S. Military Occupation and Japanese Women's Enfranchisement," *American Quarterly* 57, no. 3 (September 2005): 888.
30 The uneven application of the U.S. Constitution in the territories does not mean that indigenous peoples lack power and sovereignty, as with American Sāmoa, where chiefs retain authority, rank, and prestige. Refer to David A. Chappell, "The Forgotten Mau: Anti-navy Protest in American Samoa, 1920–1935," *Pacific Historical Review* 69, no. 2 (May 2000): 217–260.
31 Natsu Taylor Saito, *From Chinese Exclusion to Guantánamo Bay: Plenary Power and the Prerogative State* (Boulder: University Press of Colorado, 2007), 5.
32 Amy Kaplan, "Where Is Guantánamo?," *American Quarterly* 57, no. 3 (2005): 841.
33 Kaplan, "Where Is Guantánamo?," 842.
34 Anne Perez Hattori, *Colonial Dis-ease: US Navy Health Policies and the Chamorros of Guam, 1898–1941* (Honolulu: University of Hawai'i Press, 2004), 18.
35 U.S. Department of the Navy, Office of the Chief of Naval Operations, *U.S. Navy Report on Guam, 1899–1950* (Washington, DC: Government Printing Office, 1951), 17.
36 Laura Thompson, "Guam: A Study in Military Government," *Far Eastern Survey* 13, no. 16 (August 9, 1944): 150.
37 Vicente M. Diaz, "'Fight Boys, 'til the Last . . .': Islandstyle Football and the Remasculinization of Indigeneity in the Militarized American Pacific Islands," in *Pacific Diaspora: Island Peoples in the United States and across the Pacific*, ed. Paul Spickard, Joanne L. Rondilla, and Debbie Hippolite Wright (Honolulu: University of Hawai'i Press, 2002), 180.
38 Laura Thompson, *Guam and Its People: A Study of Culture Change and Colonial Education* (San Francisco: American Council, Institute of Pacific Relations, 1941), 63.
39 Hattori, *Colonial Dis-ease*, 3.
40 U.S. Department of the Navy, Office of the Chief of Naval Operations, *U.S. Navy Report on Guam, 1899–1950*, 18.
41 Thompson, *Guam and Its People*, 65.
42 Thompson, *Guam and Its People*, 66.
43 Anne Perez Hattori, "Re-membering the Past: Photography, Leprosy and the Chamorros of Guam, 1898–1924," *Journal of Pacific History* 46, no. 3 (2011): 311.
44 Achille Mbembe, "Necropolitics," *Public Culture* 15, no. 1 (Winter 2003): 23.
45 Mbembe, "Necropolitics," 24.
46 Sinclair Dinnen, "Restorative Justice in the Pacific Islands: An Introduction," in *A Kind of Mending: Restorative Justice in the Pacific Islands*, ed. Sinclair Dinnen, Anita Jowitt, and Tess Newton Cain (Canberra: Pandanus Books, 2003), 11.
47 Keith L. Camacho, *Cultures of Commemoration: The Politics of War, Memory, and History in the Mariana Islands* (Honolulu: University of Hawai'i Press, 2011), 29–32.

48 Dirk Ballendorf, "Summary of Interviews," [no page number] [1980s?], Ballendorf, Dirk et al., "Oral Historiography," Folder 25, Box 3, MARC.
49 Manuel T. Sablan, "Messenger Boy for the Japanese Police," in *Saipan: Oral Histories of the Pacific War*, ed. Bruce M. Petty (Jefferson, NC: McFarland, 2002), 35.
50 Susan L. Burns, "Introduction," in *Gender and Law in the Japanese Imperium*, ed. Susan L. Burns and Barbara J. Brooks (Honolulu: University of Hawai'i Press, 2014), 5.
51 "A Copy of Japanese Records," trans. William S. Reyes [1975?], p. 9, Mark Peattie's Nan'yō Papers, Folder 3, Box 2, MARC.
52 Mark R. Peattie, *Nan'yō: The Rise and Fall of the Japanese in Micronesia, 1885–1945* (Honolulu: University of Hawai'i Press, 1988), 38.
53 Ching-chih Chen, "Police and Community Control Systems in the Empire," in *The Japanese Colonial Empire, 1895–1945*, ed. Ramon H. Myers and Mark R. Peattie (Princeton, NJ: Princeton University Press, 1984), 237.
54 Noah Riseman, *Defending Whose Country? Indigenous Soldiers in the Pacific War* (Lincoln: University of Nebraska Press, 2012), 27.
55 Vicente L. Rafael, "Translation, American English, and the National Insecurities of Empire," in *Formations of United States Colonialism*, ed. Alyosha Goldstein (Durham, NC: Duke University Press, 2014), 336.
56 Greg Dvorak, "'The Martial Islands': Making Marshallese Masculinities between American and Japanese Militarism," *Contemporary Pacific* 20, no. 1 (Spring 2008): 74.
57 "CAMACHO, Antonio, interrogation of," December 19, 1944, p. 2, Records of the Naval Operating Forces, RG 313, Trust Territory of the Pacific Islands, Office of the High Commissioner, General Administrative Files, ca. 1944–1951, Box 1 P35, Folder "CAMACHO, Antonio: alleged crimes," NACP.
58 "CAMACHO, Antonio, interrogation of," December 19, 1944, 3.
59 Jose P. Villagomez, Court Transcript, February 26, 1945, p. 4 (hereafter cited as Jose P. Villagomez 1945a Court Transcript), World War II Document Archive, Pacific Theater, U.S. Navy Trials (microfilm reel no. 124919), WCSC.
60 Statement of Elias P. Sablan, March 16, 1946, p. 1, Records of the Office of the Judge Advocate General (Navy), RG 125, War Crimes Branch, Records Originated by Director of War Crimes, Pacific Fleet Correspondence, 1944–1949, Box 9, NACP.
61 Robert F. Rogers, *Destiny's Landfall: A History of Guam* (Honolulu: University of Hawai'i Press, 1995), 165.
62 "CAMACHO, Antonio, interrogation of," December 19, 1944, p. 5, Records of the Naval Operating Forces, RG 313, NACP.
63 Rafael, "Translation, American English, and the National Insecurities of Empire," 337.
64 Paul W. Kahn, *Sacred Violence: Torture, Terror, and Sovereignty* (Ann Arbor: University of Michigan Press, 2008), 2.

65 Kahn, *Sacred Violence*, 23.
66 Kahn, *Sacred Violence*, 23.
67 Pedro Sablan Leon Guerrero, Court Transcript, July 2, 1945, p. 23 (hereafter cited as Pedro Guerrero Court Transcript), World War II Document Archive, Pacific Theater, U.S. Navy Trials (microfilm reel no. 137910), WCSC.
68 Justin Clemens, "Oath, Torture, Testimony: Language, Law and Life in the Work of Giorgio Agamben," *Res Publica: Revista de Filosofía Política* 28 (2012): 78.
69 Louis Fisher, *Military Tribunals and Presidential Power: American Revolution to the War on Terrorism* (Lawrence: University Press of Kansas, 2005), 148.
70 Niko Besnier, *Gossip and the Everyday Production of Politics* (Honolulu: University of Hawai'i Press, 2009), 2.
71 Besnier, *Gossip and the Everyday Production of Politics*, 2–3.
72 Christine Taitano DeLisle, "A History of Chamorro Nurse-Midwives in Guam and a 'Placental Politics' for Indigenous Feminism," *Intersections: Gender and Sexuality in Asia and the Pacific* 37 (March 2015), accessed June 22, 2016, http://intersections.anu.edu.au/issue37/delisle.htm.
73 Tiara R. Na'puti and Michael Lujan Bevacqua, "Militarization and Resistance from Guåhan: Protecting and Defending Pågat," *American Quarterly* 67, no. 3 (September 2015): 847.
74 Lilli Perez Iyechad, *An Historical Perspective of Helping Practices Associated with Birth, Marriage and Death among Chamorros of Guam* (Lewiston, NY: Edwin Mellen Press, 2001), 177.
75 Faye Untalan, interview by the author, Los Angeles, California, February 19, 2017.
76 Lawrence J. Cunningham, *Ancient Chamorro Society* (Honolulu: Bess Press, 1992), 111.
77 Cunningham, *Ancient Chamorro Society*, 111.
78 Cunningham, *Ancient Chamorro Society*, 111 (my emphasis).
79 Malia Ramirez, interview by the author, Hagåtña, Guam, February 26, 2015.
80 "Chamorro Expressions," [1910s?], Helen Paul Collection, Pacific Collections, MARC.
81 Kevin Bruyneel, *The Third Space of Sovereignty: The Postcolonial Politics of U.S.-Indigenous Relations* (Minneapolis: University of Minnesota Press, 2007), 6.
82 On Chamorro relations with the material and spiritual domains, refer to Robert Tenorio Torres, "Pre-contact Marianas Folklore, Legends, and Literature," *Micronesian: Journal of the Humanities and Social Sciences* 2, nos. 1–2 (December 2003): 3–15; and Donald Soker, "The Taotaomona Stories of Guam," *Western Folklore* 31, no. 3 (1972): 153–167.
83 Vicente M. Diaz, "Sniffing Oceania's Behind," *Contemporary Pacific* 24, no. 2 (2012): 336.
84 Tina Camacho Pablo, *Enchanting Tales of Guam* (Agaña Heights: Guamology, 2010), 6.

85 Jonathan Goldberg-Hiller and Noenoe K. Silva, "Sharks and Pigs: Animating Hawaiian Sovereignty against the Anthropological Machine," *South Atlantic Quarterly* 110, no. 2 (2011): 431.
86 Jonathan Goldberg-Hiller and Noenoe K. Silva, "The Botany of Emergence: Kanaka Ontology and Biocolonialism in Hawai'i," *Native American and Indigenous Studies* 2, no. 2 (Fall 2015): 2.
87 Goldberg-Hiller and Silva, "The Botany of Emergence," 2.
88 DeLisle, "A History of Chamorro Nurse-Midwives in Guam."
89 Michael Phillips, "Land Ownership in Guam," Guampedia, last modified on July 2, 2014, accessed May 5, 2017, www.guampedia.com/land-ownership-on-guam/.
90 Giorgio Agamben, *The Open: Man and Animal*, trans. Kevin Attell (Stanford, CA: Stanford University Press, 2004), 16.
91 Agamben, *State of Exception*, 23.
92 Elizabeth Dauphinee, "War Crimes and the Ruin of Law," *Millennium: Journal of International Studies* 37, no. 1 (2008): 51.
93 Walter Benjamin, *Reflections: Essays, Aphorisms, Autobiographical Writings*, trans. Edmund Jephcott (New York: Schocken Books, 1986), 281.
94 Benjamin, *Reflections*, 283–284.
95 Benjamin, *Reflections*, 287.
96 Marie Gottschalk, "Hiding in Plain Sight: American Politics and the Carceral State," *Annual Review of Political Science* 11 (2008): 236.
97 Laurel E. Fletcher and Eric Stover, *The Guantánamo Effect: Exposing the Consequences of U.S. Detention and Interrogation Practices* (Berkeley: University of California Press, 2009), xvi–xvii.
98 Marita Sturken, "Comfort, Irony, and Trivialization: The Mediation of Torture," *International Journal of Cultural Studies* 14, no. 4 (July 2011): 431.
99 For "rule of law," refer to Brett J. Kyle and Andrew G. Reiter, "Militarized Justice in New Democracies: Explaining the Process of Military Court Reform in Latin America," *Law and Society Review* 47, no. 2 (June 2013): 378; Muneer I. Ahmad, "Guantánamo Is Here: The Military Commissions Act and Noncitizen Vulnerability," *University of Chicago Legal Forum* 1 (2007): 7.
100 Fionnuala Ní Aoláin and Oren Gross, "Introduction: Guantánamo and Beyond: Exceptional Courts and Military Commissions in Comparative and Policy Perspective," in *Guantánamo and Beyond: Exceptional Courts and Military Commissions in Comparative Perspective*, ed. Fionnuala Ní Aoláin and Oren Gross (Cambridge: Cambridge University Press, 2013), 10.
101 Jace Weaver, *Turtle Goes to War: Of Military Commissions, the Constitution and American Indian Memory* (New Haven, CT: Trylon and Perisphere Press, 2002), xiii.
102 Weaver, *Turtle Goes to War*, 87.
103 Dauphinee, "War Crimes and the Ruin of Law," 57.
104 Catherine Lutz, "Introduction: Bases, Empire, and Global Response," in *The

Bases of Empire: The Global Struggle against U.S. Military Posts, ed. Catherine Lutz (New York: New York University Press, 2009), 19.
105 Yen Le Espiritu, Body Counts: The Vietnam War and Militarized Refuge(es) (Berkeley: University of California Press, 2014), 32.
106 D. C. Ramsey, Vice Chief of Naval Operations, to Judge Advocate General, August 1, 1946, p. 2, Records of the Naval Operating Forces, RG 313, Trust Territory of the Pacific Islands, Office of the High Commissioner, General Administrative Files, ca. 1944–1951, Box 10 P31, Folder "GUAM—EG (54)-1, 1 January 1946 through 30 June 1946 (1 of 2) [Secret]," NACP.
107 Chalmers Johnson, The Sorrows of Empire: Militarism, Secrecy, and the End of the Republic (New York: Henry Holt, 2004), 189.
108 David Vine, Island of Shame: The Secret History of the U.S. Military Base on Diego Garcia (Princeton, NJ: Princeton University Press, 2009), 42.
109 On the invisibility of U.S. militarism, refer to Kathy E. Ferguson and Phyllis Turnbull, Oh, Say, Can You See? The Semiotics of the Military in Hawai'i (Minneapolis: University of Minnesota Press, 1999).

Chapter 1. War Bodies

1 Johnson, The Sorrows of Empire, 117.
2 Alan Harris Bath, Tracking the Axis Enemy: The Triumph of Anglo-American Naval Intelligence (Lawrence: University Press of Kansas, 1998), 4.
3 Captain Ellis M. Zacharias, US Navy, to Chief of Naval Operations, US Pacific Fleet, "Selection of Officers for Intelligence Duty," January 27, 1942, Records of Naval Operating Forces, RG 313, Blue Finding Aid Folder 644, Joint Intelligence Center Pacific Ocean Areas (JICPOA), Box 7 (Old Box 5857), Folder "A8/a Intelligence General (4 of 4) [November 1941–March 1944]," NACP.
4 Zacharias, "Selection of Officers for Intelligence Duty," 1.
5 Zacharias, "Selection of Officers for Intelligence Duty," 1.
6 Zacharias, "Selection of Officers for Intelligence Duty," 3.
7 Zacharias, "Selection of Officers for Intelligence Duty," 1.
8 Zacharias, "Selection of Officers for Intelligence Duty," 1.
9 Report of Intelligence Activities in the Pacific Ocean Areas (U.S. Navy: Pearl Harbor, 1945), p. 3, Records of Naval Operating Forces, RG 313, Blue Finding Aid Folder 645, Joint Intelligence Center Pacific Ocean Areas (JICPOA), Box 1 (Old Box 5876), Folder "Report of Intelligence Activities in the Pacific Ocean Areas—15 Oct 1945," NACP.
10 Report of Intelligence Activities in the Pacific Ocean Areas, 3.
11 Report of Intelligence Activities in the Pacific Ocean Areas, 3 of 4.
12 Report of Intelligence Activities in the Pacific Ocean Areas, 3 of 4 to 4 of 4.
13 Report of Intelligence Activities in the Pacific Ocean Areas, 33.
14 Report of Intelligence Activities in the Pacific Ocean Areas, 31.

15 1st Provisional Marine Brigade in the Field, "Operations and Special Action Report," August 19, 1944, p. 9, Box Naval Operational Archives AR-42–79, AR-145–74, Folder "NOA AR 145.79 Reel 3 USMC Reports 1st Prov. Mar. Br. I.," MARC.
16 "Appendix No. 4 to Annex B, INTELLIGENCE," Intelligence Section, Third Marine Division, May 13, 1944, p. 1, Pacific Collection, Box National Archives RG 45, RG 71, RG 165, RG 225, Folder "NOA AR 145–79 Reel 3 USMC Reports 3rd Mar. Div. I.," MARC.
17 "Appendix No. 4 to Annex B, INTELLIGENCE," 1.
18 "Appendix No. 4 to Annex B, INTELLIGENCE," 1.
19 Michel Foucault, *Discipline and Punish: The Birth of the Prison*, trans. Alan Sheridan (New York: Vintage Books, 1995), 11.
20 Major General Roy S. Geiger, "Troop Instructions," [1944?], p. 1, Records of the U.S. Marine Corps, RG 127, History and Museums Division, General Subject File, 1940–1953, 5–8 to 11–8, Box 24, Folder "5–8 Operation Plan, 1–44, 1st Provisional Marine Brigade 53.8—Guam, L.C. Shepherd, Jr. Part 2 of 2," NACP.
21 Major General Roy S. Geiger, "Troop Instructions," [1944?], 3.
22 Major General Roy S. Geiger, "Troop Instructions," [1944?], 3.
23 Commanding General to All Officers Concerned, "Instructions to Military Police Concerning Treatment of Civilians and Civilian Property," May 30, 1944, p. 1, Records of the U.S. Marine Corps, RG 127, History and Museums Division, General Subject File, 1940–1953, 5–8 to 11–8, Box 24, Folder "5–8 Operation Plan, 1–44, 1st Provisional Marine Brigade 53.8—Guam, L.C. Shepherd, Jr. Part 2 of 2," NACP.
24 Commanding General to All Officers Concerned, "Instructions to Military Police Concerning Treatment of Civilians and Civilian Property," 1.
25 Commanding General to All Officers Concerned, "Instructions to Military Police Concerning Treatment of Civilians and Civilian Property," 2.
26 Commanding General to All Officers Concerned, "Instructions to Military Police Concerning Treatment of Civilians and Civilian Property," 2.
27 Commanding General to All Officers Concerned, "Instructions to Military Police Concerning Treatment of Civilians and Civilian Property," 2.
28 Nicholas T. Sablan, Court Transcript, March 30, 1945, p. 5 (hereafter cited as Nicholas T. Sablan Court Transcript), World War II Document Archive, Pacific Theater, U.S. Navy Trials (microfilm reel no. 131529), WCSC.
29 Pedro Guerrero Court Transcript, 3.
30 Pedro Guerrero Court Transcript, 3.
31 Pedro Guerrero Court Transcript, 3.
32 Pedro Guerrero Court Transcript, 3.
33 Henry S. Pangelinan, Court Transcript, May 23, 1945, p. 3 (hereafter cited as Henry S. Pangelinan Court Transcript), World War II Document Archive, Pacific Theater, U.S. Navy Trials (microfilm reel no. 135563), WCSC.

34 Pedro Guerrero Court Transcript, 3.
35 After hiding for several months, Luis C. Crisostomo surrendered to the U.S. military on January 1, 1945.
36 Pedro Guerrero Court Transcript, 3.
37 Manuel Borja Tudela, May 9, 1945, p. 5 (hereafter cited as Manuel Borja Tudela Court Transcript), World War II Document Archive, Pacific Theater, U.S. Navy Trials (microfilm reel no. 134816), WCSC.
38 "Memorandum for the Judge Advocate General," April 24, 1945, p. 1, Records of the Office of the Judge Advocate General (Navy), RG 125, War Crimes Branch, Records Regarding Pacific Area War Crimes Cases, 1944–1949, Box 1, NACP.
39 Jose P. Villagomez 1945a Court Transcript, 17.
40 Jose P. Villagomez 1945a Court Transcript, 17.
41 Commanding General to All Officers Concerned, "Instructions to Military Police Concerning Treatment of Civilians and Civilian Property," May 30, 1944, p. 3, Records of the U.S. Marine Corps, RG 127, NACP.
42 Nicholas Savage, interview by Guam Cable News [1985?], videotape, Hagåtña, Guam (copy of videotaped interview in the author's possession).
43 Major General Roy S. Geiger, "Notice for Protective Compound," [August 1944?], p. 1, Records of the U.S. Marine Corps, RG 1237, History and Museums Division, General Subject File, 1940–1953, 5–8 to 11–8, Box 24, Folder "5–8 Operation Plan, 1–44, 1st Provisional Marine Brigade 53.8—Guam, L. C. Shepherd, Jr. Part 2 of 2," NACP.
44 Major General Roy S. Geiger, "Notice for Protective Compound," [August 1944?], p. 1, Records of the U.S. Marine Corps, RG 127, NACP.
45 Rogers, *Destiny's Landfall*, 191.
46 Orlando Patterson, *Slavery and Social Death: A Comparative Study* (Cambridge, MA: Harvard University Press, 1982), 105. The six other means for enslavement include kidnapping, tribute and tax payment, debt, abandonment and sale of children, self-enslavement, and birth.
47 Patterson, *Slavery and Social Death*, 8–9.
48 Angela Y. Davis, *Are Prisons Obsolete?* (New York: Seven Stories Press, 2003), 33.
49 1st Provisional Marine Brigade in the Field, "Operations and Special Action Report," August 19, 1944, p. 9, Pacific Collection, MARC.
50 1st Provisional Marine Brigade in the Field, "Operations and Special Action Report," 9.
51 Dan Williams, "Communicating with the Enemy: Interpreters, 1942–45," in *Pacific War Stories in the Words of Those Who Survived*, ed. Rex Alan Smith and Gerald A. Meehl (New York: Abbeville Press, 2004), 203.
52 Major General Clark L. Ruffner, "Military Justice—Treatment of Military Prisoners," May 19, 1945, p. 1, Records of Naval Operating Forces, RG 313, Trust Territory of the Pacific Islands, Office of the Deputy High Commissioner, Monthly Reports POW's [Prisoners of War], Saipan (1 of 2) to Correspondence,

November 1944, Box 49 P32 Red 340, Folder "POW Correspondence, 1944–1946 [1 of 2]," NACP.

53 Colonel M. H. Silverthorn, "Instructions for Organization and Operation of Labor Pool," May 30, 1944, p. 1, Records of the U.S. Marine Corps, RG 127, History and Museums Division, General Subject File, 1940–1953, 5–8 to 11–8, Box 24, Folder "5–8 Operation Plan, 1–44, 1st Provisional Marine Brigade 53.8—Guam, L. C. Shepherd, Jr. Part 2 of 2," NACP.

54 Silverthorn, "Instructions for Organization and Operation of Labor Pool," 1.

55 E. E. Sprung to Heads of Branches, Sections and Sub-sections of SECP, July 7, 1944, p. 1, Records of the Bureau of Naval Personnel, RG 24, Naval Prisoners of War Board, Box 8, NACP.

56 Sprung to Heads of Branches, Sections and Sub-sections of SECP, 1.

57 Sprung to Heads of Branches, Sections and Sub-sections of SECP, 1.

58 "Duties of the Prisoner of War Guards," May 29, 1946, p. 1, Records of Naval Operating Forces, RG 313, Naval Government of Guam, Mariana Islands, General Correspondence, 1946–50, Box 1 of 2, Folder "A2–11(2) Island Command Memorandums," NARA-PAC.

59 "Duties of the Prisoner of War Guards," 1.

60 Angela Y. Davis, "Racialized Punishment and Prison Abolition," in *The Angela Y. Davis Reader*, ed. Joy James (Malden, MA: Blackwell, 1998), 99.

61 Major General Clark L. Ruffner, "Military Justice—Treatment of Military Prisoners," May 19, 1945, p. 1, Records of Naval Operating Forces, RG 313, NACP.

62 Silvina Charfauros-Cruz Taumomoa, 12/01/03, page 9, Guam Review War Claims, University of Guam, 2003–2004, Box 43, Rec. No. 75910, MARC.

63 "Surrender or Die, Order of DCMGO to Recalcitrant Japs: Guam's Famed Combat Patrol Again on War Path," *Guam Gazette*, October 12, 1945, 1.

64 "Special Marine, Guam Police Patrols Sweep Island in Widespread Jap Hunt," *Navy News*, December 12, 1945, 1.

65 "Intelligence Annex to Special Action Report," August 17, 1944, p. 1, Pacific Collection, University of Guam, Box Naval Operational Archives AR-42–79, AR-145–74, Folder "NOA AR 145.79 Reel 3 USMC Reports 1st Prov. Mar. Br. I.," MARC.

66 "Intelligence Annex to Special Action Report," 1.

67 "Military Government Patrols Protect Interests and Pursuits of Guam Civilians," *Navy News*, April 16, 1946, 2.

68 Adolf Sgambelluri, interview by the author, Nimitz Hill, Guam, April 22, 2006.

69 Sgambelluri, interview by the author.

70 Sgambelluri, interview by the author.

71 "Japs Still at Large, Imperil Civilian Communities," *Guam Gazette*, September 19, 1945, 1. For example, the military government awarded the Purple Heart to families of the deceased Jesus Cruz Cruz, Vicente Cruz Chargualaf, Angel L. Flores, and V. S. Sablan on April 12, 1946.

72 For a partial account of the death and capture statistics of the Guam Combat Patrol, refer to the file "U.S. Naval Government of Guam's Monthly Reports, 1946–1947," Pacific Collection, MARC.
73 Refer to Vicente M. Diaz, "Deliberating 'Liberation Day': Identity, History, Memory, and War in Guam," in *Perilous Memories: The Asia-Pacific War(s)*, ed. T. Fujitani, Geoffrey M. White, and Lisa Yoneyama (Durham, NC: Duke University Press, 2001), 155–180; and Laura Marie Torres Souder, "Psyche under Siege: Uncle Sam, Look What You've Done to Us," in *Uncle Sam in Micronesia: Social Benefits, Social Costs*, ed. Donald H. Rubinstein and Vivian L. Dames (Mangilao: Micronesia Area Research Center, 1989), 120–124.
74 Foucault, *Discipline and Punish*, 101.
75 Achille Mbembe, *On the Postcolony* (Berkeley: University of California Press, 2001), 186.
76 Secretary of the Navy James Forrestal to All Ships and Stations, Bureaus and Offices, Navy Department, "War Crimes Office, Announcement of Establishment," January 13, 1945, p. 1, Records of the Office of the Judge Advocate General (Navy), RG 125, War Crimes Branch, 1944–1949, Miscellaneous Records, From: Civil Affairs Division, Thru: Directives and Distributions, Box 3, NACP.
77 Secretary of the Navy James Forrestal, "War Crimes Office, Announcement of Establishment," 1.
78 United States War Department, "Reporting of War Crimes and Identification of Suspects," August 1945, pp. 1–2, Records of the Office of the Judge Advocate General (Navy), RG 125, War Crimes Branch, Miscellaneous Records, 1944–1949, Box 5, NACP.
79 United States War Department, "Reporting of War Crimes and Identification of Suspects," August 1945, pp. 3–4, Records of the Office of the Judge Advocate General (Navy), RG 125, NACP.
80 Secretary of the Navy James Forrestal, "War Crimes Office, Announcement of Establishment," 1..
81 "Memorandum describing functions of Navy personnel in Navy Division, War Crimes Office," [1944?], p. 2, Records of the Office of the Judge Advocate General (Navy), RG 125, War Crimes Branch, 1944–1949, Miscellaneous Records, From: War Crimes Office, Thru: War Crimes Officers, Box 15, NACP.
82 George E. Erickson, "United States Navy War Crimes Trials (1945–1949)," *Washburn Law Journal* 5, no. 1 (1965): 95.
83 Secretary of the Navy James Forrestal, "War Crimes Office, Announcement of Establishment," 1.
84 Officer-in-Charge to Officer-in-Charge, Joint Intelligence Center Pacific Ocean Areas, "Advance Intelligence Center, brief history of," September 5, 1945, p. 1, Records of Naval Operating Forces, RG 313, Blue Finding Aid Folder 644, Joint Intelligence Center Pacific Ocean Areas (JICPOA), Box 7 (Old Box 5857), Folder "A3/AIC-Organization (AIC-General) [1945]," NACP.

85 "Monthly Progress and Work Report," June 2, 1947, p. 6, Records of the Office of the Judge Advocate General (Navy), RG 125, War Crimes Branch, Records Originated by Director of War Crimes, Pacific Fleet, Confidential Correspondence, 1945–1948, Box 1, NACP.
86 "Monthly Progress and Work Report," June 2, 1947, 6.
87 The Secretary of the Navy (Office of the Judge Advocate General) to Commandant, U.S. Marine Corps, "Procedure for Investigation and Report of War Crimes," [April?] 1945, pp. 1–2, Records of the Office of the Judge Advocate General (Navy), RG 125, War Crimes Branch, Miscellaneous Records, 1944–1949, From: War Crimes Office, Thru: War Crimes Officers, Box 15, NACP.
88 Supreme Commander for the Allied Powers, "Standard Operating Procedures for Investigation of War Crimes and Atrocities," April 29, 1946, p. 1, RG 331, Records of Allied Operational and Occupational Headquarters, Supreme Commander for the Allied Powers, Legal Section, Investigation Division, Summary of Cases, 1945–1949, #3–16, Box 1852, Folder "Investigation Div., Admin.—S.O.P. IV.," NACP.
89 Commander George H. Brereton, "Outline of Investigation Methods and Techniques," [1945?], p. 1, RG 331, Records of Allied Operational and Occupation Headquarters, World War II, Supreme Commander for the Allied Powers, Legal Section, Investigation Division, Summary of Cases, 1945–1949, #3–16, Box 1852, RG 331, Folder "Investigation Div., Admin.—S.O.P. IV.," NACP.
90 The Secretary of the Navy, "Procedure for Investigation and Report of War Crimes," p. 4.
91 John D. Murphy, US Navy War Crimes Program Final Report (Washington, DC: Department of the Navy, 1950), 42.
92 Johnson, The Sorrows of Empire, 120.
93 Peter B. Kraska, "Crime Control as Warfare: Language Matters," in Militarizing the American Criminal Justice System: The Changing Roles of the Armed Forces and the Police, ed. Peter B. Kraska (Boston: Northeastern University Press, 2001), 21.
94 Commander George H. Brereton, "Outline of Investigation Methods and Techniques," [1945?], p. 1, RG 331, Records of Allied Operational and Occupation Headquarters, NACP.
95 Brereton, "Outline of Investigation Methods and Techniques," 2.
96 Luis C. Crisostomo, June 4, 1945, p. 67 (hereafter cited as Luis C. Crisostomo Court Transcript), World War II Document Archive, Pacific Theater, U.S. Navy Trials (microfilm reel no. 136369), WCSC.
97 Luis C. Crisostomo Court Transcript, 71.
98 Commander George H. Brereton, "Interrogation of Witnesses and Suspects," [1945?], p. 2, RG 331, Records of Allied Operational and Occupation Headquar-

ters, World War II, Supreme Commander for the Allied Powers, Legal Section, Investigation Division, Summary of Cases, 1945–1949, #3–16, Box 1852, Folder "Investigation Div., Admin.—S.O.P. IV," NACP.
99 Brereton, "Interrogation of Witnesses and Suspects," 1–2.
100 From Commander in Chief, U.S. Pacific Fleet and Pacific Ocean Areas to Commander Marianas et al., September 4, 1945, p. 1, RG 125, Records of the Office of the Judge Advocate General (Navy), War Crimes Branch, Records Originated by Director of War Crimes, Pacific Fleet, Confidential Correspondence, 1945–1948, Box 1, NACP.
101 From Commander in Chief, U.S. Pacific Fleet and Pacific Ocean Areas to Commander Marianas et al., September 4, 1945, 2.
102 From Commander in Chief, U.S. Pacific Fleet and Pacific Ocean Areas to Commander Marianas et al., September 4, 1945, 2.
103 Brereton, "Outline of Investigation Methods and Techniques," 3.
104 Brereton, "Outline of Investigation Methods and Techniques," 5.
105 Adolf Sgambelluri, interview by the author, Nimitz Hill, Guam, April 22, 2006.
106 Kanzo Kawachi Court Transcript, September 17, 1945, p. 15 (hereafter cited as Kanzo Kawachi Court Transcript), World War II Document Archive, Pacific Theater, U.S. Navy Trials (microfilm reel no. 144575), WCSC.
107 Captain Charles H. Kraus, "Personal Observations of Civil Affairs Activities in the Guam Operation and Comments and Recommendations Concerning Civil Affairs Organization and Operation in the Marine Corps," 1944, p. 42, RG 313, Records of the Naval Operating Forces, Trust Territory of the Pacific Islands, Office of the High Commissioner, General Administrative Files, ca. 1944–1951, Box 9 P31, Folder "EG-54-(1) Observations on CA activities in Guam Operation," NACP.
108 Kraus, "Personal Observations of Civil Affairs Activities in the Guam Operation," 42.
109 Kraus, "Personal Observations of Civil Affairs Activities in the Guam Operation," 43.
110 Kraus, "Personal Observations of Civil Affairs Activities in the Guam Operation," 43.
111 Kraus, "Personal Observations of Civil Affairs Activities in the Guam Operation," 43.
112 Kraus, "Personal Observations of Civil Affairs Activities in the Guam Operation," 64.
113 Kraus, "Personal Observations of Civil Affairs Activities in the Guam Operation," 64.
114 Franquez, Rita Torres, November 29, 2003, p. 2, Guam Review War Claims 2003–2004, Box 12, Rec. No. 32100, MARC.
115 Franquez, Rita Torres, November 29, 2003, 4.

116 Franquez, Rita Torres, November 29, 2003, 4.
117 Franquez, Rita Torres, November 29, 2003, 2.
118 Franquez, Rita Torres, November 29, 2003, 2.
119 Franquez, Rita Torres, November 29, 2003, 2.
120 Rear Admiral John D. Murphy to Commander Marianas, March 31, 1948, p. 3, RG 125, Records of the Office of the Judge Advocate General (Navy), War Crimes Branch, Records Originated by Director of War Crimes, Pacific Fleet, Secret Correspondence, 1945–1949, Box 3, NACP.
121 Statement of Hubert R. Brinkley, P. F. C. (973877) USMC, SS. June 17, 1946, p. 1, RG 125, Records of the Office of the Judge Advocate General (Navy), War Crimes Branch, Records Originated by the Director of War Crimes, Pacific Fleet, Confidential Correspondence, 1945–1948, Box 2, NACP.
122 Commander Marianas to Island Commander, GUAM, September 25, 1945, p. 1, RG 125, Records of the Office of the Judge Advocate General (Navy), War Crimes Branch, Records Originated by the Director of War Crimes, Pacific Fleet, Confidential Correspondence, 1945–1948, Box 2, NACP.
123 Rear Admiral John D. Murphy to Commander Marianas, March 31, 1948, p. 3, RG 125, Records of the Office of the Judge Advocate General (Navy), War Crimes Branch, Records Originated by Director of War Crimes, Pacific Fleet, Secret Correspondence, 1945–1949, Box 3, NACP.
124 The navy sometimes flew witnesses from Japan, Rota, and Saipan to Guam for them to testify in its military trials, at which point the witnesses were made to reside in the War Criminals Stockade. Naval documents reveal little about the living conditions of the witnesses other than to indicate that they were segregated from the prisoners.
125 "Instructions for Conduct of Accused and Convicted War Criminals," November 1, 1947, p. 1, RG 125, Records of the Office of the Judge Advocate General (Navy) War Crimes Branch, Records Originated by Director of War Crimes, Pacific Fleet, Correspondence, 1944–1949, Box 12, NACP.
126 Statement of Hubert R. Brinkley, P. F. C. (973877) USMC, SS. June 17, 1946, p. 1, RG 125, Records of the Office of the Judge Advocate General (Navy), War Crimes Branch, Records Originated by the Director of War Crimes, Pacific Fleet, Confidential Correspondence, 1945–1948, Box 2, NACP.
127 "Instructions for Conduct of Accused and Convicted War Criminals," 1.
128 Commanding Officer to Commander Marianas, July 22, 1946, pp. 1–4, RG 125, Records of the Office of the Judge Advocate General (Navy), War Crimes Branch, Records Originated by the Director of War Crimes, Pacific Fleet, Confidential Correspondence, 1945–1948, Box 2, NACP.
129 Statement of Kaoru Arima, July 2, 1946, p. 1, RG 125, Records of the Office of the Judge Advocate General (Navy), War Crimes Branch, Records Originated by the Director of War Crimes, Pacific Fleet, Confidential Correspondence, 1945–1948, Box 2, NACP.

130 Statement of Kaoru Arima, July 2, 1946, 1.
131 Statement of Tsugio Asanuma, [June or July?] 1946, p. 1, RG 125, Records of the Office of the Judge Advocate General (Navy), War Crimes Branch, Records Originated by the Director of War Crimes, Pacific Fleet, Confidential Correspondence, 1945–1948, Box 2, NACP.
132 John D. Murphy to Captain Moriarty, August 20, 1946, p. 1, RG 125, Records of the Office of the Judge Advocate General (Navy), War Crimes Branch, Records Originated by the Director of War Crimes, Pacific Fleet, Confidential Correspondence, 1945–1948, Box 2, NACP.
133 Statement of Private David N. Morris, [June 14, 1946?], p. 1, RG 125, Records of the Office of the Judge Advocate General (Navy), War Crimes Branch, Records Originated by the Director of War Crimes, Pacific Fleet, Confidential Correspondence, 1945–1948, Box 2, NACP.
134 Statement of Private Donald Purcell, June 14, 1946, p. 1, RG 125, Records of the Office of the Judge Advocate General (Navy), War Crimes Branch, Records Originated by the Director of War Crimes, Pacific Fleet, Confidential Correspondence, 1945–1948, Box 2, NACP.
135 Statement of Captain John N. Rentz, U.S. Marine Corps Reserve, [June or July 1946?], p. 1, RG 125, Records of the Office of the Judge Advocate General (Navy), War Crimes Branch, Records Originated by the Director of War Crimes, Pacific Fleet, Confidential Correspondence, 1945–1948, Box 2, NACP.
136 The Barracks Surgeon to Commanding Officer, Marine Barracks, July 16, 1946, p. 1, RG 125, Records of the Office of the Judge Advocate General (Navy), War Crimes Branch, Records Originated by the Director of War Crimes, Pacific Fleet, Confidential Correspondence, 1945–1948, Box 2, NACP.
137 Commander Marianas to Commanding Officer, July 22, 1946, p. 1, RG 125, Records of the Office of the Judge Advocate General (Navy), War Crimes Branch, Records Originated by the Director of War Crimes, Pacific Fleet, Confidential Correspondence, 1945–1948, Box 2, NACP.
138 Statement of Private Raymond L. Romero, U.S.M.C., [June or July 1946?], p. 1, RG 125, Records of the Office of the Judge Advocate General (Navy), War Crimes Branch, Records Originated by the Director of War Crimes, Pacific Fleet, Confidential Correspondence, 1945–1948, Box 2, NACP.
139 Captain J. A. Moriarty, Jr., to Legal Section, Major C. A. Reinhard, September 2, 1946, p. 1, RG 125, Records of the Office of the Judge Advocate General (Navy), War Crimes Branch, Records Originated by the Director of War Crimes, Pacific Fleet, Confidential Correspondence, 1945–1948, Box 2, NACP.
140 Captain J. A. Moriarty, Jr., to Rear Admiral J. D. Murphy, October 13, 1947, p. 1, RG 125, Records of the Office of the Judge Advocate General (Navy), War Crimes Branch, Records Originated by the Director of War Crimes, Pacific Fleet, Confidential Correspondence, 1945–1948, Box 2, NACP.

141 CHIBA Eigo, Affidavit, October 22, 1947, p. 2, RG 125, Records of the Office of the Judge Advocate General (Navy), War Crimes Branch, Records Originated by the Director of War Crimes, Pacific Fleet, Confidential Correspondence, 1945–1948, Box 2, NACP.
142 HATAOKA Hideo, Affidavit, October 20, 1947, p. 1, RG 125, Records of the Office of the Judge Advocate General (Navy), War Crimes Branch, Records Originated by the Director of War Crimes, Pacific Fleet, Confidential Correspondence, 1945–1948, Box 2, NACP.
143 HATAOKA Hideo, Affidavit, October 20, 1947, 2.
144 HATAOKA Hideo, Affidavit, October 20, 1947, 2.
145 Statement of Sub. Lieutenant 1st Class IJIMA, Mayuki, [May 25 to May 27, 1947?], p. 1, RG 125, Records of the Office of the Judge Advocate General (Navy), War Crimes Branch, Records Originated by the Director of War Crimes, Pacific Fleet, Confidential Correspondence, 1945–1948, Box 2, NACP.
146 FUJINO, Yoshio, Affidavit, October 20, 1947, p. 1, RG 125, Records of the Office of the Judge Advocate General (Navy), War Crimes Branch, Records Originated by the Director of War Crimes, Pacific Fleet, Confidential Correspondence, 1945–1948, Box 2, NACP.
147 FUJINO, Yoshio, Affidavit, October 20, 1947, 2.
148 YATSUHASHI, Shigeru, Affidavit, October 20, 1947, p. 2, RG 125, Records of the Office of the Judge Advocate General (Navy), War Crimes Branch, Records Originated by the Director of War Crimes, Pacific Fleet, Confidential Correspondence, 1945–1948, Box 2, NACP.
149 Captain J. A. Moriarty, Jr., to Rear Admiral J. D. Murphy, October 13, 1947, p. 1, RG 125, Records of the Office of the Judge Advocate General (Navy), War Crimes Branch, Records Originated by the Director of War Crimes, Pacific Fleet, Confidential Correspondence, 1945–1948, Box 2, NACP.
150 Captain J. A. Moriarty, Jr., to Rear Admiral J. D. Murphy, October 13, 1947, 1.
151 Captain J. A. Moriarty, Jr., to Rear Admiral J. D. Murphy, October 13, 1947, 2.
152 LCDR. H. W. Buckingham to Deputy Chief of Staff for Planning, March 29, 1948, p. 1, RG 125, Records of the Office of the Judge Advocate General (Navy), War Crimes Branch, Records Originated by Director of War Crimes, Pacific Fleet, Secret Correspondence, 1945–1949, Box 3, NACP.
153 LCDR. H. W. Buckingham to Deputy Chief of Staff for Planning, March 29, 1948, 1.
154 Rear Admiral John D. Murphy to Commander Marianas, March 31, 1948, p. 3, RG 125, Records of the Office of the Judge Advocate General (Navy), War Crimes Branch, Records Originated by Director of War Crimes, Pacific Fleet, Secret Correspondence, 1945–1949, Box 3, NACP.
155 LCDR. H. W. Buckingham to Deputy Chief of Staff for Planning, March 29, 1948, 1.

Chapter 2. War Crimes

1. Sheldon Glueck, *What Shall Be Done with War Criminals?* (Washington, DC: United States War Department, 1944), 23.
2. Glueck, *What Shall Be Done with War Criminals?*, 38.
3. Glueck, *What Shall Be Done with War Criminals?*, 38–39.
4. Glueck, *What Shall Be Done with War Criminals?*, 39.
5. Elizabeth M. DeLoughrey, *Routes and Roots: Navigating Caribbean and Pacific Island Literatures* (Honolulu: University of Hawai'i Press, 2007), 8.
6. Glueck, *What Shall Be Done with War Criminals?*, 3.
7. Yuma Totani, *The Tokyo War Crimes Trial: The Pursuit of Justice in the Wake of World War II* (Cambridge, MA: Harvard University Asia Center, 2008), 102.
8. Robert H. Jackson, "Address Before the American Society of International Law, Washington, DC," April 13, 1945, p. 8, RG 125, Records of the Office of the Judge Advocate General (Navy), Miscellaneous Records, 1944–1949, From: Von Mackensen Papers, Thru: War Crimes (5) Law Briefs, Box 13, NACP.
9. Jackson, "Address Before the American Society of International Law, Washington, DC," 8.
10. Jackson, "Address Before the American Society of International Law, Washington, DC," 8.
11. Jackson, "Address Before the American Society of International Law, Washington, DC," 7.
12. Jackson, "Address Before the American Society of International Law, Washington, DC," 9.
13. Jackson, "Address Before the American Society of International Law, Washington, DC," 9.
14. Jackson, "Address Before the American Society of International Law, Washington, DC," 9.
15. Jackson, "Address Before the American Society of International Law, Washington, DC," 9.
16. Robert A. Williams Jr., *Like a Loaded Weapon: The Rehnquist Court, Indian Rights, and the Legal History of Racism in America* (Minneapolis: University of Minnesota Press, 2005), 23.
17. Dennis J. Hutchinson, "'The Achilles Heel' of the Constitution: Justice Jackson and the Japanese Exclusion Cases," *Supreme Court Review* 2002 (2002): 455.
18. Williams, *Like a Loaded Weapon*, 23.
19. The Marshall cases include *Johnson v. McIntosh* (1823), *Cherokee Nation v. Georgia* (1831), and *Worcester v. Georgia* (1832). Reflecting on the racisms of these rulings, Robert A. Williams Jr. argued that the rulings "developed a legal model of Indian rights that relied upon the same basic language that the Founders had used in defining the first U.S. Indian policy. As used in Marshall's model of Indian rights under U.S. law, this language served to justify the legal imposition

of the white racial dictatorship over the tribes that had been envisioned as the ultimately intended goal of the Founders' inaugural Indian policy paradigm of treating 'the Savage as the Wolf.' . . . The model of inferior and diminished Indian rights under the Constitution and laws of the United States laid out in these three seminal cases continues to define the Court's approach to all questions of Indian tribal rights" (Williams, *Like a Loaded Weapon*, 49).

20 Williams, *Like a Loaded Weapon*, 23.
21 Williams, *Like a Loaded Weapon*, 23.
22 Jackson, "Address Before the American Society of International Law, Washington, DC," 8.
23 Jackson, "Address Before the American Society of International Law, Washington, DC," 2.
24 Jackson, "Address Before the American Society of International Law, Washington, DC," 11.
25 Hutchinson, "'The Achilles Heel' of the Constitution," 488.
26 Justice Robert H. Jackson to the President, June 7, 1945, p. 5, Martin Emilius Carlson Papers, Box 2, Hoover Institution Archives, Stanford University, Stanford, CA.
27 Address by Lieutenant Commander James J. Robinson, U.S.N.R., Office of the Judge Advocate General of the Navy before Joint Meeting of the Military and Naval Law Committees of the American Bar Association and the Federal Bar Association, Washington, D.C., April 20, 1945, p. 2, John Damian Murphy Papers, Box 8, Folder 18, Hoover Institution Archives, Stanford University, Stanford, CA.
28 Address by Lieutenant Commander James J. Robinson, 3.
29 Address by Lieutenant Commander James J. Robinson, 3.
30 Address by Lieutenant Commander James J. Robinson, 3.
31 Larry May, *War Crimes and Just War* (Cambridge: Cambridge University Press, 2007), 305.
32 Gerry J. Simpson, "War Crimes: A Critical Introduction," in *The Law of War Crimes: National and International Approaches*, ed. Timothy L. H. McCormack and Gerry J. Simpson (The Hague: Kluwer Law International, 1997), 16.
33 Shannon Lee Dawdy and Joe Bonni, "Towards a General Theory of Piracy," *Anthropology Quarterly* 85, no. 3 (Summer 2012): 675.
34 Gerry Simpson, *Law, War and Crime: War Crimes Trials and the Reinvention of International Law* (Cambridge: Polity Press, 2007), 161.
35 Simpson, *Law, War and Crime*, 162.
36 Rear Admiral Arthur G. Robinson, "War Crimes Speech" (1948?), p. 32, John Damian Murphy Papers, Box 13, Folder 1896–, Hoover Institution Archives, Stanford University, Stanford, CA.
37 Alexander Sebastian Dent, "Introduction: Understanding the War on Piracy,

Or Why We Need More Anthropology of Pirates," *Anthropology Quarterly* 85, no. 3 (Summer 2012): 666.
38 Dent, "Introduction," 666.
39 Lisa Yoneyama, "Traveling Memories, Contagious Justice: Americanization of Japanese War Crimes at the End of the Post–Cold War," *Journal of Asian American Studies* 6, no. 1 (February 2003): 65.
40 U.S. Bureau of Naval Personnel, *Naval Justice* (Washington, DC: Standards and Curriculum Division and Training, U.S. Bureau of Naval Personnel, 1945), 1.
41 U.S. Bureau of Naval Personnel, *Naval Justice*, 2.
42 O. S. Colclough, "Naval Justice," *Journal of Criminal Law and Criminology* 38, no. 3 (September–October 1947): 205.
43 Colclough, "Naval Justice," 201.
44 U.S. Bureau of Naval Personnel, *Naval Justice*, 2 (emphasis in original).
45 Michel Foucault, *Power: Essential Works of Michel Foucault, 1954–1984*, vol. 3, ed. James D. Faubion, trans. Robert Hurley et al. (London: Penguin Books, 1994), 52.
46 Weaver, *Turtle Goes to War*, 34.
47 Fisher, *Military Tribunals and Presidential Power*, xi.
48 Sheldon Glueck, "By What Tribunal Shall War Offenders Be Tried?," *Harvard Law Review* 56, no. 7 (June 1943): 1073.
49 A. Wigfall Green, "The Military Commission," *American Journal of International Law* 42, no. 4 (October 1948): 834.
50 Green, "The Military Commission," 834.
51 United Nations War Crimes Commission (UNWCC), ed., *Law Reports of Trials of War Criminals*, vol. 3 (London: His Majesty's Stationery Office, 1948), 104.
52 UNWCC, *Law Reports of Trials of War Criminals*, 104.
53 Colclough, "Naval Justice," 200.
54 UNWCC, *Law Reports of Trials of War Criminals*, 112.
55 UNWCC, *Law Reports of Trials of War Criminals*, 112–113.
56 UNWCC, *Law Reports of Trials of War Criminals*, 113.
57 U.S. Bureau of Naval Personnel, *Naval Justice*, 6.
58 U.S. Department of the Navy, *Naval Courts and Boards* (Washington, DC: Government Printing Office, 1937), 490.
59 Secretary of the Navy to All Ships and Stations, Bureaus and Offices, Navy Department. January 13, 1945, p. 1, RG 125, Records of the Office of the Judge Advocate General (Navy), War Crimes Branch, 1944–1949, Miscellaneous Records, From Civil Affairs Divisions Thru Directives and Distributions, Box 3, NACP.
60 Secretary of the Navy to All Ships and Stations, Bureaus and Offices, Navy Department. January 13, 1945, 1,
61 Robinson, "War Crimes Speech," 8.
62 Robinson, "War Crimes Speech," 8.

63 Yuki Tanaka, *Hidden Horrors: Japanese War Crimes in World War II* (Boulder, CO: Westview Press, 1996), 2.
64 Murphy, *US Navy War Crimes Program Final Report*, 29a.
65 Dylan Rodríguez, *Forced Passages: Imprisoned Radical Intellectuals and the U.S. Prison Regime* (Minneapolis: University of Minnesota Press, 2006), 44.
66 Murphy, *US Navy War Crimes Program Final Report*, 81.
67 Philip R. Piccigallo, *The Japanese on Trial: Allied War Crimes Operations in the East, 1945–1951* (Austin: University of Texas Press, 1979), 35.
68 Piccigallo, *The Japanese on Trial*, 40.
69 Memorandum: Proposed plan for establishment of a war crimes office in the Pacific Ocean Areas and integration of Army (with Air Force), Navy, and Marine Corps personnel into both Army and Navy war crimes branches, July 24, 1945, p. 2, RG 125, Records of the Office of the Judge Advocate General (Navy), War Crimes Branch, Miscellaneous Records, 1944–1949, From: War Crimes Office Thru: War Crimes Officers, Box 15, NACP.
70 Erickson, "United States Navy War Crimes Trials (1945–1949)," 95.
71 As quoted in UNWCC, *Law Reports of Trials of War Criminals*, the SCAP classifications on war crimes reads as follows: "(a) The planning, preparation, initiation or waging of war of aggression or a war in violation of international treaties, agreements or assurances, or participation in a common plan or conspiracy for the accomplishment of any of the foregoing. (b) Violations of the laws or customs of war. Such violations shall include, but not be limited to, murder, ill-treatment or deportation to slave labour or for any other purpose of civilian population of or in occupied territory; murder or ill-treatment of prisoners of war or internees or persons on the seas or elsewhere; improper treatment of hostages; plunder of public or private property; wanton destruction of cities, towns or villages; or devastation not justified by military necessity. (c) Murder, extermination, enslavement, deportation and other inhuman acts committed against any civilian population before or during war, or persecutions on political, racial or religious grounds in execution of, or in connection with, any crime defined herein, whether or not in violation of the domestic laws of the country where perpetrated" (106).
72 UNWCC, *Law Reports of Trials of War Criminals*, 106.
73 State-War-Navy Coordinating Subcommittee for the Far East: The Apprehension and Punishment of War Criminals, September 12, 1945, p. 14, RG 125, Records of the Office of the Judge Advocate General (Navy), War Crimes Branch, Miscellaneous Records, 1944–1949, From: State-War-Navy Coord. S.C. for Far East, Proceedings Thru: Uniform of the Day, Box 12, NACP (emphasis in original).
74 Green, "The Military Commission," 842.
75 Robinson, "War Crimes Speech," 31.
76 Robinson, "War Crimes Speech," 31.

77　Saito, *From Chinese Exclusion to Guantánamo Bay*, 14.
78　Saito, *From Chinese Exclusion to Guantánamo Bay*, 41.
79　U.S. Department of the Navy, Office of the Chief of Naval Operations, *U.S. Navy Report on Guam, 1899–1950*, 17.
80　Roy E. James, "The Island Possession of Guam," in *America's Pacific Dependencies: A Survey of American Colonial Policies and of Administration and Progress toward Self-Rule in Alaska, Hawaii, Guam, Samoa and the Trust Territory*, ed. Rupert Emerson, Lawrence S. Finkelstein, E. L. Bartlett, George H. McLane, and Roy E. James (New York: American Institute of Pacific Relations, 1949), 79.
81　James, "The Island Possession of Guam," 79.
82　Charles A. Pownall, "Navy Day Speech—27 October 1948," p. 1, Charles A. Pownall Papers, Box 1, Hoover Institution Archives, Stanford University, Stanford, CA.
83　Rogers, *Destiny's Landfall*, 195.
84　Admiral C. W. Nimitz, "Proclamation No. 4, EXCEPTIONAL MILITARY COURTS," July 21, 1944, p. 1, RG 125, Records of the Office of the Judge Advocate General (Navy), War Crimes Branch, Records Regarding Pacific Area War Crimes Cases, 1944–1949, Box 1, NACP.
85　Robinson, "War Crimes Speech," 26.
86　T. L. Sprague, "Length of Tours of Duty for Naval Personnel at Overseas Bases," [1947?], p. 1, RG 313, Records of the Naval Operating Forces, Naval Government Unit, Guam, Mariana Islands, General Correspondence, 1946–1950, Box 8 of 12, Folder "P14-2 Retention of Officers and Enlisted Men," NARA-PAC.
87　Murphy, *US Navy War Crimes Program Final Report*, 43.
88　Murphy, *US Navy War Crimes Program Final Report*, 43.
89　Rear Admiral C. A. Pownall to Commander in Chief Pacific and U.S. Pacific Fleet, October 28, 1949, p. 1, RG 125, Records of the Office of Judge Advocate General (Navy) War Crimes Branch, Records Originated by Director of War Crimes, Pacific Fleet, Correspondence, 1944–1949, Box 13, NACP.
90　Murphy, *US Navy War Crimes Program Final Report*, 32.
91　Murphy, *US Navy War Crimes Program Final Report*, 32.
92　Murphy, *US Navy War Crimes Program Final Report*, 65.
93　Murphy, *US Navy War Crimes Program Final Report*, 65.
94　Murphy, *US Navy War Crimes Program Final Report*, 108.
95　Murphy, *US Navy War Crimes Program Final Report*, 108.
96　Murphy, *US Navy War Crimes Program Final Report*, 108.
97　Murphy, *US Navy War Crimes Program Final Report*, 108.
98　Jorge Cristobal, "War as Island Natives Saw It, 1942–45," in *Pacific War Stories in the Words of Those Who Survived*, ed. Rex Alan Smith and Gerald A. Meehl (New York: Abbeville Press, 2004), 401.
99　Cristobal, "War as Island Natives Saw It," 402.
100　Cristobal, "War as Island Natives Saw It," 402.

101 Jorge Cristobal, interview by the author, Tumon, Guam, May 4, 2006 (emphasis added).
102 First Report on War Crimes, Navy Division, December 7, 1945, pp. 120–121, RG 125, Records of the Office of the Judge Advocate General (Navy), War Crimes Branch, Miscellaneous 1944–1949, From: Naval Bombardment and Aerial Attacks Thru: Pacific Ocean Areas, Box 9, NACP.
103 Chief of Naval Operations to Commander in Chief, U.S. Pacific Fleet and Pacific Ocean Areas, November 28, 1945, p. 1, RG 125, Records of the Office of the Judge Advocate General (Navy), War Crimes Branch, Records Originated by Director of War Crimes, Pacific Fleet, Confidential Correspondence, 1945–1948, Box 1, NACP.
104 The Commander Marianas Area to Rear Admiral G. Robinson, U.S. Navy, April 5, 1946, p. 1, Martin Emilius Carlson Papers, Box 1, Hoover Institution Archives, Stanford University, Stanford, CA.
105 David Cohen, interview by the author, Honolulu, Hawai'i, February 23, 2006.
106 Hal M. Friedman, "The Beast in Paradise: The United States Navy in Micronesia, 1943–1947," *Pacific Historical Review* 62, no. 2 (May 1993): 189.
107 Murphy, *US Navy War Crimes Program Final Report*, 80.
108 Murphy, *US Navy War Crimes Program Final Report*, 80 (emphasis mine).
109 In December 1944, the navy held three war crimes trials in Kwajalein, Marshall Islands, and one civil crimes trial in Guam. With respect to Kwajalein, the cases concerned the Japanese murder of American prisoners of war and Marshallese natives during the war, whereas in Guam the trial regarded a Guamanian-on-Guamanian murder case during the U.S. reoccupation of the island. Based on my review of documents from the U.S. War Crimes Office and the United Nations, I have not come across any explanation for why the navy sponsored only three trials in Kwajalein. I speculate that the navy withdrew its tribunal from Kwajalein knowing that its presence in a Japanese colony, while justifiable in U.S. naval law, would attract international criticism.
110 Takashi Fujitani, *Race for Empire: Koreans as Japanese and Japanese as Americans during World War II* (Berkeley: University of California Press, 2011), 13.
111 Murphy, *US Navy War Crimes Program Final Report*, Appendix K-6-e, p. 1.
112 "Memorandum for the Judge Advocate General," April 24, 1945, section Q.1, p. 1, RG 125, Records of the Office of the Judge Advocate General (Navy), War Crimes Branch, Records Regarding Pacific Area War Crimes Cases, 1944–1949, Box 1, NACP.
113 "Memorandum for the Judge Advocate General," April 24, 1945, section Q.1, p. 1,
114 "Memorandum for the Judge Advocate General," April 24, 1945, section Q.4, p. 2,
115 "Memorandum for the Judge Advocate General," April 24, 1945, section Q.2, p. 1.

116 Michel Foucault, *Security, Territory, Population: Lectures at the Collège de France, 1977–1978*, ed. Michel Senelart, trans. Graham Burchell (New York: Palgrave Macmillan, 2007), 126.
117 "Memorandum for Commander Dangerfield," May 8, 1945, p. 2, RG 125, Records of the Office of the Judge Advocate General (Navy), War Crimes Branch, Records Regarding Pacific Area War Crimes Cases, 1944–1949, Box 1, NACP.
118 "Memorandum for the Judge Advocate General," April 24, 1945, section Q.7, p. 1, RG 125, Records of the Office of the Judge Advocate General (Navy), War Crimes Branch, Records Regarding Pacific Area War Crimes Cases, 1944–1949, Box 1, NACP.
119 Lieutenant Commander Francis Whitehair to Captain J. J. Robinson, USNR, July 24, 1945. p. 3–4, RG 125, Records of the Office of the Judge Advocate General (Navy), War Crimes Branch, Miscellaneous 1944–1949, Box 9, NACP.
120 Foucault, *Security, Territory, Population*, 169.
121 Rear Admiral Charles A. Pownall, "INAUGURAL ADDRESS," May 30, 1946, p. 2, Charles A. Pownall Papers, Box 1, Hoover Institution Archives, Stanford University, Stanford, CA.
122 Foucault, *Security, Territory, Population*, 169.
123 Murphy, *US Navy War Crimes Program Final Report*, 42.
124 Robinson, "War Crimes Speech," 24.
125 Tim Maga, *Judgment at Tokyo: The Japanese War Crimes Trials* (Lexington: University Press of Kentucky, 2001), 118.
126 Robinson, "War Crimes Speech," 20.
127 Murphy, *US Navy War Crimes Program Final Report*, 1.
128 Murphy, *US Navy War Crimes Program Final Report*, 80.
129 Murphy, *US Navy War Crimes Program Final Report*, 204.

Chapter 3. Native Assailants

1 "Memorandum for Admiral Gatch," Office of the Judge Advocate General, March 1945, p. 2, RG 125, Records of the Office of the Judge Advocate General (Navy), War Crimes Branch, Records Regarding Pacific Area War Crimes Cases, 1944–1949, Box 1, NACP.
2 Stephen B. Robinson, comp., *The Penal Code of Guam* (Manila: Bureau of Printing, 1933), 72.
3 Memorandum for Major General Larsen, USMC, Office of the Judge Advocate General, April 23, 1945, p. 1, RG 125, Records of the Office of the Judge Advocate General (Navy), War Crimes Branch, Records Regarding Pacific Area War Crimes Cases, 1944–1949, Box 1, NACP.
4 Miguel A. Cruz, Court Transcript, March 22, 1945, p. 3 (hereafter cited as Miguel A. Cruz Court Transcript), World War II Document Archive, Pacific Theater, U.S. Navy Trials (microfilm reel no. 126322), WCSC.

5 Pedro C. Sanchez, *Guahan Guam: The History of Our Island* (Agaña: Sanchez Publishing House, 1987), 195.
6 Miguel A. Cruz Court Transcript, 22.
7 Miguel A. Cruz Court Transcript, 22.
8 Miguel A. Cruz Court Transcript, 23.
9 With one exception, every Rotanese and Saipanese identified Japan as their host country responsible for granting them rights as prisoners of war under the United States. For unknown reasons, only Pedro Sablan Leon Guerrero requested Spain as his "protecting power."
10 Judith Gardam, "Gender and Non-combatant Immunity," *Transnational Law and Contemporary Problems* 3 (1993): 351.
11 Kushner, *Men to Devils, Devils to Men*, 14.
12 Henry S. Pangelinan Court Transcript, 6.
13 May, *War Crimes and Just War*, 93.
14 May, *War Crimes and Just War*, 93.
15 Pedro Guerrero Court Transcript, 12.
16 Antonio Camacho and Juan Reyes, April 27, 1945, p. 15 (hereafter cited as Antonio Camacho and Juan Reyes Court Transcript), World War II Document Archive, Pacific Theater, U.S. Navy Trials (microfilm reel no. 130525), WCSC.
17 Riseman, *Defending Whose Country?*, 225.
18 Pedro Guerrero Court Transcript, 12.
19 Gardam, "Gender and Non-combatant Immunity," 348.
20 Gardam, "Gender and Non-combatant Immunity," 348.
21 Joseph Pugliese, *State Violence and the Execution of Law* (New York: Routledge, 2013), 41.
22 Pugliese, *State Violence and the Execution of Law*, 41.
23 Helen M. Kinsella, "Securing the Civilian: Sex and Gender in the Laws of War," in *Power in Global Governance*, ed. Michael Barnett and Raymond Duvall (Cambridge: Cambridge University Press, 2005), 271 (emphasis in original).
24 May, *War Crimes and Just War*, 168.
25 "War Criminals," March 1945, p. 2, RG 125, Records of the Office of the Judge Advocate General (Navy), War Crimes Branch, Records Regarding Pacific Area War Crimes Cases, 1944–1949, Box 1, NACP.
26 Nicholas T. Sablan Court Transcript, 8.
27 Nicholas T. Sablan Court Transcript, 17.
28 Nicholas T. Sablan Court Transcript, 17.
29 Nicholas T. Sablan Court Transcript, 17.
30 Lisa Hajjar, *Courting Conflict: The Israeli Military Court System in the West Bank and Gaza* (Berkeley: University of California Press, 2005), 68.
31 Nicholas T. Sablan Court Transcript, 24.
32 Nicholas T. Sablan Court Transcript, 22.
33 Nicholas T. Sablan Court Transcript, 27.

34 Nicholas T. Sablan Court Transcript, 28.
35 Rogers, *Destiny's Landfall*, 174.
36 Robinson, *The Penal Code of Guam*, 69.
37 Nicholas T. Sablan Court Transcript, 30.
38 Nicholas T. Sablan Court Transcript, 30.
39 Zillah Eisenstein, "Resexing Militarism for the Globe," in *Feminism and War: Confronting U.S. Imperialism*, ed. Robin L. Riley, Chandra Talpade Mohanty, and Minnie Bruce Pratt (London: Zed Books, 2008), 39.
40 Nicholas T. Sablan Court Transcript, 35.
41 Nicholas T. Sablan Court Transcript, 36.
42 Nicholas T. Sablan Court Transcript, 32.
43 Nicholas T. Sablan Court Transcript, 32.
44 Nicholas T. Sablan Court Transcript, 32.
45 Nicholas T. Sablan Court Transcript, 32.
46 Nicholas T. Sablan Court Transcript, 32.
47 Nicholas T. Sablan, "Written statement of the accused," April 5, 1945, p. 1, Nicholas T. Sablan Court Transcript.
48 Alexander Akerman, Jr., "Accused's written argument," April 5, 1945, p. 1, Nicholas T. Sablan Court Transcript.
49 Agueda I. Johnston, "Tweed," 1963, p. 1, Johnston, A. I., Publishing Companies, Box 7, Folder 53, 5 of 7, MARC.
50 Jose P. Villagomez 1945a Court Transcript, 103.
51 Jose P. Villagomez 1945a Court Transcript, 103.
52 Jose P. Villagomez 1945a Court Transcript, 103.
53 Teller Ammons, Judge Advocate's written opening argument, May 29, 1945, p. "S," Henry S. Pangelinan Court Transcript.
54 Henry S. Pangelinan Court Transcript, 22.
55 "War Criminals," March 1945, p. 4, RG 125, Records of the Office of the Judge Advocate General (Navy), War Crimes Branch, Records Regarding Pacific Area War Crimes Cases, 1944–1949, Box 1, NACP.
56 Henry S. Pangelinan Court Transcript, 9.
57 Henry S. Pangelinan Court Transcript, 18.
58 Translation of the accused's written statement, May 29, 1945, p. "R," Henry S. Pangelinan Court Transcript.
59 Henry S. Pangelinan, Written Statement, May 29, 1945, p. "Q(1)," Henry S. Pangelinan Court Transcript, my translation.
60 Henry S. Pangelinan Court Transcript, 17.
61 Henry S. Pangelinan Court Transcript, 17.
62 Henry S. Pangelinan Court Transcript, 20.
63 Pedro Sablan Leon Guerrero Court Transcript, 77.
64 Pedro Sablan Leon Guerrero Court Transcript, 57.
65 Pedro Sablan Leon Guerrero Court Transcript, 16.

66 Pedro Sablan Leon Guerrero Court Transcript, 20.
67 Pedro Sablan Leon Guerrero Court Transcript, 17–18.
68 Pedro Sablan Leon Guerrero Court Transcript, 61.
69 Pedro Sablan Leon Guerrero Court Transcript, 32.
70 Pedro Sablan Leon Guerrero Court Transcript, 30.
71 Pedro Sablan Leon Guerrero Court Transcript, 30.
72 Pedro Sablan Leon Guerrero Court Transcript, 63.
73 Pedro Sablan Leon Guerrero Court Transcript, 80.
74 Kahn, *Sacred Violence*, 25.
75 "From Pedro Sablan Leon Guerrero to the Island Commander, 24 August 1945," Pedro Guerrero Court Transcript, 1.
76 Pedro Guerrero Court Transcript, 109.
77 Jose C. Cabrera Court Transcript, September 26, 1945, p. 8 (hereafter cited as Jose C. Cabrera Court Transcript), World War II Document Archive, Pacific Theater, U.S. Navy Trials (microfilm reel no. 144764), WCSC.
78 Jose C. Cabrera Court Transcript, 5.
79 Jose C. Cabrera Court Transcript, 27.
80 Jose C. Cabrera Court Transcript, 27.
81 Jose C. Cabrera Court Transcript, 28.
82 Jose C. Cabrera Court Transcript, 15.
83 Jose C. Cabrera Court Transcript, 13.
84 Jose C. Cabrera Court Transcript, 38.
85 Jose C. Cabrera Court Transcript, 38.
86 Jose C. Cabrera Court Transcript, 39.
87 Domingo S. Quintanilla Court Transcript, October 15, 1945, p. 18 (hereafter cited as Domingo S. Quintanilla Court Transcript), World War II Document Archive, Pacific Theater, U.S. Navy Trials (microfilm reel no. 144031), WCSC.
88 Domingo S. Quintanilla Court Transcript, 15.
89 Domingo S. Quintanilla Court Transcript, 18.
90 Robinson, *The Penal Code of Guam*, 89.
91 Robinson, *The Penal Code of Guam*, 89.
92 Domingo S. Quintanilla Court Transcript, 9.
93 Domingo S. Quintanilla Court Transcript, 9.
94 Domingo S. Quintanilla Court Transcript, 9.
95 Domingo S. Quintanilla Court Transcript, 10.
96 Domingo S. Quintanilla Court Transcript, 11.
97 Robert Aldrich, *Colonialism and Homosexuality* (London: Routledge, 2003), 250.
98 Domingo S. Quintanilla Court Transcript, 19.
99 Domingo S. Quintanilla Court Transcript, 20.
100 Fritz Angocio Mendiola Court Transcript, October 18, 1945, p. 32 (hereafter cited as Fritz Angocio Mendiola Court Transcript), World War II Document Archive, Pacific Theater, U.S. Navy Trials (microfilm reel no. 141745), WCSC.

101 Fritz Angocio Mendiola Court Transcript, 25.
102 Fritz Angocio Mendiola Court Transcript, 20.
103 Fritz Angocio Mendiola Court Transcript, 35.
104 Fritz Angocio Mendiola Court Transcript, 35.
105 Jose P. Villagomez Court Transcript, October 22, 1945, p. 15 (hereafter cited as Jose P. Villagomez 1945b Court Transcript), World War II Document Archive, Pacific Theater, U.S. Navy Trials (microfilm reel no. 142103), WCSC.
106 Nicholas T. Sablan Court Transcript, 13.
107 Jose P. Villagomez 1945b Court Transcript, 5.
108 Jose P. Villagomez 1945b Court Transcript, 10.
109 Jose P. Villagomez 1945b Court Transcript, 17.
110 Francisco P. Sablan Court Transcript, October 22, 1945, p. 51 (hereafter cited as Francisco P. Sablan Court Transcript), World War II Document Archive, Pacific Theater, U.S. Navy Trials (microfilm reel no. 142104), WCSC.
111 Francisco P. Sablan Court Transcript, 30.
112 Francisco P. Sablan Court Transcript, 33.
113 Francisco P. Sablan Court Transcript, 11.
114 Robinson, *The Penal Code of Guam*, 98.
115 Francisco P. Sablan Court Transcript, 5.
116 Francisco P. Sablan Court Transcript, 5.
117 Francisco P. Sablan Court Transcript, 23.
118 Francisco P. Sablan Court Transcript, 42.
119 Francisco P. Sablan Court Transcript, 52.
120 Henry S. Pangelinan Court Transcript, R.
121 Jose P. Villagomez 1945b Court Transcript, P(1).
122 Nicholas T. Sablan Court Transcript, U.
123 Domingo S. Quintanilla Court Transcript, T(1).
124 Fritz Angocio Mendiola Court Transcript, S.
125 Francisco P. Sablan Court Transcript, T(1).
126 Henry S. Pangelinan Court Transcript, R.
127 Foucault, *Discipline and Punish*, 11.
128 Michael Salman, *The Embarrassment of Slavery: Controversies over Bondage and Nationalism in the American Colonial Philippines* (Berkeley: University of California Press, 2003), 266.
129 Khalil Gibran Muhammad, *The Condemnation of Blackness: Race, Crime, and the Making of Modern Urban America* (Cambridge, MA: Harvard University Press, 2010), 139.

Chapter 4. Native Murderers

1 U.S. Department of the Navy, *Naval Courts and Boards*, 52.
2 Robinson, *The Penal Code of Guam*, 63.

3 Robinson, *The Penal Code of Guam*, 63–64.
4 Robert Asher, Lawrence B. Goodheart, and Alan Rogers, "Adjudicating Homicide: The Legal Framework and Social Norms," in *Murder on Trial: 1620–2002*, ed. Robert Asher, Lawrence B. Goodheart, and Alan Rogers (Albany: State University of New York Press, 2005), 14.
5 Juan Muña Dueñas, Court Transcript, December 28, 1944, p. 11 (hereafter cited as Juan Muña Dueñas Court Transcript), World War II Document Archive, Pacific Theater, U.S. Navy Trials (microfilm reel no. 117509), WCSC.
6 Juan Muña Dueñas Court Transcript, 5.
7 Juan Muña Dueñas Court Transcript, 9.
8 Sanchez, *Guahan Guam*, 15.
9 Sanchez, *Guahan Guam*, 52.
10 Robinson, *The Penal Code of Guam*, 72.
11 Robinson, *The Penal Code of Guam*, 63.
12 T. L. Gatch to Secretary of the Navy, March 22, 1945, p. 1, RG 125, Records of the Office of the Judge Advocate General (Navy), War Crimes Branch, Records Regarding Pacific Area War Crimes Cases, 1944–1949, Box 1, NACP.
13 T. L. Gatch to Secretary of the Navy, March 22, 1945, 1.
14 Jose P. Villagomez 1945a Court Transcript, 112.
15 Jose P. Villagomez 1945a Court Transcript, 112.
16 Jose P. Villagomez 1945a Court Transcript, 23.
17 Jose P. Villagomez 1945a Court Transcript, 22.
18 Jose P. Villagomez 1945a Court Transcript, 44.
19 Jose P. Villagomez 1945a Court Transcript, 82.
20 Jose P. Villagomez 1945a Court Transcript, 82.
21 Elaine Scarry, *The Body in Pain: The Making and Unmaking of the World* (New York: Oxford University Press, 1985), 27–28.
22 Jose P. Villagomez 1945a Court Transcript, 22.
23 Jose P. Villagomez 1945a Court Transcript, 51.
24 Jose P. Villagomez 1945a Court Transcript, 53.
25 Jose P. Villagomez 1945a Court Transcript, 67.
26 Jose P. Villagomez 1945a Court Transcript, 55.
27 Jose P. Villagomez 1945a Court Transcript, 65.
28 Jose P. Villagomez 1945a Court Transcript, 73.
29 Jose P. Villagomez 1945a Court Transcript, 74.
30 Jose P. Villagomez 1945a Court Transcript, 71.
31 Jose P. Villagomez 1945a Court Transcript, 105.
32 Jose P. Villagomez 1945a Court Transcript, 107.
33 Jose P. Villagomez 1945a Court Transcript, 46.
34 Jose P. Villagomez 1945a Court Transcript, 46.
35 Juan Villagomez, October 31, 1945, p. 34 (hereafter cited as Juan Villagomez

Court Transcript), World War II Document Archive, Pacific Theater, U.S. Navy Trials (microfilm reel no. 142374), WCSC.
36 Juan Villagomez Court Transcript, 13.
37 Juan Villagomez Court Transcript, 21.
38 Juan Villagomez Court Transcript, 22.
39 Juan Villagomez Court Transcript, 23.
40 Juan Villagomez Court Transcript, 25.
41 Juan Villagomez Court Transcript, 26.
42 Antonio Camacho and Juan Reyes, April 27, 1945, p. 5 (hereafter cited as Antonio Camacho and Juan Reyes Court Transcript), World War II Document Archive, Pacific Theater, U.S. Navy Trials (microfilm reel no. 130525), WCSC.
43 Antonio Camacho and Juan Reyes Court Transcript, 22.
44 Antonio Camacho and Juan Reyes Court Transcript, 23.
45 Antonio Camacho and Juan Reyes Court Transcript, 25.
46 Antonio Camacho and Juan Reyes Court Transcript, 39.
47 Antonio Camacho and Juan Reyes Court Transcript, 31.
48 Antonio Camacho and Juan Reyes Court Transcript, 31.
49 Antonio Camacho and Juan Reyes Court Transcript, 29.
50 Antonio Camacho and Juan Reyes Court Transcript, 28.
51 Antonio Camacho and Juan Reyes Court Transcript, 32
52 Antonio Camacho and Juan Reyes Court Transcript, 18.
53 Antonio Camacho and Juan Reyes Court Transcript, 23.
54 Antonio Camacho and Juan Reyes Court Transcript, 48.
55 Antonio Camacho and Juan Reyes Court Transcript, 45.
56 Antonio Camacho and Juan Reyes Court Transcript, 53.
57 Antonio Camacho and Juan Reyes Court Transcript, 56.
58 Manuel Borja Tudela Court Transcript, 21.
59 Manuel Borja Tudela Court Transcript, 21.
60 Manuel Borja Tudela Court Transcript, 24.
61 Manuel Borja Tudela Court Transcript, 24.
62 Manuel Borja Tudela Court Transcript, 41.
63 Manuel Borja Tudela Court Transcript, 42.
64 Manuel Borja Tudela Court Transcript, 11.
65 Rogers, *Destiny's Landfall*, 173.
66 Manuel Borja Tudela Court Transcript, 11.
67 Manuel Borja Tudela Court Transcript, 28.
68 Manuel Borja Tudela Court Transcript, 28.
69 Manuel Borja Tudela Court Transcript, 12.
70 Manuel Borja Tudela Court Transcript, 26.
71 Manuel Borja Tudela Court Transcript, 26.
72 Manuel Borja Tudela Court Transcript, 34.
73 Manuel Borja Tudela Court Transcript, 18.

74 Manuel Borja Tudela Court Transcript, 31.
75 Manuel Borja Tudela Court Transcript, 32.
76 Manuel Borja Tudela Court Transcript, 40.
77 Manuel Borja Tudela Court Transcript, 40.
78 Ann Laura Stoler, "Tense and Tender Ties: The Politics of Comparison in North American History and (Post) Colonial Studies," in *Haunted by Empire: Geographies of Intimacy in North American History*, ed. Ann Laura Stoler (Durham, NC: Duke University Press, 2006), 42.
79 Manuel Borja Tudela Court Transcript, 46.
80 Manuel Borja Tudela Court Transcript, 44.
81 Manuel Borja Tudela Court Transcript, 40.
82 Manuel Borja Tudela Court Transcript, 41.
83 Manuel Borja Tudela Court Transcript, 41.
84 Manuel Borja Tudela Court Transcript, 50.
85 Manuel Borja Tudela Court Transcript, 51.
86 Manuel Borja Tudela Court Transcript, 38.
87 Manuel Borja Tudela Court Transcript, 51.
88 Manuel Borja Tudela Court Transcript, 52.
89 Manuel Borja Tudela Court Transcript, "P(3)."
90 Luis C. Crisostomo, June 4, 1945, p. 35 (hereafter cited as Luis C. Crisostomo Court Transcript), World War II Document Archive, Pacific Theater, U.S. Navy Trials (microfilm reel no. 136369), WCSC.
91 Lin Poyer, Suzanne Falgout, and Laurence Marshall Carucci, *The Typhoon of War: Micronesian Experiences of the Pacific War* (Honolulu: University of Hawai'i Press, 2001), 233.
92 Luis C. Crisostomo Court Transcript, 32
93 Luis C. Crisostomo Court Transcript, 33.
94 Luis C. Crisostomo Court Transcript, 43.
95 Luis C. Crisostomo Court Transcript, 42.
96 Edward L. G. Aguon, Guam War Claims Review Commission Survivor's Questionnaire, November 29, 2003, p. 2, Guam Review War Claims 2003–2004, Edward L. G., 11/29/03, Box 1, Rec. 2090, MARC.
97 Luis C. Crisostomo Court Transcript, 54.
98 Luis C. Crisostomo Court Transcript, 57.
99 Luis C. Crisostomo Court Transcript, 58.
100 Luis C. Crisostomo Court Transcript, 56.
101 Luis C. Crisostomo Court Transcript, 67.
102 Luis C. Crisostomo Court Transcript, 67.
103 Luis C. Crisostomo Court Transcript, 72.
104 Luis C. Crisostomo Court Transcript, 61.
105 Kahn, *Sacred Violence*, 27.
106 Luis C. Crisostomo Court Transcript, 76.

107 Kahn, *Sacred Violence*, 27.
108 Kahn, *Sacred Violence*, 27.
109 Luis C. Crisostomo Court Transcript, 64.
110 Luis C. Crisostomo Court Transcript, 64.
111 Luis C. Crisostomo Court Transcript, 68.
112 Luis C. Crisostomo Court Transcript, 76.
113 Scott Richard Lyons, *X-Marks: Native Signatures of Assent* (Minneapolis: University of Minnesota Press, 2010), 2–3.
114 Paul A. Kramer, *The Blood of Government: Race, Empire, the United States, and the Philippines* (Chapel Hill: University of North Carolina Press, 2006), 140.
115 Luis C. Crisostomo Court Transcript, 82.
116 Luis C. Crisostomo Court Transcript, 82.
117 Tony Palomo, *An Island in Agony* (Agaña: Tony Palomo, 1984), 140.
118 Luis C. Crisostomo Court Transcript, 87.
119 Luis C. Crisostomo Court Transcript, 86.
120 Luis C. Crisostomo Court Transcript, 86.
121 Luis C. Crisostomo Court Transcript, 86.
122 Luis C. Crisostomo Court Transcript, 83.
123 Luis C. Crisostomo Court Transcript, 95.
124 Luis C. Crisostomo Court Transcript, 89.
125 Luis C. Crisostomo Court Transcript, 100.
126 Luis C. Crisostomo Court Transcript, 100.
127 Luis C. Crisostomo Court Transcript, 100.
128 Luis C. Crisostomo Court Transcript, 112.
129 Luis C. Crisostomo Court Transcript, P-1.
130 Luis C. Crisostomo Court Transcript, 111.
131 Luis C. Crisostomo Court Transcript, 115.
132 Juan B. Manibusan, "Three Obnoxious Saipanese Escape Death," *Guam Gazette*, February 1, 1946, 1.
133 Jose P. Villagomez to the Secretary of the Navy, July 19, 1951, p. 1, Jose P. Villagomez 1945a Court Transcript.
134 Luis C. Crisostomo, Antonio Camacho, and Juan Reyes to the Honorable Secretary of the Navy, October 22, 1951, p. 1, Antonio Camacho and Juan Reyes Court Transcript.
135 The Warden, A. A. Jackson, to the Honorable Secretary of the U.S. Navy, October 23, 1951, p. 1, Antonio Camacho and Juan Reyes Court Transcript.

Chapter 5. Japanese Traitors

1 Caroline Chung Simpson, *An Absent Presence: Japanese Americans in Postwar America* (Durham, NC: Duke University Press, 2001), 80.
2 Rogers, *Destiny's Landfall*, 157.

3. Rogers, *Destiny's Landfall*, 164.
4. Rogers, *Destiny's Landfall*, 157; Maga, *Judgment at Tokyo*, 108.
5. Translation of Affidavit of MIWA, Kyomon, by Lt. Eugene Kerrick, Jr., USNR. October 17, 1946, p. 1, World War II Document Archive, Pacific Theater, U.S. Navy Trials (microfilm reel no. 144704), Samuel T. Shinohara (28 Jul 1945), WCSC.
6. Wakako Higuchi, *The Japanese Administration of Guam, 1941–1944: A Study of Occupation and Integration Policies, with Japanese Oral Histories* (Jefferson, NC: McFarland, 2013), 195.
7. Exhibit No. 7a: Offender Samuel T. Shinohara, Island Command Stockade, Guam [1945?], p. 1, RG 125, Records of the Office of the Judge Advocate General (Navy), War Crimes Branch, Records Regarding Pacific Area War Crimes Cases, 1944–1949, Box 1, NACP.
8. Exhibit No. 7a: Offender Samuel T. Shinohara, 1.
9. Exhibit No. 7a: Offender Samuel T. Shinohara, 2.
10. Exhibit No. 7a: Offender Samuel T. Shinohara, 2.
11. Exhibit No. 7a: Offender Samuel T. Shinohara, 1.
12. Naoko Shibusawa, *America's Geisha Ally: Reimagining the Japanese Enemy* (Cambridge, MA: Harvard University Press, 2006), 143.
13. Suzanne Kelly Babb, "Fear and Loathing in America: Application of Treason Law in Times of National Crisis and the Case of John Walker Lindh," *Hastings Law Journal* 54, no. 6 (August 2003): 1732
14. Memorandum for the Judge Advocate General, April 24, 1945, p. 2, RG 125, Records of the Office of the Judge Advocate General (Navy), War Crimes Branch, Records Originated by the Director of War Crimes, Pacific Fleet, Correspondence, 1944–1948, Box 4, NACP.
15. H. N. Stent to The Island Commander, June 20, 1945, p. 1, RG 125, Records of the Office of the Judge Advocate General (Navy), War Crimes Branch, Records Originated by the Director of War Crimes, Pacific Fleet, Confidential Correspondence, 1945–1948, Box 1, NACP.
16. H. N. Stent to The Island Commander, June 20, 1945, 1
17. H. N. Stent to The Island Commander, June 20, 1945, 2.
18. The Island Commander to Lieutenant Colonel Teller Ammons, January 23, 1945, p. 2, RG 125, Records of the Office of the Judge Advocate General (Navy), War Crimes Branch, Records Originated by the Director of War Crimes, Pacific Fleet, Correspondence, 1944–1949, Box 6, NACP.
19. Charges and specifications in the case of Samuel T. Shinohara, an inhabitant and resident of Guam, May 12, 1945, p. 1, World War II Document Archive, Pacific Theater, U.S. Navy Trials (microfilm reel no. 144704), Samuel T. Shinohara (28 Jul 1945), WCSC.
20. Samuel T. Shinohara, Court Transcript, July 28, 1945, p. 2 (hereafter cited as Shinohara Court Transcript), World War II Document Archive, Pacific Theater,

U.S. Navy Trials (microfilm reel no. 144704), Samuel T. Shinohara (28 Jul 1945), WCSC.
21 Additional charges and specifications in the case of Samuel T. Shinohara, an inhabitant and resident of Guam, July 20, 1945, p. 1, World War II Document Archive, Pacific Theater, U.S. Navy Trials (microfilm reel no. 144704), Samuel T. Shinohara (28 Jul 1945), WCSC.
22 Shinohara Court Transcript, 2.
23 Shinohara Court Transcript, 6.
24 Cheryl I. Harris, "Whiteness as Property," *Harvard Law Review* 106, no. 8 (June 1993): 1716.
25 Harris, "Whiteness as Property," 1721.
26 Additional charges and specifications in the case of Samuel T. Shinohara, July 20, 1945, 1.
27 Robinson, *The Penal Code of Guam*, 160.
28 Shinohara Court Transcript, 11.
29 Shinohara Court Transcript, 13.
30 Shinohara Court Transcript, 14.
31 Heon Stevenson, *American Automobile Advertising, 1930–1980: An Illustrated History* (Jefferson, NC: McFarland, 106.
32 Shinohara Court Transcript, 20.
33 Shinohara Court Transcript, 22.
34 Charges and specifications in the case of Samuel T. Shinohara, May 12, 1945, 2.
35 Robinson, *The Penal Code of Guam*, 72.
36 Robinson, *The Penal Code of Guam*, 72
37 Shinohara Court Transcript, 33.
38 Rogers, *Destiny's Landfall*, 75.
39 Shinohara Court Transcript, 37.
40 Shinohara Court Transcript, 39.
41 Shinohara Court Transcript, 40.
42 Additional charges and specifications in the case of Samuel T. Shinohara, July 20, 1945, 3.
43 Robinson, *The Penal Code of Guam*, 93.
44 Shinohara Court Transcript, 45.
45 It is not clear, however, if or why the prosecutors prepared their witnesses to mention late 1943 or December 1943 when the charge listed "in or about the month of February or March 1942" as the time frame to consider. Even with more than a year's difference between these two generalized dates, the witnesses may have followed the prosecution's lead concerning the desecration of the U.S. flag.
46 Charges and specifications in the case of Samuel T. Shinohara, May 12, 1945, 2.
47 Robinson, *The Penal Code of Guam*, 78.
48 Robinson, *The Penal Code of Guam*, 80.

49 Rhonda Copelon, "Surfacing Gender: Reconceptualizing Crimes against Women in Time of War," in *The Women and War Reader*, ed. Lois Ann Lorentzen and Jennifer Turpin (New York: New York University Press, 1998), 65.
50 U.S. military documents refer to the governor aide-de-camp only as Sakai. No other name is provided.
51 C. Sarah Soh, *The Comfort Women: Sexual Violence and Postcolonial Memory in Korea and Japan* (Chicago: University of Chicago Press, 2008), 115.
52 Shinohara Court Transcript, 70.
53 Shinohara Court Transcript, 65.
54 Shinohara Court Transcript, 65.
55 Iyechad, *An Historical Perspective of Helping Practices*, 101.
56 Iyechad, *An Historical Perspective of Helping Practices*, 101.
57 Shinohara Court Transcript, 58.
58 Shinohara Court Transcript, 59.
59 Shinohara Court Transcript, 63.
60 Seungsook Moon, "Regulating Desire, Managing the Empire: U.S. Military Prostitution in South Korea, 1945–1970," in *Over There: Living with the U.S. Military Empire from World War Two to the Present*, ed. Maria Höhn and Seungsook Moon (Durham, NC: Duke University Press, 2010), 65.
61 Shinohara Court Transcript, 62.
62 Sarah Kovner, "Base Cultures: Sex Workers and Servicemen in Occupied Japan," *Journal of Asian Studies* 68, no. 3 (August 2009): 780.
63 Kovner, "Base Cultures," 780.
64 Shinohara Court Transcript, 73.
65 Shinohara Court Transcript, 73.
66 Ibid., Shinohara Court Transcript, 77.
67 Shinohara Court Transcript, 77.
68 Shinohara Court Transcript, 78.
69 Shinohara Court Transcript, 77.
70 Shinohara Court Transcript, 78.
71 Shinohara Court Transcript, 74.
72 "The Judge Advocate's Written Opening Argument," p. T(5), World War II Document Archive, Pacific Theater, U.S. Navy Trials (microfilm reel no. 144704), Samuel T. Shinohara (28 Jul 1945), WCSC.
73 Robinson, *The Penal Code of Guam*, 56–57.
74 Robinson, *The Penal Code of Guam*, 57.
75 Sonya O. Rose, "The 'Sex Question' in Anglo-American Relations in the Second World War," *International History Review* 20, no. 4 (December 1998): 890.
76 Fujitani, *Race for Empire*, 83.
77 Greg Robinson, *A Tragedy of Democracy: Japanese Confinement in North America* (New York: Columbia University Press, 2009), 61.
78 Robinson, *The Penal Code of Guam*, 24.

79 Robinson, *The Penal Code of Guam*, 24.
80 "The Judge Advocate's Written Opening Argument," T(17).
81 Wakako Higuchi identifies the organization as "Dai Niseikai," which conscripted at least 214 children from Chamorro-Japanese families in Guam. But because the Chamorro-Japanese and Japanese witnesses in Shinohara's case used "Dai Nisei" and "Dai Nisei Young Men's Association" to describe their affiliation with or opposition to this group, this chapter will privilege their choice of terms. Refer to Higuchi, *The Japanese Administration of Guam, 1941–1944*, 72–78.
82 Shinohara Court Transcript, 109.
83 Shinohara Court Transcript, 81.
84 Shinohara Court Transcript, 81.
85 Shinohara Court Transcript, 81.
86 Shinohara Court Transcript, 89, 90.
87 Shinohara Court Transcript, 95, 96.
88 Shinohara Court Transcript, 112.
89 Shinohara Court Transcript, 112.
90 Shinohara Court Transcript, 115.
91 Shinohara Court Transcript, 119.
92 Shinohara Court Transcript, 125.
93 Shinohara Court Transcript, 125.
94 Shinohara Court Transcript, 125.
95 Shinohara Court Transcript, 142.
96 Shinohara Court Transcript, 140.
97 Shinohara Court Transcript, 156.
98 Shinohara Court Transcript, 181.
99 Shinohara Court Transcript, 188.
100 Vicente Calvo Aflague, a silversmith and witness for the defense, also argued that Samuel T. Shinohara never stole Lieutenant James E. Davis's vehicle. Aflague likewise stated that other Japanese officials had utilized the American automobile, implying that the Minseibu had seized these and other cars for administrative purposes.
101 Shinohara Court Transcript, 170.
102 Shinohara Court Transcript, 226.
103 Shinohara Court Transcript, 225.
104 Eyal Benvenisti, *The International Law of Occupation* (Princeton, NJ: Princeton University Press, 1993), 9.
105 Benvenisti, *The International Law of Occupation*, 10.
106 Shinohara Court Transcript, 224 (emphasis added by the defense counsel).
107 Shinohara Court Transcript, 224.
108 Yoram Dinstein, *The International Law of Belligerent Occupation* (Cambridge: Cambridge University Press, 2009), 218.
109 Shinohara Court Transcript, 232.

110 Shinohara Court Transcript, 228.
111 Shinohara Court Transcript, 230.
112 William P. Oliver Jr., "International Law: Treason against the United States by Alien Enemy," *George Washington Law Review* 17, no. 2 (February 1949): 284.
113 Shinohara Court Transcript, 239 (emphasis in original).
114 James Snedeker, Chief, Division I, to Office of the Judge Advocate General, July 4, 1946, p. 1, World War II Document Archive, Pacific Theater, U.S. Navy Trials (microfilm reel no. 144704), Samuel T. Shinohara (28 Jul 1945), WCSC.
115 James Snedeker, Chief, Division I, to Office of the Judge Advocate General, July 4, 1946, 1.
116 James Snedeker, Chief, Division I, to Office of the Judge Advocate General, July 4, 1946, 7.
117 James Snedeker, Chief, Division I, to Office of the Judge Advocate General, July 4, 1946, 7.
118 James Snedeker, Chief, Division I, to Office of the Judge Advocate General, July 4, 1946, 8.
119 James Snedeker, Chief, Division I, to Office of the Judge Advocate General, July 4, 1946, 8.
120 The two witnesses were Felix Flores Sakai and Jesus B. Sayama. Refer, for example, to the Affidavit of Felix Flores Sakai, October 18, 1946, World War II Document Archive, Pacific Theater, U.S. Navy Trials (microfilm reel no. 144704), Samuel T. Shinohara (28 Jul 1945), WCSC.
121 Samuel T. Shinohara, Affidavit, November 3, 1946, p. 1, World War II Document Archive, Pacific Theater, U.S. Navy Trials (microfilm reel no. 144704), Samuel T. Shinohara (28 Jul 1945), WCSC.
122 Samuel T. Shinohara, Affidavit, November 3, 1946, 4.
123 Samuel T. Shinohara, Affidavit, November 3, 1946, 4.
124 Samuel T. Shinohara, "Petition of Samuel T. Shinohara to The Honorable Secretary of the Navy," January 2, 1947, p. 26, World War II Document Archive, Pacific Theater, U.S. Navy Trials (microfilm reel no. 144704), Samuel T. Shinohara (28 Jul 1945), WCSC.
125 Shinohara, "Petition of Samuel T. Shinohara to The Honorable Secretary of the Navy," 17.
126 Shinohara, "Petition of Samuel T. Shinohara to The Honorable Secretary of the Navy," 35.
127 Shinohara, "Petition of Samuel T. Shinohara to The Honorable Secretary of the Navy," 6.
128 Shinohara, "Petition of Samuel T. Shinohara to The Honorable Secretary of the Navy," 6.
129 Shinohara, "Petition of Samuel T. Shinohara to The Honorable Secretary of the Navy," 6.

130 Shinohara, "Petition of Samuel T. Shinohara to The Honorable Secretary of the Navy," 7.
131 Shinohara, "Petition of Samuel T. Shinohara to The Honorable Secretary of the Navy," 41.
132 Shinohara, "Petition of Samuel T. Shinohara to The Honorable Secretary of the Navy," 4.
133 Shinohara, "Petition of Samuel T. Shinohara to The Honorable Secretary of the Navy," 1.
134 Shinohara, "Petition of Samuel T. Shinohara to The Honorable Secretary of the Navy," 2.
135 "Mil: Com.—SHINOHARA, Samuel T./A17–20," Navy Department, Office of the Judge Advocate General, April 28, 1948, p. 3, World War II Document Archive, Pacific Theater, U.S. Navy Trials (microfilm reel no. 144704), Samuel T. Shinohara (28 Jul 1945), WCSC.
136 John Nicholas Brown, Acting Secretary of the Navy, to The Judge Advocate General, July 8, 1948, p. 1, World War II Document Archive, Pacific Theater, U.S. Navy Trials (microfilm reel no. 144704), Samuel T. Shinohara (28 Jul 1945), WCSC.
137 G. L. Russell, Judge Advocate General of the U.S. Navy, Memorandum for the Secretary of the Navy, July 26, 1948, p. 3, World War II Document Archive, Pacific Theater, U.S. Navy Trials (microfilm reel no. 144704), Samuel T. Shinohara (28 Jul 1945), WCSC.
138 "Mil. Com.—SHINOHARA, Samuel T./A17–10/OQ," Navy Department, Secretary of the Navy, August 24, 1948, p. 1, World War II Document Archive, Pacific Theater, U.S. Navy Trials (microfilm reel no. 144704), Samuel T. Shinohara (28 Jul 1945), WCSC.
139 Rogers, *Destiny's Landfall*, 206.
140 Gary Y. Okihiro, *Margins and Mainstreams: Asians in American History and Culture* (Seattle: University of Washington Press, 2014 [1994]), 138.
141 Simpson, *An Absent Presence*, 80.

Chapter 6. Japanese Militarists

1 Frank H. Wu, *Yellow: Race in America beyond Black and White* (New York: Basic Books, 2002), 96.
2 Anicée Van Engeland, *Civilian or Combatant? A Challenge for the Twenty-First Century* (Oxford: Oxford University Press, 2011), 15.
3 Tanaka, *Hidden Horrors*, 201.
4 Akiyoshi Hosokawa Court Transcript, September 12, 1945, p. 10 (hereafter cited as Akiyoshi Hosokawa Court Transcript), World War II Document Archive, Pacific Theater, U.S. Navy Trials (microfilm reel no. 144574), WCSC.
5 Akiyoshi Hosokawa Court Transcript, 4.

6 Kanzo Kawachi Court Transcript, 11.
7 Kanzo Kawachi Court Transcript, 10.
8 Kanzo Kawachi Court Transcript, 14.
9 Kanzo Kawachi Court Transcript, 14.
10 Kanzo Kawachi Court Transcript, 44.
11 Kanzo Kawachi Court Transcript, 44,
12 Kanzo Kawachi Court Transcript, 44.
13 Kanzo Kawachi Court Transcript, 6.
14 Kanzo Kawachi Court Transcript, 8.
15 Kanzo Kawachi Court Transcript, 6–7.
16 Lisa Hajjar, *Torture: A Sociology of Violence and Human Rights* (New York: Routledge, 2013), 22.
17 Kanzo Kawachi Court Transcript, 18.
18 Paul J. Bordallo, Guam War Claims Review Commission Survivor's Questionnaire, December 1, 2003, p. 2, Guam Review War Claims 2003–2004, Bordallo, Paul Joseph 12/01/03, Box 4, Rec. 9830, MARC.
19 Kanzo Kawachi Court Transcript, 22.
20 Bordallo, Guam War Claims Review Commission Survivor's Questionnaire, 2.
21 Kanzo Kawachi Court Transcript, G-1.
22 Shinohara Court Transcript, 35.
23 Shinohara Court Transcript, 42.
24 Kyomon Miwa Court Transcript, September 20, 1945, p. 5 (hereafter cited as Kyomon Miwa Court Transcript), World War II Document Archive, Pacific Theater, U.S. Navy Trials (microfilm reel no. 140600), WCSC.
25 Kyomon Miwa Court Transcript, 5.
26 Kyomon Miwa Court Transcript, 4.
27 Okihiro, *Margins and Mainstreams*, 138.
28 Matsukichi Kobayashi Court Transcript, April 10, 1945, p. 4 (hereafter cited as Matsukichi Kobayashi Court Transcript), World War II Document Archive, Pacific Theater, U.S. Navy Trials (microfilm reel no. 128473), WCSC.
29 Matsukichi Kobayashi Court Transcript, 18.
30 Matsukichi Kobayashi Court Transcript 18.
31 Matsukichi Kobayashi Court Transcript, 18.
32 Matsukichi Kobayashi Court Transcript, 16.
33 Matsukichi Kobayashi Court Transcript, 23.
34 Matsukichi Kobayashi Court Transcript, 23.
35 Matsukichi Kobayashi Court Transcript, 8.
36 Matsukichi Kobayashi Court Transcript, 27.
37 Matsukichi Kobayashi Court Transcript, 27.
38 Matsukichi Kobayashi Court Transcript, T-1.
39 Matsukichi Kobayashi Court Transcript, 29.
40 Matsukichi Kobayashi Court Transcript, V.

41 Tadao Igawa Court Transcript, February 8, 1946, p. 18 (hereafter cited as Tadao Igawa Court Transcript), World War II Document Archive, Pacific Theater, U.S. Navy Trials (microfilm reel no. 158039), WCSC.
42 Tadao Igawa Court Transcript, 18.
43 Tadao Igawa Court Transcript, 14.
44 Tadao Igawa Court Transcript, 35.
45 Tadao Igawa Court Transcript, 34.
46 Tadao Igawa Court Transcript, 26.
47 Tadao Igawa Court Transcript, 39.
48 Tadao Igawa Court Transcript, 21.
49 Tadao Igawa Court Transcript, 21.
50 Tadao Igawa Court Transcript, 39.
51 Tadao Igawa Court Transcript, 40.
52 Tadao Igawa Court Transcript, E (2).
53 Tadao Igawa Court Transcript, 41.
54 Tadao Igawa Court Transcript, 42.
55 Tadao Igawa Court Transcript, H (2).
56 Tadao Igawa Court Transcript, H (5).
57 John W. Dower, *War without Mercy: Race and Power in the Pacific War* (New York: Pantheon Books, 1986), 46.
58 Tadao Igawa Court Transcript, G (3).
59 Tadao Igawa Court Transcript, G (3).
60 Lieutenant Colonel George R. Newton to Island Command Provost Marshal, September 25, 1947, p. 1, Tadao Igawa Court Transcript.
61 Director of Security to Commander Marianas Area, October 7, 1947, p. 2, Tadao Igawa Court Transcript.
62 Lieutenant Colonel George R. Newton to Island Command Provost Marshal, September 25, 1947, p. 1, Tadao Igawa Court Transcript.
63 Last Letters of Tadao Igawa, September 24, 1947, p. 1, Tadao Igawa Court Transcript.
64 Last Letters of Tadao Igawa, September 24, 1947, 1.
65 Lieutenant Colonel George R. Newton to Island Command Provost Marshal, September 25, 1947, p. 2, Tadao Igawa Court Transcript.
66 Commander Marianas Area to Secretary of the Navy, p. 2, October 30, 1947, Tadao Igawa Court Transcript.
67 As per naval policy in Guam, two individuals assisted the executioner in the hanging of convicted war criminals.
68 Adolf Sgambelluri, interview by the author, Nimitz Hill, Guam. April 22, 2006.
69 Rear Admiral John D. Murphy to Commander in Chief Pacific and United States Pacific Fleet, April 7, 1949, p. 1, Akira Tokunaga, Shigeo Koyama, and Yoshio Takahashi Court Transcript (hereafter cited as Tokunaga et al. Court

Transcript), World War II Document Archive, Pacific Theater, U.S. Navy Trials (microfilm reel no. 167716), WCSC.
70 Rear Admiral John D. Murphy to Commander in Chief Pacific and United States Pacific Fleet, April 7, 1949, 3.
71 Yukiko Koshiro, *Trans-Pacific Racisms and the U.S. Occupation of Japan* (New York: Columbia University Press, 1999), 16.
72 Dirk Anthony Ballendorf, "Guam Military Action in World War II," in *Guam History: Perspectives*, ed. Lee D. Carter, William L. Wuerch, and Rosa Roberto Carter (Mangilao: Richard F. Taitano Micronesian Area Research Center, 1997), 1:235.
73 Saito, *From Chinese Exclusion to Guantánamo Bay*, 41.
74 Carl Schmitt, *The Nomos of the Earth in the International Law of the Jus Publicum Europaeum*, trans. G. L. Ulmen (New York: Telos Press, 2003), 46.
75 Rear Admiral C. A. Pownall to Rear Admiral Arthur G. Robinson, January 19, 1949, p. 2, Tokunaga et al. Court Transcript.
76 David Hanlon, *Remaking Micronesia: Discourses over Development in a Pacific Territory, 1944–1982* (Honolulu: University of Hawai'i Press, 1998), 52.
77 Hanlon, *Remaking Micronesia*, 51–52.
78 Maga, *Judgment at Tokyo*, 113.
79 William A. Schabas, *An Introduction to the International Criminal Court* (Cambridge: Cambridge University Press, 2003), 47.
80 Tokunaga et al. Court Transcript, 89.
81 Tokunaga et al. Court Transcript, 90.
82 Tokunaga et al. Court Transcript, 91.
83 Tokunaga et al. Court Transcript, B (3).
84 Tokunaga et al. Court Transcript, D (1).
85 Tokunaga et al. Court Transcript, D (1)-D (2).
86 Tokunaga et al. Court Transcript, D (1).
87 Tokunaga et al. Court Transcript, T (1).
88 Tokunaga et al. Court Transcript, HH (1).
89 Tokunaga et al. Court Transcript, AA (2).
90 Tokunaga et al. Court Transcript, AA (2).
91 Tokunaga et al. Court Transcript, CC (1).
92 Renato Rosaldo, "Imperialist Nostalgia," *Representations* 26 (Spring 1989): 107.
93 Rosaldo, "Imperialist Nostalgia," 108.
94 W. M. Peck, "Rota's War Years Examined," p. 9, Pacific Collections, Peattie, Nan'yō, William Peck Papers, Various Writings on Rota and Micronesia, Box 4, Folder 19, MARC.
95 Peck, "Rota's War Years Examined," 4.
96 W. M. Peck, "The Pit . . . Another Version," p. 3, Pacific Collections Peattie, Nan'yō, William Peck Papers, Japanese Colonialism: Japanese in Micronesia Project (1985–86), Box 2, Folder 13, MARC.

97   Peck, "The Pit . . . Another Version," 3
98   Peck, "The Pit . . . Another Version," 4.
99   Peck, "The Pit . . . Another Version," 4.
100 Peck, "Rota's War Years Examined," 6.
101 Peck, "Rota's War Years Examined," 6
102 Aileen Moreton-Robinson, "Virtuous Racial States: The Possessive Logic of Patriarchal White Sovereignty and the United Nations Declaration on the Rights of Indigenous Peoples," *Griffith Law Review* 20, no. 3 (2011): 649.
103 Tokunaga et al. Court Transcript, T (1).
104 Tokunaga et al. Court Transcript, T (1).
105 M. E. Currie to Rear Admiral John D. Murphy, August 18, 1948, p. 2, Tokunaga et al Court Transcript.
106 Tokunaga et al. Court Transcript, 109.
107 Tokunaga et al. Court Transcript, 110.
108 Tokunaga et al. Court Transcript, 110.
109 Tokunaga et al. Court Transcript, 110.
110 Tokunaga et al. Court Transcript, 11.
111 Tokunaga et al. Court Transcript, 12.
112 Tokunaga et al. Court Transcript, 18.
113 Tokunaga et al. Court Transcript, 12.
114 Kenichi Hosoya, Affidavit, March 30, 1948, p. 3, RG 125, Records of the Office of the Judge Advocate General (Navy), War Crime Branch, Records Originated by Director of War Crimes, Pacific Fleet Correspondence: 1944–1949, Box 8, NACP.
115 Yoshimaro Sato, Affidavit, March 15, 1948, p. 4, RG 125, Records of the Office of the Judge Advocate General (Navy), War Crime Branch, Records Originated by Director of War Crimes, Pacific Fleet Correspondence: 1944–1949, Box 8, NACP.
116 Tokunaga et al. Court Transcript, 23.
117 Tokunaga et al. Court Transcript, 23–24.
118 Tokunaga et al. Court Transcript, 24.
119 Tokunaga et al. Court Transcript, 45.
120 Tokunaga et al. Court Transcript, 33.
121 Tokunaga et al. Court Transcript, 33.
122 Tokunaga et al. Court Transcript, 55.
123 Tokunaga et al. Court Transcript, 68.
124 Tokunaga et al. Court Transcript, 115.
125 Tokunaga et al. Court Transcript, 122.
126 Tokunaga et al. Court Transcript, AA (1).
127 Tokunaga et al. Court Transcript, 115.
128 Tokunaga et al. Court Transcript, 115.
129 Tokunaga et al. Court Transcript, Exhibit 10 (a) (2).
130 Tokunaga et al. Court Transcript, 116.

131 Tokunaga et al. Court Transcript, 116.
132 Tokunaga et al. Court Transcript, 102.
133 Tokunaga et al. Court Transcript, 102.
134 Tokunaga et al. Court Transcript, 102.
135 Tokunaga et al. Court Transcript, 117.
136 Tokunaga et al. Court Transcript, AA (3).
137 Tokunaga et al. Court Transcript, AA (3).
138 Tokunaga et al. Court Transcript, KK (9).
139 Tokunaga et al. Court Transcript, KK (8).
140 Tokunaga et al. Court Transcript, KK (5).
141 Tokunaga et al. Court Transcript, H (12).
142 Tokunaga et al. Court Transcript, H (4).
143 Tokunaga et al. Court Transcript, H (4).
144 Tokunaga et al. Court Transcript, 139.
145 Tokunaga et al. Court Transcript, 139.
146 Tokunaga et al. Court Transcript, 139.
147 Tokunaga et al. Court Transcript, 139.
148 Tokunaga et al. Court Transcript, 139.
149 Tokunaga et al. Court Transcript, Exhibit 17 (a).
150 Tokunaga et al. Court Transcript, Exhibit 20 (a).
151 Tokunaga et al. Court Transcript, Exhibit 21 (a) (1).
152 Natsu Taylor Saito, *Meeting the Enemy: American Exceptionalism and International Law* (New York: New York University Press, 2010), 250.
153 Tokunaga et al. Court Transcript, T (2).
154 Peck, "The Pit . . . Another Version," 2.
155 Peck, "The Pit . . . Another Version," 2.
156 Peck, "The Pit . . . Another Version," 2.
157 Peck, "The Pit . . . Another Version," 2.
158 Peck, "The Pit . . . Another Version," 2.
159 Peck, "The Pit . . . Another Version," 2.
160 Peck, "The Pit . . . Another Version," 2.
161 Hirose Ogawa Court Transcript, October 12, 1945, p. T (1) (hereafter cited as Hirose Ogawa Court Transcript), World War II Document Archive, Pacific Theater, U.S. Navy Trials (microfilm reel no. 144577), WCSC.
162 Hirose Ogawa Court Transcript, T (1).
163 Kanzo Kawachi Court Transcript, E.
164 Carl Schmitt, *The Concept of the Political*, trans. George Schwab (Chicago: University of Chicago Press, 2007), 49.
165 Fujitani, *Race for Empire*, 76.

Conclusion

1. Amy Kaplan, "Violent Belongings and the Question of Empire Today: Presidential Address to the American Studies Association," *American Quarterly* 56, no. 1 (March 2004): 14.
2. Rodríguez, *Forced Passages*, 28.
3. Koshiro, *Trans-Pacific Racisms*, 3.
4. Shibusawa, *America's Geisha Ally*, 144.
5. Fujitani, *Race for Empire*, 118.
6. Moreton-Robinson, "Virtuous Racial States," 656.
7. "War Crimes Trials," *Navy News*, October 26, 1947, 4.
8. Gardam, "Gender and Non-combatant Immunity," 349.
9. Leo T. S. Ching, *Becoming "Japanese": Colonial Taiwan and the Politics of Identity Formation* (Berkeley: University of California Press, 2001), 7.
10. Alexander Laban Hinton, *Why Did They Kill? Cambodia in the Shadow of Genocide* (Berkeley: University of California Press, 2005), 236.
11. Hinton, *Why Did They Kill?*, 236.
12. Brendan Hokowhitu, "Producing Elite Indigenous Masculinities," *Settler Colonial Studies* 2, no. 2 (2012): 29.
13. R. W. Connell and James W. Messerschmidt, "Hegemonic Masculinity: Rethinking the Concept," *Gender and Society* 19, no. 6 (2005): 846.
14. Cynthia Enloe, *Bananas, Beaches and Bases: Making Feminist Sense of International Politics* (Berkeley: University of California Press, 2014), 150.
15. Hokowhitu, "Producing Elite Indigenous Masculinities," 33.
16. Anne McClintock, "Paranoid Empire: Specters from Guantánamo and Abu Ghraib," *Small Axe* 13, no. 1 (2009): 59 (emphasis in original).
17. Muhammad, *The Condemnation of Blackness*, 5.
18. Angela Y. Davis, "Race, Gender, and Prison History: From the Convict Lease System to the Supermax Prison," in *Prison Masculinities*, ed. Don Sabo, Terry A. Kupers, and Willie London (Philadelphia: Temple University Press, 2001), 36.
19. David Sablan, "Arrested by the Kempeitai," in *Saipan: Oral Histories of the Pacific War*, ed. Bruce M. Petty (Jefferson, NC: McFarland, 2002), 43.
20. Antonio Shimabukuro Borja, "Digging Tunnels on Rota," in *Saipan: Oral Histories of the Pacific War*, ed. Bruce M. Petty (Jefferson, NC: McFarland, 2002), 63–64.
21. "Two Members of Guam Police Force Commended," *Guam Gazette*, November 17, 1945, 1–2.
22. Escolastica Tudela Cabrera, "Escolastica," in *Saipan: Oral Histories of the Pacific War*, ed. Bruce M. Petty (Jefferson, NC: McFarland, 2002), 26.
23. Agueda I. Johnston, "Mr. Jose Villagomez," [1963?], p. 8, Working Papers no. 69, Inventory of the Papers of Agueda I. Johnston Compiled by W. L. W. and C. F. Q., General Box 14, (1 of 1) Folder 14, 8, MARC.
24. Crisostomo, "The Interpreter's Wife," 85. On the Central Intelligence Agency

in Saipan, refer to Richard A. Falk, "CIA Covert Action and International Law," *Society* 12, no. 3 (March–April 1975): 39–44.
25 Sablan, "Arrested by the Kempeitai," 44.
26 Borja, "Digging Tunnels on Rota," 64.
27 Don Sabo, Terry A. Kupers, and Willie London, "Gender and the Politics of Punishment," in *Prison Masculinities*, ed. Don Sabo, Terry A. Kupers, and Willie London (Philadelphia: Temple University Press, 2001), 5.
28 McClintock, "Paranoid Empire," 54 (emphasis in original).
29 Murphy, *US Navy War Crimes Program Final Report*, 203.
30 Murphy, *US Navy War Crimes Program Final Report*, 203.
31 "CAMACHO, Antonio, interrogation of," December 23, 1944, p. 1, RG 313 Records of the Naval Operating Forces, Trust Territory of the Pacific Islands, Office of the High Commissioner, General Administrative Files, ca. 1944–1951, Box 1 P35, Folder "CAMACHO, Antonio: alleged crimes," NACP.
32 Cary Wolfe, *Before the Law: Humans and Other Animals in a Biopolitical Frame* (Chicago: University of Chicago Press, 2013), 10.
33 Lisa Yoneyama, *Cold War Ruins: Transpacific Critique of American Justice and Japanese War Crimes* (Durham, NC: Duke University Press, 2016), 9.
34 Maria Höhn and Seungsook Moon, "Introduction: The Politics of Gender, Sexuality, Race, and Class in the U.S. Military Empire," in *Over There: Living with the U.S. Military Empire from World War Two to the Present*, ed. Maria Höhn and Seungsook Moon (Durham, NC: Duke University Press, 2010), 5.

Bibliography

Archival Collections

Ballendorf, Dirk, et al. "Oral Historiography." Manuscript Collection. Richard F. Taitano Micronesian Area Research Center, University of Guam.

Charles A. Pownall Papers. Hoover Institution Archives, Stanford University, Stanford, CA.

Guam Review War Claims, 2003–2004. Richard F. Taitano Micronesian Area Research Center, University of Guam.

Helen Paul Collection. Pacific Collections. Richard F. Taitano Micronesian Area Research Center, University of Guam.

Inventory of the Papers of Agueda I. Johnston. Compiled by W. L. W. and C. F. Q. General Box 14, (1 of 1) Folder 14, 8. Richard F. Taitano Micronesian Area Research Center, University of Guam.

John Damian Murphy Papers. Hoover Institution Archives, Stanford University, Stanford, CA.

Martin Emilius Carlson Papers. Hoover Institution Archives, Stanford University, Stanford, CA.

Naval Operational Archives. Pacific Collection. Richard F. Taitano Micronesian Area Research Center, University of Guam.

Peattie, Mark. Nan'yō Papers. Manuscript Collection. Richard F. Taitano Micronesian Area Research Center, University of Guam.

Records of the Allied Operational and Occupation Headquarters, World War II. Record Group 331. Supreme Commander for the Allied Powers, Legal Section, Investigation Division, Summary of Cases, 1945–1949. National Archives at College Park, College Park, MD.

Records of the Bureau of Naval Personnel. Record Group 24. Naval Prisoners of War Board. National Archives at College Park, College Park, MD.

Records of the Naval Operating Forces, Naval Government of Guam, Mariana Islands, General Correspondence, 1946–50. Record Group 313. National Archives and Records Administration–Pacific Region (San Francisco), San Bruno, CA.

Records of the Naval Operating Forces, Trust Territory of the Pacific Islands, Office of the High Commissioner, General Administrative Files, ca. 1944–1951. Record Group 313. National Archives at College Park, College Park, MD.

Records of the Office of the Judge Advocate General (Navy), Miscellaneous Records, 1944–1949, Von Mackensen Papers. National Archives at College Park, College Park, MD.

Records of the Office of the Judge Advocate General (Navy), Navy JAG Case Files of Pacific Area War Crimes Trials, 1944–1949. 16 rolls, 35mm, Scholarly Resources. Pacific Theater Document Archive. War Crimes Studies Center, University of California, Berkeley, Berkeley, CA.

Records of the Office of the Judge Advocate General (Navy), War Crimes Branch, 1944–1949. Miscellaneous Records. Record Group 125. National Archives at College Park, College Park, MD.

Records of the Office of the Judge Advocate General (Navy), War Crimes Branch, Records Originated by the Director of War Crimes, Pacific Fleet, Confidential Correspondence, 1945–1948. Box 1. Record Group 125. National Archives at College Park, College Park, MD.

Records of the Office of the Judge Advocate General (Navy), War Crimes Branch, Records Originated by Director of War Crimes, Pacific Fleet Correspondence, 1944–1949. Record Group 125. National Archives at College Park, College Park, MD.

Records of the Office of the Judge Advocate General (Navy), War Crimes Branch, Records Regarding Pacific Area War Crimes Cases, 1944–1949. Box 1. Record Group 125. National Archives at College Park, College Park, MD.

Records of the U.S. Marine Corps. Record Group 127. National Archives at College Park, College Park, MD.

U.S. Navy Trials, Court Transcripts. World War II Document Archive, Pacific Theater. War Crimes Studies Center, University of California, Berkeley, Berkeley, CA.

Primary and Secondary Sources

Agamben, Giorgio. *Homo Sacer: Sovereign Power and Bare Life.* Translated by Daniel Heller-Roazen. Stanford, CA: Stanford University Press, 1998.

Agamben, Giorgio. *Means without End: Notes on Politics.* Translated by Vincenzo Binetti and Cesare Casarino. Minneapolis: University of Minnesota Press, 2000.

Agamben, Giorgio. *The Open: Man and Animal.* Translated by Kevin Attell. Stanford, CA: Stanford University Press, 2004.

Agamben, Giorgio. *Remnants of Auschwitz: The Witness and the Archive.* Translated by Daniel Heller-Roazen. New York: Zone Books, 2002.

Agamben, Giorgio. *State of Exception.* Translated by Kevin Attell. Chicago: University of Chicago Press, 2005.

Ahmad, Muneer I. "Guantánamo Is Here: The Military Commissions Act and Noncitizen Vulnerability." *University of Chicago Legal Forum* 1 (2007): 1–25.
Aldrich, Robert. *Colonialism and Homosexuality*. London: Routledge, 2003.
Anderson, Warwick. *Colonial Pathologies: American Tropical Medicine, Race, and Hygiene in the Philippines*. Durham, NC: Duke University Press, 2006.
Asher, Robert, Lawrence B. Goodheart, and Alan Rogers. "Adjudicating Homicide: The Legal Framework and Social Norms." In *Murder on Trial: 1620–2002*, edited by Robert Asher, Lawrence B. Goodheart, and Alan Rogers, 3–30. Albany: State University of New York Press, 2005.
Attell, Kevin. *Giorgio Agamben: Beyond the Threshold of Deconstruction*. New York: Fordham University Press, 2015.
Babb, Suzanne Kelly. "Fear and Loathing in America: Application of Treason Law in Times of National Crisis and the Case of John Walker Lindh." *Hastings Law Journal* 54, no. 6 (August 2003): 1721–1744.
Bailey, Beth, and David Farber. *The First Strange Place: Race and Sex in World War II Hawaii*. Baltimore: John Hopkins University Press, 1992.
Balce, Nerissa S. "The Filipina's Breast: Savagery, Docility, and the Erotics of American Empire." *Social Text* 24, no. 2 (Summer 2006): 89–110.
Ballendorf, Dirk Anthony. "Guam Military Action in World War II." In *Guam History: Perspectives*, edited by Lee D. Carter, William L. Wuerch, and Rosa Roberto Carter, 1:219–238. Mangilao: Richard F. Taitano Micronesian Area Research Center, 1997.
Bath, Alan Harris. *Tracking the Axis Enemy: The Triumph of Anglo-American Naval Intelligence*. Lawrence: University Press of Kansas, 1998.
Benjamin, Walter. *Reflections: Essays, Aphorisms, Autobiographical Writings*. Translated by Edmund Jephcott. New York: Schocken Books, 1986.
Benvenisti, Eyal. *The International Law of Occupation*. Princeton, NJ: Princeton University Press, 1993.
Bérubé, Allan. *Coming Out under Fire: The History of Gay Men and Women in World War Two*. New York: Free Press, 1990.
Besnier, Niko. *Gossip and the Everyday Production of Politics*. Honolulu: University of Hawai'i Press, 2009.
Bignall, Simone, and Marcelo Svirsky. "Introduction: Agamben and Colonialism." In *Agamben and Colonialism*, edited by Marcelo Svirsky and Simone Bignall, 1–14. Edinburgh: Edinburgh University Press, 2012.
Borja, Antonio Shimabukuro. "Digging Tunnels on Rota." In *Saipan: Oral Histories of the Pacific War*, edited by Bruce M. Petty, 62–63. Jefferson, NC: McFarland, 2002.
Bruyneel, Kevin. *The Third Space of Sovereignty: The Postcolonial Politics of U.S.-Indigenous Relations*. Minneapolis: University of Minnesota Press, 2007.
Burns, Susan L. "Introduction." In *Gender and Law in the Japanese Imperium*, edited by Susan L. Burns and Barbara J. Brooks. Honolulu: University of Hawai'i Press, 2014.

Byrd, Jodi A. *Transit of Empire: Indigenous Critiques of Colonialism.* Minneapolis: University of Minnesota Press, 2011.

Cabrera, Escolastica Tudela. "Escolastica." In *Saipan: Oral Histories of the Pacific War*, edited by Bruce M. Petty, 24–26. Jefferson, NC: McFarland, 2002.

Camacho, Keith L. *Cultures of Commemoration: The Politics of War, Memory, and History in the Mariana Islands.* Honolulu: University of Hawai'i Press, 2011.

Chappell, David A. "The Forgotten Mau: Anti-navy Protest in American Samoa, 1920–1935." *Pacific Historical Review* 69, no. 2 (May 2000): 217–260.

Chen, Ching-chih. "Police and Community Control Systems in the Empire." In *The Japanese Colonial Empire, 1895–1945*, edited by Ramon H. Myers and Mark R. Peattie, 213–239. Princeton, NJ: Princeton University Press, 1984.

Ching, Leo T. S. *Becoming "Japanese": Colonial Taiwan and the Politics of Identity Formation.* Berkeley: University of California Press, 2001.

Clemens, Justin. "Oath, Torture, Testimony: Language, Law and Life in the Work of Giorgio Agamben." *Res Publica: Revista de Filosofía Política* 28 (2012): 77–99.

Cohen, David. Interview by the author. Honolulu, Hawai'i. February 23, 2006.

Colclough, O. S. "Naval Justice." *Journal of Criminal Law and Criminology* 38, no. 3 (September–October 1947): 198–205.

Comaroff, Jean, and John Comaroff. "Law and Disorder in the Postcolony." *Social Anthropology* 15, no. 2 (June 2007): 133–152.

Connell, R. W., and James W. Messerschmidt. "Hegemonic Masculinity: Rethinking the Concept." *Gender and Society* 19, no. 6 (December 2005): 829–859.

Copelon, Rhonda. "Surfacing Gender: Reconceptualizing Crimes against Women in Time of War." In *The Women and War Reader*, edited by Lois Ann Lorentzen and Jennifer Turpin, 63–79. New York: New York University Press, 1998.

Crisostomo, Marikita Palacios. "The Interpreter's Wife." In *Saipan: Oral Histories of the Pacific War*, edited by Bruce M. Petty, 82–85. Jefferson, NC: McFarland, 2002.

Cristobal, Jorge. Interview by the author. Tumon, Guam. May 4, 2006.

Cristobal, Jorge. "War as Island Natives Saw It, 1942–45." In *Pacific War Stories in the Words of Those Who Survived*, edited by Rex Alan Smith and Gerald A. Meehl, 397–406. New York: Abbeville Press, 2004.

Cunningham, Lawrence J. *Ancient Chamorro Society.* Honolulu: Bess Press, 1992.

Damai, Puspa. "The Killing Machine of Exception: Sovereignty, Law, and Play in Agamben's *State of Exception*." Review of *State of Exception*, by Giorgio Agamben, trans. Kevin Attell. *CR: The New Centennial Review* 5, no. 3 (Winter 2005): 255–276.

Dauphinee, Elizabeth. "War Crimes and the Ruin of Law." *Millennium: Journal of International Studies* 37, no. 1 (2008): 49–67.

Davis, Angela Y. *Are Prisons Obsolete?* New York: Seven Stories Press, 2003.

Davis, Angela Y. "Race, Gender, and Prison History: From the Convict Lease System to the Supermax Prison." In *Prison Masculinities*, edited by Don Sabo, Terry A. Kupers, and Willie London, 35–45. Philadelphia: Temple University Press, 2001.

Davis, Angela Y. "Racialized Punishment and Prison Abolition." In *The Angela Y. Davis Reader*, edited by Joy James, 96–109. Malden, MA: Blackwell, 1998.

Dawdy, Shannon Lee, and Joe Bonni. "Towards a General Theory of Piracy." *Anthropological Quarterly* 85, no. 3 (Summer 2012): 673–699.

DeLisle, Christine Taitano. "A History of Chamorro Nurse-Midwives in Guam and a 'Placental Politics' for Indigenous Feminism." *Intersections: Gender and Sexuality in Asia and the Pacific* 37 (March 2015). Accessed June 22, 2016. http://intersections.anu.edu.au/issue37/delisle.htm.

DeLoughrey, Elizabeth M. *Routes and Roots: Navigating Caribbean and Pacific Island Literatures*. Honolulu: University of Hawai'i Press, 2007.

Dent, Alexander Sebastian. "Introduction: Understanding the War on Piracy, Or Why We Need More Anthropology of Pirates." *Anthropological Quarterly* 85, no. 3 (Summer 2012): 659–672.

Diaz, Vicente M. "Deliberating 'Liberation Day': Identity, History, Memory, and War in Guam." In *Perilous Memories: The Asia-Pacific War(s)*, edited by T. Fujitani, Geoffrey M. White, and Lisa Yoneyama, 155–180. Durham, NC: Duke University Press, 2001.

Diaz, Vicente M. "'Fight Boys, 'til the Last . . .': Islandstyle Football and the Remasculinization of Indigeneity in the Militarized American Pacific Islands." In *Pacific Diaspora: Island Peoples in the United States and across the Pacific*, edited by Paul Spickard, Joanne L. Rondilla, and Debbie Hippolite Wright. Honolulu: University of Hawai'i Press, 2002.

Diaz, Vicente M. "Sniffing Oceania's Behind." *Contemporary Pacific* 24, no. 2 (2012): 323–344.

Dinnen, Sinclair. "Restorative Justice in the Pacific Islands: An Introduction." In *A Kind of Mending: Restorative Justice in the Pacific Islands*, edited by Sinclair Dinnen, Anita Jowitt, and Tess Newton Cain, 1–34. Canberra: Pandanus Books, 2003.

Dinstein, Yoram. *The International Law of Belligerent Occupation*. Cambridge: Cambridge University Press, 2009.

Dower, John W. *War without Mercy: Race and Power in the Pacific War*. New York: Pantheon Books, 1986.

Dvorak, Greg. "'The Martial Islands': Marking Marshallese Masculinities between American and Japanese Militarism." *Contemporary Pacific* 20, no. 1 (Spring 2008): 55–86.

Eisenstein, Zillah. "Resexing Militarism for the Globe." In *Feminism and War: Confronting U.S. Imperialism*, edited by Robin L. Riley, Chandra Talpade Mohanty, and Minnie Bruce Pratt, 27–46. London: Zed Books, 2008.

Enloe, Cynthia. *Bananas, Beaches and Bases: Making Feminist Sense of International Politics*. Berkeley: University of California Press, 2014.

Erickson, George E. "United States Navy War Crimes Trials (1945–1949)." *Washburn Law Journal* 5, no. 1 (1965): 89–111.

Espiritu, Yen Le. *Body Counts: The Vietnam War and Militarized Refuge(es)*. Berkeley: University of California Press, 2014.

Falk, Richard A. "CIA Covert Action and International Law." *Society* 12, no. 3 (March–April 1975): 39–44.

Ferguson, Kathy E., and Phyllis Turnbull. *Oh, Say, Can You See? The Semiotics of the Military in Hawaiʻi*. Minneapolis: University of Minnesota Press, 1999.

Fisher, Louis. *Military Tribunals and Presidential Power: American Revolution to the War on Terrorism*. Lawrence: University Press of Kansas, 2005.

Fletcher, Laurel E., and Eric Stover. *The Guantánamo Effect: Exposing the Consequences of U.S. Detention and Interrogation Practices*. Berkeley: University of California Press, 2009.

Foucault, Michel. *Discipline and Punish: The Birth of the Prison*. Translated by Alan Sheridan. New York: Vintage Books, 1995.

Foucault, Michel. *Power: Essential Works of Michel Foucault, 1954–1984*. Vol. 3. Edited by James D. Faubion. Translated by Robert Hurley et al. London: Penguin Books, 1994.

Foucault, Michel. *Security, Territory, Population: Lectures at the Collège de France, 1977–1978*. Edited by Michel Senelart. Translated by Graham Burchell. New York: Palgrave Macmillan, 2007.

Friedman, Hal M. "The Beast in Paradise: The United States Navy in Micronesia, 1943–1947." *Pacific Historical Review* 62, no. 2 (May 1993): 173–195.

Frost, Tom. "The *Dispositif* between Foucault and Agamben." *Law, Culture and the Humanities* 15, no. 1 (2015): 151–171.

Fujitani, Takashi. *Race for Empire: Koreans as Japanese and Japanese as Americans during World War II*. Berkeley: University of California Press, 2011.

Gardam, Judith. "Gender and Non-combatant Immunity." *Transnational Law and Contemporary Problems* 3 (1993): 345–370.

Glueck, Sheldon. "By What Tribunal Shall War Offenders Be Tried?" *Harvard Law Review* 56, no. 7 (June 1943): 1059–1089.

Glueck, Sheldon. *What Shall Be Done with War Criminals?* Washington, DC: United States War Department, 1944.

Goldberg-Hiller, Jonathan, and Noenoe K. Silva. "The Botany of Emergence: Kanaka Ontology and Biocolonialism in Hawaiʻi." *Native American and Indigenous Studies* 2, no. 2 (Fall 2015): 1–26.

Goldberg-Hiller, Jonathan, and Noenoe K. Silva. "Sharks and Pigs: Animating Hawaiian Sovereignty against the Anthropological Machine." *South Atlantic Quarterly* 110, no. 2 (2011): 429–446.

Gottschalk, Marie. "Hiding in Plain Sight: American Politics and the Carceral State." *Annual Review of Political Science* 11 (2008): 235–260.

Green, A. Wigfall. "The Military Commission." *American Journal of International Law* 42, no. 4 (October 1948): 832–848.

Gupta, Akhil. *Red Tape: Bureaucracy, Structural Violence, and Poverty in India*. Durham, NC: Duke University Press, 2012.

Hajjar, Lisa. *Courting Conflict: The Israeli Military Court System in the West Bank and Gaza*. Berkeley: University of California Press, 2005.

Hajjar, Lisa. *Torture: A Sociology of Violence and Human Rights*. New York: Routledge, 2013.

Hanlon, David. *Remaking Micronesia: Discourses over Development in a Pacific Territory, 1944–1982*. Honolulu: University of Hawai'i Press, 1998.

Harris, Cheryl I. "Whiteness as Property." *Harvard Law Review* 106, no. 8 (June 1993): 1707–1791.

Hattori, Anne Perez. *Colonial Dis-ease: U.S. Navy Health Policies and the Chamorros of Guam, 1898–1941*. Honolulu: University of Hawai'i Press, 2004.

Hattori, Anne Perez. "Re-membering the Past: Photography, Leprosy and the Chamorros of Guam, 1898–1924." *Journal of Pacific History* 46, no. 3 (December 2011): 293–318.

Havemann, Paul. "Denial, Modernity and Exclusion: Indigenous Placelessness in Australia." *Macquarie Law Journal* 5 (2005): 57–80.

Higuchi, Wakako. *The Japanese Administration of Guam, 1941–1944: A Study of Occupation and Integration Policies, with Japanese Oral Histories*. Jefferson, NC: McFarland, 2013.

Hinton, Alexander Laban. *Why Did They Kill? Cambodia in the Shadow of Genocide*. Berkeley: University of California Press, 2005.

Höhn, Maria, and Seungsook Moon. "Introduction: The Politics of Gender, Sexuality, Race, and Class in the U.S. Military Empire." In *Over There: Living with the U.S. Military Empire from World War Two to the Present*, edited by Maria Höhn and Seungsook Moon, 1–36. Durham, NC: Duke University Press, 2010.

Hokowhitu, Brendan. "Producing Elite Indigenous Masculinities." *Settler Colonial Studies* 2, no. 2 (2012): 23–48.

Hutchinson, Dennis J. "'The Achilles Heel' of the Constitution: Justice Jackson and the Japanese Exclusion Cases." *Supreme Court Review* 2002 (2002): 455–494.

Inglis, Kerry A. *Ma'i Lepera: Disease and Displacement in Nineteenth-Century Hawai'i*. Honolulu: University of Hawai'i Press, 2013.

Iyechad, Lilli Perez. *An Historical Perspective of Helping Practices Associated with Birth, Marriage and Death among Chamorros of Guam*. Lewiston, NY: Edwin Mellen Press, 2001.

James, Roy E. "The Island Possession of Guam." In *America's Pacific Dependencies: A Survey of American Colonial Policies and of Administration and Progress toward Self-Rule in Alaska, Hawaii, Guam, Samoa and the Trust Territory*, edited by Rupert Emerson, Lawrence S. Finkelstein, E. L. Bartlett, George H. McLane, and Roy E. James, 77–93. New York: American Institute of Pacific Relations, 1949.

"Japs Still at Large, Imperil Civilian Communities." *Guam Gazette*, September 19, 1945.

Johnson, Chalmers. *The Sorrows of Empire: Militarism, Secrecy, and the End of the Republic.* New York: Henry Holt, 2004.

Kahn, Paul W. *Sacred Violence: Torture, Terror, and Sovereignty.* Ann Arbor: University of Michigan Press, 2008.

Kaplan, Amy. "Violent Belongings and the Question of Empire Today: Presidential Address to the American Studies Association." *American Quarterly* 56, no. 1 (March 2004): 1–18.

Kaplan, Amy. "Where Is Guantánamo?" *American Quarterly* 57, no. 3 (September 2005): 831–858.

Kinsella, Helen M. "Securing the Civilian: Sex and Gender in the Laws of War." In *Power in Global Governance*, edited by Michael Barnett and Raymond Duvall, 249–272. Cambridge: Cambridge University Press, 2005.

Koshiro, Yukiko. *Trans-Pacific Racisms and the U.S. Occupation of Japan.* New York: Columbia University Press, 1999.

Kovner, Sarah. "Base Cultures: Sex Workers and Servicemen in Occupied Japan." *Journal of Asian Studies* 68, no. 3 (August 2009): 777–804.

Kramer, Paul A. *The Blood of Government: Race, Empire, the United States, and the Philippines.* Chapel Hill: University of North Carolina Press, 2006.

Kraska, Peter B. "Crime Control as Warfare: Language Matters." In *Militarizing the American Criminal Justice System: The Changing Roles of the Armed Forces and the Police*, edited by Peter B. Kraska, 14–28. Boston: Northeastern University Press, 2001.

Kushner, Barak. *Men to Devils, Devils to Men: Japanese War Crimes and Chinese Justice.* Cambridge, MA: Harvard University Press, 2015.

Kyle, Brett J., and Andrew G. Reiter. "Militarized Justice in New Democracies: Explaining the Process of Military Court Reform in Latin America." *Law and Society Review* 47, no. 2 (June 2013): 375–407.

Lutz, Catherine. "Introduction: Bases, Empire, and Global Response." In *The Bases of Empire: The Global Struggle against U.S. Military Posts*, edited by Catherine Lutz, 1–44. New York: New York University Press, 2009.

Lyons, Scott Richard. *X-Marks: Native Signatures of Assent.* Minneapolis: University of Minnesota Press, 2010.

Maga, Tim. *Judgment at Tokyo: The Japanese War Crimes Trials.* Lexington: University Press of Kentucky, 2001.

Manibusan, Juan B. "Three Obnoxious Saipanese Escape Death." *Guam Gazette*, February 1, 1946, 1.

May, Larry. *War Crimes and Just War.* Cambridge: Cambridge University Press, 2007.

Mbembe, Achille. "Necropolitics." *Public Culture* 15, no. 1 (Winter 2003): 11–40.

Mbembe, Achille. *On the Postcolony.* Berkeley: University of California Press, 2001.

McClintock, Anne. "Paranoid Empire: Specters from Guantánamo and Abu Ghraib." *Small Axe* 13, no. 1 (2009): 50–74.

"Military Government Patrols Protect Interests and Pursuits of Guam Civilians." *Navy News*, April 16, 1946.

Mills, Catherine. *The Philosophy of Agamben*. Stocksfield, UK: Acumen, 2008.
Moon, Seungsook. "Regulating Desire, Managing the Empire: U.S. Military Prostitution in South Korea, 1945–1970." In *Over There: Living with the U.S. Military Empire from World War Two to the Present*, edited by Maria Höhn and Seungsook Moon, 39–77. Durham, NC: Duke University Press, 2010.
Moreton-Robinson, Aileen. "Virtuous Racial States: The Possessive Logic of Patriarchal White Sovereignty and the United Nations Declaration on the Rights of Indigenous Peoples." *Griffith Law Review* 20, no. 3 (2011): 641–658.
Muhammad, Khalil Gibran. *The Condemnation of Blackness: Race, Crime, and the Making of Modern Urban America*. Cambridge, MA: Harvard University Press, 2010.
Murphy, John D. *US Navy War Crimes Program Final Report*. Washington, DC: Department of the Navy, 1950.
Na'puti, Tiara R., and Michael Lujan Bevacqua. "Militarization and Resistance from Guåhan: Protecting and Defending Pågat." *American Quarterly* 67, no. 3 (September 2015): 837–858.
Ní Aoláin, Fionnuala, and Oren Gross. "Introduction: Guantánamo and Beyond: Exceptional Courts and Military Commissions in Comparative and Policy Perspective." In *Guantánamo and Beyond: Exceptional Courts and Military Commissions in Comparative Perspective*, edited by Fionnuala Ní Aoláin and Oren Gross, 1–34. Cambridge: Cambridge University Press, 2013.
Norris, Andrew. "Introduction: Giorgio Agamben and the Politics of Living Dead." In *Politics, Metaphysics, and Death: Essays on Giorgio Agamben's Homo Sacer*, edited by Andrew Norris, 1–30. Durham, NC: Duke University Press, 2005.
Okihiro, Gary Y. *Margins and Mainstreams: Asians in American History and Culture*. Seattle: University of Washington Press, 2014 [1994].
Oliver, William P., Jr. "International Law: Treason against the United States by Alien Enemy." *George Washington Law Review* 17, no. 2 (February 1949): 283–285.
Pablo, Tina Camacho. *Enchanting Tales of Guam*. Agaña Heights: Guamology, 2010.
Palomo, Tony. *An Island in Agony*. Agaña: Tony Palomo, 1984.
Patterson, Orlando. *Slavery and Social Death: A Comparative Study*. Cambridge, MA: Harvard University Press, 1982.
Peattie, Mark R. *Nan'yō: The Rise and Fall of the Japanese in Micronesia, 1885–1945*. Honolulu: University of Hawai'i Press, 1988.
Phillips, Michael. "Land Ownership in Guam." Guampedia. Last modified July 2, 2014. Accessed May 5, 2017. www.guampedia.com/land-ownership-on-guam/.
Piccigallo, Philip R. *The Japanese on Trial: Allied War Crimes Operations in the East, 1945–1951*. Austin: University of Texas Press, 1979.
Povinelli, Elizabeth A. *The Cunning of Recognition: Indigenous Alterities and the Making of Australian Multiculturalism*. Durham, NC: Duke University Press, 2002.
Poyer, Lin, Suzanne Falgout, and Laurence Marshall Carucci. *The Typhoon of War: Micronesian Experiences of the Pacific War*. Honolulu: University of Hawai'i Press, 2001.

Pugliese, Joseph. *State Violence and the Execution of Law*. New York: Routledge, 2013.

Rafael, Vicente L. "Translation, American English, and the National Insecurities of Empire." In *Formations of United States Colonialism*, edited by Alyosha Goldstein, 335–359. Durham, NC: Duke University Press, 2014.

Ramirez, Malia. Interview by the author. Hagåtña, Guam. February 26, 2015.

Reddy, Chandan. *Freedom with Violence: Race, Sexuality, and the US State*. Durham, NC: Duke University Press, 2011.

Rifkin, Mark. "On the (Geo)Politics of Belonging: Agamben and the UN Declaration on the Rights of Indigenous People." *Settler Colonial Studies* (2015): 1–10. Accessed June 14, 2016. doi: 10.1080/2201473X.2015.1090527.

Riseman, Noah. *Defending Whose Country? Indigenous Soldiers in the Pacific War*. Lincoln: University of Nebraska Press, 2012.

Robinson, Greg. *A Tragedy of Democracy: Japanese Confinement in North America*. New York: Columbia University Press, 2009.

Robinson, Stephen B., comp. *The Penal Code of Guam*. Manila: Bureau of Printing, 1933.

Rodríguez, Dylan. *Forced Passages: Imprisoned Radical Intellectuals and the U.S. Prison Regime*. Minneapolis: University of Minnesota Press, 2006.

Rogers, Robert F. *Destiny's Landfall: A History of Guam*. Honolulu: University of Hawaiʻi Press, 1995.

Rosa, John P. *Local Story: The Massie-Kahahawai Case and the Culture of History*. Honolulu: University of Hawaiʻi Press, 2014.

Rosaldo, Renato. "Imperialist Nostalgia." *Representations* 26 (Spring 1989): 107–122.

Rose, Sonya O. "The 'Sex Question' in Anglo-American Relations in the Second World War." *International History Review* 20, no. 4 (December 1998): 884–903.

Ross, Alison. "Agamben's Political Paradigm of the Camp: Its Features and Reasons." *Constellations* 19, no. 3 (2012): 421–434.

Sablan, David. "Arrested by the Kempeitai." In *Saipan: Oral Histories of the Pacific War*, edited by Bruce M. Petty, 40–45. Jefferson, NC: McFarland, 2002.

Sablan, Manuel T. "Messenger Boy for the Japanese Police." In *Saipan: Oral Histories of the Pacific War*, edited by Bruce M. Petty, 34–38. Jefferson, NC: McFarland, 2002.

Sabo, Don, Terry A. Kupers, and Willie London. "Gender and the Politics of Punishment." In *Prison Masculinities*, edited by Don Sabo, Terry A. Kupers, and Willie London, 3–18. Philadelphia: Temple University Press, 2001.

Saito, Natsu Taylor. *From Chinese Exclusion to Guantánamo Bay: Plenary Power and the Prerogative State*. Boulder: University Press of Colorado, 2007.

Saito, Natsu Taylor. *Meeting the Enemy: American Exceptionalism and International Law*. New York: New York University Press, 2010.

Salman, Michael. *The Embarrassment of Slavery: Controversies over Bondage and Nationalism in the American Colonial Philippines*. Berkeley: University of California Press, 2003.

Sanchez, Pedro C. *Guahan Guam: The History of Our Island*. Agaña: Sanchez Publishing House, 1987.

Savage, Nicholas. Interview by Guam Cable News. [1985?]. Videotape. Hagåtña, Guam. Copy of videotaped interview in the author's possession.

Scarry, Elaine. *The Body in Pain: The Making and Unmaking of the World*. Oxford: Oxford University Press, 1985.

Schabas, William A. *An Introduction to the International Criminal Court*. Cambridge: Cambridge University Press, 2003.

Schmitt, Carl. *The Concept of the Political*. Translated by George Schwab. Chicago: University of Chicago Press, 2007.

Schmitt, Carl. *The Nomos of the Earth in the International Law of the Jus Publicum Europaeum*. Translated and annotated by G. L. Ulmen. New York: Telos Press, 2003 [1950].

Sgambelluri, Adolf. Interview by the author. Nimitz Hill, Guam. April 22, 2006.

Shibusawa, Naoko. *America's Geisha Ally: Reimagining the Japanese Enemy*. Cambridge, MA: Harvard University Press, 2006.

Shigematsu, Setsu, and Keith L. Camacho. "Introduction: Militarized Currents, Decolonizing Futures." In *Militarized Currents: Toward a Decolonized Future in Asia and the Pacific*, edited by Setsu Shigematsu and Keith L. Camacho, xv–xlviii. Minneapolis: University of Minnesota Press, 2010.

Simpson, Caroline Chung. *An Absent Presence: Japanese Americans in Postwar America*. Durham, NC: Duke University Press, 2001.

Simpson, Gerry. *Law, War and Crime: War Crimes Trials and the Reinvention of International Law*. Cambridge: Polity Press, 2007.

Simpson, Gerry J. "War Crimes: A Critical Introduction." In *The Law of War Crimes: National and International Approaches*, edited by Timothy L. H. McCormack and Gerry J. Simpson, 1–30. The Hague: Kluwer Law International, 1997.

Soh, C. Sarah. *The Comfort Women: Sexual Violence and Postcolonial Memory in Korea and Japan*. Chicago: University of Chicago Press, 2008.

Soker, Donald. "The Taotaomona Stories of Guam." *Western Folklore* 31, no. 3 (July 1972): 153–167.

Souder, Laura Marie Torres. "Psyche under Siege: Uncle Sam, Look What You've Done to Us." In *Uncle Sam in Micronesia: Social Benefits, Social Costs*, edited by Donald H. Rubinstein and Vivian L. Dames, 120–124. Mangilao: Micronesia Area Research Center, 1989.

Souder, Laura M. Torres. "Unveiling Herstory: Chamorro Women in Historical Perspective." In *Pacific History: Papers from the 8th Pacific History Association Conference*, edited by Donald H. Rubinstein. Mangilao: Press and University of Guam Richard F. Taitano Micronesian Area Research Center, 1992.

Spade, Dean. *Normal Life: Administrative Violence, Critical Trans Politics, and the Limits of Law*. New York: South End Press, 2011.

"Special Marine, Guam Police Patrols Sweep Island in Widespread Jap Hunt." *Navy News*, December 12, 1945.

Stevenson, Heon. *American Automobile Advertising, 1930–1980: An Illustrated History*. Jefferson, NC: McFarland, 2008.

Stoler, Ann Laura. "Tense and Tender Ties: The Politics of Comparison in North American History and (Post) Colonial Studies." In *Haunted by Empire: Geographies of Intimacy in North American History*, edited by Ann Laura Stoler, 23–69. Durham, NC: Duke University Press, 2006.

Sturken, Marita. "Comfort, Irony, and Trivialization: The Mediation of Torture." *International Journal of Cultural Studies* 14, no. 4 (July 2011): 423–440.

"Surrender or Die, Order of DCMGO to Recalcitrant Japs: Guam's Famed Combat Patrol Again on War Path." *Guam Gazette*, October 12, 1945.

Svirsky, Marcelo, and Simone Bignall, eds. *Agamben and Colonialism*. Edinburgh: Edinburgh University Press, 2012.

Tanaka, Yuki. *Hidden Horrors: Japanese War Crimes in World War II*. Boulder, CO: Westview Press, 1996.

Tengan, Ty P. Kāwika. "Re-membering Panalā'au: Masculinities, Nation, and Empire in Hawai'i and the Pacific." *Contemporary Pacific* 20, no. 1 (Spring 2008): 27–53.

Thompson, Laura. *Guam and Its People: A Study of Culture Change and Colonial Education*. San Francisco: American Council, Institute of Pacific Relations, 1941.

Thompson, Laura. "Guam: A Study in Military Government." *Far Eastern Survey* 13, no. 16 (August 9, 1944): 149–154.

Torres, Robert Tenorio. "Pre-contact Marianas Folklore, Legends, and Literature." *Micronesian: Journal of the Humanities and Social Sciences* 2, nos. 1–2 (December 2003): 3–15.

Totani, Yuma. *The Tokyo War Crimes Trial: The Pursuit of Justice in the Wake of World War II*. Cambridge, MA: Harvard University Asia Center, 2008.

"Two Members of Guam Police Force Commended." *Guam Gazette*, November 17, 1945.

United Nations War Crimes Commission (UNWCC), ed. *Law Reports of Trials of War Criminals*. Vol. 3. London: His Majesty's Stationery Office, 1948.

Untalan, Faye. Interview by the author. Los Angeles, California. February 19, 2017.

U.S. Bureau of Naval Personnel. *Naval Justice*. Washington, DC: Standards and Curriculum Division and Training, U.S. Bureau of Naval Personnel, 1945.

U.S. Department of the Navy. *Naval Courts and Boards*. Washington, DC: Government Printing Office, 1937.

U.S. Department of the Navy, Office of the Chief of Naval Operations. *U.S. Navy Report on Guam, 1899–1950*. Washington, DC: Government Printing Office, 1951.

Van Engeland, Anicée. *Civilian or Combatant? A Challenge for the Twenty-First Century*. Oxford: Oxford University Press, 2011.

Vine, David. *Island of Shame: The Secret History of the U.S. Military Base on Diego Garcia*. Princeton, NJ: Princeton University Press, 2009.

"War Crimes Trials." *Navy News*, October 26, 1947.

Weaver, Jace. *Turtle Goes to War: Of Military Commissions, the Constitution and American Indian Memory*. New Haven, CT: Trylon and Perisphere Press, 2002.

Williams, Dan. "Communicating with the Enemy: Interpreters, 1942–45." In *Pacific War Stories in the Words of Those Who Survived*, edited by Rex Alan Smith and Gerald A. Meehl, 198–208. New York: Abbeville Press, 2004.

Williams, Robert A., Jr. *Like a Loaded Weapon: The Rehnquist Court, Indian Rights, and the Legal History of Racism in America*. Minneapolis: University of Minnesota Press, 2005.

Wolfe, Cary. *Before the Law: Humans and Other Animals in a Biopolitical Frame*. Chicago: University of Chicago Press, 2013.

Wu, Frank H. *Yellow: Race in America beyond Black and White*. New York: Basic Books, 2002.

Yoneyama, Lisa. *Cold War Ruins: Transpacific Critique of American Justice and Japanese War Crimes*. Durham, NC: Duke University Press, 2016.

Yoneyama, Lisa. "Liberation under Siege: U.S. Military Occupation and Japanese Women's Enfranchisement." *American Quarterly* 57, no. 3 (September 2005): 885–910.

Yoneyama, Lisa. "Traveling Memories, Contagious Justice: Americanization of Japanese War Crimes at the End of the Post–Cold War." *Journal of Asian American Studies* 6, no. 1 (February 2003): 57–93.

Index

Note: Page numbers followed by *f* indicate illustrations.

Advance Intelligence Center (AIC), 46
Aflague, Inocencio, 102
Aflague, Vicente Calvo, 259n100
Afleje, Vincent, 108
Agamben, Giorgio, 1, 20; on Auschwitz, 9; on bare life, 167; biopower, theories of, 5, 7, 226n18; on *bios*, 1, 3, 5, 7–8, 223; on the camp, 7, 9, 26; on *homo sacer*, 3, 8–9; on state of exception, 3, 7, 22; on *zoē*, 1, 3, 5, 7–8, 223
Aguigui, Maria C., 133
Aguigui, Rosa, 137
Aguon, Francisco Santos, 158
Aguon, Jose P., 106
Aguon, Juan U., 42, 43*f*
Akatani, Kan, 79
Akatani, Yoshio, 79
Akerman, Alexander, Jr.: Crisostomo murder defense, 141–142; Cruz defense, 90; Jose Villagomez defense, 123; Juan Reyes defense, 128; Kobayashi defense, 189; Nicholas Sablan defense, 97–98; Tudela defense, 135
American exceptionalism, 223
American Indians, rights of, 241n19
Ammons, Teller, 219–220; on American justice, 110; Cabrera prosecution, 105; Cruz prosecution, 91; Francisco Sablan prosecution, 97; Jose Villagomez prosecution, 119; Juan Reyes prosecution, 128–130; Leon Guerrero prosecution, 103; Mendiola prosecution, 109; Nicholas Sablan prosecution, 97; Quintanilla prosecution, 107; Shinohara prosecution, 155, 165, 167, 174; Tedula prosecution, 132, 135
Anderson, Lourdes, 172
Anderson, Margaret, 172
animals: in Chamorro culture, 20–21. See also ko'ko (bird) and hilitai (lizard) proverb; ko'ko-hilitai relation
anticolonialism: and American racism, 167; of Rotanese, 201
Arima, Kaoru, 54
Articles for the Government of the Navy, 71
Asanuma, Tsugio, 54
assault and battery, defined, 89, 157
assault trials: "American" as signifier in, 109; confessions in, 94–95; and torture, 110, 111. *See also individual defendants*
Atoigue, Antonio Toves, 99
authenticity, indigenous claims to, 8

Babauta, Ana Sahagon, 122
Babauta, Antonio M., 130–131

Babauta, Juan C., 136
Babauta, Vincente Sahagon, 123; murder of, 119; torture of, 120, 124
Bakewell, Henry P.: Cabrera defense, 105; Kawachi defense, 185–186; Quintanilla defense, 107
Barcinas, Cerilo Reyes, 138, 139
Barcinas, Joaquin A., 136
Bath, Alan Harris, 30
Baza, Beatrice, 188
Baza, Ramon S., 101
Baza, Teresa, 188
Baza, Vicente Sablan, 188–189, 190, 191
Benavente, Juan C., 106
Benjamin, Walter, on violence, 22–23
Besnier, Niko, 17
Bevacqua, Michael Lujan, 18
Bignall, Simone, 9
biopolitics, 8, 213, 223; of exception and inclusion, 9
biopower, 1, 5, 7, 226n18; and colonialism, 8, 223; decolonization of, 223; and interrogation, 85; of modern democracy, 8; normalization of, 24; and war criminality, 26
bios, 1, 3, 5, 7–8, 223; gossip as, 26; of indigenous Chamorros, 44; of Japanese, 44, 149, 215, 216; and *ko'ko-hilitai* relation, 5; of war criminality, 18. *See also* Agamben, Giorgio; *zoē*
Blanco, Ramon B., 204–205, 206
Blanco, Vicente Flores, 161
Blas, Jose Caesarius, 167
Bonni, Joe, 68
Bordallo, Baltazar Jerome, 183, 185, 186
Bordallo, Carlos, 168
Borja, Antonio Shimabukuro, 219
Borja, Eugenio B., 158
Borja, Jesus C., 102, 103
Borja, Juan, 111
Borja, Manuel M., 141
Borja, Martin, 15

Brereton, George H., 48
Brinkley, Hubert R., 53
Brown, John Nicholas, 178–179
Brunton, Maria, 94, 96
Buckingham, H. W., 58
Buckles, William A., 193
Bush, George W., 24
Butler, Chester, 168
Butler, Ignacia Bordallo, 150, 154, 168, 173

Cabrera, Jose C., 15, 93; assault trial of, 103–105
Camacho, Antonio, 15, 116, 121, 190; civilian status of, 125; confession of, 222; death sentence, commutation of, 143; as *homo sacer*, 122; murder trial of, 123–130; plea for leniency, 144–145
Camacho, Antonio R., 190
Camacho, Jose Rivera, 140–141
Camacho, Luis Cruz, 89–90, 110
Camacho, Mabel, 183–184, 186
Camacho, Pedro Dueñas, 50, 95, 183–184, 185–186
Camacho, Ramon, S. N., 102
Carbullido, Antonio B., 130–131, 132–133
Carbullido, Baltazar, 135
Carlson, Martin E., 198, 199, 209
Carpenter, Edmund S., 192
Castro, Ignacio T., 111
Castro, Juan, 167
Chamorros: as American wards, 89, 115; antagonisms among, 50–51; *bios* of, 44; Chamorro women as U.S. property, 159–160, 161, 162, 165; citizenship of, 10, 89, 213; civil rights of, 10; criminalization of, 37, 72; dehumanization of, 45; emasculation of, 39, 59, 96; feminization of, 92–93; inclusive exclusion of, 22; interrogation of, 101; under Japanese colonial rule, 11–12; as nonsubjects, 89; nurses, 127*f*;

pastoral duty of, 84; on Rota, 200–201; term, usage of, 225n2; torture of, 2, 5, 16–17, 23, 101; as *zoē*, 93. *See also* Guamanians; Rotanese; Saipanese
Charfauros, Jesus B., 133
Charfauros, Joaquin A., 187
Chiba, Eigo, 57
Chiguina, Jesus Mantanona, 110
chilin guaka, 17, 102
citizenship: of Chamorros, 10, 89, 213; and espionage, 211; and *homo sacer*, 9; of Rotanese, 199; of Shinohara, 154–155, 182; and treason, 152–153, 174; and War Crimes Tribunals Program, 5, 17, 20
civil rights: of Chamorros, 10; of civilian internees and detainees, 65, 114–115; of Japanese Americans, 65
Clark, Eugene F., 79
Colclough, O. S., 69
Cold War: and anticommunism, 25; and humanitarianism, 25; and Japan–U.S. relations, 149, 180, 221; treason trials during, 152
colonialism: and biopower, 8, 223; in Guam, 11, 25, 82; Japanese, 13, 24, 223; and masculinity, 2; and military tribunals, 24; and sovereignty, 11; U.S., 24–25, 223; and war criminals, 68
Combado, Juan, 125
comfort system, Japanese, 37, 160, 218
Concepcion, Jose A., 111
Concepcion, Soledad Lizama, 192
confessions, 217; in assault cases, 94–95; court-induced, 213; forced, 102; as sin, acknowledgment of, 16, 222; and torture, 16–17; of war crimes defendants, 117, 138–139, 222
criminalization: of Chamorros, 37, 72; of Guamanians, 72; of homosexuality, 106–107; of indigenous bodies, 46; Japanese, 11, 151, 212,

213; and JICPOA, 32; of Rotanese, 219; of Saipanese, 100, 219; of settler bodies, 46
Crisostomo, Jose P., 157
Crisostomo, Luis C., 1–3, 9, 36, 116, 220–221; assault allegations against, 136; confession of, 138–139; death sentence, commutation of, 143; defense against murder charge, 141–142; as *homo sacer*, 143; murder trial of, 130, 136–143; as nonsacrifice, 3, 143; plea for leniency, 144–145
Crisostomo, Marikita Palacios, 1, 2
Crisostomo, Rafael C., 108
Cristobal, Jorge E., 79–80, 170
Cruz, Catalina Degracia, 137
Cruz, Dolores Santos, 95–96, 98
Cruz, Flora C., 136
Cruz, Ignacio, 211–212
Cruz, Isabel Taitano, 183, 184, 186
Cruz, Jose B., 108
Cruz, Jose Diaz, 100
Cruz, Juan, 96
Cruz, Juan B., 101, 103
Cruz, Manuel B., 102, 103, 187
Cruz, Miguel A., 114; trial of, 89–91, 93
Cruz, Nicolas, 108–109
Cruz, Ramon Lizama, 136
Cruz, Vicente Reyes, 111, 112
Cruz, Vicente Sablan, 111
Cunningham, Lawrence J., 18

Dai Nisei, 154, 166–168, 171–174, 259n81
Damian, Celestine B., 109
d'Aquino, Toguri (Tokyo Rose), 151
Davis, Angela Y., 40–41
Davis, James E., 156, 172, 259n100
Dawdy, Shannon Lee, 68
De Jager v. Attorney General of Natal, 174
De La Cruz, Edward (Toshiwo Tamaoki), 13

de la Cruz, Ignacio, 196, 202; execution of, 204–205; murder of, 206
Delgado, Jose, 104
DeLisle, Christine Taitano, 18, 21
DeLoughrey, Elizabeth M., 62
detainees: civil rights of, 114–115; exploitation of, 39; as status, 92
De Vries, Ralph, 48, 138, 139
Diaz, Vicente M., 44
Diego, Agueda Dueñas, 96–98
Dueñas, Francisco S., 109
Dueñas, Jesus Baza, 15
Dueñas, Juan Muña, 116; confession of, 117; murder trial of, 117–118
Dumanal, Pedro G., 136, 139, 141; murder of, 140
Dunbar, Calvin W., 192

Eclevea, Gonzalo, 123, 124–125, 151
Eclevea, Jose Miner, 111, 112, 120, 121
Eisenstein, Zillah, 96
emasculation: of Chamorros, 39, 59, 96; of Japanese, 29; of war criminals, 61, 220. *See also* masculinity
enslavement, 38
Espinosa, Jose E., 102
Estebes, Bonifacio, 196, 202, 212
executions: spectacle of, 188; of war criminals, 189–192, 194, 204–205
Executive Order 9066, 65

Farfan, Rosa C., 121–122
Fejeran, Juan, 191
Fernandez, Jesus L., 159
Fisher, Louis, 70
Fletcher, Laurel E., 23
Flores, Alfonsina, 159–162, 164, 173–174; as property, 161, 162, 165
Flores, Alice, 162, 174
Flores, Francisco T., 154, 156, 171
Flores, Grace Taitano, 97
Flores, Jose Dueñas, 160–161

Flores, Juan Flores, 100, 110, 111
Flores, Rafaela San Flores, 161–162
Forrestal, James, 45, 176; War Crimes Office, founding of, 71–72
Foucault, Michel: on the inquiry, 70; on pastoral power, 83–85; on the prison, 44; on punishment, 33; on suspended rights, 114
Franquez, Maria T., 51–52
Franquez, Rita T., 51–52
Friedman, Hal M., 81
Frost, Tom, 7–8
Fujino, Yoshio, 57
Fujitani, Takashi, 213

gallows, 195*f*
Garrido, Fecundo B. D., 109
Garrido, Miguel, 111
Garrido, Ramon C., 107
Gatch, Thomas Leigh, 77, 118–119
Geiger, Roy S., 37
Geneva Convention of 1929, 62, 67, 91
Glueck, Sheldon, 60, 61–62, 67
Goldberg-Hiller, Jonathan, 21
Gomez, Jose R., 106
gossip: as *bios*, 26; and *inafa'maolek*, 18; and retribution, 20–21, 41, 219; in Rota, 203; about Shinohara, 151; as testimony, 17–18; and War Crimes Tribunals Program, 5, 17, 20
Grey, Concepcion, 141–142
Gross, Oren, 24
Guam: colonialism in, 11, 25, 82; as exceptional, 223; internment camps in, 25–38; Japanese invasion of (1941), 14–16; Japanese nationals in, 11; maps of, 4*f*, 6*f*; as military colony, 9, 22–23, 73; military courts on, 76–88; state of exception in, 11; U.S. bombardment of, 184, 188, 190; and U.S. hegemony, 68–69, 75–77; and U.S. military intel-

ligence, 29, 33; U.S. naval rule of, 9–11; U.S. sovereignty over, 34, 82
Guamanians: criminalization of, 72; inclusive exclusion of, 116; as ko'ko, 29; as loyal wards, 115, 153; and military intelligence, 34; and racism, 26; and retribution, 181; settler, 29, 32–34, 38, 44–47, 60, 223; settler Asian, 38, 44; as U.S. subjects, 34. See also Chamorros
Guam Combat Patrol, 41, 43f, 44, 220f; murder of Japanese "stragglers," 42–43
Guantánamo Bay, 23–24; as exceptional, 24
Guantánamo effect, 23–24
Guerrero, Jose, 15
Guerrero, Jose C., 123, 124
Gupta, Akhil, 226
Gutierrez, Jose T., 153
Guzman, Jose C., 136

Hague Convention of 1907, 67, 173, 198, 207
Hajjar, Lisa, 185
Halsey, William, 79
Hanlon, David, 197
Hara, Jesus Cruz, 167
Harris, Cheryl I., 155
Hataoka, Hideo, 57
Havemann, Paul, 8
Hayashi, Hiroshi, 160, 162
Herrero, Vicente, P., 157
hilitai: Rotanese and Saipanese as, 216. See also ko'ko (bird) and hilitai (lizard) proverb; ko'ko-hilitai relation
Hines, Arturo C., 102
homo sacer, 3; as bare life, 7–8; and citizenship, 9; manifestations of, 8–9; origins of, 7; political life, foreclosure of, 44; Rotanese and Saipanese as, 105; war crimes defendants as, 122, 135, 143, 149–150, 192

homosexuality: criminalization of, 106–107; as war crime, 85–86
Hosokawa, Akiyoshi, 181, 190–191; trial of, 182–183
Hosoya, Kenichi, 204

ianjos, 156, 160, 163–164
Igawa, Tadao, 53, 181, 188, 190; death sentence of, 193; defense of, 192–193; execution of, 194; as homo sacer, 192; murder trial of, 189–193; as nonsacrifice, 194
Igawa, Yukiko, 193–194
Iglesias, Tomas A., 79
Ijima, Mayuki, 57
Imagawa, Shigeo, 203
imperialism: imperialist nostalgia, 200; Japanese, 83, 103, 121, 149, 197, 211; U.S., 22, 201, 211; and war criminality, 60, 83, 86, 89, 107, 115, 134, 213
inafa'maolek, 3, 18, 218; and birthing practices, 21; and gossip, 18; and reciprocity, 20
Indian rights, 241n19
international law: and occupation, 173; and rape, 160; and Rota, 211; and sovereignty, 82–83; and treason, 175; and war crimes, 67–68, 77–78
internment, Japanese American, 63–64; Executive Order 9066, 65; *Korematsu v. United States*, 63–65
internment camps: in Guam, 25, 38; as symbolic instruments of enslavement, 38
interpreters, Chamorro, 13–16, 50–51; as civilians, 22; conscription of, 1–2; internment of, 37–39; under Japanese rule, 101; processing of, 35–36; Rotanese, 108, 220–221; Saipanese, 220–221
interpreters, in war crimes tribunals, 78–79

interrogation: and biopower, 85; of Chamorros, 101; and fear, 80; of Japanese military officers, 39; of prisoners of war, 46–49; and war crimes investigations, 47–49, 73, 85
Ishizaki, Joaquina M., 128
Island Command Prisoner of War Camp, 44, 52, 52f; screening of war criminals at, 46

Jackson, Robert H., 62–63; *Korematsu* dissent, 63–64; on war criminality, 64–65, 67
James, Rita Gogue, 122, 126–127
James, Roy, E., 76
Japanese: *bios* of, 44, 149, 215–216; and Cold War, 149, 221; criminalization of, 11, 151, 212, 213; emasculation of, 29; internment of, 44, 52; prisoners of war, 40f, 182, 187f; racialization of, 149, 181, 187, 212, 221–222; racism against, 36–37, 42–44
Japanese Americans: civil rights of, 65; and Cold War, 149, 221; exclusion of, 216; internment of, 63–65
Japanese Society of Guam (Nihon Jin Kai), 171
Johnson, C. B., 95
Johnston, Agueda Iglesias, 52, 98, 151
Johnston, Herbert, 159
Joint Intelligence Center Pacific Ocean Areas (JICPOA), 31, 46; and criminalization, 32; propaganda of, 32
jurisdiction: of military police, 35; over Rota, 198–199, 210; of SCAP, 74–75; of War Crimes Office, 45–46

Kahn, Paul W., 16, 103, 139
Kaikan, Omiya, 159
Kaplan, Amy, 10
Kawachi, Kanzo, 101, 181, 213; trial of, 183–186

Kawakita, Tomoya, 152
Kerner, Albert, 160
Kerner, Mercedes T., 160
kino lau, 21
Kinsella, Helen M., 93
Kobayashi, Masashi, 54, 56
Kobayashi, Matsukichi, 181, 188, 190; murder trial of, 188–189
ko'ko (bird) and *hilitai* (lizard) proverb, 5, 18, 19f, 20–21
ko'ko-hilitai relation, 5, 21, 89, 212; and *bios*, 5; Guamanians as *ko'ko*, 29; and Rotanese murder trials, 202; as testimony, 216; as torture trial testimony, 216; and War Crimes Tribunals Program, 216
Korematsu v. United States, 63–64, 65
Koshiro, Yukiko, 196
Kovner, Sarah, 163
Koyama, Hideko, 98, 114
Koyama, Shigeo, 182, 195, 205, 208, 209; clemency plea of, 212; murder trial of, 202; as nonsacrifice, 211
Kraus, Charles H., 50, 51
kuchōs, 90, 104, 217
Kumai, George, 79
Kwajalein, Marshall Islands, war crimes trials in, 246n109

labor: forced, 106; and imprisonment, 40; prisoners of war, exploitation of, 39–41, 53
Leon Guerrero, Jose Iglesias, 138, 139
Leon Guerrero, Pedro Sablan, 35–36, 93, 120–121, 183–184, 190, 248n9; assault trial of, 100–103; as *zoē*, 103
leprosy (Hansen's disease), 11
Limtiaco, Joaquin Aflague, 17, 101, 110, 183, 187
Lizama, Manuel Q., 182
Lizama, Vicenta Q., 190, 192

Lizama, Vicente, 188–192; execution of, 189–192, 194
Lizama, Vicente D., 137–138
Lyons, Scott Richard, 139

MacArthur, Douglas, 74–75
Mafnas, Joaquin: murder of, 136, 137, 140; torture of, 140
Maga, Tim, 85, 150
Manglona, Ignacio, 211–212
Mangloña, Jose L., 95
Manglona, Tomas Cruz, 204–205
Manibusan, Antonio, 43f
Manibusan, Francisco, 109
Manibusan, Juan, 15, 79, 117
Manibusan, Juan B. (editor), 143
Manibusan, Juan Blas, 99–100
Mantanona, Manuel Pablo, 117–118
Mantanoña, Pedro, 153
Mantanona, Ricardo T., 107
Mariana Islands, 30; as exceptional, 223; JICPOA propaganda in, 32
Marshall, John, 64, 241n19
Martinez, Jose M., 123, 125
masculinity: and colonialism, 2; and empire, 218; Japanese, emasculation of, 29; militarized, 217–218, 221; and noncombatant status, 92; and prisoner of war labor, 39; and torture, 217; and War Crimes Tribunals Program, 59, 81, 105, 111
Matanane, Maria Quintanilla, 122
Mbembe, Achille: on colonial subjects, 45; on the colony, 11
McClintock, Anne, 218–219
McMillin, George J., 150, 156, 171; "assaults" on, 157–158, 172, 177, 178; U.S. property, as embodiment of, 157
Mendiola, Fritz Angocio, 105, 114; assault trial of, 108–109
Mendiola, Geronimo, 153
Mendiola, Jose Mafnas, 111

Mendiola, Nicholasa P., 159–160, 163–165, 174; as "modern girl," 163, 164; as property, 165
Mesa, Juan L. G., 101
Mesa, Juan R., 105
military commissions: history of, 26; "justice" under, 110; scholarship on, 23–24; and sovereignty, 5. See also military tribunals; U.S. Navy's War Crimes Tribunals Program
military police, jurisdiction of, 35
military tribunals: and civil liberties, 70; judicial review, lack of, 70–71; jurisdiction of, 74–75; and retribution, 86; as state of exception, 22; types of, 71. See also U.S. Navy's War Crimes Tribunals Program
Minseibu, 2, 35, 93–94, 150; American sentences, recognition of, 99; former police officers, testimony by, 120; interpreters of, 51
Miwa, Kyomon, 150–151, 176, 181; murder trial of, 186–187
modernity, colonial, 2; and the white body, 33–34
Moreton-Robinson, Aileen, 201
Mori, Kunizo, 54
Moriarty, J. A., Jr., 56, 58
Morris, David N., 55
Morris, Emory L., Shinohara defense, 154, 171, 173–174, 176
Muña, Joaquin M., 109
Murphy, John D., 73f; *The Final Report*, 86; on the Japanese, 221–222; on war crimes testimony, 73; War Criminals Stockade, praise for, 58
Murphy, John K., 80

Nanyō-chō (Japanese South Seas Government), 11
Na'puti, Tiara R., 18
Nauta, Felix Q., 157–158

Naval Courts and Boards, 25, 198; murder definition of, 116
naval intelligence, U.S., 29–33; in Guam, 33; officer training, 30–31; post–9/11, 30
naval justice: defined, 69; deterrent theory of punishment, 69–70; as exceptional, 86; and whiteness, 86
Navy, U.S.: anti-Japanese racism of, 36–37, 42–44
Nededog, Ignacio, 111
Newton, George R., 193, 194
Ní Aoláin, Fionnuala, 24
Nihon Jin Kai (Japanese Society of Guam), 171
Nimitz, C. W., 76, 197
1947 Trusteeship Agreement, 197–198
Nishi Gunzō, 4
Northern Mariana Islands: map of, 4f; U.S. sovereignty in, 22
nostalgia, imperialist, 200

Office of Naval Intelligence (ONI), 30
Ogawa, Hirose, 181, 213; murder trial of, 187–188
Ogawa, Tsutomu, 55
Ogo, Manuel M., 200, 201
Okada, Jose S., 168–169
Okada, Juan Santos, 176
Okada, Shintaro, 151
Okiyama, Jesus C., 133
Okiyama, Jesus Carbullido, 167, 172
Olano, Miguel Angel, 172
Onedera, Juan S., 153

Pablo, Jose A., 105
Pablo, Tina Camacho, 21
Pangelinan, Felix Torres, 137–138
Pangelinan, Henry S., 36, 93, 112; assault trial of, 98–100; leniency, plea for, 113
Pangelinan, Maria, 135

Pangelinan, Vicente, 111
Patterson, Orlando, 38
Pearl Harbor, bombing of, 150
Penal Code of Guam, The, 25, 35; assault definition, 157; "crimes against nature" in, 106; death penalty under, 118; gambling under, 112; intent to rape under, 95–96; under the Minseibu, 99; murder, definition of, 116; prostitution under, 159–160, 165; and Rota, 198; treason under, 166
Perez, Isabel T., 79
Perez, Joaquin C., 79
Perez, Juan N., 111
Perez, Pedro D., 103
Phillips, Michael, 21
Piacente, Rocco L., 54
piracy, 82; and war criminality, 68
plenary power doctrine, U.S., 10, 25; and acquisitiveness, 76; Guam, 75–77; and whiteness, 75–76
Posse Comitatus Act of 1878, 48
Povinelli, Elizabeth, 8
Pownall, Charles A., 77, 84–85, 197
prisoner of war camps, 84
prisoners of war, 246n109; guard abuse, allegations of, 54–55; incarceration of, 38; interrogation of, 46–49; Japanese, 40f, 182, 187f; labor exploitation of, 39–41, 53
Proclamation No. 4 ("Exceptional Military Courts"), 22, 76, 197
property: Chamorro women as, 159–160, 161, 162, 165; and race, 155; and whiteness, 149, 155–156, 215
property rights, U.S., 155, 157, 216
prostitution, 159, 165; under Penal Code of Guam, 159, 160, 165; in Shinohara case, 160–166, 173–174
proverbs, Chamorro, 1, 3, 5, 20–21; about hilitai, 20. See also ko'ko (bird) and hilitai (lizard) proverb

Punciano, Lorenzo, 140–141, 142
punishment, 33; under naval justice, 69–70; in Rota, 207–209; for war crimes, 61; and white supremacy, 181. See also Foucault, Michel; *Penal Code of Guam, The*
Purcell, Donald W., 54, 55

Quinata, Jesus A., 106
Quinata, Jose Q., 128
Quintanilla, Domingo S., 113; assault trial of, 105–108; crimes against nature accusations, 106–107
Quitugua, Jesus P., 101
Quitugua, Miguel, 104

Rabago, Enrique, 111
race: and deviance, 25; and property, 155; and war criminality, 48, 60
racialization: of Japanese, 149, 181, 187, 221–222; of Rotanese, 48, 192, 219; of Saipanese, 192, 219
racism: American, 26, 36–37, 42–44, 177, 215; and anticolonialism, 167; anti-Japanese, 36–37, 42–44; Chamorro, 177, 215; Guamanian, 26; and Japanese American internment, 64; and retribution, 26; in Shinohara trial, 177; among U.S. Navy staff, 36–37, 42–44, 77–78; and War Crimes Tribunals Program, 115
Rafael, Vicente, 16
Ramirez, Malia, 20
Ramsey, D. C., 25
rape: and feminization, 96; and international law, 160; in Nicholas Sablan case, 95–98; under *Penal Code of Guam*, 95–96; and property, 160; same-sex, 107
reciprocity: and *inafa'maolek*, 18, 20; and obligation, 44; and power, 217; retribution, 5, 45, 216, 218

recognition, 8
Regan, Joseph A., 198, 202, 210
Rentz, John N., 55
retribution: as core Chamorro value, 18; and gossip, 20–21, 41, 219; in Guam, 181; and racism, 26; and reciprocity, 5, 45, 216, 218; and translation, 16; and tribunals, 86; and violence, 29, 59
Rexroad, Charles C., 194
Reyes, Antonio, 136
Reyes, Jose Cruz, 136
Reyes, Juan, 116, 121; civilian status of, 125; death sentence of, 129f; death sentence, commutation of, 143; murder trial of, 123–130; plea for leniency, 144–145
Reyes, Juan Taijito, 138, 139
Reyes, Theresa Pablo, 105
Reyes, Vicente C., 79; Crisostomo murder defense, 141–142; Jose Villagomez, defense of, 123; Juan Reyes, defense of, 128; Shinohara defense, 154, 176; Tudela defense, 135
Rios, Beatrice Santos, 159
Rivera, Juan G., 126
Rivera, Juan R., 167
Riverin, Ignacio, 43f
Roberto, Juan A., 120, 122, 219
Robinson, Arthur G., 72, 76–77; on territorial jurisdiction, 75; on war crimes, 68
Robinson, James J., 66–67
Rodríguez, Dylan, 72, 215
Rodriguez, Jesus B., 94
Rogers, Robert F., 150
Romero, Raymond L., 54, 56
Rosaldo, Renato, 200
Rosario, Juan B., 106
Rosario, Manuel, 111
Rota: colonial rule of, 11, 13; espionage on, 203; gossip in, 203; and international law, 211; Japanese claim to, 211;

Rota (continued)
Japanese-era police officers, 35; Japanese military law in, 207; as "Japanized" island, 50; jurisdiction over, 198–199, 210; map of, 197f; treason punishment in, 207–209; U.S. appropriation of, 196–197; U.S. bombardment of, 200, 204; U.S. claim to, 211; as U.S. military colony, 195; as U.S. possession, 212; yellow peril in, 182
Rotanese: anticolonialism of, 201; assault cases of, 89; and citizenship, 199; civilian detainee status of, 92; criminalization of, 219; feminization of, 92–93, 149; as *homo sacer*, 105; internment of, 52; interpreters, 108, 220–221; jurisdiction over, 209–210; as noncitizen subjects of Japan, 199; noncombatant status of, 92, 216; racialization of, 48, 192, 219; as *zoē*, 216
rumor, 20; and War Crimes Tribunals Program, 5, 17, 20. *See also* gossip
Russell, G. L., 179

Sablan, Cencilio, 131
Sablan, Elias Parong, 221
Sablan, Francisco C., 131–133
Sablan, Francisco P., 15, 105, 114, 130; assault trial of, 110–113
Sablan, Jose Santos, 108, 109
Sablan, Nicholas T., 35, 93, 188, 189, 190–191; assault trial of, 93–98; intent to commit rape charge, 95–98; leniency, plea for, 113
Sablan, Pedro Gogue, 125, 126
Sablan, Segundo, 15
Saipan: colonial rule of, 11, 13; Japanese colonial rule of, 14f, 144; Japanese-era police officers, 35; as "Japanized" island, 50; map of, 12f
Saipanese: assault cases of, 89; civilian detainee status of, 92; criminalization of, 100, 219; feminization of, 92–93, 149; as *homo sacer*, 105; internment of, 52; interpreters, 220–221; as noncombatants, 92, 216; racialization of, 192, 219; war criminals, 143; as *zoē*, 216
Salas, Francisco Cruz: murder of, 130; torture of, 131–132
Salas, Galo Lujan, 169–170
Salas, Joaquin Aquiningnoc, 133–134
Salas, Joaquin Santos, 182
Salas, Jose G., 94
Salas, Juan Muña, 136
Salas, Juan S., 104
Salas, Rosa Aquiningnoc, 132
San Augustine, Vicente, 90
Sanagi, Sadamu, 198
Sanchez, Pedro C., 90, 117
Sanchez, Pedro Q., 187
Sanchez, Vicente S., 187
San Nicholas, Pedro, 43f
San Nicolas, Jesus M., 109
Santos, Gervacio Ignacio, 137
Santos, Inecto Degracia, 137
Santos, Olita T., 159
Santos, Ramon Cruz, 122
Sarmiento, Juan, 141
Sato, Yoshimaro, 204
Savage, Nicholas, 37, 42, 91–92
Savory, Frederick A., 79
Sayama, Jesus Baza, 167, 168
Sayama, Jesus S., 171
Scarry, Elaine, 121
Schmitt, Carl, 197
segregation: of Chamorro schools, 10–11; of civilian war crimes suspects, 50–51
Seinendan (Chamorro Young Men's Association), 13–14, 105, 171
Sgambelluri, Adolf, 42
Sgambelluri, Adolfo C., 42, 50, 122–123, 163, 194, 219–220
Sgambelluri, Hector C., 119–120

Shibusawa, Naoko, 152
Shinohara, Carmen Torres, 51, 150, 152f, 172
Shinohara, Cecilia, 150, 161, 172
Shinohara, Gil, 150, 156
Shinohara, Samuel Takekuna, 26, 51, 53, 152f, 210, 257n45; "assault" on McMillan, 157–158, 172, 177, 178; citizenship of, 154–155, 182; death sentence of, 174–175; defense of, 154, 171–174, 176; early biography of, 150–151; gossip regarding, 151; as *homo sacer*, 149–150, 166–167, 174–175, 179; inclusive exclusion of, 166–167; as Japanese American, 180; as nonsacrifice, 175, 181; petition to Forrestal, 176–178; prostitution charges against, 160–166, 173–174; and racism, 151, 177; treason charges against, 153–154, 166–172, 175, 177–179; treason trial of, 155–174
Siguenza, Maria C., 186
Silva, Noenoe K., 21
Simpson, Gerry J., 67–68
Smith, Ralph C., 128
Snedeker, James, 175, 178
sonchōs, 89, 90–91, 102–103, 217
Souder, Laura Marie Torres, 44
sovereignty, 22; and belligerent occupancy, 83; and colonialism, 11; over Guam, 34, 82; and Igawa case, 190; and international law, 82–83; and military commissions, 5; in Northern Mariana Islands, 22; and torture, 218; and whiteness, 26, 166
stare decisis, 24; and racial discrimination, 64
state of exception, 3, 65; in Guam, 11; military tribunals as, 22; as paradigm of government, 7; zone of indifference in, 22
Stoler, Ana Laura, 134

Stover, Eric, 23
Sullivan, John L., 143
Supreme Commander of Allied Powers (SCAP), 244n71; war crimes jurisdiction of, 74–75
surveillance, 83; racialized, 85–86; and war crime interrogations, 47–48
Suss, Fredrick, 175–177
Svirsky, Marcelo, 9

Taimanglo, Blas T., 123, 125
Taimanglo, Vicente M., 170
Taitano, Francisco, 102
Taitano, Jesusa, 163
Taitingfong, Antonia, 93
Tajalle, Francisco M., 109
Takahashi, Yoshio, 182, 195, 200, 209; clemency plea of, 210–211; murder trial of, 202; as nonsacrifice, 211; statement to American intelligence, 198–199
Takano, Junjiro, 198, 209–210
Takeshina, Takeshi, 191, 193
Taumomoa, Silvina Charfauros-Cruz, 41
Tedpago, Jose Espinosa, 106
Tedtaotao, Juan C., 111, 112
Tenorio, Juan Santos, 111
Terlaje, Jose Salas, 101
Terlaje, Vicente Blanco, 138, 139
Thompson, Laura, 10
Timoner, Miguel, 202; execution of, 205
Tinian, 11, 13
Tokuichi, Yoshizaki, 205
Tokunaga, Akira, 53, 182, 195, 200, 209; clemency plea of, 210; military career of, 206; murder trial of, 202; as nonsacrifice, 211; as senior official of Rota, 206–208
Tokyo Rose (Toguri d'Aquino), 151
Topasna, Jose F., 187
Topasna, Jose Q., 187
Torres, Celeste, 15

Torres, Maria U., 132
torture: and American/Japanese rule, 223; in assault cases, 110, 111; of Chamorros, 2, 5, 16–17, 23, 101; and confession, 16–17; and conversion, 121; and empire, 217; and forced labor, 106; as form of sacrifice, 103; and imperial power, 121–122; under Japanese rule, 23, 113–114; ko'ko-hilitai relation, 216; and masculinity, 217; in murder cases, 119–120, 124, 131–132, 140; and political power, 103; and sovereignty, 218; as spectacle, 103; and translation, 16; "water cure," 139–140, 142
Toves, Albert (Kondo Akira), 200–201, 211–212
translation: in military tribunals, 78–79; and political agency, 15–16; and retribution, 16; in Shinohara trial, 176; and torture, 16
treason: and citizenship, 152–153, 174; and Cold War, 82; and international law, 175; under *Penal Code of Guam*, 166; punishment in Rota for, 207–209. *See also* Shinohara, Samuel Takekuna; *and individual defendants*
Trust Territory of the Pacific Islands (TTPI), 197, 198
Tsuji, Kimio, 79
Tudela, Manuel Borja, 37, 116; death sentence, commutation of, 143; defense of, 134–135; as *homo sacer*, 135; murder trial of, 130–135
Tweed, George, 181, 183, 184–185
Tyson, A. J., 95

Ulloa, Vicente, 104–105
Untalan, Fay, 18
Upingco, Felipe Aguon, 110
U.S. Navy's War Crimes Tribunals Program, 3–4, 8, 58; and *bios* of Japanese, 215–216; establishment of, 82–83; gossip as testimony under, 17; interpreters in, 78–79; interrogations of, 73, 85; Japanese, racialization of, 181, 187; on Japanese military torture, 23; Japanese war criminals, 182; and ko'ko-hilitai relation, 216; "loyal native" trope of, 120; and masculinity, 59, 81, 105, 101; origins of, 26; Proclamation No. 4, 22; racialized surveillance of, 85–86; and racism, 115; and rule of law, 63, 67, 222; and rumor, 5, 17, 20; selective prosecution of, 115; treason, interpretation of, 152–153; and U.S. property, 216; and U.S. sovereignty, 22, 83, 86, 222; war crimes cases of, 85–86; white possession, logics of, 216
Uson, Maria Arriola, 122

Villagomez, Jose P., 14, 15, 105, 188–189, 190, 220; American conversion of, 143–144; assault trial of, 109–110; defense of, 122–123; leniency, plea for, 113; murder trial of, 116, 119–125; sentence of, 143; treason charges against, 153
Villagomez, Jose Quidachay, 126, 128
Villagomez, Juan, 53, 105, 116, 120; murder trial of, 123–125; sentence of, 143
violence: and acknowledgement, 16; and empire, 221; and the law, 22–23, 65; militarized, 65; and retribution, 29, 59

war crimes, 22; classifications of, 82, 244n71; definitions of, 67, 74; homosexuality as, 85–86; and international law, 67–68, 77–78; interrogation techniques of, 48–49; investigation of, 47–49; jurisdiction over, 74–75;

punishments for, 61. *See also* U.S. Navy's War Crimes Tribunals Program
war crimes cases, prisoner of war status petitions, 91–92, 248n9. *See also individual defendants*
War Crimes Office, 45, 71–74, 81–82; and authority of a victor, 72; branches of, 74; founding of, 71–72; jurisdiction of, 45–46; murder trials of, 116–118; prisoner of war status petitions, 91–92, 248n9; whiteness, privileging of, 81
war crimes tribunals: and citizenship, 5, 17, 20; gossip in, 5, 17, 20; and ko'ko-hilitai relation, 216; and nationalism, 65; and politics, 63; and precedent, 91, 118; and whiteness, 81. *See also* U.S. Navy's War Crimes Tribunals Program
war criminality, 44–52, 60–61, 67, 188; and biopower, 26; *bios* of, 18; definitions of, 62; and imperialism, 60, 83, 86, 89, 107, 115, 134, 213; and nationalism, 65; and piracy, 68; and race, 48, 60
war criminals: bodies of, 59; disciplining of, 53–54; emasculation of, 61, 220; executions of, 189–192, 194, 204–205; feminization of, 103; German, 61; Japanese, racialization of, 149; Saipanese, 143; and U.S. legitimacy, 29
War Criminals Stockade, 53, 55f, 78f, 83, 144f; investigation of, 54–56; prisoner abuse at, 54–58, 77; same-sex rape at, 107; staffing of, 80; witnesses housed at, 238n124
War on Terror, 23
Weaver, Jace, 24
Whitehair, Francis, 84

whiteness: and civil rights, 81–82; and modernity, 33–34; and naval justice, 86; and plenary power, 75–76; as property, 149, 155–156, 215; and sovereignty, 26; as sovereignty, 166; and victimhood, 81; and War Crimes Office, 81; and war crimes tribunals, 81; and war crime victims, 47
white possession, 215–216
white supremacy: and justice, 110; and law, 65; and punishment, 181; and War Crimes Tribunals Program, 60
Wiig, Jon, 118
Williams, Franklin, 80
Williams, Robert A., Jr., 64, 241n19
Wolfe, Cary, 223
Wusstig, Felix, 111, 112

x-marks, 139

Yasui, Yukio, 203–204
Yatsuhashi, Shigeru, 57
yellow peril, 151, 179; and Japanese war criminals, 188; in Rota, 182
Yoneyama, Lisa, 68
Yoshimura, Suekichi, 206
Yosida, Jesus, 43f

Zacharias, Ellis M., 30
Zafra, Isabel Perez, 79
Zafra, Vicente, 170
Zamora, Dorothy, 111
Zamora, Pedro, 36
Zimmerman, Harry M., 135
zoē, 1, 3, 5, 7–8, 223; Chamorro men as, 93; and ko'ko-hilitai, 5; Rotanese and Saipanese as, 216; war crimes defendants as, 103; of war criminality, 18. *See also* Agamben, Giorgio; *bios*

www.ingramcontent.com/pod-product-compliance
Lightning Source LLC
Chambersburg PA
CBHW030524230426
43665CB00010B/760